Worlding the Brain

Experimental Practices

ENCOUNTERS ACROSS ARTS, SCIENCES AND HUMANITIES

General Editors

Stephan Besser (*University of Amsterdam*)
Christoph Brunner (*University of Leuphana, Lüneburg*)
Delphine Chapuis Schmitz (*Zurich University of the Arts*)
Christine Goding-Doty (*The New School, New York*)

Advisory Board

Erin Manning (*Concordia University Montreal*)
Alanna Thain (*McGill University Montreal*)
Sher Doruff (*Amsterdam University of the Arts*)
Yvonne Volkart (*Academy of Art and Design, FHNW Basel*)

VOLUME 3

The titles published in this series are listed at *brill.com/exp*

Worlding the Brain

Neurocentrism, Cognition, and the Challenge of the Arts and Humanities

Edited by

Stephan Besser and Flora Lysen

BRILL

LEIDEN | BOSTON

Library of Congress Cataloging-in-Publication Data

Names: Besser, Stephan, editor. | Lysen, Flora Christine, editor.
Title: Worlding the brain : neurocentrism, cognition and the challenge of the arts and humanities / edited by Stephan Besser and Flora Lysen.
Description: Leiden ; Boston : Brill, 2023. | Series: Experimental practices, 1873–8788 ; volume 3 | Includes bibliographical references and index.
Identifiers: LCCN 2023036776 (print) | LCCN 2023036777 (ebook) | ISBN 9789004681286 (hardback ; acid-free paper) | ISBN 9789004681293 (ebook)
Subjects: LCSH: Neurosciences and the arts. | Neurosciences and the humanities. | LCGFT: Essays.
Classification: LCC NX180.N48 W67 2023 (print) | LCC NX180.N48 (ebook) | DDC 001.3--dc23/eng/20230824
LC record available at https://lccn.loc.gov/2023036776
LC ebook record available at https://lccn.loc.gov/2023036777

Typeface for the Latin, Greek, and Cyrillic scripts: "Brill". See and download: brill.com/brill-typeface.

ISSN 1873-8788
ISBN 978-90-04-68128-6 (hardback)
ISBN 978-90-04-68129-3 (e-book)

Copyright 2023 by Koninklijke Brill NV, Leiden, The Netherlands.
Koninklijke Brill NV incorporates the imprints Brill, Brill Nijhoff, Brill Schöningh, Brill Fink, Brill mentis, Brill Wageningen Academic, Vandenhoeck & Ruprecht, Böhlau and V&R unipress.
All rights reserved. No part of this publication may be reproduced, translated, stored in a retrieval system, or transmitted in any form or by any means, electronic, mechanical, photocopying, recording or otherwise, without prior written permission from the publisher. Requests for re-use and/or translations must be addressed to Koninklijke Brill NV via brill.com or copyright.com.

This book is printed on acid-free paper and produced in a sustainable manner.

Contents

Acknowledgements IX
List of Illustrations X
Notes on Contributors XI

Introduction: Together again, Apart 1
   Stephan Besser and Flora Lysen

PART 1
Worlded Brains

1 "Worlding" the Brain through the Cultural Practice of Rhetorical *memoria* 19
   Michael Burke

2 The Mediated Brain
  A Case Study on Experiential Engagement with Cinematic Form 31
   Joerg Fingerhut

3 Getting a Kick out of Film
  Aesthetic Pleasure and Play in Prediction Error Minimizing Agents 49
   Mark Miller, Marc M. Anderson, Felix Schoeller, and
   Julian Kiverstein

4 Transgenerational Trauma and Worlded Brains
  An Interdisciplinary Perspective on "Post-Traumatic Slave Syndrome" 63
   Machiel Keestra

5 Beworldered
  An Autobiographical Inquiry of Epileptic Being 82
   Trijsje Franssen

6 Pedagogy and Neurodiversity
  Experimenting in the Classroom with Autistic Perception 95
   Halbe Kuipers

VI CONTENTS

PART 2
Narrative Entanglements

7 Personification as *Élanification*
Agency Combustion and Narrative Layering in Worlding Perceived Relations 113
Marco Bernini

8 Cognitive Formalism
Or, How Presence Machines are Built 129
Karin Kukkonen

9 "Watchman, What of the Night?"
Reading Uncertainty in Djuna Barnes's Nightwood 142
Shannon McBriar

10 The Unfolding Now
Narrative Sense-Making from a Neurocinematic Perspective 156
Pia Tikka and Mauri Kaipainen

PART 3
Figuring the Brain

11 Set and Setting of the Brain on Hallucinogen
Psychedelic Revival in the Acid Western 173
Patricia Pisters

12 Modeling the Model
Reflections on a 10-Year Documentary about the Blue Brain Project 188
Noah Hutton

13 A Monk in the Office
Mindfulness and the Valuation of Popular Neuroscience 201
Ties van de Werff

14 Figuring Thought
Between Experience and Abstraction 215
Ksenia Fedorova

CONTENTS VII

PART 4
Shared Patterns and Discordant Worlds

15 Circulating Neuro-Imagery: A Trilogue 236
Antye Guenther, Flora Lysen, and Alexander Sack

16 What Have the Arts and Humanities Ever Done for Us?
Disruptive Contributions and a 4E Cognitive Arts and Humanities 258
Michael Wheeler

17 Measuring Acoustic Social Worlds
Reflections on a Study of Multi-Agent Human Interaction 274
*Shannon Proksch, Majerle Reeves, Michael Spivey, and
Ramesh Balasubramaniam*

18 Harmonic Dissonance: Synchron(icit)y
*A Case Study of Experimentation at the Intersection of the Arts and
Sciences* 285
Suzanne Dikker and Suzan Tunca

19 Thanks for Sharing
Local Worlds, Xeno-Patterning, and Predictive Processing 300
Stephan Besser

Index 319

Acknowledgements

This volume emerged from exchanges and conversations facilitated by the Neurocultures and Neuroaesthetics Research Group at the University of Amsterdam, in particluar the "Worlding the Brain"-conferences and workshops that were organized between 2016 and 2019 at the University of Amsterdam and Aarhus University ("Worlding the Brain: Patterns, Rhythms and Narartives in Neuroscience and the Humanities", March 2016; "Worlding the Brain: Predictive Processing as an Interdisciplinary Concept", November 2016; "Worlding the Brain: Affect, Care and Engagement", November 2017; "Worlding the Brain: Tools of Collective Prediction – Music, Art, Literature, Religion", November 2018; "Brain-Culture Interfaces: Interdisciplinary Perspectives on the Entanglement of the Human Mind and Its Cultural Environments", February 2019).

We would like to thank all artists and scholars that have generously dedicated their time, ideas, and curiosity to these gatherings. The editors of this volume would in particular like to thank the other members of the core convening team of these exchanges: Nim Goede, Machiel Keestra, Julian Kiverstein, and Patricia Pisters. Over the years, the Worlding the Brain events have been generously supported by the Amsterdam School of Cultural Analysis (ASCA, special thanks go to Eloe Kingma), the Royal Netherlands Academy of Arts and Sciences (KNAW), the Netherlands Research School for Literary Studies (OSL), the Netherlands Research School for Cultural Analysis (NICA), the Netherlands Research School for Media Studies (RMeS), Amsterdam Brain and Cognition (ABC), Art of Neuroscience, the Amsterdam Centre for Globalization Studies (ACGS), the Netherlands Organization for Health Research and Development (ZonMw), and Stedelijk Museum Amsterdam. For the realization of this volume we owe special thanks to Maria Poulaki, Meindert Peters, Fem Eggers, and Christa Stevens.

Illustrations

2.1 Still from *Notorious* (Hitchock et al., RKO, 1946) 38

2.2 Still from *Notorious* (Hitchock et al., RKO, 1946) 38

2.3 Still from *Notorious* (Hitchock et al., RKO, 1946) 39

2.4 Still from *Notorious* (Hitchock et al., RKO, 1946) 40

6.1 The classroom as *spazze* (photographs by Halbe Kuipers, 2018) 96

6.2 The classroom as *spazze* (photographs by Halbe Kuipers, 2018) 96

6.3 Research on *patches* and *landing* (photographs by Halbe Kuipers, 2020, 2017) 106

6.4 Research on *patches* and *landing* (photographs by Halbe Kuipers, 2020, 2017) 107

7.1 Diagram of Élanification processes 120

7.2 Woods in Durham, UK (photograph by Marco Bernini) 123

8.1 Curve of a snail's house according to the logic of the Fibonacci sequence (Wikimedia Commons) 134

12.1 Fly-through of the rat neocortex as projected in the Blue Brain Project's visitor screening room in 2010 (courtesy of Couple 3 Films) 189

12.2 Graphic designer Nicolas Antille regards "Virtual Golgi Staining," a poster in the lobby of the Blue Brain Project's headquarters in Geneva (courtesy of Couple 3 Films) 191

14.1 *Index of figures I* (Gansterer, *Drawing a Hypothesis*) 217

14.2 "Questions of Order and Relational Characteristics of Figures of Thought" (Gansterer, *Drawing a Hypothesis*) 221

14.3 *Key Lines* (Gansterer et al., *Choreo-graphic Figures*) 222

14.4 Method Lab, scores of attention (Gansterer, *Choreo-graphic Figures*) 225

14.5 Method Lab, scores of attention (Gansterer, *Choreo-graphic Figures*) 226

14.6 "Figure of Spiraling Momentum" (Gansterer et al., *Choreo-graphic Figures*) 227

14.7 "Figure of Spiraling Momentum" (Gansterer et al., *Choreo-graphic Figures*) 228

18.1 (a) Taxonomy of synchron(icit)y (Workshop I); (b) Sequences "tuning" and "together vs. simultaneous" (Workshop II); (c) Stills from ID-Lab performance (Workshop III); (d) Experiment design (courtesy of Suzanne Dikker and Nadine Hottenrott) 287

18.2 Performance of *Harmonic Dissonance: Synchron(icit)y* at the Ballet National de Marseille (courtesy of Matthias Oostrik) 288

19.1 "Cultural Affordances: Scaffolding Local Worlds through Shared Intentionality and Regimes of Attention" (Ramstead et al., "Cultural Affordances") 303

Notes on Contributors

Marc M. Anderson

is an Associate Professor at the Department of Culture, Cognition & Computation and at the Interacting Minds Center, Aarhus University. He is also a member of the Recreational Fear Lab at Aarhus University, Denmark. His research is concerned with the cognitive and physiological underpinnings of play in humans and with the development of methodologies to study play in experimental and ecological field settings.

Ramesh Balasubramaniam

is a Professor of Cognitive and Information Sciences at the University of California, Merced. He received his PhD from the University of Connecticut in 2000. The primary aim of his research is to understand the organization of human action, with the eventual goal of developing a comprehensive theory of embodied cognition. Dr. Balasubramaniam's research program uses methods from complex dynamical systems, robotics, neuroimaging, and statistical physics to study human movement production at the cognitive, neurophysiological, and ecological levels of analysis. His work is supported by several grants from the National Science Foundation and other funding agencies.

Marco Bernini

is Associate Professor in Cognitive Literary Studies in the Department of English Studies at Durham University. He is a narrative theorist working on the relationship between mind and narrative and on how fictional narratives explore and model cognitive processes. He has also worked on the extended mind theory, on empirical studies on readers, on theories of complexity and emergence, and on consciousness and mind wandering. He has a recently published monograph for Oxford University Press on Beckett and cognition (*Beckett and the Cognitive Method: Mind, Models, and Exploratory Narratives*, 2021), and co-directed an interdisciplinary project on dreams, narrative, and liminal cognition (thresholdworlds.org.uk). He leads the newly established "Narrative and Cognition Lab" (2023-2030) at the Durham Institute for Medical Humanities.

Stephan Besser

is Assistant Professor of Literary Studies and Modern Dutch Literature at the University of Amsterdam. He is a researcher at the Amsterdam School for Cultural Analysis (ASCA) and a former fellow of the Netherlands Institute for Advanced Study (NIAS). Stephan is the author of *Pathographie der Tropen: Literatur, Medizin und Kolonialismus um 1900* (Königshausen und Neumann, 2013).

Michael Burke

is Professor of Rhetoric at University College Roosevelt, Utrecht University. He is the author of *Literary Reading Cognition and Emotion: An Exploration of the Oceanic Mind* (Routledge, 2011) and a co-editor, together with Emily T. Troscinako, of *Cognitive Literary Science: Dialogues between Literature and Cognition* (OUP, 2017).

Suzanne Dikker

merges cognitive and environmental neuroscience, performance art and education in her work. She uses a crowdsourcing neuroscience approach to bring human brain and behavior research out of the lab, into real-world, everyday situations, with the goal to characterize the brain basis of dynamic human social communication. As a Research Professor at the Max Planck - NYU Center for Language, Music and Emotion and member of the art/science collective HARMONIC DISSONANCE, Suzanne leads various research projects, including MindHive, a community science platform that supports community-based initiatives and student-teacher-scientist partnerships for human brain and behavior research.

Ksenia Fedorova

(PhD) is Assistant Professor at Leiden University, NL. She is the author of *Tactics of Interfacing: Encoding Affect in Art and Technology* (MIT Press, 2020) and the co-editor of *Media: Between Magic and Technology* (2014, in Russian); other publications of hers appeared in *Leonardo Electronic Almanac, Media & Culture Journal, Acoustic Space*, and *Dialog of Arts*. In 2007–2011, she led the "Art. Science. Technology" program at the Ural branch of the National Center for Contemporary Arts (Ekaterinburg, RU). Ksenia's interests encompass media art theory and history, aesthetics, philosophy, science and technology, and visual culture studies, with a focus on the effects of technologies on human perception and interaction.

Joerg Fingerhut

heads the "Arts and Minds Lab" at the Berlin School of Mind and Brain, Humboldt-Universität (Berlin). Previously, he was Deputy Professor of Philosophy of Mind at Ludwig Maximilian University (Munich). As an empirically engaged philosopher of mind and aesthetics he works, theoretically and experimentally, on embodied theories of cultural artifacts. Those span from architecture and urbanism to pictures and moving images. Moreover, he is interested in the potential of art to change our perspective on the world and explores this topic within the European H2020-consortium ARTIS (Art and Research on Transformations of Individuals and Societies).

Trijsje Franssen

is Assistant Professor and Post-doc researcher in Philosophy of Technology and Ethics at Delft University of Technology. She obtained her PhD in Philosophy at the University of Exeter (UK). A central theme in her research is the human/technology relationship. She focuses on the posthuman, human enhancement, and cyborgs, and the role of myths, narratives, and (science) fiction in this context. Within this framework, neurotechnology is of particular importance. Franssen approaches this topic from an autobiographical viewpoint as someone who has close personal experience with the chronic disease of epilepsy as well as deep brain research and brain surgery.

Antye Guenther

is a visual artist and researcher. She is currently a PhD in the Arts Candidate at the Maastricht Experimental Research in and through the Arts Network (MERIAN). In her performance and installation works she draws on her education in photography as well as on experiences in former East Germany, studies in medicine, and military training. She addresses themes such as (non)biological intelligence and supercomputers, human enhancement and posthumanism, technological imaginaries and science fiction.

Noah Hutton

is a filmmaker and independent researcher based in New York. He was nominated for a 2021 Independent Spirit Award for Best First Screenplay for *Lapsis*, a sci-fi feature film he wrote, directed, scored, and edited. In 2020 he completed *In Silico*, a ten-year documentary begun in 2009 and supported by Sandbox Films and the Alfred P. Sloan Foundation about a ten-year project to simulate the human brain on supercomputers. He has authored chapters for *The Cambridge Handbook of the Imagination* (2020) and the *Springer Series on Bio- and Neurosystems* (2019).

Mauri Kaipainen

PhD, Adjunct Professor of Cognitive Science at the University of Helsinki, is a former Professor of Media Technology at Södertörn University (Sweden), Professor of New Media at Tallinn University, and Professor of Applied Cognitive Science at the Media Lab of the University of Art and Design Helsinki (today Aalto University). He studied education, musicology, and cognitive science at the University of Helsinki, earning his PhD in 1994 on a computational model description of musical knowledge ecology. As Professor of New Media at Tallinn University (2005–08) he established the international master program Interactive Media and Knowledge Environments. At the Media Lab of the University of Art and Design Helsinki he contributed to a number of media projects, including research on narrative spaces and logics, e-participation, cultural heritage, and language technology. At the heart of his research agenda lies the systemic characterization of conceptualization and narration, conceived of as core cognitive functions.

Machiel Keestra
is Central Diversity Officer, philosopher at the Institute for Interdisciplinary Studies, and researcher at the Institute for Logic, Language and Computation at the University of Amsterdam. He has published on human action and tragedy, the history and philosophy of science, interdisciplinarity and transdisciplinarity, metacognition and reflection, and dialogue and narrative identity. Keestra has been president of the International Association for Interdisciplinary Studies and a founding board member of the global Interdisciplinary and Transdisciplinary Alliance. He co-initiated the Keti Koti Table, a reflection and dialogue method that focuses on the shared history of slavery and its aftermath, with over 30.000 participants so far in the Netherlands and abroad.

Julian Kiverstein
is Senior Researcher in the Department of Psychiatry at Amsterdam University Medical Research Center. He is trained as a philosopher of mind and works at the intersection of philosophy of mind, phenomenology, embodied cognitive science, and cognitive neuroscience. He has published widely on issues relating to 4E (embodied, extended, ecological, and enactive) cognition. He is co-author (with Michael Kirchhoff) of the monograph *Extended Consciousness and Predictive Processing: A Third-Wave View* (Routledge, 2019).

Halbe Kuipers
(PhD University of Amsterdam, 2022) investigates the work of perspectivism: its different philosophical conceptualizations, its deployment in different fields such as anthropology, environmental studies, disabilities studies, and film studies, and, above all, its practical and ethical implications in regard to us as Moderns. He has been a long standing (or sitting, and at times rolling) collaborator of the Montréal Experimental Laboratory for Research Creation, SenseLab. He is currently employed at the University of Amsterdam as a Lecturer in Film Studies.

Karin Kukkonen
is Professor in Comparative Literature at the University of Oslo. She leads the interdisciplinary initiative Literature, Cognition and Emotions (2019–2023), a prioritized area of research and teaching at the Humanities Faculty at the

University of Oslo. Her research focuses on links between the study of literary form and cognitive approaches to literature, including cognitive poetics and narratology. Her most recent publications include *With Bodies: Narrative Theory and Embodied Cognition* (with Marco Caracciolo, Ohio State UP, 2021), *Probability Designs: Literature and Predictive Processing* (OUP, 2020), *4E Cognition and Eighteenth-Century Fiction: How the Novel Found its Feet* (OUP, 2019), and *A Prehistory of Cognitive Poetics: Neoclassicism and the Novel* (OUP, 2017).

Flora Lysen

is an Assistant Professor at Maastricht University, where she researches past and present (media) technologies embedded in scientific research, particularly in the field of medical imaging and brain science. In her most recent book *Brainmedia: One Hundred Years of Performing Live Brains*, 1920–2020 (Bloomsbury, 2022), she examines ways in which scientists, science educators, and artists use new media to conceptualize, examine, and demonstrate the "brain at work". In her current research she focuses on the history of artificial intelligence in the field of automating (medical) image reading in the post-WWII period.

Shannon McBriar

(MPhil, DPhil Oxford) is a Lecturer in Literature at Amsterdam University College and a research affiliate at the Amsterdam School for Cultural Analysis at the University of Amsterdam. Her research interests lie at the crossroads of literary modernism, literary ecologies, and the cognitive humanities. She was a contributor to Hubbub, an interdisciplinary residency at The Wellcome Collection in London, exploring the phenomenon of mind wandering within the context of attention and rest. Her current research focuses on the dynamics of uncertainty in modernist fiction in dialogue with a range of cognitive and ecological frameworks. Most recently, she has guest edited, with Meindert Peters (University of Oxford), a special issue of *Symbiosis: Transatlantic Literary and Cultural Relations* on transatlantic cognitive cultures (2022).

Mark Miller

is a philosopher of cognition. His research explores what recent advances in neuroscience can tell us about happiness and well-being, and what it means to live well in our increasingly technologically-mediated world. Mark is currently a Senior Research Fellow at Monash University's *Centre for Consciousness and Contemplative Studies*, a Research Fellow at the University of Toronto's Psychology Department, and a visiting researcher at Hokkaido University's *Center for Human Nature, Artificial Intelligence and Neuroscience*.

Patricia Pisters

is Professor of Film, Media and Culture at the Department of Media Studies of the University of Amsterdam. She is one of the co-founding editors of *Necsus: European Journal of Media Studies* and a board member of The Open Foundation that promotes scientific research into psychedelics and the psychedelic experience from a multidisciplinary perspective. Her previous books include *The Matrix of Visual Culture* (Stanford UP, 2003) and *The Neuro-Image: A Deleuzian Film-Philosophy of Contemporary Screen Culture* (Stanford UP, 2012). Her latest book is *New Blood in Contemporary Cinema: Women Directors and the Poetics of Horror* (Edinburgh UP, 2020).

Shannon Proksch

is an Assistant Professor of Psychology at Augustana University in Sioux Falls, South Dakota. She received her PhD in Cognitive and Information Sciences at the University of California, Merced in 2022. She holds a BA in Music from Texas A&M University, Corpus Christi and an MSc in Mind, Language and Embodied Cognition from the University of Edinburgh. Her research blends empirical and philosophical methods from the dynamical systems and predictive processing frameworks to examine the neural, behavioral, and social dynamics of music cognition—from lower-level beat processing to higher-level coordination and social interaction. Her work has been supported, in part, by a National Science Foundation Traineeship in Intelligent and Adaptive Systems.

Majerle Reeves

focuses in her research on building mathematical models to solve active problems in Public Health and Cognitive Science. She received her PhD in Applied Mathematics at the University of California, Merced in 2023. She earned a BA in Mathematics and a BSc in Mechanical Engineering from California State University, Fresno in 2017. Her past research work includes building more equitable machine learning and statistical models to predict suicide death from administrative patient records, parameter estimation for stochastic processes, and system identification using neural networks. Her work was supported, in part, by a National Science Foundation Traineeship in Intelligent and Adaptive Systems.

Alexander Sack

is a Professor of Brain Stimulation and Applied Cognitive Neuroscience at the Faculty of Psychology & Neuroscience, Maastricht University. He is an expert in noninvasive brain stimulation, fundamental and applied cognitive neuroscience, and clinical brain research. Sack has become an influential leader in brain stimulation research by combining and developing new tools to uncover the brain dynamics underlying human cognition and behavior and by translating these findings into clinical applications for treating various neuropsychiatric disorders.

Felix Schoeller

is a cognitive scientist with expertise in emotion, mental health, and human-computer interaction. His work concerns synthetic emotions and their therapeutic applications. Felix is a member of the American Psychological Association, the Association for Computing Machinery, and the IEEE Computational Intelligence Society. He graduated from the University of Copenhagen and holds a PhD in Cognitive Science from the School for Advanced Studies in the Social Sciences. His work was featured in *Aeon, The Verge, Rolling Stone, Big Think*, and *Ars Electronica*.

Michael J. Spivey

has a PhD in Brain and Cognitive Sciences from University of Rochester and is Professor of Cognitive Science at the University of California, Merced. After 12 years as a psychology professor at Cornell University, Spivey moved to UC Merced in 2008 to help build their Cognitive & Information Sciences PhD Program. His research uses eye-tracking, computer-mouse tracking, and dynamical systems theory to explore how brain, body, and environment work together to make a mind what it is. In 2010, Spivey received the William Procter Prize for Scientific Achievement from the Sigma Xi Scientific Research Honor Society.

Pia Tikka

PhD, is filmmaker and EU Mobilitas Research Professor at the MEDIT Centre of Excellence, Tallinn University. She holds the honorary title of Adjunct Professor of New Narrative Media at the University of Lapland. She is the founder and principal investigator of NeuroCine research group (since 2011), and a founding member of neuroscience project aivoAALTO at the Aalto University (2010–2014). Actively engaged with the film and media industry, she is a voting member of the Society for Cognitive Studies of the Moving Image and the European Film Academy. As a filmmaker, she has directed two feature films and several interactive new media works. Tikka is the author of the monograph *Enactive Cinema: Simulatorium Eisensteinense* (2008) and publishes widely on enactive media and neurocinematics studies. She currently heads an Estonian Research Council-funded research project at her Enactive Virtuality Lab at Tallinn University.

Suzan Tunca

has performed as a dancer, dance teacher, and choreographer since 1998. Since 2015 she works as a dance researcher and head of the Academy at ICK Dans Amsterdam. She implemented and develops an artistic research curriculum for BA Dance students at Codarts University of the Arts Rotterdam and coaches MA choreography students at Codarts/Fontys. She is member of DAS THIRD, a 3rd cycle research group in the performing arts at the Graduate School of Amsterdam University of the Arts and a PhD candidate at PhDArts Leiden University (NL).

Ties van de Werff

is head of the research center What Art Knows and a teacher in the interdisciplinary Bachelor iArts (both at Zuyd University of Applied Sciences, NL). Ties has a background in practical philosophy, science and technology studies, and community arts. He is interested in the ethics and aesthetics of societal engagement practices: how makers (from artists to engineers) make their work valuable and relevant to others, and how such valuation practices can be cultivated and diversified.

Michael Wheeler

is Professor of Philosophy at the University of Stirling. His primary research interests are in philosophy of science (especially cognitive science, psychology, biology, and AI) and philosophy of mind. In pursuing these interests, he often finds himself developing ideas at the interface between the analytic and the continental philosophical traditions. He has published widely on the nature of, and the prospects for, so-called 4E (embodied, embedded, extended, and enactive) cognition, with a special focus on the subtle and complex ways in which human beings intimately couple with technology to transform, enhance, and sometimes impede, psychological performance. His most recent research explores the possibility of bringing 4E cognitive science into a mutually productive relationship with the arts and humanities.

INTRODUCTION

Together again, Apart

Stephan Besser and Flora Lysen

In his poem "Biology for the Youth" (1965), Dutch-American writer and hematologist Leo Vroman (1915–2014) imagines the brain as a leaky organ that extends physically into the world. The poem starts with a consideration of human hair as a "tuber" (*knolgewas*) that sprouts from lumps of cells within the skin. The lyrical subject then looks beyond the surface of the body and projects the imagery of roots and fibers into the skull. Is the brain not also "a sac of cells," the narrator wonders, each of which is able to generate "a thousand thoughts" that protrude to the outside? Addressing an imaginative interlocutor, the narrator cautions: "my friend, let this be a sign to you/that some things might be leaking/in a manner of speech/we call this speaking"[1] (Vroman 444). But if the brain actually had hair-like extension outside the skull, the exchange would work in the opposite direction as well: then every touch of the crown of the head by another person would directly stimulate the brain and generate an abundance of thoughts and images:

> If I could stroke your tender brain
> The way I now caress your crown
> The touch that you are feeling now
> Would equal pictures beyond count[2]

The poem closes with a warning for those who might be frightened by this vision of mental stimulation through outside touch; they should keep the "box of their skull closed." But the intimacy and enchantment of the stroking gesture that Vroman envisions contradict this warning: they conjure up the image of a brain that is not isolated in the skull but connected to the world and others through material, sensory extensions, bodily exchange, and physical communication; a brain that is literally able to feel, think, and imagine

---

1 "Dit vriend zij u ten teken/dat een en ander wel eens lekt;/wij spreken dan van Spreken" (our translation).

2 "En kon ik je zachte hersenen strelen/zoals ik nu je kruintje strijk/dan stond wat je nu voelde gelijk/aan tien biljoen tafrelen" (our translation).

© KONINKLIJKE BRILL NV, LEIDEN, 2023 | DOI:10.1163/9789004681293_002

through interaction with things outside itself—or, as we suggest to say in this volume, a brain that is irreducibly *worlded*.

1   The Brain and the World

Vroman's poetic fantasy from 1965 prefigures ideas and imageries that now are a commonplace in pop and neuroculture. In the science fiction film *Avatar* (2009), for instance, the long braids of the inhabitants of the planet Pandora are extensions of their central nervous system through which they physically and mentally link up with other people and organisms. This psycho-neuronal connection contributes to the elaborate filmic depiction of the biosphere of Pandora as a giant "world brain" (Gere). Meanwhile, and with no direct connection to Vroman, the notion of the mind as a "leaky organ" (Clark, *Being There* 53) has in various ways inspired research on embodied, embedded, extended, and enactive cognition—now generally called 4E cognition—over the last quarter century. The notion was first used in philosopher Andy Clark's influential 1997 book *Being There: Putting Brain, Body, and World Together Again*, whose programmatic subtitle also offered a catchy slogan to the new movement in cognitive science, philosophy, and other fields.[3] Alluding to the famous English "Humpty Dumpty" nursery rhyme, the proclaimed intention to bring world, body, and brain "together again" is directed against a Cartesian separation of brain and mind and, to a certain extent, against computationalist approaches to cognition that are seen to distance the brain from its social and material environments by regarding it essentially as a disembodied, representationalist processing apparatus. Against this paradigm, the phrase proposes an interactive entanglement and "mingling" (Clark, *Being There* 53) of brain, body, and world, which can be spelled out in different ways. Seen as a concentric arrangement, the three-fold nestedness of brain, body, and world can support brain-centered conceptions of the "leaky mind" that seeps out into the more peripheral realms of the body and the world (Morgan 291). It can even collapse into the radically constructivist notion of the brain as creating the "appearance of a world" at the neuronal level, with no way to reach beyond this phenomenal horizon (Metzinger 15–22, 299; cf. Northoff). But (un) folded differently, the mutual nestedness of brain, body, and world can also

---

3   Cf. Wheeler 11, Clark, "Where", Clark, "Surfing", Crippen and Schulkin. In coining the phrase, Clark reached back to the phenomenological tradition (Heidegger, Merleau-Ponty, Vygotsky and the recursive understanding of self and world expounded in Varela, Thompson and Rosch's *Embodied Mind* (Varela et al. 1991).

be approached from a more distinctly phenomenological conception of the "world" as a "holistic network of contexts" (Wheeler 18) into which cognitive and neural activity are meaningfully embedded. Along these general lines, the notions of "common worlds" (Roepstorff et al. 1057) and of a "shared world" of intersubjective action and understanding gain ground, the latter being defined in terms of "collective sense-making processes manifested in dynamic forms of intercorporeality, collective body memory, artifacts, affordances, scaffolding, use of symbols" that connect multiple brains and bodies (Tewes et al. 1).

But the broader significance and epistemic relevance of brain-world relations in contemporary culture and science does not stop here. It is the appealing complexity of the term "world" that it always signifies more than one thing and thus is able to connect and confront divergent perspectives on related issues. When 4E cognition research was starting to take up speed, the brain also came to be studied as part of the "world" in a less phenomenological and more biosocial and discursive sense: it emerged as the key figure in a "neurocultural world" (Vidal and Ortega, "Approaching" 8) that includes everyday practices of subjectivation and their articulation in film, literature, and other arts as well as new diagnostic routines of the naturalized mind and the rise of a host of *neuro* disciplines across various fields of knowledge (from neuroaesthetics to neurotheology). As a guiding belief of this neurocultural world Francisco Ortega and Fernando Vidal have identified the idea that humans essentially are their brains, i.e., that they are "cerebral subjects" that are sufficiently defined by their neurological setup (Vidal, "Brainhood"; Vidal and Ortega, "Being"). Similarly, but with a stronger emphasis on a multiplicity of identity options beyond brainhood, Nikolas Rose and Joelle M. Abi-Rached have traced the various pathways through which neuroscience since the 1960s was able to "leave the lab for the world outside" (48). These trajectories include psychopharmacology and psychiatric genomics as well as the concept of neuroplasticity that opened up the brain in entirely new ways to environmental influences, training, treatment, selfcare, and other practices of governing the mind. Here, the "world" does not so much signify a neurocultural "universe" as such (Vidal and Ortega, "Approaching") but rather an extra-scientific realm of biopolitics and everyday life in which the brain emerges as an object and conduit for governing both the self and the population as a whole.

Within the frameworks of neuroculture and the "neurobiological complex" (Rose and Abi-Rached 225) various research projects and scholars over the last twenty years or so have studied the impact of the neurosciences and brain-centered ideologies on contemporary culture, policies, and lifeworlds. These initiatives include the important project of a "critical neuroscience" that situated itself "between lifeworld and laboratory" in order to understand "the situatedness, leading assumptions, conceptual and explanatory resources, historical developments, and social implications of the emerging neuroindustry" (Choudhury and Slaby 3). Other projects have focused on "brain culture" in popular media (Thornton), the emergence of specific neurodisciplines such as neuroeconomics and neuromarketing (Schneider and Wolgar), and the interaction of neuroscience and the wider public (Schregel and Broer).

2   Worlding

We believe that this double impulse to situate brains in a phenomenological and in a biosocial "world"—to oversimplify a bit—is not a mere coincidence and offers opportunities for a very productive exchange. The two movements that come together in this volume—4E cognition and critical neuroculture research—diverge in important ways with respect to their epistemic frameworks, research aims, and practices. But they also converge in rejecting conceptual dichotomies of mind and body, body and world and in their insistence on mental processes as being inherently embodied and environmentally embedded. "If it is true that experience, cognition, action, and personhood are intelligible only as constitutively *situated*," Suparna Choudhury and Jan Slaby state, "then it becomes a task of great importance to understand and analyze how all those 'cognitive extensions' are organized, how they develop and by whom they are managed" (12, emphasis added).

To bring this situatedness into sharper focus, the contributions to this volume approach the *worlding* of the brain as an active process that involves cognitive, biological, and socio-discursive factors. By extending attention form the noun "world" to the verb/gerund "worlding" they emphasize doing and (en)action instead of being. They thereby contribute to a critical reconsideration of Martin Heidegger's notion of worlding/*welten* as the opening of ways of being-in-the-world through human history and cultural practice (Heidegger). Postcolonial scholar Gayatri Spivak has practiced a deliberate "vulgarization" of Heidegger's notion in her analyses of worlding as the imperialist project of "domesticating" colonized people and territories and undoing their worlds (Spivak, "Three" 260; cf. Spivak "Critique"). Science and technology scholar Donna Haraway, in turn, resolutely distinguishes her view of worlding as a multi-species "becoming-with" from "grumpy human-exceptionalist Heideggerian worlding" (11) and instead draws on Gilles Deleuze and Félix Guattari's take on worlding/*faire monde* (Deleuze and Guattari 308).[4] Similarly, recent

---

4   In light of the current ecological crisis philosopher Timothy Morton has rejected the anthropocentric, phenomenological notion of "world" altogether (Morton 99–133).

new materialist approaches regard worlding as a more-than-human, ontological process that means a "turning of attention to a certain experience, place or encounter and our active engagement with the materiality and context in which events and interactions occur" (Palmer and Hunter).[5]

Picking up on these various impulses, the chapters in this book share a profound interest in placing brain and cognition in worldly environments and exploring their entanglements with different media, cultural practices, social processes, and power relations. "Worlding" here means, first of all, an emphasis on the process character of these entanglements. Research on neuroplasticity, for instance, has shown that the brain is always in the making and that synaptic plasticity forms the biosocial basis of cognitive functions such as learning and, more grimly, various forms of trauma (Malabou, *What Shall we Do*; Malabou, *The New Wounded*). Brains now are not just biophysical entities anymore, they are "always in process, always open to transforming themselves and being transformed" (Pitts-Taylor 18). In different but related ways, researchers and scholars working with the emerging research paradigm of predictive processing conceive of brains as constantly shaped by and enacting probabilistic regularities in their bodily environment and the "transformative structures of our material, social, and technological worlds" (Clark, *Surfing Uncertainty* 108). These exchanges are not free from biological constraints, but they make static conceptions of brain and cognition less and less plausible.

Second, worlding in this volume is also taken to refer to the irreducible plurality of worlds that emerge in the interaction of multiple brains, cognitive agents, and socio-cultural practices. The trend to study the emergence of "common worlds" through patterned socio-cultural practices (Roepstorff et al. 1057; Tewes et al.), predictive processing routines (Ramstead et al.) and inter-brain couplings that underpin the creation of "a shared social world" (Czeszumski et al. 4) insistently moves the cognitive and neurosciences beyond a solipsistic focus on individual brains. With Spivak in mind, it seems important then to keep the power relations in the construction and collisions of worlds in mind. We propose that thinking in terms of *worlding* can help not to conceive of "world" as a figure of self-contained coherence and unity—as certain phenomenological approaches tend to do—but to regard all world-making as partial, contested, and incomplete. As anthropologist Philippe Descola states, there always is a "variety in forms of worlding," dependent upon the differential

---

5   Philosopher Pascal David traces a "Germanic," phenomenological history of the concept of world that is exclusively concerned with the ontological structure of *human* existence (David 2015). Martin Heidegger famously regarded non-living objects like stones as having no world (*weltlos*), animals as poorly endowed with world (*weltarm*), and only human beings as world-forming (*weltbildend*).

actualization of the physical and mental affordances of a certain environment: "What there is, independently from us, is not a complete and self-contained world waiting to be represented or accounted for according to different viewpoints, but, most probably, a vast amount of qualities and relations that can be actualized or not by humans, within themselves and outside of them, according to how they respond to some basic ontological choices" (Descola 336).

3 Interdiscipinarity and Bricolage

This plurality, third and finally, is also reflected in the variety of approaches to worlded brains that we assemble in this book. In order to study brains and cognition as enmeshed in worldly contexts, the authors in this volume offer bricolage approaches in which different scholarly methodologies and frameworks intersect. However, to simply say that the chapters in this book therefore are examples of "interdisciplinary" research would be as appropriate as it is confounding. "Interdisciplinarity" has been—and still is—an ubiquitous buzzword in calls for a more nuanced way of examining not only cognition and the brain. Yet, as sociologists Felicity Callard and Des Fitzgerald note in *Rethinking Interdisciplinarity across the Social Sciences and Neurosciences* (2015), interdisciplinarity also is a term "that everyone invokes and none understands" (4).

Exploring the potency of inter-, trans-, and cross-disciplinary encounters has been a central tenet of the "Worlding the Brain"-conferences and workshops, organized between 2016 and 2019 at the University of Amsterdam and Aarhus University that form the springboard for this book. During these events, exchanges between researchers coming from the humanities, social sciences, and neurosciences were envisioned as explorative moments that could spark new ways of thinking and may lead to future collaborations. In such discussions, encounters of scholars with different backgrounds appeared as a way to suture questionable disciplinary divisions between the social and the biological or the material and the discursive. This imperative to "exchange" across research fields has been prompted, among others, by puzzling observations in the natural sciences regarding the way social and material aspects of environments shape human development—observations derived from the field of neuroscience, but also from endocrinology, developmental systems biology, immunology, and epigenetics (Wolfe; Roy). When trying to understand the "dynamics between embodied self and lived environment," feminist theorist Samantha Frost states, life scientists have much to learn from humanities and social science researchers, who have "anticipated" such feedback loops in their complex accounts of subject formation in particular socio-material settings and environments (897). Naturally, she contends, these disparate domains "resonate" in their call for a study of bodies in situated worlds (897). Bringing these resonances together, interdisciplinarity may thus be a key to study and understand worlding.

Yet, the magical appeal of the "inter" needs closer attention as well. As Callard and Fitzgerald note, it is important to realize that power asymmetries between the well-funded and authoritative discipline of the neurosciences and the publicly less-prestigious and underfunded humanities, social sciences, and arts have a significant impact on the practice of interdisciplinarity work. Callard and Fitzgerald sketch a situation in which humanities and social science scholars mainly take on a subordinate role, supporting neuroscientists in conceptually refining the socio-cultural constructs of their experiments. Moreover, social scientists and humanities scholars may sometimes undertake an all-too enthusiastic reading of neuroscientific findings, taking them as a given to proceed with a cultural or social analysis of new and interesting scientific facts (Fitzgerald and Callard; Papoulias and Callard). Because of the dominant position of neuroscientific discourses, Melissa Littlefield and Jennell Johnson have typified the academic landscape as characterized by a "neuroscientific turn." Part of this "turn" means that hierarchies between disciplines are warped and neuroscience becomes what they call a "translational discipline," fueling an exchange between concepts and approaches in brain science and all other disciplines (3).

Hence, approaches to worlding the brain should not unreflectively pursue a dream of collaboration between disciplines. For good reasons, feminist philosopher Cynthia Kraus has warned against a certain type of interdisciplinary research projects on the sexed brain in which social scientists and science studies scholars engage in a "preventive politics" of conflict avoidance with their neuroscience collaborators in order to keep up good communication (197). She instead proposes a "dissensus framework" for encounters between social scientists and neuroscientists during which political matters are not muffled but exacerbated instead.

The possibility and necessity of being critical—to confront, to dissent, and to clash—has been an important element of the critical neuroscience movement and, to a lesser degree, of the "critical friendship" between the life sciences and other disciplines, as proposed by Nikolas Rose, that allows for a non-reductionist articulation of human beings and other organisms in their milieu (Rose 24). The chapters in this book demonstrate varying forms of alliances, convergences, and disputes between disciplinary frameworks and approaches that are necessary to find new articulations of organisms in milieus—of brains in worlds. They make a case for the important contribution of the humanities in this context, not just as auxiliary disciplines or skeptical critics, but as genuine experts in the study of experience, co-evolution, and situated cognition (Zunshine; Starr; Otis; Caracciolo and Kukkonen). And they emphasize the role of the arts that in their own ways experiment with the entanglements of brain, body, and world.

A situated view of interdisciplinarity, beyond the rhetoric and dreams of frictionless collaboration, shows that such bricolage approaches are not easygoing assemblages. Returning to Andy Clark's vision of "putting brain, body, and world together again," cited at the beginning of this introduction, we can now start to question the restorative imagery that is implied in this phrase. Clark seems to suggest that there might be a unified and unifying theory that is able to seamlessly connect brains, bodies, and worlds (again). Contrary to Clark, the chapters in this book embody our claim that, while connections and zigzags between fields are important, it is neither possible nor desirable to suture these planes of analysis into a coherent whole or overarching approach. It is therefore worth remembering that the Humpty Dumpty rhyme that inspired Clark's motto ends in fracture rather than reconstitution: "all of the king's horses, and all of the king's men/couldn't put Humpty together again." We suggest that the action written into the project of putting things together and in worlding the brain can also signal a more open-ended, multifaceted, or bricolage approach that reconfigures the pieces without the comprehensive blueprint of a whole. For this project, the chapters in this volume happily offer their own versions—and "vulgarizations" (Spivak)—of worlding the brain.

4 Volume Overview

The chapters in the first section "Worlded Brains" explore from a variety of angles how brains and bodies are enworlded in their engagement with different media, pedagogical practice, and historical experience. The section opens with an essay by Michael Burke on the worlding of the brain through the cultural practice of rhetoric. Reflecting on his own teaching practice, Burke brings the classical method of rhetorical *memoria* into dialogue with neurocognitive memory research and the constructive episodic simulation hypothesis of memory proposed by Daniel Schacter et al. He argues that present day simulation theory can help to explain the working/functioning of classical memorizing techniques as described in the widely influential *Rhetorica ad Herennium* and that, conversely, neuroscientific memory research can benefit enormously from studying classical practices of rhetorical memory.

The next two chapters focus on film and visual media as important sites of the worlding of the brain in contemporary culture. In his consideration of the theory of embodied simulation as an innovative proposal for the study of moving images, Joerg Fingerhut uses the concept of neuromediality to capture how media and the human organism jointly bring forth meaning and affective experience. His case study examines the embodiment of camera movements in Alfred Hitchcock's *Notorious* (1946) and supports an understanding of the brain as intimately bound up with and continuously adjusting to different media settings. Similarly, Mark Miller, Marc M. Anderson, Felix Schoeller, and Julian Kiverstein explore the aesthetic pleasure experienced in watching horror films as manifestation of the embodied brain's engagement with a particular media environment. Starting from the predictive processing network, they introduce the concept of "consumable error" and posit that engaging with horror is enjoyable for an agent if it helps them to better deal with uncertainty both in filmic and real surroundings.

Machiel Keestra's chapter on the transgenerational transmission of trauma and the "post-traumatic slave syndrome" then moves the exploration of real world contexts to the historical experiences of war, violence, discrimination, and injustice. Offering an interdisciplinary approach to the "post-traumatic slave syndrome," he suggests to conceive of epigenetics as part of multimodal, mutual interactions between adaptive, embodied brains in specific historical and social contexts. The chapter insistently demonstrates that the worlding of the brain is not necessarily a connective and enabling process but can involve violence and disruption as well.

Disruptive experience of a different kind, and at an individual level, is also at the center of Trijsje Franssen's autobiographical inquiry of epileptic being and the feeling of "de-worlding" that results from her complex partial seizures. Approaching her experience from the perspective of existential phenomenology, Franssen describes how the seizures feel as reinstating boundaries of mind and body, brain, and self and can enforce a loss of the experience of the self as an embodied whole. This alienation results in a paradoxical experience of *not*-Being There (to invert Clark's programmatic title). Finally, Halbe Kuipers explores ways of being in the world that do not take the human subject as a starting point at all and show the limitations of phenomenological approaches. His chapter on neurodiverse pedagogy at the Senselab in Montréal demonstrates how autistic experience can question and expand common conceptions of learning and, more in particular, classroom settings. Brains and bodies are worlded here not so much as centers of cognition and intentionality but rather as elements in a field of "feeling" (A. N. Whitehead) that is dispersed across various entities in the world.

The second section "Narrative Entanglements" takes the exploration of the worlding of brains to the field of storytelling and narrative. In different ways, all contributors share an interest in the dyad of "worlding the story" and "storying the world," that literary scholar David Herman proposed to study the nexus of mind and narrative. While "storying the world" refers to sensemaking through narrative, "worlding the story" signifies the embedding of acts of narration in larger worlds of cultural experience, humanistic interpretation, and scientific explanation (Herman 1–15). Marco Bernini combines these two dimensions in his chapter on personification as a worlding mechanism. He proposes the concept of *élanification* for conceiving of the processes whereby humans, spontaneously or intentionally, structure relations with their world. Narrative is an important vehicle in this process, as it provides the temporal and agential frameworks through which we "world" outer elements—from human to non-human, inorganic, and even imagined matter—into a meaningful space of interactions. In her chapter on the experience of presence in and through literary narrative, Karin Kukkonen focuses on the worlding of stories by way of techniques of reflexivity and surprise. Drawing on the predictive processing framework, Kukkonen argues that it is precisely the artificiality of literary designer environments that entangles brain, body, and world and extends our minds beyond ourselves. This insight leads her to a reappraisal of literary formalism from a 4E perspective and to propose a "cognitive formalism" that studies how literary language extends embodied experience.

Shannon McBriar then continues the discussion of predictive processing and literary cognition by questioning the notion of "uncertainty" in PP accounts of reading and sense-making. In her close reading of Djuna Barnes's modernist novel *Nightwood* (1936) she demonstrates that uncertainty is not so much a catalyst for the reduction of prediction errors but rather a constant presence and open-ended affordance structure that defies progressive understanding. McBriar's conclusion is not that predictive processing should be dismissed as a framework in literary analysis but that such approaches should make more room for the disruptive character of uncertainty. Finally, Pia Tikka and Mauri Kaipainen shift focus from "worlding the story" to "storying the world" in their chapter on narrative sense making from a neurocinematic perspective. They discuss recent advances in phenomeno-physiological research on intersubjective and auto-narration in filmic experience and argue that cinematic narrative is particularly suited for the interdisciplinary study of narrative in general. From this perspective, the brain is continuously worlded inwards (through individual autonarration) and outwards (through intersubjectively shared narratives) and thus intrinsically entangled with other minds, bodies and stories.

Shifting perspective to a more neurocultural angle, the third section "Figuring the Brain" examines the tropes, images, discourses, and performances through which the brain and cognition currently materialize in artworks, films, and the world of work. Patricia Pisters investigates the "worlding of the brain on hallucinogens," prompted by a recent resurgence of scientific research into psychedelics. Zooming in on the cinematic genre of the "acid Western," a sub-genre of counterculture hippie films, she shows how (psychedelic) experiences are mediated by, and emerge through, historically changing media forms, narratives, and technologies. Psychedelic perceptions, in Pisters's analysis, reveal the feedback loops between human experiences and collective media repertoires. Brains as mediated figures are also central to Noah Hutton's chapter, in which he reflects on his ten-year long documentary film project *In Silico* (2020). The film traces the rise and partial demise of the Blue Brain Project, a multi-billion research endeavor based in Switzerland that aims to digitally model a biological brain with the help of supercomputers. The project is based on the assumption that biological variability—the complexity of the real-world "in vivo" brain—can be simulated in digital form. Hutton shows that when the validity of such modeling approaches starts to be questioned, researchers in turn rely on artful visual simulations to sustain the future promise of a completely reconstructed brain.

The figure of the "mindful brain" is central to Ties van de Werff's study of the valuation and transformation of a Buddhist conception of mindfulness in contemporary work culture. Van de Werff carefully traces the interdisciplinary "value work" through which ethical imperatives of Buddhist spirituality, the authority of brain science, and ideas about "working well" are re-assembled in the role model of the mindful, brain-trained employee, as strikingly captured in the trope of the "monk in the office". The chapter shows how a meticulous discourse analysis of the worlding of brains—in this case, in the present-day office—can reveal the ways in which brain facts are normatively mobilized and made valuable in various but always specific contexts. The concluding chapter of the section turns to the notion of the figure itself and discusses how mind, brain, and body can interact in *figuring* thought. Ksenia Fedorova defines figuring as the process in which images and cognitive schemata are enacted and performed through the body, thereby generating new forms of thought beyond abstract representation. The work of the artist Nikolaus Gansterer and his collaborators is a central example in Fedorova's analysis, as it moves from two-dimensional diagrams of mental processes to the activation of such images as choreographic scores for performers to investigate "thinking-in-action."

In the fourth and final section of this volume, "Shared Patterns and Discordant Worlds," the authors variably address a key conundrum in the worlding of the brain: how to move from investigations of single brains and individual behavior to an analysis of group level action and even social or cultural patterns of behavior? And how can approaches from different fields jointly raise new questions about these phenomena, without themselves simply subscribing to the notion of a shared, coherent world of interdisciplinary research?

In a multimodal and kaleidoscopic contribution, the artist Antye Guenther, humanities scholar Flora Lysen, and cognitive neuroscientist Alexander Sack conduct a playful experiment in image and text association, centered on the theme of imaging and imagining the brain. This bouncy way of exchanging thoughts, they propose, could serve as a model for exercising interdisciplinarity, a frisk assignment to kickstart conversations about the brain between researchers from different fields. In the next chapter, Michael Wheeler is also interested to know how arts and humanities research can be brought into mutual dialogue with cognitive science, to which the former contribute more than new data and research material for the latter. One of Wheeler's examples is the debate around the notion of "group cognition," to which classicist scholarship on Athenian political practice contributes the insight and evidence that cognition is not necessary a property of individuals. Similarly, the works of performance artists can function as psychological experiments that explore the possibility of group cognition. If 4E scholars want to develop new approaches to memory, perception, emotion, and cognition, Wheeler proposes, they can learn from arts and humanities researchers that productively "disrupt" and augment emerging approaches to worlding.

A move beyond the study of single brains is also central to the next two chapters, which analyze interpersonal interactions in the practices of musicians and dancers. Shannon Proksch, Majerle Reeves, Michael Spivey, and Ramesh Balasubramaniam study multi-agent human interaction in the case of musicians who perform a score. When uncoordinated fanfare sounds finally unify into an accomplished piece, the authors observe a type of "collective synergy." By coordinating their acoustic behaviors, the musicians are co-creating what the authors describe as a "shared musical world." In the next chapter, Suzanne Dikker and Suzan Tunca examine concepts and processes of synchronizing (both of bodily motions and brain activities) in experimental workshops with dancers. The authors deliberately foreground the ambiguous notions of "synchrony" and "synchronicity" because these terms articulate a productive friction between different disciplinary understandings, opening up a dialogue between approaches from dance research and cognitive neuroscience.

The final contribution by Stephan Besser critically questions notions of worlds that are "shared" and supposedly mutual. In 4E scholarship and predictive processing research, the term "patterned practices" refers to shared, habitual actions in specific material environments that create "common worlds." Besser argues that such notions of patterns can obscure internal conflicts, intra-cultural differences, and clashes of allegedly coherent "worlds." When studying worldings of the brain, he argues, it is important to keep in mind the plurality, irregularity, and partiality of all possible worlds as well.

References

Callard, Felicity, and Des Fitzgerald. *Rethinking Interdisciplinarity across the Social Sciences and Neurosciences*. Palgrave Macmillan, 2015.

Caracciolo, Marco, and Karin Kukkonen. *With Bodies: Narrative Theory and Embodied Cognition*. Ohio State UP, 2021.

Choudhury, Suparna, and Jan Slaby, editors. *Critical Neuroscience: A Handbook of the Social and Cultural Contexts of Neuroscience*. Wiley-Blackwell, 2011.

Clark, Andy. *Being There: Putting Brain, Body, and World Together Again*. MIT Press, 1997.

Clark, Andy. "Where Brain, Body, and World Collide." *Daedulus*, vol. 27, no. 2, 1998, pp. 257–88.

Clark, Andy. *Surfing Uncertainty: Prediction, Action, and the Embodied Mind*. Oxford UP, 2016.

Crippen, Matthew and Jay Schulkin. *Mind Ecologies: Body, Brain, and World*. Columbia UP, 2020.

Czeszumski, Artur, et al. "Hyperscanning: A Valid Method to Study Neural Inter-Brain Underpinnings of Social Interaction." *Frontiers in Human Neuroscience* vol. 14, art. 39, 2020.

David, Pascal. "Welt." *Dictionary of Untranslatables: A Philosophical Lexicon*, edited by Barbara Cassin et al., Princeton UP, 2014, pp. 1217–25.

Deleuze, Gilles, and Félix Guattari. *A Thousand Plateaus: Capitalism and Schizophrenia*. Translated by Brian Massumi, Continuum, 2004.

Descola, Phillipe, "Cognition, Perception and Worlding." *Interdisciplinary Science Reviews,* vol. 35, no. 3–4, 2010, pp. 334–40.

Durt, Christoph, et al., editors. *Embodiment, Enaction, and Culture: Investigating the Constitution of the Shared World*. MIT Press, 2017.

Fitzgerald, Des, and Felicity Callard. "Social Science and Neuroscience beyond Interdisciplinarity: Experimental Entanglements." *Theory, Culture & Society*, vol. 32, no. 1, 2015, pp. 3–32.

Frost, Samantha. "Ten Theses on the Subject of Biology and Politics: Conceptual, Methodological, and Biopolitical Considerations." *The Palgrave Handbook of Biology and Society*, edited by Maurizio Meloni et al., Palgrave Macmillan, 2019, pp. 897–923.

Gere, Charlie: "Brains-in-Vats, Giant Brains and World Brains: The Brain as a Metaphor in Digital Culture." *Studies in History and Philosophy of Biological and Biomedical Sciences*, vol. 35, no. 2, 2004, pp. 351–66.

Haraway, Donna J. *Staying with the Trouble: Making Kin in the Chthulucene*. Duke UP, 2016.

Heidegger, Martin. *Der Ursprung des Kunstwerks*. 1950. Reclam, 2012.

Herman, David. *Storytelling and the Sciences of Mind*. MIT Press, 2017.

Kraus, Cynthia. "Linking Neuroscience, Medicine, Gender and Society through Controversy and Conflict Analysis: A 'Dissensus Framework' for Feminist/Queer Brain Science Studies." *Neurofeminism: Issues at the Intersection of Feminist Theory and Cognitive Science*, edited by Robyn Bluhm et al. Palgrave Macmillan, 2012.

Littlefield, Melissa M., and Johnson, Jenell. "Introduction: Theorizing the Neuroscientific Turn-Critical Perspectives on a Translational Discipline." *The Neuroscientific Turn: Transdisciplinarity in the Age of the Brain*, edited by Melissa M. Littlefield and Jenell Johnson, U of Michigan P, 2012, pp. 1–25.

Malabou, Catherine. *What Should We Do with Our Brains?* Translated by Sebastian Rand, Fordham UP, 2008.

Malabou, Catherine. *The New Wounded: From Neurosis to Brain Damage*. Translated by Steven Miller, Fordham UP, 2012.

Metzinger, Thomas. *The Ego Tunnel: The Science of Mind and the Myth of the Self*. Basic Books, 2009.

Morgan, Ben. "Situated Cognition and the Study of Culture: An Introduction." *Poetics Today*, vol. 38, no. 2, 2017, pp. 213–33.

Morton, Timothy. *Hyperobjects: Philosophy and Ecology after the End of the World*. U of Minnesota P, 2013.

Northoff, Georg. *The Spontaneous Brain: From the Mind-Body to the World-Brain Problem*. MIT Press, 2018.

Otis, Laura. *Rethinking Thought: Inside the Minds of Creative Scientists and Artists*. Oxford UP, 2015.

Palmer, Helen, and Vicky Hunter. "Worlding." *New Materialism*, 16 Mar. 2018, https://newmaterialism.eu/almanac/w/worlding.html.

Papoulias, Constantina, and Felicity Callard. "Biology's Gift: Interrogating the Turn to Affect." *Body & Society*, vol. 16, no. 1, 2010, pp. 29–56.

Pitts-Taylor, Victoria. *The Brain's Body: Neuroscience and Corporeal Politics*. Duke UP, 2016.

Ramstead, Maxwell, et al. "Cultural Affordances: Scaffolding Local Worlds through Shared Intentionality and Regimes of Attention." *Frontiers in Psychology*, vol. 7, art. 1090, 2016.

Roepstorff, Andreas et al. "Enculturing Brains through Patterned Practices." *Neural Networks*, vol. 23, no. 8–9, 2010, pp. 1051–59.

Rose, Nikolas. "The Human Sciences in a Biological Age." *Theory, Culture & Society* vol. 30, no. 1, 2013, pp. 3–34.

Rose, Nikolas, and Joelle M. Abi-Rached. *Neuro: The New Brain Sciences and the Management of the Mind*. Princeton UP, 2013.

Roy, Deboleena. "Neuroscience and Feminist Theory: A New Directions Essay." *Signs: Journal of Women in Culture and Society*, vol. 41, no. 3, 2016, pp. 531–52.

Schneider, Tanja, and Steve Wolgar. "Neuroscience beyond the Laboratory: Neuro Knowledges, Technologies and Markets."*BioSocieties*, vol. 10, no. 4, 2015, pp. 389–99.

Schregel, Suzanne, and Tieneke Broer. "Contested Narratives of the Mind and the Brain: Neuro/psychological Knowledge in Popular Debates and Everyday Life." *History of the Human Sciences*, vol. 33, no. 5, 2020, pp. 3–11.

Spivak, Gayatri Chakravorty. "Three Women's Texts and a Critique of Imperialism." *Critical Inquiry*, vol.12, 1987, pp. 243–61.

Spivak, Gayatri Chakravorty. *A Critique of Postcolonial Reason: Toward a History of the Vanishing Present*. Harvard UP, 1999.

Starr, Gabrielle. *Feeling Beauty: The Neuroscience of Aesthetic Experience*. MIT Press, 2013.

Tewes, Christian, et al. "Introduction: The Interplay of Embodiment, Enaction, and Culture." *Embodiment, Enaction, and Culture: Investigating the Constitution of the Shared World*, edited by Christoph Durt et al., MIT Press, 2017, pp. 1–22.

Thornton, Davi. *Brain Culture: Neuroscience and Popular Media*. Rutgers UP, 2011.

Varela, Francisco J., Evan Thompson, and Eleanor Rosch. *The Embodied Mind*. MIT Press, 1991.

Vidal, Fernando. "Brainhood, Anthropological Figure of Modernity." *History of the Human Sciences*, vol. 22, no. 1, 2009, pp. 5–36.

Vidal, Fernando, and Francisco Ortega. "Approaching the Neurocultural Spectrum." *Neurocultures: Glimpses into an Expanding Universe*, edited by Francisco Ortega and Fernando Vidal, Lang, 2011, pp. 7–24.

Vidal, Fernando, and Francisco Ortega. *Being Brains: Making the Cerebral Subject*. Fordham UP, 2017.

Vroman, Leo. *Gedichten 1946–1984*. Querido, 1985.

Wheeler, Michael. *Reconstructing the Cognitive World: The Next Step*. MIT Press, 2005.

Wolfe, Cary. "'Theory,' the Humanities, and the Sciences: Disciplinary and Institutional Settings." *Journal of Literature and Science*, vol. 10, no. 1, 2017, pp. 75–80.

Zunshine, Liza, editor. *Introduction to Cognitive Cultural Studies*. Johns Hopkins UP, 2010.

PART 1

Worlded Brains

CHAPTER 1

"Worlding" the Brain through the Cultural Practice of Rhetorical *memoria*

Michael Burke

1 Introduction

Rhetoric is a core humanities subject. For hundreds of years, it made up the backbone of learning and skills acquisition in the western scholastic world, together with its two sisters: grammar and logic. Memory is a key concept in rhetorical theory and practice. It is the fourth of the five canons and it allows orators to speak persuasively, unhindered by notes and props.[1] In this study, I will begin by first reflecting on my own rhetorical teaching practice and then by describing a two thousand year old method of rhetorical memorization from a book I use in my teaching called *Rhetorica ad Herennium*. I will then consider the main two aspects from that mnemonic theory, namely *backgrounds* and *images* in the light of contemporary research on the cognitive neuroscience of memory. In particular, I will bring the ancient method of rhetorical *memoria* into a conversation with the modern theories of constructive memory and simulation theory in the hope that they may initiate a meaningful exchange on how the mind and brain may become "worlded" through the cultural practice of rhetoric.

I start with taking you back to the rhetoric classroom. It is often said of speaking in public that it is the most terrifying activity a person can engage in. Many surveys have shown that public speaking is top of the list of things that people are most afraid of; dying often comes second. That insane statistic means, as a wise person once observed, that when given a choice to give a eulogy at a funeral or be in the casket, a majority would choose the latter.[2] In that classroom, the terrified future orators wait and they contemplate how on earth they are going to be able to learn how to speak extemporaneously and persuasively for a long period of time without written notes or mnemonic prompts.

---

1 The five canons of rhetoric that have existed in this form since the Roman days of oratory are (1) invention, (2) arrangement, (3) style, (4) memory, and (5) delivery.
2 See, for example, Croston.

© KONINKLIJKE BRILL NV, LEIDEN, 2023 | DOI:10.1163/9789004681293_003

2 Rhetorical *memoria* in a Classroom Setting

When I teach *rhetorical memoria* in my freshman course *Introduction to Rhetoric and Argumentation* at University College Roosevelt in Middelburg in the Netherlands, I do my best to follow the advice laid out in the book *Rhetorica ad Herennium*, about which I will say more in the next section. Towards the end of my course, I ask the students to each deliver a ten-minute persuasive speech by heart, without notes. That speech needs to have three different arguments that will all support the main standpoint. Students are allowed to carry a small flash card in their pocket with some key bullet point concepts on it which they may take out and use in case they lose their train of thought, but, in principle, the entire speech should be delivered extemporaneously without visual aids. How do the students prepare for this feat of memorization and delivery and how can they possibly succeed? Well, I do not get them to learn the text verbatim, as, for example, a theater actor would have to. Rather, I start off my rhetorical *memoria* class by having them take the *ten animals test*.

In this visualization test, I first show the students a list of ten animals on a screen for approximately ten seconds and ask them to memorize all ten animals in the correct order in that they appear. These are: (1) pig, (2) rabbit, (3) duck, (4) cow, (5) rhino, (6) sheep, (7) monkey, (8) cat, (9) mantis, and finally, (10) elephant. I then remove the list from the screen and ask for volunteers to recall what they have remembered. Sometimes, one or two students may get five out of ten correct, and these are more or less in the correct order, but most students get just two or three right. I then tell them a tactile, sensory, vivid narrative that I deliver in an engaging storytelling-like fashion, whereby I try to enter a house and move through the hallway, then the kitchen, then up the staircase, then into the bathroom and finally into the bedroom encountering, one by one, the ten brightly colored, noisy, smelly, active animals. All senses are deployed in my narrative account: sight, sound, smell, taste, and touch. When I am finished telling this story, I ask the students to run through the story that they have just heard me tell silently in their mind's eye, only this time they make themselves the protagonist who, in a first-person narrative, goes into the house and experiences in a multi-sensual way the manifestation of the animals. Once they have done this, I ask again who can now recite the ten animals aloud in the correct order that you have encountered them. Not only can almost all students do this successfully, but when I ask them "out of the blue" to do it again at the end of the semester, some four weeks later, then most of them still can.

After this warm-up exercise, we move on to prepare more directly for the 10-minute persuasive speech that they will give. I start by asking my students to recall a real familiar location or background. This can be the layout of their current family home or their childhood home. It could even be the layout of the student dormitory at the university or one of the buildings that they often frequent for classes. They then have to enter the front door in their mind's eye, as a first-person narrator, and go into at least three rooms, one for each argument, starting from left to right. They then have to arrange their arguments (and any sub-arguments they might have) as vivid images in an orderly fashion, again from left to right. They are encouraged to use large objects as a setting/background for the argument image, like, for example, a chair or table or desk or TV. They then have to place a colorful, dynamic, and surprising image on each of these locations. The vivid image will present the argument; the more absurd, incongruent, and striking the image, the better, as this will make the argument more memorable and more easily retrievable. I also encourage students to number the arguments. For example, a student can enter their old childhood home in their visual memory and go into the room immediately to the left. This could be a dining room with three large objects, for example, a dining table, a sideboard, and a large armchair. The main argument is placed on the table and the two supporting/sub arguments are placed on the sideboard and on the chair, respectively. These are now labelled argument "one," "two" and "three." The main argument in the following room will be labelled "four" and its two sub/supporting arguments "five" and "six."

The locations in the first rooms are now all given vibrant and dynamic objects that seek to engage several of the senses. For example, on the table there could be a large black dog, sporting a bright, turquoise-colored bow instead of a collar, and jumping on bright green balloons and bursting them with its gnashing and gnarling teeth. This scene provides us input across the domains of color, sound, and movement and could, for example, represent an argument about the destruction of wind energy projects by big oil companies. Once all backgrounds have been selected for their distinction and peculiarity and all arguments have been vividly created to rest at/on these locations, students can run up and down the arguments, back and forth: first from one-to-nine and thereafter from nine-to-one. They repeat this until if I ask "which is argument number five?" they can answer almost immediately. This method tends to work with most students, certainly if they repeat the process over again, as described above. The key to this whole process of rhetorical *memoria* rests in training and in mental/visual flexibility and creativity. This idea of argument retention via mental visual means is not my own; far from it. It is based on a text in a handbook that is more than 2000 years old: the *Rhetorica ad Herennium*.

3 Rhetorical *memoria* in the *Rhetorica ad Herennium*

The *Rhetorica ad Herennium*, written in 80 BC, is the oldest surviving Latin textbook on rhetoric. The author is unknown, though it was long thought that it was written by Cicero. The book is addressed to a certain Gaius Herennius, who was perhaps a young man who was about to enter a school of rhetoric after having been in schools of first grammar and then logic. Many years later the book would be translated into many different European languages and it would be used extensively as a key rhetorical textbook in Latin schools during the Renaissance and Early Modern periods in Europe. The work is unique because not only does it have the oldest surviving systematic treatment of style (*elocutio*), which is the third canon of rhetoric, but it also includes the first complete treatment of memorization (*memoria*) via the method of loci.[3] This is to be found at the end of Book III and will be our focus of attention. At its essence, this section provides a set of memory instructions for budding public speakers. Whoever wrote the book, it is clear that he was aware of previous Greek attempts to memorize words via the creation of images, because he discusses these methods in the book and critiques them for being cumbersome and ineffective. In his own handbook, the author argues for a more image-based, rather than word-based, approach to memorization (225). This is what we will now look at more closely.

The author starts by saying that there are two types of memory: a natural type and an artificial type. The first is a kind of "everyday" memory, as we know it, and the author devotes very few lines to this. His main interest is in what he terms "artificial" memory. Artificial memory, he claims, is the kind of memory that "is strengthened by a kind of training and system of discipline" (207). He adds that memory requires training and discipline in order to reinforce and develop its natural capacities (207). The author also notes that artificial memory, i.e., rhetorical *memoria*, is principally concerned with two related matters, namely *backgrounds* and *images*. By backgrounds, he means simple, small-scale, and completed locations such as a house, an intercolumnar space, a recess, an arch, etc. By images, he means a figure or mark or characteristic of the object that we wish to remember (209). He gives a number of examples including those of a horse, a lion, and an eagle and advises his young reader, Gaius Herennius, to place them in a definite background (209). He adds that if

---

3 The method of loci stems from a story, via Plato, that is told about the Greek poet Simonides, who had been employed to recite verse to a group of guests in a house during a dinner/symposium. Simonides has to briefly leave the house and while he is outside, the building collapses and the guests are all killed by the falling masonry, and as a result their faces and bodies become unrecognizable. It is down to Simonides and his powers of locative and spatial memory to relate to the authorities who is whom. He succeeds by relying on his spatial memory of their position in the room.

we want to memorize a large number of items, then we will need a large number of backgrounds and that these items should be in a recognizable series, so that we can start at any point and go backwards or forwards (209–11). These backgrounds must be marked after every fifth one and they should be recognizable so that "they may cling lastingly in our memory" (211). They should also be devoid of people as "people confuse and weaken the impress of the images, while solitude keeps their outlines sharp" (211). The background must be neither too small nor too large. If the background is too large it will "render the images vague" (213). Backgrounds should also be neither too bright nor too dim (213). He also suggests having about thirty feet between backgrounds "for, like the external eye, so the inner eye of thought is less powerful when you have moved the object of sight too near or too far away" (213).

With regard to the second concern of artificial memory, namely images, the author of the *Herennium* says that "by properly arranging the patterns of the background, and carefully imprinting the images, we shall easily succeed in calling back to mind what we wish" (215). He notes further how ordinary images in the real world easily slip from memory, but a striking image does not. He compares the daily rising of the sun to a solar eclipse: the first is almost instantly forgettable, as it happens every day, but the second is arguably unforgettable, as it occurs so seldom and, when it does, it is prominent and noteworthy (219). He advises that we must imitate natural vision when we employ mental imagery in rhetorical mnemonic acts and use striking manifestations. We must therefore "set up images of a kind that can adhere longest in memory. And we will do so if we establish likeness as striking as possible" (221). He also advises to make these manifestations active and either extraordinarily beautiful or exceptionally ugly; to dress them in crowns and purple cloaks; to disfigure them or have them smeared with soil or blood or red paint. He adds that one can also assign some comedic effect. All these effects will make the likeness (i.e., the image of the object) more distinct to us, so that it will ensure that we can remember them more readily (221). Lastly, the author of the *Herennium* says that "everybody, therefore, should in equipping himself with images suit his own convenience" (223), by which he means that one must not take striking images "off the shelf," as it were, but construct them individually, for what may seems conspicuous or striking to one person, may not be so to another.

4 Rhetorical *memoria* in the Context of Neuro-Cognitive Memory Studies

Thus far we have looked at the rhetorical notion of what has been termed "artificial memory." We will now consider it within the modern and broader context of neuro-cognitive memory studies. Two areas that I will focus on that have emerged from the foregoing discussion are the key notions of *backgrounds* and *images*. The two questions that we will investigate are, first, what are the cognitive and neural processes that lie behind how we consciously recall and "see," in our mind's eye, much cherished buildings and locations from our past, and, second, how do we consciously construct vivid, original, and dynamic images to occupy those imagined locations?

How can we account for the notion of "backgrounds" in rhetorical *memoria* as set out in the *Rhetorica ad Herennium*? Let us begin by recalling some of the key aspects on this matter. The author states that backgrounds should ...

- be simple, small-scale, and completed locations
- occur in a series so that a person can cognitively move back and forth between them with ease
- be marked after every fifth one and be recognizable
- be devoid of people
- be neither too small nor too large
- be neither too bright nor too dim

It could be fair to say that when viewed on its own, the type of memory that the budding rhetoricians are using here in envisioning these backgrounds is as close to what the classical rhetoricians would refer to as "natural" memory, as it is to "artificial" memory. This is the case as consciously "recalling" those memories seems to dominate over any sense of having to "construct" or "create" them. Of course, such memories, for example of a childhood home, can never be wholly accurate or real or completely stable. However, for most of us, barring trauma, the effort to close our eyes and return, as it were, to the locations of our childhood home and move freely from one room to another, and back again, is a relatively artless cognitive task. The idea of backgrounds therefore does not tell us much new about memory, especially when considered in isolation. From a mainstream cognitive psychological perspective we can conclude that it is likely that episodic memory—a kind of autobiographical form of long-term memory that is both flexible and conscious—plays a key processing role here in the recollection of such backgrounds. This will be in interaction with the so-called "visuospatial sketchpad," which is located in working memory. From a neurobiological perspective, such episodic memories are believed to be mainly stored in the pre-frontal cortex (Brand and Markowitsch), though cross-cortical input from motor, audio, and visual regions will also be occurring. There is, however, an interesting observation with regard to *backgrounds* and that is when the author states that they "should be marked at every fifth one," especially if there are many. This number compares favorably with Miller's 1956 work on memory "chunks" or our capacity to process

"WORLDING" THE BRAIN THROUGH THE CULTURAL PRACTICE 25

information, where he claimed the magic number to be seven plus/minus two. This knowledge therefore appears to have been around for at least 2000 years before it was "discovered" in 20th-century cognitive psychology.

With this in mind let us now move on to consider the second component of rhetorical memory, namely images, as this promises to be a far more elucidating aspect of *memoria* for contemporary studies in neuro-cognitive memory. How can we better understand, in contemporary terms, the notion of "images" in rhetorical *memoria* as set out in the *Rhetorica ad Herennium*? As above, let us begin by recalling the key aspects on the notion of images. The author states of images that they should:

- be striking
- be made to do something
- be constructed/created and not taken "off the shelf"
- be a figure or mark or characteristic of the object that we wish to remember
- be extraordinarily beautiful or exceptionally ugly
- not be many or vague
- imitate natural vision
- have some comedic effect

The type and amount of cognitive effort needed to produce images is arguably much greater than that needed to produce backgrounds. This does not relegate backgrounds to some subdivision, as they are essential to the optimal functioning of images. Background and images are two sides of the same coin. Without backgrounding, no foregrounding is possible. In order to create an enduring image that will be placed in a designated background, an orator must start from scratch and build that image, drawing on both structural and intuitive creativity. Let me return to an example I used earlier, namely that of the large black dog that was jumping on bright green balloons and bursting them with its teeth. This, I said, represented an argument pertaining to the destruction of wind energy projects by big oil companies. So what did I do here in constructing and creating this image?

Well, I sought to make the image striking with the big black dog with his distinctive turquoise bow around his neck and the bright green balloons. I also made the dog and the balloons active—I made them do something; the dog was jumping and biting and the balloons were popping. I could also hear, in my mind's ear, the gnashing and gnarling of the dog's teeth and the loud bangs as the balloons burst. The combined senses of sound, vision, and motion are all employed here. I might have added taste and smell to amplify the effect, but on this occasion I chose not to. This dog was also not taken "off the shelf," as it were. It was not some dog that I know of, either in real life or from popular culture.

Rather, I constructed it from scratch. If I reflect now on what it looks like, it is a kind of bull mastiff/German shepherd cross. It was quite ugly, and although it was a little scary, it also had some absurdist, even ridiculous, comedic elements, which created a mildly humorous effect. This was arguably achieved by its purposely-placed incongruent huge turquoise-colored bow, instead of a black studded collar, which, drawing from popular culture, one might expect to find on such a fierce canine.

This creative-constructive process was not difficult to achieve, nor was it simple. It required some dedicated creative cognitive effort and, in a way, a method of analogical or metaphorical production. The argument had to fit the image. Hence, the men behind the big oil industry were represented by the size and the aggression of the dog, and the commodity they deal in, namely oil, was represented by the color of the animal, black. The green color of the balloons and the air/wind inside them represented the windmills of future green energy. The willful, targeted destruction of these balloons represents the obstinate delaying tactics of large oil companies who do not wish to switch to green resources. In sum, therefore, unlike *backgrounds*, which seem to rely heavily on structural recall, *images* appear to require a significant amount of constructive and creative *memory-making*. This suggests that a considerable amount of subjective agency must be involved in this type of memory. Let us investigate this idea further.

Cognitively and neurally, there is arguably much more going on with images than is the case with backgrounds. As with backgrounds, the so-called "visuospatial sketchpad," located in working memory, will be involved. However, the extent to which episodic memory is involved is uncertain, as the construction of images is not a matter of autobiographical recall but of constructive creation and event simulation. One neural area that arguably does come into play here is the so-called episodic buffer. This is a functional area that is also viewed as a third subordinate system to the central executive in working memory (in addition to the phonological loop and the visuospatial sketchpad; cf. Baddeley, "The Episodic Buffer"; Baddeley, "Working Memory"). It is housed in the pre-frontal cortex and it plays an important role in higher cognitive processes.[4] This functional area communicates between long-term and short-term memory and it acts as a buffer between the phonological loop and the visuospatial sketchpad. It also holds, and temporarily stores, integrated and assimilated episodes from both perception and long-term memory

---

4 Having said this, there is probably not a single area responsible for the episodic buffer. In an interview from 2010 on the website *Go Cognitive* Baddeley suggests that the episodic buffer arises through the emerging properties of a number of different brain areas working together.

"WORLDING" THE BRAIN THROUGH THE CULTURAL PRACTICE 27

(Baddeley, "The Episodic Buffer"; Funahashi). Among other things, the episodic buffer allows for the novel elaboration of mental imagery.

Baddeley provides us with the vivid examples of both an "ice-hockey playing elephant" and a swan doing the shopping ("Working Memory" 857). He suggests, quite rightly, that we are unlikely to have encountered such combinations in real life. Baddeley also alludes to how we can elaborate almost endlessly on these examples. We could, for instance, put the swan on a hover-board or give it a large floppy hat or paint it bright orange. Semantic, long-term memory will give us the base details: the swan, the shopping bag, the hover board, the hat, and the paint that will assist recall. However, when we combine them, something special occurs: we see a swan out getting the groceries. This is the ability to integrate and assimilate episodes from perception and long-term memory. Baddeley also explains that this is possible because humans have the ability to extend reality and in doing so create a multitude of novel, vivid mental objects and scenarios. This process of novel elaboration of mental imagery, described by Baddeley, is almost certainly the same thing as the images that I have been discussing in rhetorical *memoria* exercises and therefore, arguably, accounts for it. What we are dealing with here are constructive and simulative processes of memory. Let us explore this idea a little further.

We have known for a long time that memory is about much more than storage and retrieval, a simple "input-output" transaction the like of which Plato envisioned with his wax tablet hypothesis. Frederick Bartlett's influential work on schemas from the late 1920s is a good case in point to show just how far back such insights into memory as a constructive process go.[5] Recent work on the simulation hypothesis of memory has made this far more explicit. Schacter and Addis, for example, in their work on the *constructive episodic simulation hypothesis*, explicitly relate episodic memory to the imagination of future events. Moreover, in later work by Schacter it has been revealed that (i) episodic memory supports the construction of imagined future events, (ii) both remembering the past and imagining the future rely on many of the same cognitive processes, and (iii) episodic memory can flexibly recover and combine stored information to produce highly original scenarios of imagined future events (Madore et al.).[6]

---

5   In his experiments, participants had to read a story set in an alien culture and then recall it. They did so in their own idiosyncratic way in that they all altered unfamiliar objects, places, and concepts in the story for things that were familiar to them in their own world. This suggests a relatively subjective, culturally-driven encoding and retrieval process. "Remembering," therefore, appears to be a constructive process that draws on the expectations, ideas, and emotions of the human individual.

6   We could therefore conclude that whereas Bartlett's model is constructive, Schacter et al.'s is imaginative/simulative.

Artificial memory, as we saw earlier in citations from the *Rhetorica ad Herennium*, is a type of memory that is strengthened by systematic training and discipline. From this, we see that rhetorical memory is not just a passive disposition. What can be suggested is that backgrounds, but especially images, in rhetorical *memoria* are not "found" or "located" or "retrieved." Rather they are constructed, organized, and applied in an active fashion. This suggests further that the notion of "agency" in memory is not merely a recent phenomenon. It is one that has a tangible ancient precursor in the theory and practice of *memoria* from classical rhetoric.

If we now reflect and take stock, then what we see happening during rhetorical acts of *memoria* is an organization of the contents for later, flexible use by integrating them into a new network of semantic contents. Hence, when a public speaker constructs backgrounds and images during acts of rhetorical memory, a process is started involving the dynamic retrieval and blending of stored information. This produces highly original scenarios of imagined upcoming "events"; ones not unlike my previous example of a black dog with its turquoise bow tie, jumping and popping the bright green balloons. All this arguably requires metacognition as a precondition, something that was only recognized and labelled by American psychologist John Flavell in the 1970s, even though it appears to have been in practice already in the classical world of rhetoric two millennia ago. At its core, metacognition is an awareness of one's own thought processes; a knowledge of one's cognitive strategies. It is a higher level of cognition that can take many forms. These include problem solving and reflecting on one's own thinking patterns. Metacognition also manifests itself in self-regulating processes and in acts of thinking about one's learning and in one's memory strategies. We can postulate here that metacognition in rhetorical memory is something that distinguishes it from Schacter's et al. simulative episodic memory, as rhetorical memory is consciously manipulated, while episodic constructive memory can arguably function without metacognition. If we take this as given, then we can also now see how the rhetorical tradition makes use of the capacities of episodic memory by developing a cultural technique, or cultural practice, for oration, of which the *Rhetorica ad Herennium* handbook is a fitting example. Here, we recognize a certain cultivation, and indeed a certain worlding, of brain capacities. Moreover, in addition to the benefits and adaptive value of constructive memory, Schacter et al. also talk lengthily about memory distortions, errors, false recognition etc. Perhaps rhetorical memory could be an example where such "deficiencies" are used— and indeed cultivated—in a productive way? This is a thought-provoking by-product, as it were, that warrants further exploration in future studies.

In light of all of the above, it is plausible to argue at a meta-level that neuroscientific memory research could have made a significant leap forward, decades earlier than it actually did, both in constructive memory and in simulation theory, had it taken more seriously these ideas from the classical world of rhetorical memory and had it used them as cognitive scientific hypotheses to be tested in contemporary settings.

5   Conclusion

The preceding discussion has brought the old, i.e., ancient classical rhetoric, into a dialogue with the new, i.e., the science of neuro-cognitive memory studies. More specifically, it has focused on the concepts of rhetorical *memoria* on the one hand and constructive memory and simulation theory on the other. The bringing together of these two perspectives on memory has shown us what steps might be taken in future research towards gaining a better understanding of how past and present, humanities and science mutually influence and act upon each other. It also shows us how modern concepts in embodied cognitive neuroscience can be anchored both in the texts and in the daily crafts and practices of antiquity. I know for one that when I next teach practical *memoria* sessions in my rhetoric class, I will be seeking to introduce my students to the theory and processes of the constructive episodic simulation hypothesis. Similarly, when I engage in cognitive poetic analysis, for research purposes, from a perspective of embodied cognition, I shall seek to draw in some of the precepts and practices from classical rhetoric and especially from the domains of style, memory, and delivery. Perhaps, unbeknown to myself, I may already be in possession, via classical rhetoric, of the knowledge that I am actually seeking in the cognitive neurosciences. What has become clear in this short study is that a detailed consideration of rhetorical *memoria* in the context of neuro-cognitive memory, and vice-versa, helps us in better understanding the processes that may lie behind how the human mind and brain become "worlded." That, in itself, is an interdisciplinary goal that is well worth pursuing.

Acknowledgments

I am greatly indebted to both Machiel Keestra and Stephan Besser for input given on the first draft of this chapter. Any inaccuracies that remain in the text are the responsibility of the author.

References

Baddeley, Alan D. "Is Working Memory Still Working?" *American Psychologist*, vol. 56, no. 11, 2001, pp. 851–64.

Baddeley, Alan D. "The Episodic Buffer: A New Component of Working Memory?" *Trends in Cognitive Science*, vol. 4, no. 11, 2000, pp. 417–23.

Baddeley, Alan D. Interview PodCast. "Location of the Episodic Buffer." *Go Cognitive*, Nov. 2010, https://www.youtube.com/watch?v=KTwQX21ICIU.

Baddeley, Alan D., and Graham J. Hitch. "Working Memory." *The Psychology of Learning and Motivation*, edited by G.H. Bower, vol. 8, Academic Press, 1974, pp. 47–89.

Brand, Matthias, and Hans J. Markowitsch. "The Role of the Prefrontal Cortex in Episodic Memory." *Handbook of Behavioural Neuroscience*, vol. 18, 2008, pp. 317–41.

[Cicero]. *Rhetorica ad Herennium*. Translated by Harry Caplan, Harvard UP, 1954.

Croston, Glenn. "The Thing We Fear More Than Death." *Psychology Today*, 29 Nov. 2012, https://www.psychologytoday.com/us/blog/the-real-story-risk/201211/the-thing-we-fear-more-death.

Funahashi, Shintaro. "Working Memory in the Prefrontal Cortex." *Brain Science*, vol. 7, no. 5, 2017.

Madore, Kevin P. et al. "Constructive Episodic Simulation: Dissociable Effects of a Specificity Induction on Remembering, Imagining, and Describing in Young and Older Adults." *Journal of Experimental Psychology: Learning, Memory, and Cognition*, vol. 40, no. 3, 2014, pp. 609–22.

Miller, George A. "The Magical Number Seven, plus or Minus Two: Some Limits on Our Capacity for Processing Information." *Psychological Review*, vol. 63, no. 2, 1956, pp. 81–97.

Schacter, Daniel L., and Donna Rose Addis. "The Cognitive Neuroscience of Constructive Memory: Remembering the Past and Imagining the Future." *Philosophical Transactions of the Royal Society B: Biological Sciences*, vol. 362, art. 1481, May 2007, pp. 773–86.

CHAPTER 2

The Mediated Brain

A Case Study on Experiential Engagement with Cinematic Form

Joerg Fingerhut

1   Introduction

The cultural artifacts and media we interact with create our reality. Our cities, the architecture and design of our built environment determine our embodied actions and are themselves models of the social beings we are. The multimedia environments of digital and social media both enable and constrain our interactions with one other. And screen-based media provide us with fictional and documentary images that play a central role in mediating an understanding of ourselves and the world we live in. Recently, philosophy of mind and cognitive science have spurred new interest in topics such as media-related differences in cognition (Fingerhut, "Enacting Media"). In particular, *embodied, embedded, extended,* and *enactive,* or so-called "4E" approaches to cognitive science (Newen et al.) could play a central role in developing a theory of the ways different media co-constitute our models of the world.

This chapter will focus on embodied engagements with pictures and especially moving images. We are currently experiencing intriguing developments in the field of neuroscience of film. Besides experimental works in neuro- and psychocinematics (Hasson et al.; Shimamura), collaborations between film scholars and neuroscientists also recently led to integrative theoretical assessments, such as the *embodied simulation* theory of filmic empathy and cinematic experience, as in Vittorio Gallese and Michele Guerra's *The Empathic Screen.* Such theories employ neuroscientific evidence to defend broader film-related claims yet have also been criticized for providing a limited perspective on our filmic engagement (Turvey). I will reflect on this debate by discussing studies regarding film form and by investigating some of the contentious interpretations of the editing and camera work in Alfred Hitchcock's film *Notorious.*

Overall, I aim to demonstrate two ways of *worlding the brain.* First, recent theorizing advances an understanding of the brain as a fast and frugal engagement device that is intimately bound to its environment—*worlded,* so to

© KONINKLIJKE BRILL NV, LEIDEN, 2023 | DOI:10.1163/9789004681293_004

speak—and that constantly changes strategies of engagement according to different cultural settings and media ecologies. This is related to what has been labeled "enculturation" (Menary) and acknowledges that cognition and experience are based on culturally mediated habits and engagement skills. Here, it can be argued that such habits are co-constituted by the cultural artifacts we encounter and differentiated with respect to what kinds of engagements these artifacts afford (Fingerhut, "Habits" and "Enacting Media"). This highlights the need to address the material and structural contributions of architecture, pictures, media, and filmic works within the framework of enculturation. One upshot of such a perspective is that the brain does not *reconstruct* the external environment but rather employs it to bring forth meaning. What is more, cultural artifacts and media themselves could be seen as constituting experiential models of the world that recruit the brain and not the other way around.

Second, we can *world the brain* by means of collaborations of practitioners, humanities scholars, psychologists, and neuroscientists. This includes the planning, set up, and analysis of experiments. In experimental philosophy, there is already a growing body of work utilizing empirical methods from psychology and the social sciences to generate their own data and analyze them to tackle philosophical problems anew (so-called X-Phi; see for aesthetics Cova et al.; Fingerhut et al.). Yet, collaborations with neuroscientists remain the exception. Due to the broader availability of neuroimaging and electroencephalography (EEG) devices, these latter interdisciplinary interactions are likely to increase in the future. The worlding of the brain we jointly embark on, then, encompasses the selection of stimuli and participants targeted, the range of responses that are measured, as well as the interpretation of the experiment and of the data generated. I will report on some such interdisciplinary research and indicate future directions.

2 Embodied Enculturation

In recent decades there has been a growing understanding of the brain's adaptability and plasticity with respect to social and cultural contexts. Neuroscience approaches enculturation from the viewpoint of the brain (such as experience-driven neuroplasticity) and, in an intriguing conceptual turn, sees the brain itself as an artifact of its cultural environments (Mithen and Parsons; Gendron et al.). Enculturation is sometimes also addressed with a focus on practices and artifacts and the way they jointly contribute to the development

THE MEDIATED BRAIN

and realization of cognitive abilities. "Cognitive integration" theories, in particular, address how new artifacts (e.g., the invention of paper, printing press, and personal computers) and the novel practices related to them might have altered and enhanced the kinds of cognitive solutions humans employ, for instance the ability to solve mathematical problems (Menary).

In addition to brain enculturation (i.e., a theory of the internal set of concepts we have derived from culture) and cognitive integration (i.e., a theory of how the brain relies on social settings and external devices to realize cognitive solutions), I think it is decisive to address the ways human organisms bring forth a plurality of experiential models of the world in different cultural settings and media ecologies (Fingerhut, "Enacting Media"). In this context, I have argued that embodied predictive processing theories provide a good approximation of how the brain contributes to our engagement with culturally construed "designer environments" (Clark 275). In a sense, experiential models have been "uploaded" into the environment: they are present in cultural practices and different media, such as texts, images, film, and architecture (in very much the same way as has been argued about certain cognitive functions having been uploaded into our cognitive niches; Constant et al.). Those different media constantly entrain our brain-body nexus.

Our brains are therefore *worlded* in cultural environments. They should be understood in terms of the role they play in those more expansive habits of bringing forth meaning and experiences. Such habits can be described as explorative activities that are co-structured by the very artifacts and media ecologies that make up our culture. Understood in this way, brains do not have to mirror the different world models we encounter (or the media-specific ways they engage us). Instead, they are highly potent, action-ready devices that facilitate our engagement with the cultural models we are presented with.

3 Media Ecologies and Film Form

A key task for cognitive neuroscience is to capture the normal conditions of engaging different media ecologies. What habits of sensorimotor and affective engagement have we developed by being exposed to the built environment? How do these differ structurally from perceiving a picture or experiencing a movie? For those different exploratory habits, I suggest that *neuromediality* could be a helpful concept to capture the specific contribution of the brain to an otherwise locationally and temporally extended process that includes patterns of bodily engagement and the structures of media themselves. The aim of the concept of *neuromediality* is to acknowledge the enabling conditions of the brain, yet to focus more directly on how we enact media; that is to capture how media and organism jointly bring forth meaning and value in different media (Fingerhut, "Enacting Media").

For the remainder of this chapter, I will discuss this in the context of a neuroscience of *film form*, specifically camerawork and editing. In what ways can a neuroscientific experiment that addresses our engagement with such forms deepen our understanding of the medium of film? While such an understanding could also refer to technological developments, on the one hand, and more general questions regarding media ecologies, on the other, it is indeed within specific forms that we perceive the content, stories, and models presented in movies and TV. Therefore, while the medium as such remains imperceptible (or only becomes perceivable once it is no longer mediating its content), it is in such media-typical forms that we engage and experience the different cultural worlds surrounding us.

Form is a broad concept. Each culture (and subculture) can be understood as bringing forth specific affective forms (iconic images, styles, representations). An encompassing theory of the encultured mind should also be able to explain the impact of such culture-specific forms. Yet, as stated above, the focus of this chapter is rather on the basic conditions of our cognitive engagement with some of the basic building blocks of film. These include, among others, *mise en cadre, mise en scène,* lens- and camerawork, as well as editing. These forms can be developed into specific styles and are used in unique ways by different traditions, cultures, and filmmakers that constitute the more specific affective forms mentioned above. Just consider how editing expresses ideas (such as in Eisenstein's polyphonic montage) and can be associated with different subcultures (such as the fast, MTV-style editing of clips in the 1980s). And yet, it also determines more generally all film experience. How then might neuroscience clarify our engagement with such formal elements? How can it help to assess, for example, the way lenses and cameras are employed to tell a story or present a perspective on the world?

4 From Marks on a Surface to Cinematographic Spectatorship

The *embodied simulation* (ES) theory of cinematic spectatorship is a key example of extending neurocognitive research (in this case on the pre-motor and mirror neuron system) to a wider theory of the appreciation of cinematic works. The general idea of ES is that the brain-body system uses some of its neural resources that are related to motor-planning and processing of its own

THE MEDIATED BRAIN

actions to also map the behavior of others. When applied to film, it claims that we use ES to engage with movie characters (i.e., their actions and facial expressions) and to track the filmmakers' marks, such as lens and camera movements (i.e., film form as introduced above).

Previously, ES has been applied to our aesthetic engagement with artworks and images more generally, such as paintings and drawings (Freedberg and Gallese). Here, critics have argued that motor simulation is neither necessary nor sufficient for an understanding of our aesthetic engagements in such cases (Casati and Pignocchi). However, those critiques ignore that ES first and foremost aims to explain our more basic emotional engagement with images (i.e., how do we pick up emotions from figurative paintings or abstract forms?) and only argues, secondarily, that our felt motor or emotional responses are also a crucial element for theories of aesthetic judgment. In Freedberg and Gallese's approach, the latter step indeed remains underdeveloped, yet there are *prima facie* good reasons to assume that the embodied engagements they focus on should also figure into a theory of aesthetic experience, appreciation, and artistic practice.

The ES account of pictures includes depicted (or recognitional) elements such as bodies, faces, and gestures of people in pictures. Yet, it crucially also addresses configurations on the surface, such as brushstrokes or cuts in canvases and, therefore, the outcomes or marks of the artist's gestures. Several studies have established that the perception of such artistic signs triggers ES mechanisms and activation of the same motor centers required to produce those signs.

Similar things can now be said with respect to marks related to film form. As has been studied in EEG experiments, the succession of frames in films (and the way framing, editing, and lens- and camerawork are used to portray a scene) also employs the motor system differently for some types of filmic form compared to others (Heimann et al., "Moving Mirrors" and "Embodying"). This has been the basis for an ES account of filmic empathy defended by Gallese and Guerra (GG) and accounts of our filmic body (Fingerhut and Heimann, "Movies and the Mind").

Let's focus for now on GG's account of film and the criticism it recently faced. Film scholar Malcolm Turvey is among its harshest critics, stating that "it is mischaracterizations of artistic practice, such as the ones found in Gallese and Guerra's account, generated by the attempt to extend a controversial scientific theory to cinema, that make [him] seriously pessimistic about the role science has to play in film studies" (43).[1] Turvey separates questions regarding our engagement with film from those of the theory's potential for explaining

---

1 I will not address how controversial mirror neuron theory is as a theory of action understanding and limit myself here to a discussion of its application to cinema.

artistic achievements. In the end, for him, ES fails on both counts: it cannot properly explain central features, such as immersion in film, and is therefore also prone to misrepresenting the artistic practices underlying central movie scenes and their appreciation.

So-called anthropomorphic camera movement is a key example of this. This relates to shots made by using a handheld camera or similar techniques. According to ES theory, the perception of traces of such camera movements is underlain by embodied simulations and by activity in the pre-motor system. GG give heavy explanatory weight to the impact of such camera work: "the involvement of the average spectator is directly proportional to the intensity of camera movements" (91). Turvey here rightly objects to the generality of this statement and claims that camera movement itself is not *sufficient* for immersion: not every movie that employs a specific camera movement would succeed in engaging the viewer. Additionally, he asserts that camera movement might also not be *necessary* and that there are other routes to becoming immersed in film.

GG are a bit more cautious when it comes to neuroscientific evidence, yet they nonetheless claim that motor neuron activity is "the starting point for the study of the intensity of our experience" (55) and credit the degree of internal simulation to be a central element in the explanation of filmic engagement: "we maintain that the functional mechanism of embodied simulation expressed by the activation of the diverse forms of resonance or neural mirroring discovered in the human brain play an important role in our experience as spectators" (68). Here, Turvey criticizes a lack of evidence for such a role and an inflation of the underlying mechanism for a theory of film. Also here one might agree. It seems wrong to identify one neural mechanism as mainly responsible for a phenomenal, psychological state at the expense of discussing other, more cognitive (i.e., the conceptual grasp of a story), contextual (i.e., the implication of previous scenes for our engagement), affective (i.e., the attachment to characters), or historical and culturally mediating factors.

What I do not agree with, however, is Turvey's own overgeneralization that any motor theory is necessarily prone to mischaracterize the artistic achievements it aims to capture (more on this in a bit). Also, nothing stands in the way of engaging in a more balanced experimental assessment of the impact of context and story in relation to motor involvement. Indeed, GG never claim to *fully* explain experiences at the movies and do acknowledge the impact of the factors listed above. While Turvey might therefore rightly object to some of GG's explanation of filmic features, this does not sufficiently establish that a neuroscience of film *cannot* enrich our understanding of filmic works. The experimental neuroscience of film is still in its infancy (and more mixed

THE MEDIATED BRAIN   37

method studies are underway). And it can only become a valuable contributor to an understanding of filmic engagement if it is accompanied by theoretical discussion from adjacent fields. Yet this requires a certain openness of film scholars and a more charitable assessment of the respective studies. GG's own interpretation of some results might dissatisfy some, yet it constitutes a collaborative engagement (in this case between a film scholar and a neuroscientist) that we need more of.

What the experimental studies on motor involvement (on which GG heavily rely) already have shown is that—all things being equal—certain camera movements (e.g., a *Steadicam* vs. a *zoom*) elicit stronger responses in motor areas and a putatively stronger feeling of involvement (Heimann et al., "Embodying"). Such studies rely on controlled conditions that are void of context and use multiple repetitions of the same scene. In what ways do these settings limit their results? How might they nonetheless contribute to a general theory of our filmic engagement? These are questions that philosophers of mind and media, film theorists, psychologists, and neuroscientists can and *should* discuss collaboratively.

5   Embodying the Camera? Alfred Hitchcock's *Notorious*

I will discuss the promises and pitfalls of ES and related motor accounts by revisiting a key scene in Alfred Hitchcock et al.'s film *Notorious* (1946). The upshot will be mixed. While I support some aspects of the view in GG I think it is in need of further experimental support and some philosophical refinement.

The scene in question portrays Alicia (Ingrid Bergmann) at a central juncture of the plot in which she has been instructed by Devlin (Cary Grant) to steal a key from her husband Sebastian (Claude Rains). Possession of this key would enable Devlin to disrupt an evil conspiracy. The scene starts with an outside shot of a Spanish villa and then cuts to the inside with Alicia moving towards us. While walking, she puts on her earrings in preparation for a party that night. She slows down at a door frame close to the camera with her face in close-up (Figure 2.1). Then there is a cut to a *point of view* (POV) shot of Alicia seeing her husband's shadow on the bathroom door (Figure 2.2), followed by a cut back to her continuing her movement from the previous shot and coming to a full halt. At the end of her movement, we see her gaze drop down. After another cut, the camera moves towards a dresser in the intermediate room and pans slightly to the left coming to a rest on a close-up of a keychain on the dresser to which (we know as much at this point) the relevant key is attached (Figure 2.3). Next, we see a full body shot of Alicia standing in the doorway (Figure 2.4). She starts

FIGURE 2.1   Still from *Notorious* (Hitchock et al., RKO, 1946)

FIGURE 2.2   Still from *Notorious* (Hitchock et al., RKO, 1946)

to walk towards the camera and the dresser with the key. At the very moment she wants to pick it up, Sebastian (still out of sight) addresses her, startling her before she can grab it: "I'm surprised at Mr. Devlin coming tonight... ."

In this scene, Hitchcock and his cinematographer Ted Tetzlaff diverge significantly from Ben Hecht's original script that suggested a medium shot of Alicia moving toward the dresser and a close-up of the keys (mimicking a similar shot of the same key planned for a previous scene; Hecht 98). Instead, we see the camera movement and the panning towards the key in this scene (Figures 2.2–2.3). This becomes a prime example in GG's account, who argue that our motor simulation of the camera transports us directly to the location of the keys. They interpret this as a SPECIFIC *point of view* (POV) shot: "the spectator naturally and immediately associates it with Alicia's movements. Nothing more is needed; we attribute the immanence of a human body to that movement. Hitchcock conveys this impression even more clearly when he moves the camera to simulate the gesture of the keys being picked up; in that precise moment, the spectator has the impression that the keys have been picked up and the difficult task entrusted to Alicia has been successfully completed" (58). In their interpretation, the viewer had perceived Alicia moving to the dresser, therefore experiencing a surge of frustration upon seeing her remain stationary in the doorway (Figure 2.4).

FIGURE 2.3   Still from *Notorious* (Hitchock et al., RKO, 1946)

FIGURE 2.4   Still from *Notorious* (Hitchock et al., RKO, 1946)

6   More Is Needed: *Notorious* Revisited

GG's interpretation of this scene is a clear application of their claim that motor engagement is central for involvement and extends it to an assessment of the artistic mastery of Hitchcock and colleagues. As interesting as this is, I believe that it is inconclusive and that we should include further filmic means in the discussion of this scene as well as consider additional experimental research.

It is relatively safe to assume that the camera movement in *Notorious* elicits motor responses that are stronger compared to a scene without movement or even one with a *zoom*. The reference for this is a study, in which we used high-density EEG while participants watch clips of an empty room with different camera and lens approaches (Heimann et al., "Embodying"). There we found a stronger motor system involvement in participants watching a *Steadicam* approach towards a table compared to versions with a *still shot* or even a *zoom*. We offered multiple interpretations of these findings: the spectator might "'embody' the camera," or take "the position of a 'quasi-character' moving through the filmic scene" based on pre-motor engagement with marks of the cameraperson visible in the succession of frames (Heimann et al., "Embodying" 14).

THE MEDIATED BRAIN   41

The issue with GG is that they singled out one such interpretation for the respective *Notorious* scene. According to them, the spectator immediately anticipates Alicia's motor intentions, interprets the camera movement as hers, and is "beset of feelings of frustration" at seeing her still standing in the doorway (Figure 2.4; 58). They claim that the viewer experiences Alicia's movement toward the dresser and expects her to pick up the keys: we have been tricked into believing that Alicia has already reached the keys.

Yet, to vindicate such an interpretation (or to falsify it) a broader psychological and phenomenological assessment of such scenes is needed, potentially leading to additional experimental designs and refined hypotheses for future studies. When I tested whether audiences experience disappointment or surprise in the *Notorious* scene, viewers were split on the topic. After having seen the full scene, surveys revealed a roughly 60:40 split in favor of "no surprise" over "I was surprised" when the scene cut back to Alicia in the doorway (n = 64). Some reported that they experienced the camera movement rather as an intense gaze of Alicia. Other preliminary results from an online survey align with this finding. The mean rating of surprise (from "not at all" to "very much" on a 7-point scale) was below the midpoint (Podschun and Fingerhut, *unpublished data*).

Already those preliminary data demonstrate the need to address additional questions: would participants who saw the whole movie instead of just one scene rather lean towards a higher surprise? Did those who experienced heightened surprise also have increased motor activation during the camera movement? Would there be a difference in felt surprise in case Hitchcock et al. would have used a *zoom* (historical issues aside) instead of a *Steadicam*-like shot (with only the latter eliciting stronger motor activations)? The general challenge is how to correlate such neuronal data to experiences. In the 2019 study we also conducted short exit interviews about the participants' experiences of the conditions (participants reported to have seen "real movement" in the *Dolly Shot* but not the *zoom* condition, Heimann et al., "Embodying" 14). We since enhanced our interview techniques (employing methodologies from micro-phenomenology), which could provide an important route for future research aiming to correlate phenomenological assessments with ratings by viewers and neurological data (Fingerhut and Heimann, "Enacting Moving Images").[2]

---

2   The limitation of above EEG experiments for such questions are rather obvious. Stimuli of each condition have to be shown multiple times for robust results, ruining any chance to measure surprise. Yet more indirect measures could be conceived, such as priming some

7   Advocating Studies on Neuromediality

Turvey also discusses the *Notorious* scene. He doubts that a spatio-temporal immersion as described by GG is experienced and questions the importance of evidence derived from studies on motor (or mirror) neuron activation. His point of criticism is general: the bulk of the literature on mirror neuron stimulation focuses on the role of the motor system in basic action understanding (e.g., seeing others preparing to grasp something). He argues that if sensorimotor activity of pre-motor neurons were *sufficient* for immersion, we should also feel immersed in such extra-cinematic action understanding, but we obviously do not. Moreover, he accuses GG of interpretive bloat: the authors take the little evidence we have of engagement with traces of the kinematics of camerapersons (contained in the succession of frames) to provide a full explanation why we experience tension or even suspense while viewing the *Notorious* scene. In contrast to GG, Turvey highlights the cognitive and contextual elements that, to his mind, are much more likely to be responsible for the heightened suspense in *Notorious:* the plot, the motives of the characters involved (Alicia also happens to be in love with Devlin, so she not only wants to prevent her husband's evil plans, but also fears for Devlin), her husband Sebastian's shadow in the bathroom, etc.

Turvey's critique is a valuable assessment of potential pitfalls (such as premature *sufficiency* claims). Yet again, his remarks are insufficient to fully dismiss motor accounts of filmic engagement that might still contribute to an explanation of central components of our filmic engagement. What is more, there is a danger that the way he discusses the neuroscientific results might unduly widen the gap between the neurosciences and the humanities. By refocusing the discussion of ES onto extra-cinematic or real-world action perception, Turvey ignores the possibility that our motor system might fulfill quite different functions and contributes differently to our experience in cinematic conditions. As argued in the initial paragraphs, there is a need to understand how neural activity may have been incorporated into habits of engagement and exapted (taken on different functions compared to our everyday actions) for cultural artifacts such as film.

The concept of *neuromediality* directly aims at such an understanding and interrogation of the contribution of the brain to filmic engagements (and other media and cultural artifacts). The role the brain takes on here has evolved

---

motor engagement (which would putatively lead to heightened motor involvement with the camera work) and then assessing whether such primed participants would feel more involved and/or surprised.

THE MEDIATED BRAIN

in the process of media-organism cognitive co-development. Our habits of engagement can be seen as locationally expansive, i.e., including brain, body, and cultural artifacts as their structural features. In film, for example, the body-brain nexus becomes entrained in the filmic exploration of a scene, a process that is dominated by the medium itself, with the organisms coming along for the ride (Fingerhut, "Enacting Media"). Cinema and TV have been so pervasive, in this sense, that we should entertain the idea of a filmic body schema that is employed when we watch a movie and that allows for heightened activation of (pre-)motor areas in such cases. We surrender our embodied responses to the medium itself, while at the same time suppressing real world engagements (Fingerhut and Heimann, "Movies and the Mind"; see also the concept of "liberated embodied simulation" in Gallese and Guerra 41).

There has been significantly less research on how film form or stylistic elements engage the motor system than research on social cognition (i.e., the perception of everyday action perception and understanding of emotions). Yet, this does not mean that such research could not produce interesting insights into our encultured mind. Here, both Turvey (who wholeheartedly dismisses motor neuron accounts) and GG (who pass over more fine-grained explanations to assume a parallelism between motor engagement and phenomenal involvement) do not reach the potential of a motor account of moving images, leaving many things barely explored.

8   Twofoldness and Expanding the Motor Equation

Filmic "twofoldness" is such an underexplored component. This concept goes back to Richard Wollheim's claim that there is a specific genus of perception appropriate to pictures called "seeing-in." According to him, there is parallel perception of configurational features (the canvas, blobs on a wall) and recognitional features (the scene presented) that is also accompanied by a phenomenal awareness of both elements, i.e., a *twofold* experience. While I cannot do justice to the rich literature on seeing-in and twofoldness in this chapter, I will briefly suggest its possible extension to cinema (see also Fingerhut, "Twofoldness").

The parallel processing of movement that is perceived in the cameraperson's traces (e.g., in a *Steadicam* approach) *and* of a depicted person can be a good illustration of how twofoldness could become relevant also for empirical aesthetics focusing on mirror neurons. One can easily imagine that an embodied camera approach could also rather detract from involvement with the character in such a scene. This could result in less immersion because the motor involvement is split, so to say, between the means of depiction and what is depicted. This could be due to the parallel processing of both (based on how motor neurons might be recruited for different empathic processes) that in certain cases might also shift the awareness mostly to camerawork and to a larger extent away from the depicted person.

Heimann and colleagues found stronger motor activation in response to a *Steadicam* approach (compared to a *zoom*) for clips that included a person sitting behind a desk and performing an action (Heimann et al., "Moving Mirrors"). Yet, in the questionnaire part of their study, participants did not report increased involvement. This raises questions about how neurological, psychological, and phenomenal data relate and how experienced engagement has to be understood under the auspices of twofoldness.

This also points towards additional factors to be considered before applying such results to a broader interpretation of cinema. The scenes presented in the above experiments are without context: we simply see, for example, a person picking up a cup. In cinema, the situation is quite different: we are already invested in the plot and follow the character across different shots in a scene (to restate Turvey's point). Context also matters in another way: a *Steadicam* approach to a person might direct our attention to the camera work itself, especially if such a camera movement is rarely used throughout the movie or differs from the one used in the scene before. In such cases we might feel less immersed and rather attend to the novelty of the camera approach itself. The concept of twofoldness strengthens our understanding of these constellations. In cinema, the phenomenology of our film experience is the integrated experience of a configurational series (including framing, camera work, editing, etc.) and a recognitional series of the evolving content or story. Perhaps, as Terrone suggests, it is therefore more a "twoseriesness" that we experience in film (225).

Context in both series of the film is important. Such that what is depicted also influences how we perceive the configurational element, not only in the simultaneous perception but also with respect to what has been depicted just before a certain scene. More fine-grained elements play a role here, for example, when deciding where to cut in a movie. As the editor and film scholar Karen Pearlman has remarked, editors themselves are the sounding boards of the pre-cognitive embodied-emotional engagement that certain shots provide within a scene, since they determine "which shot, where, and how long" (Pearlman 78). Reflecting on our Hitchcock scene, she notes that just before the false POV in question, Alicia moves slightly forward before and looks down to the left. These latter frames are out of focus. Pearlman speculates that the editor, Theron Warth, might have included the last elements of this movement to create a specific effect. This includes the out of focus effect (of which Pearlman

THE MEDIATED BRAIN 45

thinks it originally probably was a mistake of the cinematographer) and the dropping of the view of the actress. Both contribute to a special form of engagement. Hence, we have two contextual elements that interact with the camera movement that follows the cut: a configurational one (the reduced focus) and a recognitional one (the drop of her gaze). It is therefore worth considering how those contribute to the experience. Is it because of the looking down that some of us experience the camera movement as an intense gaze on something (in this case the key)? Is it because some viewers miss this pivotal dropping of the gaze that they experience the camera movement as Alicia moving towards the key (and not as just looking)?

This could prompt new experimental manipulations. What would happen if we removed those few frames for one group but left them in for another? Would leaving them in elicit more or less motor activation during the camera movement? More or less experienced involvement? More or less surprise that Alicia is still at the door?

These are ways to test the impact of context and story. What plays a bigger role for our feeling of involvement: motor activation (due to configurational or depicted elements), contextual elements, or story (which both might also influence motor activation)? What mediates what in such cases? [3] Based on our expanded view of motor engagement, we can now generate further hypotheses based on onitial experimental evidence that can be weighed against other interpretations and falsified in future experiments (or limited in their generality). Such considerations should have a place within the critical repertoire of film scholars and philosophers rather than be dismissed wholeheartedly.

9 Conclusion and Outlook

I have advocated for a stronger integration between film studies, philosophy of mind, experimental aesthetics, and cognitive neuroscience. Turvey rallies for the opposite: "rather than rushing to embrace the latest scientific theory, it might be wise for film scholars to wait until it has been subjected to rigorous scrutiny by those who have the requisite expertise and neutrality to assess it properly" (43). Such a move risks that our engagement with media, and questions regarding artistic achievement will become an afterthought for neuroscience (if, e.g., most of the exploration of motor neurons will be carried out

---

3   Also GG who sometimes seem myopic with respect to one aspect (motor system activiation) acknowledge (e.g., in chapters dealing with multimodal integration) the need to study more complex processes and interactions.

within social neuroscience, with no consideration for cultural developments and aesthetic repertoires).

I have been more critical of ES and the concept of mirror neurons in theories of action understanding and of pictorial engagement than this brief essay may convey. I subscribe to an enactive-embodied perspective on ES that does not require what could be called a simulation or personal identification within the motor system itself (Fingerhut, "Enactive Aesthetics"). Additionally, instead of focusing on neural responses to pictures and moving images alone, philosophers should address the role such media play as part of a larger predictive, world-exploring engine that spans brain, body, and cultural environment.

The motor system (and ES accounts) nonetheless plays a central role in a *worlded* and enculturated understanding of the brain. It tracks opportunities for engagement and action that unfold in our environment and with respect to cultural artifacts such as pictures and movies. Notwithstanding critiques of "simulation" and "mirroring" in ES accounts, I think it is worthwhile exploring the role of the motor system in picking up elements of configuration and recognition and their contributions to a twofold filmic experience. Even Turvey's criticism might ultimately press neuroscientists to adjust their overly optimistic and sometimes carefree interpretations and guide them (and theoretical followers) towards more cautious theorizing. In the future, approaches to film (from historians, theoreticians, and practitioners) could reference several types of data (from historical sources, artists' reports, experimental philosophy, and cognitive neuro-psychology), thereby contributing to a more detailed and rewarding approach to understanding filmic engagement. As I aimed to demonstrate, an empirically engaged philosophy of film and other media can lead to new experimental settings that address relevant questions for such a theory. They also might lead to more measured interpretations of previous neuroscientific data. In such a collaborative sense, I remain a cautious optimist: only through joint inter- and transdisciplinary efforts can the field truly mature.

References

Casati, Roberto, and Alessandro Pignocchi. "Mirror and Canonical Neurons Are Not Constitutive of Aesthetic Response." *Trends in Cognitive Sciences*, vol. 11, no. 10, 2007, p. 410.

Clark, Andy. *Surfing Uncertainty: Prediction, Action, and the Embodied Mind.* Oxford UP, 2016.

Constant, Axel, et al. "Extended Active Inference: Constructing Predictive Cognition beyond Skulls." *Mind & Language*, Dec. 2019, pp. 373–94.

Cova, Florian, et al. "Experimental Philosophy of Aesthetics." *Philosophy Compass*, vol. 10, no. 12, Dec. 2015, pp. 927–39.

Fingerhut, Joerg. "Enactive Aesthetics and Neuroaesthetics." *Phenomenology and Mind*, vol. 14, 2018, pp. 80–97.

Fingerhut, Joerg. "Habits and the Enculturated Mind." *Habits: Pragmatist Approaches from Cognitive Science, Neuroscience, and Social Theory*, edited by Fausto and Italo Testa, Cambridge UP, 2020, pp. 352–75.

Fingerhut, Joerg. "Twofoldness in Moving Images: The Philosophy and Neuroscience of Filmic Experience." *Projections*, vol. 14, no. 3, 2020, pp. 1–20.

Fingerhut, Joerg, et al. "The Aesthetic Self: The Importance of Aesthetic Taste in Music and Art for Our Perceived Identity." *Frontiers in Psychology*, vol. 11, art. 577703, 2021, pp. 1–18.

Fingerhut, Joerg. "Enacting Media: An Embodied Account of Enculturation between Neuromediality and New Cognitive Media Theory." *Frontiers in Psychology*, vol. 12, art. 635993, 2021, pp. 1–25.

Fingerhut, Joerg, and Katrin Heimann. "Movies and the Mind: On Our Filmic Body." *Embodiment, Enaction, and Culture: Investigating the Constitution of the Shared World*, edited by Christoph Durt et al., MIT Press, 2017, pp. 353–77.

Fingerhut, Joerg, and Katrin Heimann. "Enacting Moving Images: Film Theory and Experimental Science within a New Cognitive Media Theory." *Projections*, vol. 16, no. 1, 2022, pp. 105–23.

Freedberg, David, and Vittorio Gallese. "Motion, Emotion and Empathy in Aesthetic Experience." *Trends in Cognitive Sciences*, vol. 11, no. 5, 2007, pp. 197–203.

Gallese, Vittorio, and Michele Guerra. *The Empathic Screen*. Oxford UP, 2019.

Gendron, Maria, et al. "The Brain as a Cultural Artifact." *Culture, Mind, and Brain*, edited by Laurence J. Kirmayer, 1st ed., Cambridge UP, 2020, pp. 188–222.

Hasson, Uri, et al. "Neurocinematics: The Neuroscience of Film." *Projections*, vol. 2, no. 1, 2008, pp. 1–26.

Hecht, Ben. *Notorious (Screen Play, RKO Pictures)*. 1946, pp. 1–158, https://rb.gy/8k26r. Accessed 16 July 2023.

Heimann, Katrin, et al. "Moving Mirrors: A High-Density EEG Study Investigating the Effect of Camera Movements on Motor Cortex Activation during Action Observation." *Journal of Cognitive Neuroscience*, vol. 26, no. 9, Sept. 2014, pp. 2087–2101.

Heimann, Katrin, et al. "Embodying the Camera: An EEG Study on the Effect of Camera Movements on Film Spectators' Sensorimotor Cortex Activation." *PLOS One*, vol. 14, no. 3, 2019.

Menary, Richard. "Cognitive Integration: How Culture Transforms Us and Extends Our Cognitive Capabilities." *The Oxford Handbook of 4E Cognition*, edited by Albert Newen et al., Oxford UP, 2018, pp. 187–216.

Mithen, Steven, and Lawrence Parsons. "The Brain as a Cultural Artefact." *Cambridge Archaeological Journal*, vol. 18, no. 3, 2008, pp. 415–22.

Newen, Albert, et al., editors. *The Oxford Handbook of 4E Cognition*. Oxford UP, 2018.

Pearlman, Karen. "Editing and Cognition beyond Continuity." *Projections*, vol. 11, no. 2, 2017, pp. 67–86.

Shimamura, Arthur P. "Psychocinematics: Issues and Directions." *Psychocinematics: Exploring Cognition at the Movies*, edited by Arthur P. Shimamura, Oxford UP, 2013, pp. 1–26.

Terrone, Enrico. "Why to Watch a Film Twice." *The Pleasure of Pictures: Pictorial Experience and Aesthetic Appreciation*, edited by Jérôme Pelletier and Alberto Voltolini, Routledge, 2018, pp. 224–45.

Turvey, Malcolm. "Mirror Neurons and Film Studies: A Cautionary Tale from a Serious Pessimist." *Projections*, vol. 14, no. 3, 2020, pp. 21–46.

Wollheim, Richard. "Seeing-as, Seeing-in, and Pictorial Representation." *Art and Its Objects*. 1980. 2nd ed., Cambridge UP, 2015, pp. 137–51.

CHAPTER 3

Getting a Kick out of Film

Aesthetic Pleasure and Play in Prediction Error Minimizing Agents

Mark Miller, Marc M. Anderson, Felix Schoeller, and Julian Kiverstein

1 Introduction

During 2020, the year in which the Covid-19 pandemic took its hold on the world, the market share of horror films doubled from 12.04% to 23.63%, by far the largest share in modern history ("Box Office Performance History for Horror Movies"). The global pandemic film *Contagion* (Soderbergh) topped the iTunes download charts. Why should a film about a global pandemic prove so popular in the midst of a pandemic? One answer that strikes us as plausible was given by a *New York Times* journalist writing at the beginning of the crisis in the US in March 2020: "The movie hit me squarely in my entertainment cortex, this funny, scary, stylish, soapy, *plausible* speculation of life during a global outbreak. The appeal now is how it's proving to be an instructive worst-case scenario of our current freak-out. We've turned to it, in part, to know how bad things could get" (Morris, our emphasis).

This explanation might strike one as surprising. One might expect comedic relief to be in high demand in these trying times, and that we would avoid exposure to unnecessarily disturbing content in the midst of an already highly volatile situation. However, recent research on recreational fear shows that quantities of fear that are "just-right" can in fact be highly enjoyable (Andersen et al.). Why do people find it enjoyable to engage with sad, frightening, or horrifying narratives? Our aim in this chapter is to open up a new perspective on this "paradox" of horror (Carroll) using an emerging theory of the brain as a prediction error minimization machine.[1]

---

1 Our aim is not to try to reductively explain the pleasure of engaging with film in terms of predictive processing. Instead, we start from predictive processing and ask how to make sense of the experience of pleasure we get from engaging with fiction from this standpoint.

© KONINKLIJKE BRILL NV, LEIDEN, 2023 | DOI:10.1163/9789004681293_005

2 On Being a Predictive Machine

The Predictive Processing Framework (PPF) is ambitious in its scope. The core idea is that the embodied brain's dynamics can be explained as an internal (generative) model making inferences about the world based on sensory information (Friston; Clark, "Whatever Next"; Clark, *Surfing Uncertainty*; Hohwy). The human brain constructs a complex, hierarchically structured model of the environment with each layer of this hierarchy predicting changing states of body and world over multiple spatial and temporal scales. This model is sometimes called "generative" because it can be interpreted as mapping how sensory states are believed to be generated by states of the environment and the agent's body. The generative model is used to predict sensory inputs based upon prior expectations. Some of these expectations are the result of learning, others are biases that have a longer evolutionary history. Prediction errors are computed by comparing predictions at each of these layers of the model with incoming sensory information at the level below. Any resulting prediction error can be used as feedback for improving the brain's future predictions. So long as prediction errors are kept to a minimum on average and over time, the brain's predictive model will maximize its usefulness for the agent.

Perception and action work together to keep prediction errors to a minimum. Perception resolves prediction errors by combining new sensory information (i.e., prediction errors) with prior expectations to infer new predictions. Action resolves prediction errors through the production of sequence of movements most likely to bring about the sensory inputs predicted by the generative model. The PPF claims that perception, action, emotion, and cognition all work together in the service of prediction error minimization.

The predictions of the generative model are organized at the lowest layers of the hierarchy of processing around the basic goal of maintaining homeostasis. What the organism cares about first of all is resisting "the natural tendency of things to go over into disorder" (Schrödinger 73). The organism should strive to maintain the stability of its internal dynamics under conditions of change (Sterling). To accomplish this goal, the organism needs a capacity for distinguishing external sensory perturbations that contribute positively to the maintenance of order and perturbations that increase disorder. Long-term prediction error (also referred to as "free energy"), is an informational quantity that serves this need. An unexpected increase in prediction error signals to the organism an increase in disorder the organism should take action to correct. Memory and imagination can be thought of as operating at higher levels of the generative model to minimize prediction errors the agent expects to encounter in the future, thereby allowing for the adaptive control of actions over longer periods of time (Metzinger; Pezzulo; Hesp et al.).

GETTING A KICK OUT OF FILM 51

Agents learn an optimal generative model through balancing an active seeking out of surprise through exploration with exploiting what is already known for the purpose of pragmatic actions. In the PPF this process of action selection is understood as the outcome of inference. Precision estimation over action policies (sequences of actions) plays a central role in this inferential process (Schwartenbeck et al.; Friston et al., "Anatomy of Choice"; Friston et al., "Active Inference"). Precision here refers to the degree of confidence in the belief that an action policy is likely to bring about expected outcomes. Predicted outcomes are understood as outcomes that are valued or rewarding such as eating when hungry. Thus, policies are weighed for precision based on expected prediction error reduction—the divergence between the valued or expected sensory outcome and the sensory outcome that is modelled as likely given one's current situation.[2]

In our earlier work, we have proposed that precision is set in part based on error dynamics—the rate of change in error reduction (Kiverstein et al., "The Feeling of Grip"). An unexpected deceleration in error reduction informs the organism that a belief in an action policy should be assigned lower confidence.[3] The agent should explore the environment for new, surprising, and novel opportunities to improve the predictions of its model. An unexpected acceleration in error reduction informs the organism that things are going better than expected and it should continue on its existing path. This drive for continual optimization means that animals like us are forever on the lookout for better-than-expected slopes of error reduction. In other words, we have evolved to be *slope-chasers*, constantly on the lookout for better and more efficient ways to resolve error (Kiverstein et al., "The Feeling of Grip," Kiverstein et al., "How Mood Tunes Prediction"; Clark, "A Nice Surprise"). The best slopes of error reduction are to be found just beyond the edge of an agent's abilities and understanding (Kiverstein et al., "The Feeling of Grip"). As slope-chasers we are motivated to actively seek out just the right quantities of error that allow for the optimal improvement of a model's predictions (Oudeyer et al.; Kidd et al.; Oudeyer and Smith; Andersen et al.; cf. Berlyne). Too much error means hard to manage environmental volatility, while too little error is boring, meaning there is little of interest for the predictive mind to learn. We call errors that are actively sought out because they have this preferred level of complexity "consumable errors."

---

2 Recall that free energy is equivalent to long-term prediction error (under certain simplifying mathematical assumptions).

3 An action policy here is defined as a path of activity or strategy that leads agents to be in states predicted by the generative model.

The tendency of humans to actively seek out consumable error is evident already from infanthood and is particularly visible in how children play (Schulz; Andersen et al., "Play in Predictive Minds"; Anderson, *Play*). In play, humans (and a series of other intelligent animals) deliberately create consumable errors. Crucially, play seems to be enjoyable for playful organisms only when there is some prediction error to be resolved. There must be some novelty or violation of expectation to pique the organism's interest. This finding may seem to create a problem for the predictive processing theory. Why would a brain that aims at prediction error minimization actively seek out error (Sun and Firestone)? However, this puzzle is only apparent. What the literature on curiosity and play suggests, is that humans and other animals remain engaged and interested only if the error encountered in play is consumable in the long run. In other words, humans and other animals prefer playing with objects that are neither too simple, nor complex, something which at times has been referred to as the "Goldilocks Principle" (e.g., Berlyne 1970; Loewenstein 1994; Kidd et al. 2012; Andersen et al., "Play in Predictive Minds")

The key idea we develop in the rest of this chapter is that media environments tend to curate a desirable supply of consumable error. Humans are prolific designers and engineers of consumable errors. We purposefully structure our environments to provide predictive brains and bodies with constant sources of new prediction error to be resolved (Clark, "A Nice Surprise"). A comparison with roller-coaster rides is instructive: we design roller-coaster rides so that errors will rise to crescendos eventually to be swiftly resolved over the course of the ride. Cultural practices ensure that our nervous systems are never done with resolving prediction errors (Kirchhoff and Kiverstein). Media of all kinds (e.g., books, films, songs, etc.) provide us with an endless source of *consumable* surprise and novelty. These curated error slopes lead us to places that offer new opportunities to learn. We argue that this curated consumable error is an important part of what makes engagement with cultural media, even horror films, sources of pleasure for us. In the next section we explain in more detail why certain surprises are more rewarding than others.

3 Enjoying Surprise: Error Dynamics and Aesthetic Pleasure

Art, film, and literature constantly surprise us—this is part of what we find entertaining about these media. We will argue that the motivation for humans to consume media that are often frustrating, problem-filled, challenging and even frightening makes complete sense from the perspective of a biological system organized to minimize *long-term prediction error*. The fact is that predictive systems like us persist over time not by trying to avoid every possible error but by remaining sensitive to opportunities where the most consumable errors can be found. Our perspective is grounded in the recent evidence that humans find pleasure in unexpected events to the extent that such experiences afford good opportunities for error reduction. There is a consensus, for instance, that jokes that elicit laughter tend to be surprising (Ritchie). But for a joke to be funny, it also must be just surprising enough that the receiver of the joke can quickly attune their prior knowledge to "get" the punchline (Schmidhuber). Similarly, in the cognitive science of music, a recent web-based study investigated the relationship between syncopations (surprising rhythmic accents or stresses relative to the main beat of the music), ratings of wanting to move, and the experience of pleasure. The study found that there was a sweet spot with a medium degree of syncopation which elicited the greatest desire to move and the most pleasure (Witek et al.).

The hypothesis that aesthetic pleasure follows an inverted U-shaped curve, reflecting the complexity of the object or event, was first introduced by Gustav Fechner (the founder of psychophysics) and subsequently taken up by Daniel Berlyne.[4] Berlyne suggested that as long as the object or event was of the right complexity and familiarity the person would enjoy a positive affective experience. They will find the object or event attractive, interesting, and pleasing, and will therefore continue to explore the object. Putting this in terms of error dynamics, what is crucial for the pleasantness of an object is that the error resulting from the novelty and complexity of the object or event is consumable. The error is consumable because through further exploration it can be resolved with the result that the hierarchical generative model is further optimized in terms of its predictions. We find ourselves drawn to places where there is consumable error because these are the places where predictions can often be improved, and progress can be made in learning.

It has been argued that error dynamics are sensed (often unconsciously) as positively and negatively valenced affective states (Kiverstein et al., "The Feeling of Grip"; Van de Cruys; Joffily and Corriceli; Hesp et al.; Wilkinson; Nave). These valenced affective states tune the agent to opportunities to do better than expected in reducing error. In other words, when we discover new

---

4   It should be noted that the concept of the aesthetic in use in Berlyne's research and those that have followed him is not reserved for the experience of artworks. The term aesthetic is used as roughly synonymous with perception that has affect at its core and does not mark any distinction between art and non-art. We are using the notion of the "aesthetic" in the same sense as Starr to refer to "the blend of sensation and knowledge such that we almost feel thought" (Starr xiv, quoting Baumgarten).

strategies, or improve on already existing strategies for error reduction, this feels good. As prediction error minimizing agents what we want and enjoy is to make progress in prediction. Humans are rewarded when they feel like they have discovered new strategies for rapid prediction error minimization. Thus, the PPF can explain why we find pleasure in encountering consumable errors. For a PP agent, pleasure is a matter of making progress in prediction. What pleases predictive agents is to be continuously improving their predictive grip on incoming sensory information in a volatile, noisy, and ambiguous world.

The phenomenon of "recreational fear" is an illustrative example of how humans are attracted to and often enjoy manageable amounts of volatility and error, even if they are associated with domains that are typically considered to be highly aversive (Clasen et al.; Andersen et al., "Playing with Fear"). Teen-agers and young adults will take white-knuckling delight in watching an alien violently burst from the chest of a spaceship crewman (Clasen). In a recent study on recreational fear (Andersen et al., "Playing with Fear"), researchers studied how 110 Danish participants equipped with HR monitors responded to a haunted house attraction and asked participants to report on the experience. Participants in the study were visitors to a Danish haunted house attraction in which actors put on a live action theatrical horror production. For example, in one location a large man wearing a pig mask emerged to chase participants with a live chainsaw. Participant's heart rate was monitored throughout their visit, and they were video-recorded at three of the locations where threatening events occurred. They were also asked to complete a questionnaire in which they were probed about their fear and enjoyment levels of each of the threat-ening events. The results were compatible with the predictive processing per-spective that aesthetic pleasure can be understood in terms of error dynamics. A moderate amount of fear and a moderate amount of small-scale heart rate fluctuations were both linked to heightened states of self-reported enjoy-ment in participants (Andersen et al., "Playing with Fear"). In other words, a U-shaped relationship between fear and enjoyment was found. Just like play, fear can be enjoyable when the eliciting event has the form of consumable error that allows the predictive agent to make further progress in learning.

4 (Horror) Films as Tools of Prediction

Films offer unique opportunities to slope-chasers like us that are drawn towards opportunities to improve our predictive grip on a volatile and noisy world. For prediction error minimizing agents finding good slopes of error is what life is all about. Given its central importance it should come as no surprise that we

GETTING A KICK OUT OF FILM

don't leave our slope-chasing to chance but are rather prolific slope creators and consumers. Our artistic, scientific, and technological endeavors are replete with examples of this drive not only to reduce error, but to create new and exciting opportunities to bend, break and update our models of the world in ways that result in new and surprising error reducing opportunities. Film is a particularly good example of this tendency.

The idea we will explore in this section is that engagement with film is an example of what we will call an "epistemic action policy." Epistemic action policies are exploratory sequences of actions the agent performs to find their way to new information that can increase the likelihood of achieving predicted outcomes in the future. Movies are examples of designed environmental structures that viewers recruit for the purpose of optimizing their generative model.

Many of us enjoy horror fiction. Yet, horror tends to evoke feelings of fear and disgust, paradigm examples of negative unpleasant emotions. How can we enjoy experiences that are supposedly intrinsically unpleasant? We speculate that we enjoy horror films because they afford opportunities to engage playfully with threatening situations, much like in the haunted house example (see also Clasen, "Why Horror Seduces"; Clasen et al.). The monsters that are at one and the same time sources of disgust, fear, and fascination in horror films are the creative constructs of our imaginings. Recall how in the PPF imagination has the function of simulating possible futures, that allow the agent to select action policies that minimize expected prediction errors (Friston et al., "Sophisticated Inference"). We suggest that watching films can offer us an opportunity to externalize the same process of exploring possible futures in imagination that also takes place internally.

Horror is enjoyable for some people because it provides them with an opportunity to play in a safe way with possibilities that scare and disgust them (Clasen, *Why Horror Seduces*; Clasen, "Very Nervous"). Horror, in other words, allows us to bring down levels of prediction error normally associated with horrifying stimuli to a consumable level. Analogously, when children play, they create their own consumable fictive errors to engage with, learn from, and enjoy. A child may for instance pretend that a banana is a smartphone and excitedly gain access to the exploration of new action patterns, forms of communication, and responses from loved ones and caregivers. Children utilize such fictive errors in their pretend play to generate novel scenarios to which they apply their existing causal knowledge. In this way children set themselves up for new possibility spaces and the generation of novel, manageable, and informative inferences (Weisberg and Gopnik; Harris). We suggest adults may also consume fiction, albeit often in more designed forms, as a rewarding way to resolve novel forms of uncertainty, discover better slopes and learn. Films for example are carefully structured, through for instance narrative and cinematography, in ways that produce errors that are temporarily frustrating or challenging but eventually are quickly resolved thereby producing pleasure.

The proposal we are making is that it is pleasurable to make progress in learning. What is it that one learns from these possible but highly improbable worlds one encounters in horror films that could account for what piques one's interest and makes the negative emotions of fear and disgust entertaining? One kind of knowledge one gains concerns the narrative itself, and the twists and turns that take place in the movie. Second, we can learn about real world situations, like in the example of *Contagion*, which offers viewers the opportunity to learn about what might happen during a global pandemic. Finally, horror films may help people to learn about themselves and their affective reaction to volatility. Some support for this prediction comes from a recent study that found horror fans and morbidly curious individuals to be more psychologically resilient during the COVID-19 pandemic (Scrivner et al.).

Horror films can offer viewers an opportunity to encounter and process anxiety-related stimuli in a safe environment. They offer an opportunity for related errors to be experienced and resolved in relatively short succession. Think again of watching the film *Contagion* during a global pandemic whose associated uncertainties are taking years to resolve. For an individual that is suffering the ongoing tension and stress of a situation that is both highly uncertain and extended over time, the opportunity to engage with errors of a similar sort, but ones which will be resolved in a short period of time, could be highly attractive, perhaps even pleasurable. More importantly however, such films may help some individuals to learn about and so better predict their own anxiety reactions to horror-inducing stimuli. They provide individuals with experiences that allow them to correctly model the arc of their own anxiety reactions when encountering high levels of uncertainty. Research suggests that individuals tend to mistakenly predict that their anxiety will escalate endlessly (see Myers and Davies). Horror movies, like all exposure therapeutic approaches to anxiety, would allow viewers to learn that anxiety doesn't necessarily accumulate but tends to rise and fall over time. When the person does a better job of predicting their own reactions this takes care of a source of error that comes with the mistaken assumption of the trajectory of their own anxiety.

5   Films, Aesthetic Chills, and Optimization

We have argued that one of the reasons horror films are enjoyable for us is because they provide us with consumable errors. In our final section, we turn to an example of how films can curate error slopes for the viewer. We focus

GETTING A KICK OUT OF FILM 57

more specifically on moments in a narrative when people report experiencing chills or goosebumps. Chills are the sensation of coldness in the back associated with shivers, a muscle tremor ordinarily involved in keeping the body's temperature stable (~37°C) across changing situations. Goosebumps also ordinarily have a thermoregulatory function, as a "second skin" that minimizes heat loss (Benedek et al.). Surprisingly, humans can experience chills and goosebumps independently of any changes in body temperature.[5] So-called *aesthetic chills* (i.e., psychogenic shivers) occur when we are reading novels, watching movies, listening to music but also when grasping a profound idea in some scientific article or taking part in a religious ritual (Schoeller, "The Shivers of Knowledge"). These chills can occur both in response to highly positive events, such as listening to a specific piece of music or a moving scene in a film (Blood and Zatorre; Schoeller, "The Shivers of Knowledge") and highly negative events, such as scenes of bodily injury or violence and highly unexpected sounds (Schoeller and Eskinazi).

It has been suggested that chills are generated when a point of dynamic equilibrium is reached (Schoeller and Perlovsky). In error dynamics terms this can be thought of as a large-scale shift in expected error reduction. For instance, when a local maximum in learning progress is reached, acceleration in error reduction reaches a peak. A positively valenced chill occurs because of the sudden insight that is gained at the highest layer of the generative model. This insight allows for a sweep of error to be resolved in one go. It is this cascade of error reduction which we are suggesting is felt in the body as a positive chill.

For example, people report experiencing chills in response to the scene in *Titanic* (Cameron) when the ship is about to sink (Schoeller and Perlovsky). The camera focuses on a mother lying in bed with her children. In this scene it is by now clear that the mother and her children will not survive. Yet, the mother continues to tell her children a good night story despite the horrendous events, hinting towards a high-level model of the situation where the relationship between the mother and her children is elevated beyond mere survival—i.e., she is lying to them, beyond her own fears, as she feels that the last moments of her children should be spent in peace rather than in the turmoil of survival (hinting that some things may be more important than life). There is thus a shift in context at the highest layer of the hierarchical model. Whereas one was holding out hope that the mother and her children

---

5   Aesthetic chills are also sometimes described using the terms "frisson" (i.e., French for shivers, Huron) and transcendent experiences (Baltes et al.). Note that the relationship between temperature and information is old. This is referred to in physiology as emotional hyperthermia or stress fever (Oka).

would survive, the film has reached a moment where this hope can no longer be sustained. What evokes the chill is how the mother responds to this situation. She knows she will not survive but she does not react with fear as one might expect. Instead, she responds with calm resignation out of love for her children. This is the prediction error, and the resolving of this prediction error is what shifts our understanding of the whole story in a powerful way. Her response gives the viewer a perspective on how they might relate to their own death and those that they love with acceptance. The viewer gains a new insight both into the lives of the people caught up in this historical event but also into something of personal significance to all of us—how we relate to our own death and those of our loved ones.

The narrative of many movies, in particular Hollywood blockbusters, are structured in such a way as to elicit aesthetic chills. An important part of the pleasure of watching Hollywood films, we contend, is chill-inducing error reduction. Note that film techniques such as editing and cinematography enable the curation of error dynamics at the lowest levels of the perceptual and memory systems, by selectively directing their attention to the important elements of the story (blurring or editing away everything unnecessary, what Hitchcock called the "dull bits of life").[6] Narrative tension increases and decreases over the course of a story, affording controlled error dynamics in the viewer. Increases in tension typically cause negative emotions and decreases in tension typically generate positive emotions. There are however moments in a story where tension peaks, defining the bounds on error dynamics within that particular story line. It is at these peak moments that aesthetic chills can occur. The storyline has reached a point of temporary equilibrium, a *dénouement*, in which the human conflicts that the narrative turns around are resolved, often after a sudden increase (and ultimately decrease) in uncertainty.

---

6 A wealth of recent studies examine how film organizes the flow of perceptual information (review in Schoeller, *La Logique du Film*). Extending the work of early pioneers such as Hugo Munsterberg, Lev Kulechov, or Rudolf Arnheim, a new theory of film emerged in recent years, describing it as an extension of perceptual and attentional processes (Cutting; Zacks). In this context, cinematography replicates, and anticipates the segregation of space (through focus, which duplicates figure, ground discrimination at the retina). Editing replaces the organization of information in time ordinarily occurring through episodic memory (mimicking the temporal organization of memory in situations or episodes). Note that our error dynamics framework accounts for this as well, film techniques resolve (low-level perceptual) uncertainty at a faster than expected rate, by preparing the incoming sensory signals as a function of relevant, meaningful information. There is in fact today a growing industry that brings together neuroscience and computational modeling techniques to better understand and create the precise flow of error creation and resolution that audiences find most appealing (see Wang and Wang).

Phenomenologically, this makes sense of the fact that chills are often surprising to the viewers. Aesthetic chills occur in response to key insights a narrative affords that one can potentially learn from.

6 Conclusion

In this chapter we explored why agents whose brains and bodies are organized to minimize prediction error would find pleasure in experiencing sad, frightening, or horrifying movies. We suggested that such movies curate consumable error slopes for viewers. One reason why predictive agents like us might enjoy fear and horror is because it provides us with the possibility to safely explore threatening uncertainties. Our chapter ended by showing how aesthetic chills—moments of peak pleasure or aversion—can be understood in terms of error dynamics as well. Films can evoke aesthetic chills because of how they curate error slopes for viewers that speak to the highest layers of our predictive generative models. Aesthetic chills mark out moments of potential insight or import for the person. They do so because for agents that aim at improving prediction in everything they do, sudden and dramatic shifts in expected error at the highest layers of the brain's predictive model constitute interesting opportunities to make progress in learning about the world and ourselves.

References

Andersen, Marc M. "Playing with Fear: A Field Study in Recreational Horror." *Psychological Science*, vol. 31, no. 12, 2020, pp. 1497–510.

Andersen, Marc M. *Play*. Aarhus Universitet Press, 2022.

Andersen, Marc M., et al. "Play in Predictive Minds: A Cognitive Theory of Play." *Psychological Review, Advance Online Publication*, 2022.

Balteş, Felicia R., et al. "Emotions Induced by Operatic Music: Psychophysiological Effects of Music, Plot, and Acting: A Scientist's Tribute to Maria Callas." *Brain and Cognition*, vol. 76, no. 1, 2011, pp. 146–57.

Baumgarten, Alexander Gottlieb. *Meditationes philosophicae de nonnullis ad poema pertinentibus = Philosophische Betrachtungen über einige Bedingungen des Gedichtes.* Edited by Heinz Paetzold, Meiner, 1983.

Benedek, Mathias, et al. "Objective and Continuous Measurement of Piloerection." *Psychophysiology*, vol. 47, no. 5, 2010.

Berlyne, Daniel E. "Novelty, Complexity, and Hedonic Value." *Perception & Psychophysics*, vol. 8, no. 5, 1970, pp. 279–86.

Blood, Anne J., and Robert J. Zatorre. "Intensely Pleasurable Responses to Music Correlate with Activity in Brain Regions Implicated in Reward and Emotion." *Proceedings of the National Academy of Sciences of the United States of America*, vol. 98, no. 20, 2011, pp. 11818–23.

"Box Office Performance History for Horror Movies." *The Numbers*, https://www.the-numbers.com/market/genre/Horror.

Carroll, Noël. *The Philosophy of Horror, or Paradoxes of the Heart*. Routledge, 1990.

Clark, Andy. "A Nice Surprise? Predictive Processing and the Active Pursuit of Novelty." *Phenomenology and the Cognitive Sciences*, vol. 17, 2018, pp. 521–34.

Clark, Andy. *Surfing Uncertainty: Prediction, Action, and the Embodied Mind*. Oxford UP, 2016.

Clark, Andy. "Whatever Next? Predictive Brains, Situated Agents, and the Future of Cognitive Science." *Behavioral and Brain Sciences*, vol. 36, no. 3, 2013, pp. 181–204.

Clasen, Mathias. *Why Horror Seduces*. Oxford UP, 2017.

Clasen, Mathias. *A Very Nervous Person's Guide to Horror Movies*. Oxford UP, 2021.

Clasen, Mathias, et al. "Adrenaline Junkies and White-Knucklers: A Quantitative Study of Fear Management in Haunted House Visitors." *Poetics,* vol. 73, 2019, pp. 61–71.

Clasen, Mathias, et al. "Horror, Personality, and Threat Simulation: A Survey on the Psychology of Scary Media." *Evolutionary Behavioral Sciences*, vol. 14, no. 3, 2020, pp. 213–230.

Contagion. Directed by Steven Soderbergh, 2011.

Cutting, James E. "Narrative Theory and the Dynamics of Popular Movies." *Psychonomic Bulletin & Review*, vol. 23, no. 6, 2016, pp. 1713–43.

Friston, Karl. "The Free-Energy Principle: A Unified Brain Theory?" *Nature Reviews Neuroscience*, vol. 11, no. 2, 2010, pp. 127–38.

Friston, Karl, et al. "The Anatomy of Choice: Dopamine and Decision-Making." *Philosophical Transactions of the Royal Society B: Biological Sciences*, vol. 369, no. 1655, 2014.

Friston, Karl, et al. "Active Inference: A Process Theory." *Neural Computation*, vol. 29, no. 1, 2017, pp. 1–49.

Friston, Karl, et al. "Sophisticated Inference." *Neural Computation*, vol. 33, no. 3, 2021, pp. 713–63.

Harris, Paul L. "Early Constraints on the Imagination: The Realism of Young Children." *Child Development*, vol. 92, no. 2, 2021, pp. 466–83.

Hesp, Casper, et al. "Deeply Felt Affect: The Emergence of Valence in Deep Active Inference." *Neural Computation*, vol. 33, no. 2, 2021, pp. 398–446.

Hitchcock, Alfred. *Interview for the BBC Programme 'Picture Parade'*. BBC, 1960.

Hohwy, Jakob. *The Predictive Mind*. Oxford UP, 2013.

Huron, David. *Sweet Anticipation: Music and the Psychology of Expectation*. MIT Press, 2006.

Joffily, Mateus, and Giorgio Corricelli. "Emotional Valence and the Free-Energy Principle." *PLOS Computational Biology*, vol. 6, art. 10030940, 2013.

Kidd, Celeste, et al. "The Goldilocks Effect: Human Infants Allocate Attention to Visual Sequences That Are Neither Too Simple nor Too Complex." *PLOS One*, vol. 7, no. 5, 2012.

Kirchhoff, Michael, and Julian Kiverstein. *Extended Consciousness and Predictive Processing: A Third Wave View*. Routledge, 2019.

Kiverstein, Julian, et al. "How Mood Tunes Prediction: A Neurophenomenological Account of Mood and Its Disturbance in Major Depression." *Neuroscience of Consciousness*, vol. 6, no. 1, 2020.

Kiverstein, Julian, et al. "The Feeling of Grip: Novelty, Error Dynamics, and the Predictive Brain." *Synthese*, vol. 196, no. 7, 2019, pp. 2847–69.

Loewenstein, George. "The Psychology of Curiosity: A Review and Reinterpretation." *Psychological Bulletin*, vol. 116, no. 1, 1994, pp. 75–98.

Metzinger, Thomas. "The Problem of Mental Action – Predictive Control without Sensory Sheets." *Philosophy and Predictive Processing*, edited by Thomas Metzinger and Wanja Wiese, MIND Group, 2017.

Morris, Wesley. "For Me, Rewatching 'Contagion' Was Fun, until It Wasn't." *The New York Times*, 10 Mar. 2020.

Myers, K. M., and M. Davis. "Mechanisms of Fear Extinction." *Molecular Psychiatry*, vol. 12, no. 2, 2007, pp. 120–50.

Nave, Kathryn, et al. "Wilding the Predictive Brain." *Wiley Interdisciplinary Reviews: Cognitive Science*, vol. 11, no. 6, art. 1542, 2020.

Oka, Takakazu. "Psychogenic Fever: How Psychological Stress Affects Body Temperature in the Clinical Population." *Temperature*, vol. 2, no. 3, 2015, pp. 368–78.

Oudeyer, Pierre-Yves, and Linda B. Smith. "How Evolution May Work through Curiosity-Driven Developmental Process." *Topics in Cognitive Science*, vol. 8, no. 2, 2016, pp. 1–11.

Oudeyer, Pierre-Yves, et al. "Intrinsic Motivation Systems for Autonomous Mental Development." *IEEE Transactions on Evolutionary Computation*, vol. 11, no. 2, 2007, pp. 265–86.

Pezzulo, Giovanni. "Tracing the Roots of Cognition in Predictive Processing." *Philosophy and Predictive Processing*, edited by Thomas Metzinger and Wanja Wiese, MIND Group, 2017.

Ritchie, Graeme D. *The Comprehension of Jokes: A Cognitive Science Framework*. Routledge, 2018.

Schmidhuber, Jürgen. "Formal Theory of Creativity, Fun, and Intrinsic Motivation (1990–2010)." *IEEE Transactions on Autonomous Mental Development*, vol. 2, no. 3, 2010, pp. 230–47.

Schoeller, Félix. "Knowledge, Curiosity, and Aesthetic Chills." *Frontiers in Psychology*, vol. 6, art. 1546, 2015.

Schoeller, Félix. "The Shivers of Knowledge." *Human and Social Studies*, vol. 4, no. 3, 2015, pp. 26–41.

Schoeller, Félix. "Physics of Mind: Experimental Confirmations of Theoretical Predictions." *Physics of Life Reviews*, vol. 25, 2018, pp. 45–68.

Schoeller, Félix. *La Loqique Du Film*. Éditions Hoosh, 2021.

Schoeller, Félix, and Mickael Eskinazi. "Psychologie du frisson esthétique." *Psychologie Française*, vol. 64, no. 3, 2019, pp. 305–12.

Schoeller, Félix, and Leonid Perlovsky. "Aesthetic Chills: Knowledge-Acquisition, Meaning-Making, and Aesthetic Emotions." *Frontiers in Psychology*, vol. 7, 2016.

Schrödinger, Erwin. *What Is Life? The Physical Aspect of the Living Cell*. Cambridge UP, 1967.

Schulz, Laura. "Infants Explore the Unexpected." *Science*, vol. 348, art. 6230, 2015, pp. 42–43.

Schwartenbeck, Philipp, et al. "The Dopaminergic Midbrain Encodes the Expected Certainty about Desired Outcomes." *Cerebral Cortex*, vol. 25, no. 10, 2015, pp. 3434–45.

Scrivner, Coltan, et al. "Pandemic Practice: Horror Fans and Morbidly Curious Individuals Are More Psychologically Resilient during the COVID-19 Pandemic." *Personality and Individual Differences*, vol. 168, art. 110397, Jan. 2021.

Starr, G. Gabrielle. *Feeling Beauty: The Neuroscience of Aesthetic Experience*. MIT Press, 2013.

Sterling, Peter. *What Is Health: Allostasis and the Evolution of Human Design*. MIT Press, 2020.

Sun, Zekun, and Chaz Firestone. "The Dark Room Problem." *Trends in Cognitive Sciences*, vol. 24, no. 5, 2020, pp. 346–48.

Titanic. Directed by James Cameron, 1997.

Van de Cruys, Sander. "Affective Value in the Predictive Mind." *Philosophy and Predictive Processing*, edited by Thomas Metzinger and Wanja Wiese, MIND Group, 2017.

Wang, Yashu, and Yiwen Wang. "A Neurocinematic Study of the Suspense Effects in Hitchcock's Psycho." *Frontiers in Communication*, vol. 5, art. 576840, 2020.

Weisberg, Deena S., and Alison Gopnik. "Pretense, Counterfactuals, and Bayesian Causal Models: Why What Is Not Real Really Matters." *Cognitive Science*, vol. 37, no. 7, 2013, pp. 1368–81.

Wilkinson, Sam, et al. "Getting Warmer: Predictive Processing and the Nature of Emotion." *The Value of Emotions for Knowledge*, edited by Laura Candiotto, Palgrave Macmillan, 2019, pp. 101–19.

Witek, Maria A. G., et al. "Syncopation, Body-movement and Pleasure in Groove Music." *PLOS One*, vol. 9, no. 4, art. 94446, 2014.

Zacks, Jeffrey M. "Events in Mind, Media, and Memory." *Representations in Mind and World*, edited by Jeffrey M. Zacks and Holly A. Taylor, Psychology Press, 2017, pp. 186–204.

CHAPTER 4

Transgenerational Trauma and Worlded Brains

An Interdisciplinary Perspective on "Post-Traumatic Slave Syndrome"

Machiel Keestra

1   Introduction

Trauma and traumatization have arguably always been part of the human experience yet have in the last few decades come to occupy a prominent place in various popular and academic contexts. This increased prominence, if not popularity, has motivated many new investigations and debates yet also raised critical questions. Observing the wide spectrum of applications of the concept of trauma in popular culture, Ruth Leys contends that "it is hard not to feel that the concept of trauma has become debased currency" (2). Others critically refer to the "postmodern trauma discourse" as a "spectacular failure [...] of scholars in the humanities and social sciences to develop a truly interdisciplinary trauma concept" (Kansteiner and Weilnböck 229). Anne Rothe diagnoses how such trauma theorizing has led to "irresponsible nonsense" that eclectically borrows from empirical trauma studies while in fact blurring differences between the lived experience of and the more indirect contact with trauma, as well as between the positions of victim, witness, and perpetrator (Rothe 181).

Heeding such warnings, this chapter offers an interdisciplinary and comparative investigation of trauma and traumatization in different historical contexts. More specifically, my aim is to discuss whether the rich bodies of research in trauma and traumatization in Holocaust survivors and their descendants yield relevant insights for post-slavery contexts. This comparative and interdisciplinary approach is partly motivated by my personal background as the child of a Jewish mother who was born one week before Nazi-Germany invaded the Netherlands. Her parents were murdered in 1943 in Sobibor and the aftermath of the Holocaust has strongly affected her life and our family. Reflections on that biography have been enriched since 20 years by the ongoing conversations with my Surinamese-Dutch wife, Mercedes Zandwijken, whose ancestors were enslaved until the abolition of slavery in Suriname in 1863, when her great-grandmother was "emancipated". Together, we developed the Keti Koti Table, a facilitated and ritualized dialogue method addressing among others post-slavery topics, which has enabled exchanges of personal experiences,

© KONINKLIJKE BRILL NV, LEIDEN, 2023 | DOI:10.1163/9789004681293_006

emotions and insights between some 18.000 participants—among whom descendants of former enslaved people, white participants, and those with other colors.[1] These personal and professional experiences and insights have motivated me to think about differences and similarities between the continuing impacts of traumatization in post-Holocaust and post-slavery contexts. It has been shown that children of Holocaust survivors suffer from stress and other symptoms related to their parents' traumatization, which influence the interactions with their environments (Danieli et al.; Kellermann; Wetter). Such results made me wonder whether the traumatic impact of chattel slavery—which has been abolished some 160 years ago—might have a similar impact, yet now across several generations.

I am aware that this question is not a scientific question alone, and maybe not even in the first place. Issues of the transmission and current persistence of trauma are inherently linked to questions of social justice, recognition and reparations (Craemer; Graff). Yet, the science regarding transgenerational transmission of trauma is itself also debated. The field of epigenetics, for example, has made important contributions to the study of transgenerational trauma in the descendants of enslaved people (Jackson et al.) but is also contested as a form of knowledge that may generate new forms of biopolitics and discrimination itself (Meloni and Testa). Although I suggest to consider epigenetics as one among several factors in transgenerational traumatization, I offer this chapter not primarily as a contribution to these debates but rather as an exploration of interdisciplinary connections that should be studied in concert to account for the traumatic impact of historical and present day experiences.

This interdisciplinary perspective also makes my exploration a study of the *worlding* of the brain. It means investigating the brain's functioning in worldly contexts, involving multimodal and mutual interactions between adaptive brains and bodies in specific historical, cultural, and social environments (cf. Besser et al. 1). Replacing the traditional view of a brain that functions independently from its environments as an input-output machine, cognitive neuroscientific research has integrated insights from phenomenology and hermeneutics and shown the brain to be fundamentally embodied, enactive, embedded, and social (Varela et al.; Kiverstein and Clark; Di Paolo). Moreover, it shows how our cognition and behavior is shaped—or "sculpted"—in response to factors which are affecting us in unexpected ways, which can be difficult to control (Keestra). Consequently, this chapter asks how a traumatic worlding of brains and bodies can occur across generations.

---

1   See https://www.ketikotitafel.nl/ for information and resources in Dutch and English.

To address this question, I first discuss the concepts of trauma and post-traumatic stress disorder and then explore the phenomenon of the inter- and transgenerational transmission of trauma, relying in part on the important body of research conducted on families of Holocaust survivors. I then turn to the much less researched "post-traumatic slave syndrome" (DeGruy) and discuss two factors that might contribute to the transgenerational transmission of trauma in the families of former enslaved: epigenetics and the continuation of traumatization even after the abolition of slavery as articulated in Historical Trauma theory.

2 Post-Traumatic Stress: from War Victimization to Indirect Traumatization

Long before the concept of Post-Traumatic Stress Disorder (PTSD) was introduced, people have been bewildered by the long-lasting psychological impact of extremely agonizing or fearful events. War provided many examples, such as the poor soldier described by Herodotus, who survived the Battle of Marathon in 490 BC but had gone blind from fear (Morris 63). Some of the trauma syndromes discussed in modern times—such as the so-called "railway spine" of the 1860s (cf. Leys 3)—arguably have been less dramatic, but war remained an important factor in the history of trauma research, for instance when soldiers were diagnosed with "shell-shock" during and after WWI. However, it was not until many American Vietnam war veterans showed a specific set of symptoms that a new disorder called PTSD was included in the *Diagnostic and Statistical Manual of Mental Disorders*, in the third edition published in 1980 (Young).

The concept of trauma itself has a complex history that I can only briefly allude to here. Psychoanalysis presents two different views, for example. Freud influentially insisted that the "work of mourning" is necessary to avoid continuing suffering from traumas from the past (Freud). Subsequent psychoanalysts assumed that traumatized patients are in a constant state of anxiety and that their symptoms—such as nightmares and intrusive memories—contribute to their ongoing state of preparedness for responding to future triggers (Young). General stress theory, in contrast, posits that a stressful event can shake up an organism only *temporarily* as it returns to a homeostatic balance as soon as the stressor ceases. Reflecting this view, the first edition of the DSM (published in 1952) only contained the diagnosis of a "gross stress reaction" which—in the case of long-lasting symptoms—was replaced with "neurotic reaction" (Friedman et al.). More recently, PTSD changed from an anxiety disorder to a "Trauma- or stress-related disorder" (North et al.). From this early stage on, these three phenomena—stress in response to specific events, traumatization due to stressful events in the past, and an associated anxiety for future similar experiences—have been investigated together.

With much about the etiology, underlying mechanisms, and treatment still unclear, PTSD is currently diagnosed according to the DSM 5 (2013) in adults who suffer for more than one month from at least: an avoidance symptom (refraining from an activity associated with the trauma), two arousal and reactivity symptoms (feeling stressed and becoming angry easily), two cognition and mood symptoms (thinking badly about oneself and no longer being interested in pleasurable activities), and a re-experiencing symptom like flashbacks and nightmares (Nat. Institute of Health).

Importantly, reactivations also raise the issue of different types of trauma exposure, included as "criterion A" in the DSM since its III-R edition of 1987. Direct exposure to a life-threatening event forms one end of the spectrum, but the classification now also includes *indirect* traumatization, for example through observing close family, relatives, or friends to be traumatized or even hearing later about their traumatization (North et al.).[2]

3 Inter- and Transgenerational Transmission of Trauma in Post-Holocaust and Other Contexts

Such indirect exposure also suggests the possibility of a transmission of trauma to the next generation (intergenerational) or across several generations (transgenerational). An expansion of the trauma diagnosis to those not directly affected was first discussed in the 1960s when clinicians noted a high incidence of the children of Holocaust survivors seeking their help (Rakoff et al.). Absent direct traumatization, these children were found "to have consciously and unconsciously absorbed their parents' Holocaust experiences into their lives" and to "manifest Holocaust-derived behaviors, particularly on the anniversaries of their parents' traumata. Moreover, some have internalized as parts of their identity the images of those who perished" (Danieli 5). Research showed that children of Holocaust survivors were more vulnerable to developing a range of psychiatric disorders including PTSD than a control group (Yehuda, et al.) and that the public recognition of the Holocaust and its aftermath in

---

2 "Secondary" or indirect traumatization according to the DSM 5 seems to assume that traumatic experiences are explicitly shared or told between individuals. In many cases, though, such knowledge is only implicitly shared or indeed replaced by an "all-consuming silence", as Horesh critically notes (347).

some countries such as Israel correlated with less severe symptoms (Danieli et al.). Summing up the results of 23 selected studies on the intergenerational transmission of Holocaust-related traumas, Dashorst et al. confirm that the children of survivors are indeed more susceptible to multiple psychiatric symptoms including PTSD.

Such intergenerational traumatization is found in other contexts, too. This holds, for example, for the children of survivors of WW II in the Dutch colony of Indonesia (Aarts), for children of victims of political oppression in the Soviet Union (Krahn), and in refugee families (Sangalang and Vang). Given that a recent *World Mental Health Survey* conducted by the WHO suggests that seven out of ten subjects experience at least one traumatizing event at some point in their life—with three subjects even suffering from four or more such events—it is even more urgent to study the transmission of trauma (Benjet et al.).

A crucial question in this context is whether this transmission continues across multiple generations or abates after two generations: is trauma transmission restricted to an intergenerational process or does it also occur *transgenerationally*, i.e., over more than two generations? For the post-Holocaust context the impact of trauma over several generations has meanwhile been recognized—even though Danieli notes in this context that a "conspiracy of silence is the most prevalent and effective mechanism for the transmission of trauma on all dimensions," which she interprets as demonstration of the lack of integration of the trauma into the lives of survivors and their families (Danieli 678).[3] This was confirmed by studies from the early 1990s showing that not only the children but also the grandchildren of Holocaust survivors reported more psychopathology than control subjects (Rubenstein et al.). Another study more specifically observed increased levels of anxiety among grandchildren of Holocaust survivors, for example (Wetter).

More recent studies and reviews show more mixed results when it comes to the traumatic impact of the Holocaust on later generations. In one meta-analysis the authors did not find significant evidence of transmitted trauma to the grandchildren of Holocaust survivors in general (Sagi-Schwartz et al.). However, this result might be due to the criteria used for assessing traumatization. Indeed, an earlier research survey by the same authors indicated that

---

3   The Keti Koti Table is a personal dialogue intervention that Mercedes Zandwijken and I developed in order to break a similar silence between people of color and white participants about the shared legacy of slavery and enhance mutual empathy and understanding (Keestra and Zandwijken). Meanwhile, it has been embraced as one of few effective interventions to combat racism and discrimination (Felten and Taouanza).

children of non-clinical Holocaust survivors, while not suffering from secondary traumatization, did show an elevated vulnerability and more difficulties in coping with stressful events than controls (van Ijzendoorn et al.).[4]

Such findings of more nuanced patterns of vulnerability and potential protective factors in subsequent generations are common. They confirm the suggestion to distinguish between investigating the *contents* of what is transmitted from investigating features of the *process* itself (Kellermann). For example, research in children and grandchildren of Holocaust survivors showed that they did experience traumatic stress related to the survivors' stress, moderated by the emotional exchanges and reactivity in their relations (Giladi and Bell). Indeed, although survivors might be successful in "encapsulating" potentially risky elements of trauma, under specific circumstances these might later resurface and affect their children or grandchildren (Shmotkin et al.). Specific features of parenting—like stress about survival, separation and loss—influenced this transmission process (Scharf and Mayseless). Explaining the differences between groups of respondents found in such studies, another study found a correlation between the salience or "event centrality" of the Holocaust in families of survivors with PTSD influences and the degree of traumatization of the next two generations (Greenblatt-Kimron et al.). This emphasizes how indirect traumatization is not just dependent upon the horrifying contents related to the original trauma but also upon the specific properties of the processes involved in sharing those contents between generations.

4 Transgenerational Trauma in Post-Slavery Contexts

Turning now to the issue of transgenerational traumatization in the descendants of former enslaved, we are confronted with a lack of empirical research on the one hand and the complexity of dealing with an extended period of time that passed since the end of slavery on the other.[5] Still, a debate emerged

---

4 Another researcher explicitly expressed their surprise about the unexpected outcome of two dissertation projects into tertiary traumatization in Holocaust families: "I went into the studies expecting, as [the graduate students] did, that there would be transfer to the third generation (…) but we didn't find that in either study. Believe me, that is not what we were looking for and not what we expected" (Nathan-Kazis).

5 The difference in number of studies pertaining to the transmission of trauma due to the Holocaust versus the aftermath of slavery is striking. A quick search for publications from the period 1975–2021 with the keywords "transmission AND trauma AND holocaust" versus "transmission AND trauma AND slavery" yielded: 202 versus 14 in Web of Science and 69 versus 1 (a study on Japanese Military Sexual Slavery in WW II) in Pubmed. Larger numbers

relatively early between two explanations that both could account for its occurrence. One explanation entailed the traumatization effects on the dispositions of the descendants, affecting their family and marital relations. Psychoanalyst Abram Kardiner, for example, argued that the period of slavery had undermined the "most rudimentary type of family organization" in African American communities with continuing effects (Kardiner and Ovesey 45). Rejecting this notion of a "tangle of pathology," Herbert George Gutman pointed out how after the Emancipation African Americans were still subject to challenging conditions like poverty, migration, discrimination, and violence (Gutman xviii). This latter view insists on the fact that even after the abolition of slavery the descendants of former enslaved would still experience consequences of the racism upon which slavery rested.

By introducing the concept of "post-traumatic slave syndrome" (PTSS), clinical psychologist and social work expert Joy DeGruy recently intervened in this debate. Defending the existence of a syndrome connecting present day symptoms with events that traumatized people numerous generations earlier, DeGruy seeks support from research on transgenerational traumatization: "While the direct relationship between the slave experience of African Americans and the current major social problems facing them is difficult to empirically substantiate, we know from research conducted on other groups who experienced oppression and trauma that survivor syndrome is pervasive in the development of the second and third generations" (DeGruy 135).[6] In line with this, several symptoms DeGruy describes are comparable to those in Holocaust survivors and their offspring.

DeGruy mentions three crucial patterns of cognition and behavior associated with PTSS: vacant esteem, ever-present anger, and racist socialization. Vacant esteem is described as "the state of believing oneself to have little or no worth, exacerbated by the group and societal pronouncement of inferiority" (DeGruy 140). The "ever-present anger" is due to the "anger at the violence,

---

and a much smaller disparity was visible in the results from a search in Google Scholar which returned 17.800 versus 16.400, similar to the results from JSTOR, which yielded 1638 versus 1274 entries. Yet, these results contained many more publications from the humanities and social sciences than previous ones, suggesting that the disparities are particularly prominent in medical and related fields. Difficult as it is to assess these differences, since 15 million enslaved were brought to the America's via the transatlantic "middle passage" during the 16–19th centuries (UNESCO), a sizeable population potentially suffering from the aftermath of the historical trauma of slavery would benefit from more research.

6 The research on other groups to which DeGruy alludes is presented in the "International Handbook of Multigenerational Legacies of Trauma", to the introduction of which she refers (Danieli).

70   KEESTRA

degradation, and humiliation visited upon us, our ancestors, and our children"
(148).[7] Thirdly, DeGruy regards PTSS as an effect of racist socialization, "due
to centuries of systematic and traumatic programming of inferiority, covering all aspects of one's being" (152).[8] These three patterns bear resemblance
to the four domains affected by post-traumatic stress in Holocaust survivors
and their descendants: self, cognition, affectivity, and interpersonal functioning (Kellermann).

My focus here, however, is not primarily on the contents of these syndromes
but rather on the possible *reactivation* of symptoms in the transgenerational
transmission of trauma in the post-slavery context and on the indirect exposure to traumatizing experiences of previous generations. DeGruy adds an
important factor to the etiology of post-traumatic slave syndrome that is relevant here. Defining PTSS, she states that "multigenerational trauma together
with continued oppression and absence of opportunity to access the benefits
available in the society lead to … Post Traumatic Slave Syndrome" (DeGruy
136). In other words, she contends that it is relevant that this trauma is transmitted during a continuing history of oppression, which is related to a "real or
imagined lack of access" to societal benefits, which further contributes to the
syndrome (136). This points to the necessity of a multicausal account of transgenerational trauma to which I turn now.

5   Causal Pluralism in Indirect Traumatization

In his discussion of the transmission of Holocaust trauma, Nathan Kellermann
insightfully points to a complex interaction between "biological predisposition, individual developmental history, family influences, and social situation" as key factors in direct traumatization (Kellermann 265). These factors
represent and integrate three different modes of explanation, that can be distinguished as *constitutive, etiological,* and *contextual* explanation respectively
(Craver; Menken and Keestra). PTSD is accordingly produced by a mechanism
that is *constituted* by multiple levels of components and relations, like brain

---

7   Carter does also include anger in the list of discrimination and race-related stress, grouping
     it with other responses like fear, anxiety, and sadness (Carter). Sule et al. confirm how the
     ongoing denial and ignorance towards of the struggle of African Americans contribute to
     such anger. In addition, they point out that it might be interpreted as what the DSM 5 calls
     "arousal and reactivity symptoms" of PTSD (Sule et al.).
8   Obviously, the self-denigrating contents of the racist values internalized by descendants of
     the enslaved do have a negative impact upon self-identification and developmental processes
     (Jernigan and Daniel).

networks and their interactions. Since these networks develop over time, *etiology* matters, too. Indeed, etiological explanation might refer to parental genetic influences or to an individual's own traumatic experiences over time. Finally, *contextual* explanation considers the context in which a mechanism operates, such as interpersonal and social contexts that can trigger reactivations or give rise to lasting traumas. These three modes of explanation being often interdependent, I will focus here on two factors in particular that integrate these: first, epigenetics as a form of biological predisposition (*constitution*) across generations and, second, historical context (*context*) as a factor that over time might lead to indirect traumatization of those with such predispositions (*etiology*).

5.1 Epigenetics as a Constitutive Factor in Trauma Transmission

Epigenetics is generally defined as "the study of cellular variations that are caused by external, environmental factors that 'switch' genes 'on' and 'off,' making changes in the phenotype of genetic expression without concomitant changes in the DNA sequence or genotype" (Krippner and Barrett 53). Such epigenetic changes are probably "ubiquitous" in various taxa, although they are more common in plants and fungi than in animals (Jablonka and Raz). This is not surprising, given the potential advantage if adaptation to, especially, risks provided by the environment is inheritable to next generations. For this mechanism to work, epigenetic changes have to be translated to changes in the germline (Lim and Brunet). Since DNA regulates both the development and functioning of brains in sometimes very specific ways, epigenetic modulation of gene expression can influence behavior and cognition (Ryan and Kuzawa). Strikingly, it can even produce inheritable patterns of behavior and cognition provoked by specific contexts across generations.

War has again provided an important source of research and insights. For instance, Dutch children who were born months after the so-called Hunger Winter of 1944–1945—as well as their children—were found to display specific inheritable physiological properties such as obesity, glucose intolerance, and coronary heart disease (Lacal and Ventura; cf. Roseboom et al.). Epigenetic changes were found to have an impact during embryonic development upon a specific gene coding for a growth factor. Confirming the transient nature that epigenetic influences often have, these effects were transmitted only over a few generations (Krippner and Barrett). Epigenetics thus allows temporary changes in response to a traumatic stressor that can be transmitted to next generations.

Given these properties of epigenetics, it is not surprising that DeGruy has included a section on "Epigenetics of PTSD" in the 2017 edition of her book on the post-traumatic slave syndrome (132–36). However, that section does not contain any discussion of epigenetics (but instead considers the role of parenting in trauma transmission). Taking up on DeGruy's suggestion, I argue that epigenetics does potentially play a role in the alleged post-traumatic slave syndrome and its persistence across several generations—especially if accompanied by certain contextual factors.[9] For my argument it is important to understand epigenetics as fetal or inter-generational programming, potentially transmitting specific stress responses to next generations. Animal studies confirm that parental stress leads to programming of stress-related systems and their response profiles in next generations (Bowers and Yehuda). A recent study in rodents, for example, found that after exposure up to three subsequent generations of rats displayed a rat phenotype characterized by specific stress responses due to an abnormal regulation of the hypothalamus-pituitary-adrenal or HPA axis (Ambeskovic et al.). Reviewing research in the inheritability of stress responsivity across generations in animals and humans including PTSD, epigenetic influences on stress-related systems were found to be a relevant factor (Yehuda and Lehrner; cf. Dashorst et al.; Ramo-Fernandez et al.).

An important question is whether changes transmitted across generations via epigenetics remain adaptive, or not—as these are related to an original traumatic event or experience (Ryan and Kuzawa). The principle of "epigenetic plasticity" suggests that "changes to the epigenome might reset when the environmental insults are no longer present, or when we have changed sufficiently to address environmental challenges in a new way" (Yehuda and Lehrner 253). An exceptional animal study that subjected animals to extinction training did indeed find such a reset of epigenetic changes upon extinguishing an acquired stress response (Aoued et al.). However, we should not conclude that epigenetic changes always reset after a traumatic event, since so-called "epigenetic recall" might occur even after a period in which these changes have remained dormant. Epigenetic changes entail a form of "neural sensitization," yielding "inherited, partial epigenetic patterns that facilitate a response" even if the stressor is weaker than the one experienced by the previous generation (Jablonka and Raz 160). Such epigenetic recall could imply that under triggering circumstances, some descendants of traumatized generations could display stronger stress responses as well. The brains and bodies of members of next generations might thus potentially be "neurally sensitized" through epigenetic changes.

---

9 A similar conclusion is drawn in the review of epigenetics research relevant to the "trauma and stress of enslavement and institutionalized racism", which lists potential epigenetic effects according to specific life stages from pregnancy to adulthood (Jackson et al.).

5.2 Historical Trauma as a Contextual Factor in Indirect Traumatization

With this possibility in mind I turn now to the historical and contextual dimension of transgenerational trauma and discuss in which ways post-slavery generations are exposed to worldly stressors that might reactivate epigenetic changes. Given the prominence of post-Holocaust studies of transgenerational transmission of trauma it is perhaps not surprising that several studies on other cases of transgenerational trauma transmission make efforts to differentiate their approaches form this research. Studies on intergenerational trauma in refugee families, for example, emphasize the role of migration and instability for these groups (Sangalang and Vang) while research on the historical traumatization of indigenous peoples underscores the extended period of time in which it occurred (O'Neill et al.). Colonization is also key factor in a recent review of transgenerational trauma in Latin American migrants to North America and their descendants, for which the authors regard "the cyclical reproduction of colonial and racialized violence continues to impact communities across the globe, including Latin Americans and Latinxs" as essential (Cerdeña et al 3).

Integrating etiological, constitutive, and contextual explanations, Historical Trauma theory aims to account for the impact of such long-lasting cultural, social, and historical contexts on traumatization processes that affect certain groups and which tend to be overlooked by explanations that exclusively focus on individual risk factors and parenting contexts. This theory initially emerged from research on, and social work practices in, American Indian and Alaska Native communities (cf. Hartman and Gone). As complicated as it is to integrate evidence about historical oppression with research on psychological trauma, the concept of Historical Trauma has informed research on how historically traumatized people are showing vulnerabilities that extend to generations that are not directly affected by it. While recognizing the risk of victimization and acknowledging that there are different ways of coping with such historical traumata, research does confirm that these can have effects on physical and mental health across generations (Prussing).

However, it is essential to keep in mind the complexities involved in comparing different historical traumata. Importantly, there are several structural differences between the trauma of the Holocaust and the so-called Historical Trauma experienced by indigenous and colonized populations. Leaving unattended the centuries of endemic antisemitism preceding it, one could refer to the Holocaust as "a time-limited series of events covering about a decade, [whereas] the events that constitute historical trauma for Indigenous peoples in the Americas lasted hundreds of years" (Kirmayer et al. 305). The latter holds largely for the former enslaved as well, being exposed to the dehumanization of enslavement for centuries. Moreover, the abolition has almost nowhere led to the immediate equal participation of the formerly enslaved and their descendants in society without further violence, oppression, and discrimination—on the contrary.[10] Indeed, researchers have introduced the notion of African American Historical Trauma in order to account for "the symptoms that can result from the long-lasting effects of trauma stemming from slavery, racism, and discrimination, in addition to the cultural, historical, and intergenerational trauma that African Americans have had to endure" (Williams-Washington and Mills 247).

Historical Trauma generally is defined by four main factors: 1) a subdominant group is systematically traumatized by a dominant group; 2) traumatization occurs on a long-term scale; 3) consequently, the target group has a "universal experience of trauma"; 4) traumatization causes a trans-generational legacy of "physical, psychological, social and economic disparities" (Sotero 95). The interaction between these factors can lead to "snowballing" effects such as unexpected peaks of traumatization in a community (Hartmann and Gone).

Questioning the notion that Historic Trauma necessarily implies a "universal experience of trauma," it is important to acknowledge the differences in vulnerabilities and resilience between individuals. In addition, even though there are cases in which contemporary events are continuous with historical traumata and might as such be considered re-traumatizing, in others we should appreciate the *discontinuity* between past and present traumatization. Distinctions like these enable us to take seriously the warnings about ill-defined concepts that I started this chapter with. Hence, we again need to consider the specific constitution, context, and etiology as factors when accounting for complex patterns of indirect traumatization. An individual's personal appraisal of a stressor and their capability of coping with stress, for example, influences to a large extent the experienced impact of external stressors (Jones et al.).[11] Another strategy mitigating the negative outcomes of perceived racism entails a stronger identification with an identity group which might "buffer the negative effects of discrimination and increase self-esteem"

---

10   Wekker uses the concept "cultural archive", introduced by Edward Said, to refer to the legacy of centuries of slavery, racism, and discrimination in terms of the stereotypes, attitudes, prejudices that did not at once disappear with the abolition of slavery (Wekker).

11   An fMRI study of survivors of sexual trauma suggests that resilience can consist of a cognitive strategy according to which individuals focus on and downregulate negative emotions associated with the trauma (New et al.).

(Harrell 51). In addition, connection to family and community, and optimism can form protective factors (Danzer et al.).

Yet, if epigenetic recall *does* lead to increased sensitization such efforts and strategies might be less effective as an individual may be predisposed to enhanced reactivity to external stressors, and in turn to potential re-traumatization (Jablonka and Raz). Indeed, children do not only inherit specific epigenetic patterns, they also learn cognitive schemata from their parents. Parents suffering from PTSD do influence the appraisal of stressors by offspring, indirectly traumatizing them (Yahyavi et al.). More specifically related to our context is the observation of increased levels of stress in response to perceived racism in the offspring of African American descendants of former enslaved (Anderson). Hence, it is important take into account that the post-slavery periods carry and continue to carry "trauma potential in their own right," as Cross notes in his chapter on "black psychological functioning and the legacy of slavery" (Cross 388). Events with such trauma potential might occur in some countries more than others, yet the psychological distress experienced by many people of color upon the brutal murder of George Floyd by US police—which motivated Black Lives Matter demonstrations across the globe—suggests that this "trauma potential" is felt elsewhere, too. These demonstrations testify to the continuing history of structural and ideologically motivated violence and discrimination, which have a great impact on mental health (Weine et al.). More recently, the disproportionate harm by the COVID-19 pandemic experienced by Black communities is related to their traumatic histories with subsequent health disparities (Leitch et al.) In sum, the Historical Trauma of centuries of slavery, interacting with contemporary events that for some groups and individuals are related to that trauma, can feed into the transgenerational transmission of trauma, sometimes possibly enhanced by epigenetic factors.

6   Concluding Remarks

One year after the Black Lives Matter demonstrations, questions about the legacy of centuries of racism and slavery in our societies are becoming more urgent—questions which might be challenging existing scientific insights and requiring new answers. Integrating insights from different fields of research—in post-traumatic stress, in transgenerational traumatization in Holocaust families, in epigenetics, and in Historic Trauma—I have proposed an interdisciplinary approach to work in this direction. I have attempted to integrate three different types of explanation which all lend themselves for further empirical investigation and articulate features of the "worlding the brain" process. Environmental conditions are included in a contextual explanation of the emergence of epigenetic changes but also of cognitive and behavioral patterns, which in turn have an impact on inheritable patterns of brain development, cognition, and behavior. Brain development and functioning are implied in a constitutive explanation of post-traumatic stress responses in traumatized individuals. Finally, etiological explanation is involved here in the impact of historical trauma on certain communities and individuals across generations. This potentially includes specific properties of brain development and functioning and the interactions of individuals with their worlds.

Obviously, various lines of research are needed to fill in the many large gaps in knowledge on the transgenerational transmission of trauma. Even if this affects only a limited number of individuals and families, it is important to recognize that the aftermath of slavery can still be experienced in such intricate ways by some until this very day. Indeed, the complex process underlying this phenomenon needs further scrutiny not just to better understand its complexity and dynamics, but also to develop interventions, and help breaking the chains of such traumatization across generations.

Acknowledgements

This chapter is based upon a presentation on this topic held at the 2017 "Worlding the Brain: Affect, Care, and Engagement" conference in Amsterdam. I would like to thank Julian Kiverstein, Mercedes Zandwijken, and other participants for their comments.

References

Aarts, Petra G. H. "Intergenerational Effects in Families of World War II Survivors from the Dutch East Indies." *International Handbook of Multigenerational Legacies of Trauma*, edited by Yael Danieli, Springer, 1998, pp. 175–87.

Ambeskovic, Mirela, et al. "Ancestral Stress Alters Lifetime Mental Health Trajectories and Cortical Neuromorphology via Epigenetic Regulation." *Scientific Reports*, vol. 9, no. 1, 2019, pp. 1–14.

Anderson, Kathryn Freeman. "Diagnosing Discrimination: Stress from Perceived Racism and the Mental and Physical Health Effects*." *Sociological Inquiry*, vol. 3, no. 1, 2013, pp. 55–81.

Aoued, Hadj S., et al. "Reversing Behavioral, Neuroanatomical, and Germline Influences of Intergenerational Stress." *Biological Psychiatry*, vol. 85, no. 3, 2019, pp. 248–56.

Benjet, Corina, et al. "The Epidemiology of Traumatic Event Exposure Worldwide: Results from the World Mental Health Survey Consortium." *Psychological Medicine*, vol. 46, no. 2, 2016, pp. 327–43.

Besser, Stephan, et al. Worlding the Brain: Patterns, Rhythms, Narratives in Neuroscience and the Humanities. Conference Program. Amsterdam, 2016.

Bowers, Mallory E., and Rachel Yehuda. "Intergenerational Transmission of Stress in Humans." *Neuropsychopharmacology: Official Publication of the American College of Neuropsychopharmacology*, vol. 41, no. 1, 2016, pp. 232–44.

Carter, Robert T. "Racism and Psychological and Emotional Injury: Recognizing and Assessing Race-Based Traumatic Stress." *The Counseling Psychologist*, vol. 35, no. 1, 2007, pp. 13–105.

Cerdeña, Jessica P., et al. "Intergenerational Trauma in Latinxs: A Scoping Review." *Social Science & Medicine*, vol. 270, 2021, pp. 1–22.

Craemer, Thomas. "Comparative Analysis of Reparations for the Holocaust and for the Transatlantic Slave Trade." *The Review of Black Political Economy*, vol. 45, no. 4, 1. Dec. 2018, pp. 299–324.

Craver, Carl. *Explaining the Brain: Mechanisms and the Mosaic Unity of Neuroscience.* Oxford UP, 2007.

Cross, William E. Jr. "Black Psychological Functioning and the Legacy of Slavery. Myths and Realities." *International Handbook of Multigenerational Legacies of Trauma*, edited by Yael Danieli, Springer, 1998, pp. 387–400.

Danieli, Yael, et al. "Multigenerational Legacies of Trauma: Modeling the What and How of Transmission." *American Journal of Orthopsychiatry*, vol. 86, no. 6, 2016, pp. 639–51.

Danieli, Yael, et al. "Conclusion and Future Directions." *International Handbook of Multigenerational Legacies of Trauma*, edited by Yael Danieli, Springer, 1998, pp. 669–89.

Danieli, Yael, et al. "Introduction." *International Handbook of Multigenerational Legacies of Trauma*, edited by Yael Danieli, Springer, 1998, pp. 1–17.

Danzer, Graham, et al. "White Psychologists and African Americans' Historical Trauma: Implications for Practice." *Journal of Aggression, Maltreatment & Trauma*, vol. 25, no. 4, 2016, pp. 351–70.

Dashorst, Patricia, et al. "Intergenerational Consequences of the Holocaust on Offspring Mental Health: A Systematic Review of Associated Factors and Mechanisms." *European Journal of Psychotraumatology*, vol. 10, no. 1, 2019, pp. 1–29.

DeGruy, Joy. *Post Traumatic Slave Syndrome: America's Legacy of Enduring Injury and Healing.* Uptone Press, 2017.

Di Paolo, Ezequiel. "Editorial: The Social and Enactive Mind." *Phenomenology and the Cognitive Sciences*, vol. 8, no. 4, 2009, pp. 409–15.

Felten, Hanneke, and Ikram Taouanza. *Wat Werkt Bij Het Verminderen Van Discriminatie?* Utrecht: Kennisplatform Integratie en Samenleving, 2018.

Freud, Sigmund. "Mourning and Melancholia." *The Standard Edition of the Complete Psychological Works of Sigmund Freud*, Volume XIV (1914–1916): On the History of the Psycho-Analytic Movement, Papers on Metapsychology and Other Works, edited by James Strachey et al., Hogarth Press, 1957, pp. 237–58.

Friedman, Matthew J., et al. "Considering PTSD for DSM-5." *Depression and Anxiety*, vol. 28, no. 9, 2011, pp. 750–69.

Giladi, Lotem, and Terece S. Bell. "Protective Factors for Intergenerational Transmission of Trauma among Second and Third Generation Holocaust Survivors." *Psychological Trauma: Theory, Research, Practice, and Policy*, vol. 5, no. 4, 2013, pp. 384–91.

Graff, Gilda. "The Intergenerational Trauma of Slavery and Its Aftereffects: The Question of Reparations." *Journal of Psychohistory*, vol. 44, no. 4, Spring 2017, pp. 256–68.

Greenblatt-Kimron, Lee, et al. "Event Centrality and Secondary Traumatization among Holocaust Survivors' Offspring and Grandchildren: A Three-Generation Study." *Journal of Anxiety Disorders*, vol. 81, 2021, pp. 1–29.

Gutman, Herbert George. *The Black Family in Slavery and Freedom, 1750–1925*. Pantheon Books, 1977.

Harrell, Shelly P. "A Multidimensional Conceptualization of Racism-Related Stress: Implications for the Well-Being of People of Color." *American Journal of Orthopsychiatry*, vol. 70, no. 1, 2000, pp. 42–57.

Hartmann, William E., and Joseph P. Gone. "American Indian Historical Trauma: Community Perspectives from Two Great Plains Medicine Men." *American Journal of Community Psychology*, vol. 54, no. 3–4, 2014, pp. 274–88.

Horesh, D. "The Reconstruction of Criterion a in DSM-5: Is It a True Incorporation of Secondary Traumatization into the PTSD Diagnosis?" *Journal of Loss & Trauma*, vol. 21, no. 5, 2016, pp. 345–49.

Ijzendoorn, Marinus H., et al. "Are Children of Holocaust Survivors Less Well-Adapted? A Meta-Analytic Investigation of Secondary Traumatization." *Journal of Traumatic Stress*, vol. 16, no. 5, 2003, pp. 459–69.

Jablonka, Eva, and Gal Raz. "Transgenerational Epigenetic Inheritance: Prevalence, Mechanisms, and Implications for the Study of Heredity and Evolution." *The Quarterly Review of Biology*, vol. 84, no. 2, 2009, pp. 131–76.

Jackson, Fatimah, et al. "Developmental Stage Epigenetic Modifications and Clinical Symptoms Associated with the Trauma and Stress of Enslavement and Institutionalized Racism." *Journal of Clinical Epigenetics*, vol. 4, no. 2, 2018, pp. 1–11.

Jernigan, Maryam M., and Jessica Henderson Daniel. "Racial Trauma in the Lives of Black Children and Adolescents: Challenges and Clinical Implications." *Journal of Child & Adolescent Trauma*, vol. 4, no. 2, 2011, pp. 123–41.

Jones, Shawn C. T., et al. "From 'Crib to Coffin': Navigating Coping from Racism-Related Stress throughout the Lifespan of Black Americans." *American Journal of Orthopsychiatry*, vol. 90, no. 2, 2020, pp. 267–82.

Kansteiner, Wulf, and Harald Weilnböck. "Against the Concept of Cultural Trauma (or How I Learned to Love the Suffering of Others without the Help of Psychotherapy)." *Cultural Memory Studies: An International and Interdisciplinary Handbook*, edited by Astrid Erll and Nünning Ansgar, De Gruyter, 2008, pp. 229–40.

Kardiner, Abram, and Lionel Ovesey. *The Mark of Oppression: Explorations in the Personality of the American Negro*. Norton, 1951.

Keestra, Machiel. *Sculpting the Space of Actions: Explaining Human Action by Integrating Intentions and Mechanisms*. ILLC Dissertation Series. Amsterdam: Institute for Logic, Language and Computation, 2014.

Keestra, Machiel, and Mercedes Zandwijken. "A Juneteenth Haggadah for a New Ritual Meal." *Forward*, 2020, https://forward.com/scribe/449765/a-juneteenth-haggadah-for-a-new-ritual-meal.

Kellermann, Natan P. F. "Transmission of Holocaust Trauma – an Integrative View." *Psychiatry: Interpersonal and Biological Processes*, vol. 64, no. 3, 2001, pp. 256–67.

Kirmayer, Laurence J., et al. "Rethinking Historical Trauma." *Transcultural Psychiatry*, vol. 51, no. 3, 2014, pp. 299–319.

Kiverstein, Julian, and Andy Clark. "Introduction: Mind Embodied, Embedded, Enacted: One Church or Many?" *Topoi*, vol. 28, no. 1, 2009, pp. 1–7.

Krahn, Elizabeth. "Lifespan and Intergenerational Legacies of Soviet Oppression: An Autoethnography of Mennonit Women and Their Adult Children." *Journal of Mennonite Studies*, vol. 29, 2011, pp. 21–43.

Krippner, Stanley, and Deirdre Barrett. "Transgenerational Trauma: The Role of Epigenetics." *Journal of Mind & Behavior*, vol. 40, no 1, 2019, pp. 53–62.

Lacal, Irene, and Rossella Ventura. "Epigenetic Inheritance: Concepts, Mechanisms and Perspectives." *Frontiers in Molecular Neuroscience*, vol. 11, art. 292, 2018, pp. 1–22.

Leitch, Stephanie, et al. "Black Lives Matter in Health Promotion: Moving from Unspoken to Outspoken." *Health Promotion International*, vol. 36, no. 4, 2020, pp. 1160–69.

Leys, Ruth. *Trauma – a Genealogy*. U of Chicago P, 2010.

Lim, Jana P., and Anne Brunet. "Bridging the Transgenerational Gap with Epigenetic Memory." *Trends in Genetics*, vol. 29, no. 3, 2013, pp. 176–86.

Meloni, Maurizion, and Giuseppe Tesat. "Scrutinizing the Epigenetics Revolution." *BioSocieties*, vol. 9, no. 4, 2014, pp. 431–56.

Menken, Steph, and Machiel Keestra, editors. *An Introduction to Interdisciplinary Research: Theory and Practice*. Amsterdam University Press, 2016.

Morris, David J. *The Evil Hours: A Biography of Post-Traumatic Stress Disorder*. Houghton Mifflin Harcourt, 2015.

Nathan-Kazis, Josh. "Can Holocaust Trauma Affect 'Third Generation'?". *The Awareness Center*, 2012, https://theawarenesscenter.blogspot.com/2012/09/can-holocaust-trauma-affect-third.html.

National Institute of Mental Health. *Post-Traumatic Stress Disorder*. 2019, https://www.nimh.nih.gov/health/topics/post-traumatic-stress-disorder-ptsd/index.shtml.

New, Antonia S., et al. "A Functional Magnetic Resonance Imaging Study of Deliberate Emotion Regulation in Resilience and Posttraumatic Stress Disorder." *Biological Psychiatry*, vol. 66, no. 7, 2009, pp. 656–64.

North, Carol S., et al. "The Evolution of PTSD Criteria across Editions of DSM" *Annals of Clinical Psychiatry*, vol. 28, no. 3, 2016, pp. 197–208.

O'Neill, Linda, et al. "Hidden Burdens: A Review of Intergenerational, Historical and Complex Trauma, Implications for Indigenous Families." *Journal of Child & Adolescent Trauma*, vol. 11, no. 2, 2018, pp. 173–86.

Prussing, Erica. "Historical Trauma: Politics of a Conceptual Framework." *Transcultural Psychiatry*, vol. 51, no. 3, 2014, pp. 436–58.

Rakoff, Vivian, et al. "Children and Families of Concentration Camp Survivors." *Canada's Mental Health*, vol. 14, no. 4, 1966, pp. 24–26.

Ramo-Fernandez, Laura, et al. "Epigenetic Alterations Associated with War Trauma and Childhood Maltreatment." *Behavioral Sciences & the Law*, vol. 33, no. 5, 2015, pp. 701–21.

Roseboom, Tessa J., et al. "Effects of Prenatal Exposure to the Dutch Famine on Adult Disease in Later Life: An Overview." *Molecular and Cellular Endocrinology*, vol. 185, no. 1–2, 2001, pp. 93–98.

Rothe, Anne. "Irresponsible Nonsense: An Epistemological and Ethical Critique of Postmodern Trauma Theory." *Interdisciplinary Handbook of Trauma and Culture*, edited by Yochai Ataria et al. Springer International Publishing, 2016, pp. 181–94.

Rubenstein, Israel, et al. "Multigenerational Occurrence of Survivor Syndrome Symptoms in Families of Holocaust Survivors." *OMEGA – Journal of Death and Dying*, vol. 20, no. 3, 1990, pp. 239–44.

Ryan, Calen P., et al. "Germline Epigenetic Inheritance: Challenges and Opportunities for Linking Human Paternal Experience with Offspring Biology and Health." *Evolutionary Anthropology: Issues, News, and Reviews*, vol. 29, no. 4, 2020, pp. 180–200.

Sagi-Schwartz, Abraham, et al. "Does Intergenerational Transmission of Trauma Skip a Generation? No Meta-Analytic Evidence for Tertiary Traumatization with Third Generation of Holocaust Survivors." *Attachment & Human Development,* vol. 10, no. 2, 2008, pp. 105–21.

Sangalang, Cindy C., and Cindy Vang. "Intergenerational Trauma in Refugee Families: A Systematic Review." *Journal of Immigrant and Minority Health*, vol. 19, no. 3, 2017, pp. 745–54.

Scharf, Miri, and Ofra Mayseless. "Disorganizing Experiences in Second- and Third-Generation Holocaust Survivors." *Qualitative Health Research*, vol. 21, no. 11, 2011, pp. 1539–53.

Shmotkin, Dov, et al. "Resilience and Vulnerability among Aging Holocaust Survivors and Their Families: An Intergenerational Overview." *Journal of Intergenerational Relationships*, vol. 9, no. 1, 2011, pp. 7–21.

Sotero, Michelle M. "A Conceptual Model of Historical Trauma: Implications for Public Health Practice and Research." *Journal of Health Disparities Research and Practice*, vol. 1, no. 1, 2006, pp. 93–108.

Sule, Ejim, et al. "The Past Does Matter: A Nursing Perspective on Post Traumatic Slave Syndrome (PTSS)." *Journal of Racial and Ethnic Health Disparities*, vol. 4, no. 5, 2017, pp. 779–83.

UNESCO. "Breaking the Silence: The Transatlantic Slave Trade Education Project." *Unesco*, 2004, https://unesdoc.unesco.org/ark:/48223/pf0000137805. Accessed July 9, 2023.

Varela, Francisco J., et al. *The Embodied Mind: Cognitive Science and Human Experience*. MIT Press, 1993.

Watson, Marlene F., et al. "Covid-19 Interconnectedness: Health Inequity, the Climate Crisis, and Collective Trauma." *Family Process*, vol. 59, no. 3, 2020, pp. 832–46.

Weine, Stevan, et al. "Justice for George Floyd and a Reckoning for Global Mental Health." *Global Mental Health*, vol. 7, 2020, pp. 1–5.

Wekker, Gloria. *White Innocence: Paradoxes of Colonialism and Race*. Duke UP, 2016.

Wetter, Michael G. *The Intergenerational Transmission of Increased Anxiety Traits in Third-Generation Holocaust Survivors*. 1999. Pepperdine University, PhD dissertation.

Yahyavi, Seyyed Taha, et al. "A Review on the Evidence of Transgenerational Transmission of Posttraumatic Stress Disorder Vulnerability." *Brazilian Journal of Psychiatry*, vol. 36, 2014, pp. 89–94.

Yehuda, Rachel, and Amy Lehrner. "Intergenerational Transmission of Trauma Effects: Putative Role of Epigenetic Mechanisms." *World Psychiatry: Official Journal of the World Psychiatric Association (WPA)*, vol. 17, no. 3, 2018, pp. 243–57.

Yehuda, Rachel, et al. "Vulnerability to Posttraumatic Stress Disorder in Adult Offspring of Holocaust Survivors." *American Journal of Psychiatry*, vol. 155, no. 9, 1998, pp. 1163–71.

Young, Allan. "Our Traumatic Neurosis and Its Brain." *Science in Context*, vol. 14, no. 4, 2001, pp. 661–83.

CHAPTER 5

Beworldered

An Autobiographical Inquiry of Epileptic Being

Trijsje Franssen

*Be*ing

in a ***world***

of ***all***-encompassing

be***wild***erment

I ***am***

Beworldered

"I think you had a seizure."

I was 22 years old and thought to be healthy, but that night in the spring of 2004, unexpectedly and inexplicably, I became epileptic. It marks a profound turn in my life, which has since that very moment been divided into a "before" and "after." It radically changed my relation to my brain, body, self, and world. In fact, I could call it a division between a pre-epileptic and epileptic form of *being*, for it would turn out to be a fundamental existential change.

This essay is an autobiographical inquiry of that existential change and its outcome. It aims to understand the experience and meaning of becoming as well as being epileptic. It aims to express this experience, despite its ineffable

© KONINKLIJKE BRILL NV, LEIDEN, 2023 | DOI:10.1163/9789004681293_007

nature. Rather than about "worlding" a brain it is about the "*de*-worlding" of a brain. A brain that, in various ways, loses its embeddedness in the world. This essay is about what I call *beworlderment*: an experience of *being* in the "real" *world*, but in a state of intense *bewilderment*.

I am inspired by existential phenomenology and in particular by Vivian Sobchack and Edmund Husserl. Sobchack uses existential phenomenology as an empirical method. She wrote a "phenomenological autobiography" of the experience of having her leg amputated and of what she calls "*living* a phantom limb" (52). I will start with an explanation of this approach and its relevance for my inquiry of the experience of *living* an epileptic body. Further, I will consider Husserl's distinction between *Leib* and *Körper* to make sense of my experiences. As we will see, the phenomenological approach is useful but has its shortcomings as well. I will show how, through critical and creative use, it can be made suitable to investigate epilepsy.

An overarching theme throughout this essay is the blurring of boundaries of traditional dualisms, such as body/mind, reality/appearance, self/other, subject/object, etc. The boundaries between the physical and the mental faded when surgical scalpels shaped what should be the physical part of my embodied consciousness. The human/machine dichotomy dissipated when brain research was done with implanted electrodes.

Paradoxically, what I call the *de-blurring* of such dualisms is just as characteristic for my experience of epilepsy. I started my inquiry from the phenomenological assumption that there is no clear boundary between body and mind. However, as my essay developed, more and more I started to realize how much I need to speak in terms of dualisms in order to describe my experiences. As a dysfunctional organ, my brain becomes an object, an Other that opposes itself to me as subject, as Self. During a seizure, my consciousness somehow disappears and seems to leave my body behind. As will become clear, in the following there will be several other examples and forms of blurring and de-blurring of such boundaries. First, simply because I need the discourse of dualisms in order to express the ambiguity of my experience. Second, because the experience of becoming epileptic, being epileptic, and concrete experiences of single seizures are all of a dynamic nature. My embodied being is sometimes split into body and mind, the world moves back and forth between reality and appearance, my brain is subject and object, depending on the situation, and so on. Therefore, I ask you not to expect this essay to be a coherent and consistent whole, because the experience of epilepsy is not, and nor *am* I.

Precisely because this text concerns something seemingly inexpressible, its form, language and symbols are of significant importance. It is a personal narrative and a philosophical inquiry as well as a tentative experiment with the traditional form of an essay.

1 A Phenomenological Approach

One could ask, if this brain disorder changed my *being*, does that inversely mean that I *am* my brain? A materialist neuroscientist such as Joseph LeDoux boldly states that "you are your synapses" (ix), and so does the Dutch neuroscientist Dick Swaab:

> Everything we think, do, and refrain from doing is determined by the brain. The construction of this fantastic machine determines our potential, our limitations, and our characters; *we are our brains*. (3)

If I would follow their line of thought, *I am nothing but that dysfunctional organ*.

As said, becoming epileptic has been an existential change. However, to reduce my very *being* to my brain is too simplistic, reductionistic, and deterministic. These neurocentric theories soft-*head*edly assume that brain, mind, consciousness, selfhood, and identity are all just synonyms for "being". They do not take into account the essential role of our embodied relation to and interaction with the world when it comes to what we are. If we wish to understand what it means to be epileptic, a more fruitful approach to start with is one that does emphasize the importance of embodiment: existential phenomenology.

Existential phenomenology studies the conscious experience of concrete human existence, as experienced from the first person point of view. Its core idea is that existence is essentially situated, characterized by an openness, "intentionality," or "directedness" towards the world. The world appears to us in a certain way, through "phenomena" or appearances, and the human is inextricably bound up with it. Existence is essentially timely and spatial and, in Heidegger's words, means *Being-in-the-world* (*In-der-Welt-Sein*, 52).

Being-in-the-world is a valuable concept that I will employ in this essay, but other phenomenologists, and particularly Merleau-Ponty, put much more emphasis on the body than Heidegger, which is crucial in my case. Each human is an embodied being, a lived body, and an embodied consciousness. Merleau-Ponty states that the inherent relationship between us and the world is based on a primordial, bodily experience of those "phenomena." It is the *lived* space and temporality, our bodily situatedness, and the field of perception that all constitute this primordial awareness, which precedes any reflection. However, this is not to say that it lacks meaning. On the contrary: the fact that the lived body is intentionally directed towards the world makes that primordial awareness always already meaningful. Finding, understanding, and expressing this meaning is the objective of phenomenological inquiry. It seeks to investigate and interpret structures of the experience of the embodied being, from a first-person perspective.

Following Sobchack, I will try to use existential phenomenology as an empirical method. This means that in "the intimate laboratory" (Sobchack 52) of my embodied self I will explore "lived" experiences. The method starts with a particular experience, which in my case is, first, becoming epileptic, and then "living" an epileptic body. Research material thus consists of living epilepsy in its many different forms—seizures, surgery, memory gaps and more. The aim is to interpret my perceptions in order to better understand what "epileptic being" *means* and, importantly, to *express* them. Hence, it is not only about understanding a personal experience but, in Sobchack's words, also an attempt "to describe and explicate the *general* or *possible* structures of that experience so as to make it resonant and comprehensible to others" (54). Indeed, throughout my investigation I intend to uncover more general existential structures that are hopefully meaningful and recognizable to others as well, and not just epileptic persons.

Since meaning is fundamental in existential phenomenology, so is language. It is not just a tool. Language, including imagination and discourse, makes it possible to not only report but also *shape* subjective experiences in various ways. By meticulously observing and describing a seizure in the way I do below, the experience as such is taking shape. Creating the neologisms of "de-blurring", "de-worlding," and "beworlderment" enables me to express something seemingly ineffable. The act of writing itself is essential. The process of putting my experiences into words and using language creatively, working with style, form, and font, in fact is an existential investigation. According to Sobchack, language is vital for existence as such, "an elaboration or extension of being." It provides the opportunity to "figure out" oneself as being, "beyond the temporal and spatial boundaries" of the lived-body experience" (54).

The importance of language, the body, and the general structure within my personal experience come together in the fact that I emphatically speak of *being* epileptic instead of *having* epilepsy. Crucial for existential phenomenology is that one does not *have* a body, one *is* the body one has. Founder of phenomenology Edmund Husserl makes a distinction between *Körper* and *Leib* (143–61). Both words officially translate as "body," but *Körper* is the physical body or body-as-object, whereas *Leib* is a lived-through body, the phenomenal body, or body-as-subject. To perceive one's body as *Körper* implies a distance from one's own body. To perceive it as a thing, just as other things in the environment. *Leib*, however, means to experience one's body through sensations, perceptions, as one's "own". *Körper* and *Leib* represent the experience of *having* a body and *being* a body respectively.

To clarify the difference, Husserl uses the following example. If I touch my left hand with my right hand, there are two ways to perceive my left hand. On the one hand, it is a touched object with particular characteristics, such as roughness or softness. On the other, I feel with my left hand that I am being touched—I experience this touch "from within." My left hand is thus material (*Körper*) as well as "feeling" (*Leib*) (Husserl 144–45).

Importantly, Husserl's distinction should not be understood as a new kind of dualism. *Leib* always implies *Körper*, for to experience being touched there needs to be a physical body that is touchable. It is a physical experience of being-myself, a form of self-perception that opens up *on* as well as *within* the body.

The approach, methods, and concepts of existential phenomenology are useful to start exploring what it means to "live" my epileptic body. However, in my view they do not suffice to fully express the experience of epilepsy. One of the most important shortcomings of the theory is that the lived body is confined to *conscious* embodiment, which excludes the semi-/trans-/ or unconscious perception of a seizure. Therefore, below I will extend classical existential phenomenology with concepts such as *Hirn* and beworlderment. My aim is to enrich the vocabulary, so that I may express the experience of living epilepsy as best as possible. In what follows, I will respectively describe becoming epileptic, undergoing brain research, and brain surgery, and end by exploring in detail what it means to live a seizure.

2 Hirn: *Leib* nor *Körper*

Until that night in 2004, I considered human existence as embodied consciousness and situated in the world. The traditional dualisms of body/mind, physical/mental, subject/object, and self/other to me were nothing but artificial means to categorize the world. Personally, I had indeed never experienced my body as an entity separable from my mind, nor did I distinguish between body and brain.

BEWORLDERED
87

However, that first seizure aggressively tore them a   part and destroyed all intertwinement. My **brain** separated itself from my   **body** as well as from my mind.

It was an event of irreversible alienation   for whereas before "I" —or what was left of it—identified with my **brain**   as belonging to my *Leib*, and thus the whole of my   lived **body**, now I no longer did. I *had* a **brain**, but certainly *wasn't*.

Not that I had ever been my **brain** in the neurocentric sense, but I used   to be my lived **body** that included my **brain** before. Now, in terms of *Körper*   and *Leib* my **brain** had become—and remained—a piece of pure *Körper*.

Husserl's original understanding of *Körper* and *Leib* does not cover this bodily experience. To express the aggressive, de-blurring experience of living epilepsy something is missing, since *Leib* always implies *Körper*. I argue therefore that this two-fold distinction should be extended by what I call *Hirn* ("brain" in German). *Hirn* is the brain-as-*Körper*, yet independent of the rest of my *Körper*. Even though obviously still physically there, my brain had disentangled itself from my body-as-subject and positioned itself opposite to what I thought to be my embodied self. Paradoxically, *Hirn* thus no longer belongs to either *Leib* or *Körper*. Rather, it is both, in the sense that it is *disembodied*, but a subject nevertheless. An actor with its own powers and autonomy that could take control of the leftover of my body and mind whenever it wanted. An opponent, no longer part of *me*. A stranger.

> In an attempt to express my experience, I take the risk of overwhelming you with yet another theoretical concept. A similar kind of stranger is graphically described by Jean-Luc Nancy in his essay "The Intruder" ("l'Intrus", 2000), which is a philosophical reflection on his heart transplant. I immediately recognized the similarities between *Hirn* and the intruder. The intruder is a figure for Nancy to understand the process of transplantation, and the experience of strangeness and unintelligibility that comes with it. The stranger's heart implanted in his body is an intruder. However, he says, in fact his own heart, the dysfunctional organ itself was the first intruder.
>
> > If my heart was giving up and going to drop me, to what degree was it an organ of "mine," my "own"? [...] It was becoming a stranger to me, intruding through its defection—almost through rejection, if not dejection. (3)

Nancy thus conceptualizes his heart as a subject who does not come from the outside to invade an integral entity but from within. If I replace "heart" with "brain," this quote perfectly reflects my own experience. For one, with the first seizure I was *rejected* and a stranger entered to end my pre-epileptic being. Shortly after I became epileptic, I was on my way home and my brain literally *dropped* me when it threw me off my bike. Later, it pushed me out of my bed while I was sleeping. My sister found me in a pool of blood and panicked, not knowing yet I had "only" broken my nose. Through its defection, my brain had become *Hirn*, an intruder.

3   De-Worlded

My experiences are complex and contradictory. For, although a subject as autonomous actor and *intruder*, in the medical environment *Hirn* was an object above all. The neurologist's perspective was one from the outside, a third-person view. Discussing which chemicals to use to fight the failure of its synaptic activity, my brain turned into nothing but an object of observation. Objectifying it like this was another form of alienation. My brain was pure matter, nothing but a dysfunctional lump of flesh that needed to be fixed. In fact, it was not only the rationalist medical perspective, but also the very way my brain appeared to me that made me experience it as such. For as far as I was still an embodied being or *Leib*, this lump surely no longer took part of it. The MRI images on the neurologist's screen were pictures of an object at a distance. As said, rather than "worlding" my brain, this was a case of "*de*-worlding." Both as a subject and an object, my brain had separated itself from the world I considered to be the one of my lived body. While my brain, simultaneously subject and object, seemed to be blurring the distinction subject-object within itself, at the same time the distance between me as a lived body in-the-world and that brain "out there" completely *de*-blurred that distinction. It drew a harsh line between

subject (me) // object (my brain), and in parallel here // there; Self // Other; material // immaterial; and, obviously, mind // brain.

The first scans showed I had a cerebral cyst, but the neurologists were not able to prove it was the actual source of epileptic activity. I tried many different kinds of medication and moved to a different clinic to consult another neurologist. The seizures had diminished but not disappeared. A four-day EEG at the clinic had not provided new insights.

Twelve years after the first seizure my neurologist suggested to start an extensive research process in order to localize the source. If localized, it could possibly be removed through brain surgery which, in the best case scenario, would end the seizures.

I took the chance and was hospitalized for fourteen days to make a deep brain EEG. I had to quit medication so that as many seizures as possible could be registered. Ten electrodes were placed under my skull, on the surface of my brain, and another two led, through small holes in the back of my head, all the way to my hippocampus. My brain was thus directly connected to that machine through electrical wires. It literally created a *mind*-bending situation that led to my experience of my brain in various and contradictory appearances.

On the one hand, it confirmed my brain as *Hirn* in its disembodied sense: a de-worlded object, still purely on the material side of the material-immaterial dichotomy. It was just a chunk of cells, mechanically producing electrical signals that led to the machine next to my bed. At the same time, another traditional boundary had blurred: the one between organism and machine. Possibly, "I was my synapses" (LeDoux) after all, for if I would identify myself with my brain, now neither self nor brain was more than an assemblage of electrical signals. Nothing but incoming data fed into the computer that trans- lated them into the patterns on its screen. A machine itself, one might say, although I wouldn't call it a "fantastic" one like Swaab. I did not feel that these data had anything to do with my lived body or being.

On the other hand, it confirmed *Hirn* as subject, as it was invaded by the electrodes to attach and thereby subject it to that machine. Simultaneously, it was a strange form of extension: being physically connected to something in the "outside world" extended my brain. In a way, being subjected to it together somehow unified me and my brain, which in that sense, despite everything, extended *us*. Even if pure matter, we were inseparable and thus shared the inability to free ourselves from our common invader-intruder, if you will. Somehow, my brain functioned as intermediate. It had an existential function which, ironically, is perfectly reflected by the word "synapse." The Greek term *synapsis* (συνάψις) means "conjunction." It is based upon the verb συνάπτειν, which consists of the words "together" (συν) and "to fasten" (ἅπτειν). Attached to the machine, while incorporated in my body, my brain created an existential *conjunction, fastening* the outside world and "me" *together*.

All that blurring, unifying, and incorporating did, however, not mean my brain lost its *Hirn* power over me. And neither was it supposed to. Unimpeded by medication, it took its chance and invited me to its Great Seizure Party. About twenty-five seizures of all sorts, apparently. I barely remember anything. As far as I do, it consists of fragments, shreds, and rags of the experiences I describe in the next section—times twenty-five.

The outcome of this research was that the cyst was *probably* the source of my seizures. Neurologist and neurosurgeon did not completely agree, however. The latter thought it had something to do with an area close to my hippocampus. As if it were a gamble, I got to choose between three options. Would I prefer to (a) get rid of the cyst; (b) get rid of that area deep down in my brain; (c) do nothing at all. I chose option (a), so a few months later that cyst was removed through brain surgery. This time it were scalpels that intruded my brain, shaping the physical part of my embodied consciousness. The removal of that cerebral cyst left a gap. Ironically, it created a physical space for phenomenal gaps to reside—memory gaps, explanatory gaps, and existential gaps.

4　Disappearances

Perhaps the neurosurgeon had actually been right, because although they did diminish, my seizures did not disappear. Unfortunately, for in terms of "intrusion" it is the seizure that is the worst one. An attack each and every time. Physically the seizure is obviously due to the dysfunctional brain. Yet, much more than *Hirn* or *Körper*, the experience of a seizure involves my phenomenal body, my *Leib*. It concerns the lived experience of **appear**ing, *dis*ap*pear*ing, and *reappear*ing.

The "tonic clonic seizure," the "complex partial seizure" and "absence" all contain distinct kinds of experience, but they have in common that they are opaque appearances. They remain unclear and indistinct because, despite there being some semi-embodied perceptions, they never involve full consciousness, let alone my cogito. Therefore, I call them *dis*appearances instead. Rather than the *phenomena* of traditional phenomenology, a seizure is the lived experience of *dis*appearance. Moreover, I am rather an embodied *un*consciousness, or, as I will explain, *transconsciousness*.

The absence is the lightest and shortest kind of seizure that involves "reduced consciousness" in medical terms. It is a moment of estrangement, but only for a few seconds. The complex partial seizure also carries the medical label of "reduced consciousness," but takes more time. The tonic clonic seizure evokes a completely unconscious state and involves full body spasm (tonic), followed by rhythmic shocks (clonic) of limbs and head. This seizure usually occurs while I am asleep, and without exception results in a severe headache,

BEWORLDERED

biting my tongue, and sometimes wetting my pants. In fact, when I step out of bed, the first thing that makes me realize I had such a sei*z*ure is a heavy body. I feel as if I weigh twice as much as I actually do.

Though physically the most extreme and painful, the tonic clonic sei*z*ures are not the ones that hurt the most, because I am lucky to have those almost always at night. The most agonizing is the complex partial sei*z*ure, which can catch me anytime a day. I experience it as a dynamic process, that consists of several stages and levels of (un)consciousness. It lasts for about twenty minutes in total. I feel it coming, and remember coming back to a "normal" state of consciousness afterwards, but I don't have any memory of the time in between. A black gap.

Because of its process-like character, the description "reduced conscious-ness" is not completely accurate. It is not a static mental state but, as said, consists of various phases. Moreover, "reduced" does not cover the lived, emotional aspect of the experience. "Reduced" suggests that consciousness is somehow quantifiable, whereas "living" a sei*z*ure is obviously not. Therefore, I will call the phase during the black gap "absent," which is emphatically not a state of mind but of *being*. I wish to point out that it is not the same as an "abs*En*ce," which is a much lighter sei*z*ure. The term is valid though, because the two forms share absence in the sense of not-being-present—in Heidegger-ian terms, a "not-Being-There."

When I feel the sei*z*ure coming, as soon as possible I sit down somewhere where I cannot hurt myself. Importantly, tonic clonic sei*z*ures start with this same awareness, and I am never sure whether it will become one of those. Suddenly everything is different. Unwillingly, I make an awkward kind of "huh!-huh!"-sound. As if having an independent will of its own, my arm makes a random move. What follows can be described as a moment where the world twists. All my senses seem to be distorted so that everything feels other than usual. It is like a voice that is distorted, yet strangely this distortion also applies to what I see, touch, smell, and taste. Furthermore, a layer of icy light, as if from a fluorescent tube, starts covering everything I perceive, including what I hear, touch, smell, and taste.

One might conceive of this experience as an "atmosphere," because of its all-encompassing character. During this phase of the sei*z*ure I would not call myself conscious, nor unconscious—or subconscious, for that matter—but *transconscious*. Not in a religious or psychoanalytic sense, but because it is a temporary mental state in a fluid process of *trans*ition from consciousness to "reduced consciousness."

I always immediately recognize this uncanny feeling. Because of its mysteri-ous familiarity, this transconscious atmosphere is similar to a déjà-vu. It seems like a memory, as if I have lived through this experience before, as if I am able to predict every detail from second to second. However, it appears a memory only in the moment as such, for while I am writing this down it is impossible to invoke it for myself. Another way to characterize it is that the experience has a certain rhythm. Thoughts and perceptions appear and disappear in a certain pattern, which is like a melody I know by heart because I feel I can "sing along". It is, however, anything but pleasant, let alone beautiful and soon transforms into full disorientedness. Although at the start of the seizure, I am still relatively at ease on a mental level, my body is overwhelmed by a purely physical state of anxiety. A wave of heat flies through my backbone, floods my shoulders and pulls back my cheeks, and soon takes control of me as a whole— physically, mentally, spiritually, and in whatever other sense. "Damn," I think, "once again!" In this alienated, disoriented, anxious state I quickly try to find a place where I can safely disappear, leave this world and enter the world of the **black gap.**

Then slowly, I am "coming-back" or "waking up". Imagine that the moment you wake up from sleep, usually probably only a few seconds, lasts for five minutes. Again I would call my mental state transconscious, this time gradually returning from reduced consciousness to consciousness. It starts with what appear to be normal sensations, but I cannot put them into context in any way. I see the room where I am and it does seem familiar somehow. However, the fact that the room is situated in a house and that house in a world—the fact that there is something "out-there" in the first place—is completely unknown to me. The same goes for time—what hour, what day is it, what date? I have no clue. In other words, I experience disappearances. Most striking is that I am not aware of the fact that my state of being is abnormal. I do not realise that I do not realise where, when and how I am. I am perfectly capable of getting out of bed and walking around. It is as if I purely function upon instinct or, one could say, pure *Körper*. Then rags of memory start reappearing, until I finally recall where I am, when and how. It is only at that point that I **realize I was attacked** by one of those ruthless sei*z*ures.

BEWORLDERED

Every time again the process of "coming back" leads to complete estrangement, for no matter how often it has happened, the experience is never stored. My memory is not working yet, so I do not recognize the experience. Therefore, though painless, every time the blow is as heavy. In fact, it is precisely the absence of pain that makes the complex partial sei*Z*ure hurt the most. If I feel physical pain as in the tonic clonic sei*Z*ure, at least there is some-*thing* that hurts—it is tangible, demonstrable, and concrete. The former sei*Z*ure however, is cruelly untouchable, ineffable, and incomprehensible, which is why it has much more impact than what, when I wake up after a tonic clonic sei*Z*ure, often feels only like a hangover. Each and every time I come back, I am thus in a state of thorough alienation. This is what I call *beworldered*. *Be*ing back in the "real" *world*, but profoundly *bewildered*.

5   Beworldered

Rather than a temporary state, beworlderment marks my new way of Being-in-the-World as such. Epilepsy brought about permanent bewilderment, alienation from, and distrust towards my brain, body, and self. Or better in plural—my bodies, selves, and new ways of being, for my embodied self is no longer one integrated whole. Sobchack describes how after the amputation and the experience of her "phantom" leg she incorporated the prosthetic and developed "another form of bodily incorporation and integrity, another sense of myself 'as a whole'" (61–62). I, however, did not develop a new sense of wholeness, on the contrary. The experience of a sei*Z*ure remains ungraspable, unfathomable for myself as a lived body—including my world. I seem to be split up into a "real" or "present" self and an "absent" self. The real self is a lived body, a *Leib*, but in the process of transconsciousness it loses its embodiment and therewith transforms into an absent self. While Husserl emphasizes that there is no *Leib* without *Körper*, I think of the experience of an absent self as exactly that: a *Leib-ohne-Körper*. Just like *Hirn* and the transconscious experience of disappearance, the lived experience of *Leib-ohne-Körper* discloses a void in classical phenomenology. For during the sei*Z*ure I do experience something "out there" that somehow **appears**, dis*ap*P*ea*rs and reappears to me, but my physical body is no longer part of it, let alone my *Hirn*. Paradoxically, it definitely is a state of being—otherwise how could I experience anything in the first place?—but it is an absent state, a negation of presence, it is a "not-Being-There." I am disembodied, as well as de-worlded.

My being thus consists of an eccentric form of fragmentation. I can never experience the two *Leiber*—with and without *Körper*—at the same time, for each has her own way of Being and her own world. There is an insurmountable existential, perceptive, and explanatory gap between the two. The absent self or *Leib-ohne-Körper* cannot describe, let alone explain, the present self or the embodied *Leib* her disembodied-yet-"lived" experience of (dis)appearances. To be beworldered is inexplicable to the de-worlded self.

Nevertheless, the latter is exactly what I aimed to do in this essay: express the beworldering experience of being both *Leiber*. Importantly, I am certain that the beworldered way of being is not only characteristic of epileptic being but of other experiences of *Leib-ohne-Körper* as well. One may think of depression, hallucination, or dreams. I therefore hope to have unfolded a more general existential structure, which makes this narrative meaningful and potentially recognizable to others as well—be they epileptic or not.

References

Heidegger, Martin. *Sein und Zeit.* 1926. Max Niemeyer Verlag, 1963.

Husserl, Edmund. *Ideen zu einer reinen Phänomenologie und phänomenologischen Philosophie.* Vol. 2 (Phänomenologische Untersuchungen zur Konstitution), edited by Marly Biemel, Nijhoff, 1952.

LeDoux, Joseph. *Synaptic Self: How Our Brains Become Who We Are.* Viking Penguin, 2002.

Merleau-Ponty, Maurice. *Phenomenology of Perception.* 1945. Taylor & Francis, 2005.

Nancy, Jean-Luc. "The Intruder." *Corpus.* Fordham University Press, 2000/2008.

Sobchack, Vivian. "Living a 'Phantom Limb': On the Phenomenology of Bodily Integrity." *Body & Society*, vol. 16, no. 3, 2010, pp. 51–67.

Swaab, Dick. *We Are Our Brains: A Neurobiography of the Brain, from the Womb to Alzheimer's.* Transl. Jane Hedley-Prôle, Spiegel & Grau, 2014.

CHAPTER 6

Pedagogy and Neurodiversity
Experimenting in the Classroom with Autistic Perception

Halbe Kuipers

It is not uncommon for someone to enter the university classroom of the experimental lab for research-creation, SenseLab at Concordia University Montreal, and halt in their tracks.[1] Seeing all the things populating this space—a huge playground-like space chockfull of materials and compositions—they would often be taken aback (Figures 6.1 & 6.2). Is this really a classroom? Having found their bearings again, they would go up to one of the persons at work there, asking what this is all about. The more adventurous would perhaps even ask whether they can touch or move something: is the material meant to be interactive? The response would often be something along the lines of "why don't you ask spazze itself?" Or, as the French philosopher Étienne Souriau would say, "ask the virtual" (cited in Lapoujade 34).

At first sight, this anecdote might not reveal much about what is going on in this not so typical classroom. It is, however, the strongest sign of a "neurodiverse" pedagogy tending to an environmental awareness practiced in this space. While giving the sense of an any-thing-whatsoever, of more chaos than order, the things here are in fact arranged carefully and the space is attentively tended to. Much like how the world of a child is not "just play," even when seeming so from the perspective of an adult (Lapoujade 33).

The play, however, also attunes to how different modes of experience come to matter in processes of learning (Manning and Massumi 4). Erin Manning and Brian Massumi, who lead the SenseLab, work with a process philosophy foregrounding indeed *processes* rather than the substantive, be it subjects or objects. The play and the materials in the classroom are therefore part and parcel of how processes of learning take place in spazze. Moreover, these compositions foreground what Manning calls "autistic perception," which hones into

---

1 SenseLab is "a laboratory for thought in motion" which is made up of "an international network of artists and academics, writers and makers, from a wide diversity of fields, working together at the crossroads of philosophy, art, and activism. (...) The SenseLab's event-based projects are collectively self-organizing. Their aim is to experiment with creative techniques for thought in the act. The SenseLab's product is its process, which is meant to disseminate" (*Senselab.ca*).

© KONINKLIJKE BRILL NV, LEIDEN, 2023 | DOI:10.1163/9789004681293_008

FIGURE 6.1

The classroom as spazze
PHOTOGRAPHS BY HALBE KUIPERS, 2018

FIGURE 6.2

The classroom as spazze
PHOTOGRAPHS BY HALBE KUIPERS, 2018

an experiental dimension that conventionally does not seem to matter in such an educational space. The question driving the experiment is thus: *what would a more neurodiverse pedagogy look like in the context of a classroom*? All too often, pedagogy and education privilege neurotypicality through approaches that favor a reflective mode of thought and rely on a deficit model of education wherein those that do not fit its demands are of a "second order."[2] This mode also reflects in the classroom itself, in how it is "spacing" bodies and their relations and how the space itself is felt. Within neurodiverse pedagogy, I argue, the classroom itself is felt in its full qualitative nature and not separated from the process of learning. This classroom experiment—variably named "spazze",

---

2 Following Manning, when I am referring to a reflective mode of thought or more generally consciousness, I mean this as "reflective consciousness" in which "there is a tuning toward cognition and language to represent what is felt" (Manning, *Minor Gesture* 237). This stands in contrast to what Henri Bergson calls "immediate consciousness" (cited in Manning, *Minor Gesture* 237) which, as I will unfold below, Manning argues is in proximity to autistic perception.

"spazz," or "spaZe"—shows that learning thrives in multiple different modes of experience and knowledge. I will unfold this idea in two steps: First, I offer a critique of the common conception of the classroom and its privileging of the reflective mode. This critique aims to show how the experiential dimension can become productive in the classroom. Second, by foregrounding process philosophy, through Brian Massumi and Erin Manning's reading, I question phenomenological perspectives, i.e., "bottom-up" approaches which *do* address experience (and notably autistic experience) but still pertain to the notion of a subject and a particular mode of consciousness, even if this mode is an intentional rather than a reflective one.[3] With Manning's concept of autistic perception I demonstrate how experience is in the world—*worlding*—and thus shapes the learning processes. If it seems strange to focus on the classroom itself in the context of learning, this only attests to the strong split of mind and matter present in education. A neurodiverse pedagogy might be an interesting antidote to this split and the deficit model that comes with it.

1 A Critique on the Typical Model of the Classroom

The classroom is all too often but an extension of the dominant mode of knowledge and its production. From the teacher to the students and from the tables to the chairs, everything tends to learning as knowledge transfer. As Manning notes, "[most] of our education systems are based on starting from stillness. [...] Reason is aligned with keeping the body still" (*Minor Gesture* 122). Paulo Freire calls this mode the "banking" of knowledge (58). As Freire argues, the banking makes students but receptors of knowledge transmitted centrally from the front of the classroom and "equally" distributed to the students. The ideal form of transmission is clarity and discreteness: knowledge should be transmitted and processed as efficiently as possible. This demands a certain way of learning through attention. We can think here of aspects such as frontality (demanding face to face communication) and an emphasis on the clarity of speaking out and presenting; the sitting in an arrangement of desks and chairs that are all directed towards the front of the classroom, holding bodies in check, straight and still; and the teacher's place at the front of the classroom

---

3   Manning speaks of the triad grounding the centrality of human narratives, and thus neurotypicality, as that of "agency, volition, and intentionality" (Manning, *Minor Gesture* 19). While agency is the composite of these dimensions, grounding the human individual in free will, I see volition and intentionality to coincide respectively the mode of reflection and the mode of intentionality I mention.

as one of explication, demanding directed attention without deviation. We can say that the banking of knowledge forms bodies and "banks" them equally in this particular mode of learning and its idealization.

Of course, this model never works absolutely nor does every classroom resemble it.[4] Even in its strictest form, there is always movement that exceed its demands, particularly with younger bodies. Moreover, throughout education from primary school to universities, these demands loosen up and a bit of wriggling in a chair is hardly a concern. We might thus wonder whether an actual classroom ever really resembles the banking model and yet the ideal somehow perseveres. The model in general aims at a particular form *of* learning: through the intellect and by virtue of cognition. This reflects in the spatial arrangement of the classroom, enacting the narrowness of the model. The model "parses" the classroom unidirectionally, only positioning the teacher in the space of explication and the students in the space of reflection.[5] Spaces are parsed in order to "filter out" as many distracting stimuli as possible so as to heighten the focus and facilitating the effective processing of knowledge. If we can call this model one of Reason, as Manning suggests, it is because—in line with the modern conception of the human and its capacity for *cogitare*—it privileges the functioning of the intellect as the base of (human) interaction, extending into capacities such as empathy, morality, and a sense of self. From this perspective, different forms of classrooms are quickly seen as of lesser value or simply deviations from the model, i.e., as "special" (think of education for the "mentally disabled," such as autistics).

Manning and Massumi suggest that this model falls together with what they call "entrainment" (7). Entrainment marks the "for-ness" of any particular field. When certain bodies enter a classroom for instance, they will immediately see the tables and the chairs and its particular setup. Affordances are thus formed and the bodies will align with them by virtue of entrainment. Entrainment, however, also makes certain bodies unfit, because their structuring of perception does not go as easily—or works in the same way—as with so-called neurotypicals (8). Think of an autistic body simply unfit for the restraint of hours of sitting in a chair in one go. This raises the more general question—which I discuss in the following section—whether if by adhering to this dominant

---

4   There are plenty of alternative pedagogies that have very different manners and styles in teaching and pedagogy more generally. One can here think of Montessori, Freinet, or Reggio Emilia pedagogy. The latter might be closest to the neurodiverse pedagogy here unfolded.

5   For a critique of pedagogy as explication see Jacques Rancière's *The Ignorant Schoolmaster: Five Lessons in Intellectual Emancipation*. Rancière unveils how learning does not only have to be about explication in a particular teacher/student relation and in fact can find very different ways to unfold wherein the teacher is not by definition the one holding knowledge.

mode we not all too easily submit to a deficit model of learning and fail to see and appreciate many other modes of knowledge.[6]

Importantly, such a deficit model needs to be questioned in order to think of a more inclusive classroom.[7] Yet, reflecting on its dominance can also reveal the blindness towards forms of learning that exceed the model of knowledge transfer and production. Like Manning and Massumi, I turn to neurodiversity, the body, and the experiential dimension that shapes learning processes to problematize this model. The aim is to not only question its material form but also to problematize the (philosophical) presuppositions grounding it. Neurodiversity offers an interesting opening for such a critique because it addresses the differential filtering and processing of knowledge not merely as divergences from the norm but as essential for what makes each body different in a complex of feeling.

2 The Movement of Neurodiversity and the Experiential Dimension: Bottom-Up?

The term neurodiversity was first introduced in the late 1990s by sociologist Judy Singer and furthered by influential autistic self-advocates such as Jane Meyerding. Since then the term has wildly grown in its uses, creating a field brimming with debate not without dispute (Pripas-Kapit). The field ranges from on the one hand a relation to disability studies to a focus on neurological discourses and their mobilization for autistic identity on the other. Neurodiversity activist and self-advocates first and foremost foreground that difference needs to be seen through the body and how it is "wired," obviously involving the brain (Walker; "What is Autism"). Neurodiversity is about refusing to see certain bodies as dependent and requiring a cure in any way—every body is different in a complex of feeling and existence. This strongly contrasts with common conceptions of autistics as lacking certain abilities such as empathy, control, intellect, etc. (e.g., see Sacks). Neurotypicality, the counter-pole of neurodiversity, foregrounds only a certain mode of existence centered on capacities such as empathy, control, and intellect. These neurotypical competences are, according to Manning, based on agency, volition, and intentionality (*Minor*

---

6 For more on the notion of a deficit model in regard to neurodiversity see Dinishak "The Deficit View and Its Critics."

7 Francisco Trento's work is a good example of this (see "On Unconditional Hos(ti)pitality"). Trento thinks with the experiment of spazze to argue for the necessity of creating a more inclusive space for other modes of existence.

Gesture 19). Such foregrounding is not absolute, however, nor should we see it as entirely grounded in some sense of nature or genetics: neurotypicals carry neurodiverse tendencies too. While the spectrum of neurodiversity is without a doubt diverse and complex (including people with Asperger's, ADHD, low-functioning and high-functioning autistics, non-speaking people etc.), and certainly not all matters are agreed upon within the movement, generally the neurodiversity movement fights to amplify the voices of those that can be considered being on the spectrum of neurodiversity.

Neurodiversity questions what it is to be human in this world. Simply said, neurotypicality tends to be human-centered precisely in the way Manning argues by linking neurotypicality to the supposed capacities and related narratives of agency, volition, and intentionality. "When failing to perform typical human emotions and interactions, the subject risks failing to qualify for the 'human club,' and instead is seen as something other than human, in some cases coming close to the category of animal" (Bergenmar et al. 8–9). For what is meant when we in general say "human"? According to autism activist Mel Baggs, we certainly don't mean "autistic" (but "real people"). We mean "neurotypical," we mean expressing oneself predominantly in spoken language. We mean "being focused on humans to the detriment of other elements in the environment" (Manning and Massumi 5). As Baggs notes, "[t]hey [neurotypicals] judge my existence, awareness, and personhood on which of a tiny and limited part of the world I appear to be reacting to" ("In My Language"). Or, as social scientist Anna Stenning paraphrases:

> Autistic people have been denied characteristics that are commonly considered part of what it is to be fully human, including empathy, morality, a sense of self, imagination, narrative identity, integrity; introspection, self-hood, personhood; rhetoricity, gender, meaning-making, sociality, or flourishing. (1)

Clearly a broad plethora of qualities attributed to "normal" human beings or neurotypicals is being denied at least to some degree to autistics. On top of that, the autist tends to be rendered flat in a stereotype as a sort of dysfunctional, or at best deviating being (Bergenmar et al).[8] The flourishing autobiographical and fictional literature on and by autistic subjects problematizes

---

8 A much noted "problem" with autistics is that they seem like automatons devoid of emotion. For example, Oliver Sacks says precisely this about autistic Dawn Temple in his well-known book *An Anthropologist on Mars*. The question is whether the seeming lack of emotion Sacks

such a stereotype by describing and showing that while it is easy to portray them as dysfunctional, they might in fact concern different ways of seeing the world, with a different logic of sense. This brings us to the pivotal point where the experiential dimension takes on relevance. Pivotal insofar as in describing this dimension it becomes apparent that it indeed is possible to describe it (a crucial criterion for validating oneself as a human being). At the same time, these descriptions shift and displace common modes of experience. In the autistic literature, boundaries between human, animals, and things blur, as Bergenmar et al. note (213); narrative temporality is prone to shifts as the descriptions frequently do not accommodate a common sense rhythm; often there is a strong attention and focus on the immediate qualities of the environment. These are but a few aspects of this literature, but they surely warrant seeing the neurodiverse experience as interesting and relevant in itself instead of merely as dysfunctional or impaired.

I turn to this literature, albeit briefly, precisely to question the interpretation of such descriptions. As noted above, what is often foregrounded is the mere fact of description (Bergenmar et al.). That is to say, the author is capable of describing the experience which gives the experience its validity. These sort of "bottom-up" approaches might challenge the typical and stereotypical conceptions and "established theory and methodology" (Stenning 1) based in reflective consciousness, but they are at the same time validated by the very cognitive capacities and phenomenological qualities they mean to overturn: agency, volition, and intentionality. The question is, how to interpret and value these descriptions differently in order to not subsume them once again under the label of "human capacities" but rather as different modes of existence?

It is important to note that such questioning circumvents an entire area of focus on autistic identity and neurodiversity. A bottom-up conception of autistic experience, which grounds itself in the subjects of autism, has its academic counterpart in the tracing of these different descriptions and routes of autistic identity. Fernando Vidal and Francisco Ortega, for instance, give an interesting "travelogue" of the movement in terms of its discursive efficacy, focused on the usage of the "neuro"-term and its relation to neuroscience (6; 167–188). While there is surely merit to these descriptions and their critical explorations, the concern is precisely, as aired above, that they might end up reaffirming the very basis they mean to undo. Perhaps the question is simply, what if these

---

sees also means that there is no feeling, or if the feeling simply diverges from the recognizable forms we have come to see as emotion.

experiences are mobilized, but not as expressions of "the human" and the triad of agency, volition, and intentionality that grounds it?

3 Autistic Perception and Processes of Sense Making as More-Than Reflection

Erin Manning proposes the concept of autistic perception, moving with the activist field of neurodiversity. She foregrounds the experiential dimension and a multiplicity of ways of being in the world precisely to decenter the human and its dominant modes (Manning, *Always More*; Manning, *Minor Gesture*). The proposition of autistic perception is simple yet profound: neurodiversity "parses experience" differently. What is in play in neurodiverse experience is precisely what tends to be left out of experience in more neurotypical perception (Manning, *Always More* 176–7). Where neurotypicality centers on cognition, and cognition presumes that what there is—at least for humans, as that is its presumed cut-off point—and what cognition can apprehend, in autistic perception such filtering might work differently. Manning defines autistic perception as "a tendency in perception shared by all that privileges complexity of experience over category" (*Minor Gesture* 112). As a tendency, it is not just a matter of filtering out external stimuli or not, which would all too easily lead to a naturalistic view and cast autism as a biological defect and thus deficit. To make her point, Manning deploys the notion of "chunking", as conceived by autistic writer Anne Corwin. Corwin describes chunking in terms of a "slowness" of experiencing (Corwin). Manning elaborates, "the autistic's entry into an environment begins not with a perception of objects (chairs, tables) or of subjects (people) but with an edging into form, a tending of light and shadow, and color. While this does eventually lead to the taking-shape of the environment, to its parsing, autistics benefit from the direct perception of the active ecologies of experience in-forming" (*Minor Gesture* 112). Where filtering (out) designates a certain selection of external stimuli (or not), chunking concerns the process of how experience shapes what is seen and how perception is structured. Chunking foregrounds an active role of that which in filtering would be relegated out in favor of the discreteness of cognition. While chunking certainly involves the discreteness of things, it concerns before all the process of their shaping, of how they come into shape, and not merely whether or not they are discrete, as is apparent in Corwin's claim regarding the slowness in chunking. From the perspective of agency, volition, and intentionality, this slowness of chunking troubles straightforward acts, and thus attests to the

PEDAGOGY AND NEURODIVERSITY   103

difficulty autistics can have in following the pace of the neurotypical world.[9] However, unlike filtering, chunking involves a process of sensemaking which opens up to a plurality of ways experience shapes seeing the world. Corwin's slowness in chunking is key here, because what she foregrounds is precisely a different mode of experience that is *qualitatively different* rather than merely quantitatively different. It is not just a matter of seeing more or less, it is a matter of seeing differently. This gives a glimpse of what a different mode of experience can do beyond seeing it as mere deficit.

Manning and Massumi further unfold the processual workings of the qualitative difference in perception by approaching it as "a dance of perception":

> To experience the texture of the world "without discrimination" is not indifference. Texture is patterned, full of contrast and movement, gradients and transitions. It is complex and differentiated. To attend to everything "the same way" is not an inattention to life. It is to pay equal attention to the full range of life's texturing complexity, with an entranced and unhierarchized commitment to the way in which the organic and the inorganic, colour, sound, smell, and rhythm, perception and emotion, intensely interweave into the "aroundness" of a textured world, alive with difference. (4)

The qualitative multiplicity of experience that Manning and Massumi emphasize brings to the foreground that what is in play in chunking in contrast to filtering cannot simply be relegated to an external dimension as separate from consciousness or cognition.[10] What constitutes chunking is as much physical as mental, concrete as abstract, or actual as virtual.[11] Chunking as such

---

9   Manning states that "[t]he neurotypical, as real contributor to society and to humanity in general, is strongly paired with a notion of independence understood according to normative definitions of ability and able-bodiedness framed by what I call the volition-intentionality-agency triad" (*Minor Gesture* 5–6).

10 The notion of "qualitative multiplicity" comes from Henri Bergson and his study on immediate experience and "duration" (Bergson). Bergson argues that qualitative multiplicity is the heterogeneity of time that is not able to be spatialized and quantified.

11 In process philosophy the experience is not grounded in a subject, as is the case with phenomenology. This makes of the affects and percepts—or "feeling," as Alfred North Whitehead calls it—not something "presubjective" but rather places the subjective in the processes. Manning (and Massumi) here work through Whitehead's conception of "subjective form" in the concrescence of an occasion of experience. See, for instance, Manning (*Minor Gesture* 247). The subjective becomes here first orientation (subjective aim) and then force (subjective intensity), which is to say, intensity in the field of feeling.

involves how discrete things come to be seen, that is, how they group into single "chunks" rather than being seen as a multiplicity. This process is thoroughly explained by cognitive science (e.g., Johnson), but Corwin and Manning mobilize it not as mere information grouping but always underway in a process of seeing. Manning also speaks of a "parsing of experience," which more than chunking might express how perception not only structures in grouping discrete things but also compresses. It is like a wrapping of experience, which in more neurotypical perception is precisely more narrow, more straight, and stricter. Parsing out thus more emphasizes an environmental dimension that foregrounds the affective tonality that is felt with a thing seen. It is not unlike the focused attention on knowledge transfer in the classroom that Manning describes where it is not merely about the focus on discrete things but also about how this focus can sustain itself. This more neurotypical mode of perception, as we can call such parsing out, which chunks discrete things and makes a sequence of them in quantitative terms, comes with an offshoot: "What is felt as quantitative effort is felt consciously, backgrounding not only the qualitative complexity in the event, but intensity's own qualitative multiplicity. In the parsing occurring with consciousness, a certain poverty of complexity has been chosen over the confused heap" (*Minor Gesture* 17). In short, we can say that neurotypical perception tends to filter our external stimuli, chunk perception, and parses out of experience a large part of sense data. While these three aspects might seem close, the differences are essential to grasp neurodiverse modes of experience: the slowness Corwin speaks of can potentially also allow a person to perceive qualities within a thing otherwise parsed out.

This finally brings us back to the differentiation Manning and Massumi make between "entrainment" and "entertainment". Entrainment creates a field saturated with "for-ness": the field is subjected to the function and utility of things as seen: something is *for* something within the field of perception: a chair is for sitting, affording "sit-ability." This parses out of the field its potential as contrasts. With entertainment on the other hand, there is a "foregrounding of the immediate field of experience" (4). The field of experience is rich in texture, in qualities and contrasts. The potential is marked by what is not held in the "for-ness" of the field; what emerges is not predetermined by any form *yet*. Of course openness is not easy; normal ways of learning are not just unsettled, they are practically rendered impossible:

> It is no doubt easier to habitually cross into a room that itself habitually chunks into chairs and tables, then to begin with the whole-field pattern as yet unresolved into objects. Rather than chunking, what occurs on the

autistic spectrum of neurodiversity is an immediate entertainment of modalities of relation. Pattern, an interplay of contrasts, comes before familiar use and describable chunking. (18)

Entertainment comes with a wonder and a curiosity rich with the texture of experience. When the field is not yet caught within a "for-ness" the potential exceeds each individual form, or what Souriau called "the virtual." In this way Manning and Massumi also speak of experience as *worlding*. If we take this back to the classroom, it necessarily involves the environment of the classroom as much as the subject of learning. That said, it seems we have ventured far away from any actual learning by diving into perception as such. How can we see the "entertainment of modalities of relation" in relation to learning?

4 The Classroom Experiment Called *spazze* and Its Neurodiverse Pedagogy

While there are plenty of techniques practiced in spazze in line with a neurodiverse pedagogy,[12] I want to focus on one in particular that concerns the *entry of a body* into the classroom. There are always a diverse amount of bodies entering the classroom at different times: not only students but also a wide variety of people interested in the subjects of art, philosophy and indeed neurodiversity. Amongst those bodies are elderly and children but also bodies with disabilities or other sorts of complexities. Many bodies in some way carry neurodiverse tendencies, also because this classroom is one of the few places in the university where neurodiversity is studied and practiced as a pedagogy. As explained above through chunking and parsing, neurodiverse bodies do not enter a space the same way as neurotypicals do, as they tend to not perceive its *for-ness* in a discrete manner. What neurodiversity teaches us here is that entering a room is not merely a physical and neurobiological concern, as if the diversity of this experience could be reduced to neurology. Rather, every body enters with a different complex of feeling, some edging more towards the physical, others to the mental. Manning speaks of "thresholds" as that what is crossed in entering ("How the Minor Moves Us"). Thresholds are as much abstract as they are concrete, such as the feeling of uneasiness when having to enter a space in which you know you are not welcome. But it also exceeds conscious knowing and reflection, reaching down more into a visceral intuition

---

12 For more writings on spazze and the techniques developed see Trento ("On Unconditional Hos(ti)pitality") and Manning (*For a Pragmatics*).

or simply feeling. This conception opens up to other sensibilities that don't need to be confined to autistic experience but considers the experience of entering a classroom in general. Indeed, while entirely specific to each entry, each crossing is general insofar as every body has to cross a threshold to enter the classroom; it is just that for some bodies this is not as easy as for others. This is key to grasping autistic perception: the sense data that is being filtered, chunked, and parsed (out) concerns as much abstractions as it does "concrete" matters. It is all material, so to say, and as such it is the material for experimentation in this spazze. This means that the abstractions that come with a classroom—i.e., our presuppositions and our opinions about it—matter on a material level as well.

Above I referred to three aspects aligned with Reason: frontality, arrangement, and directedness. When the entry of a body is taken seriously in the complex of feeling, it becomes clear that while a typical setup of the classroom can be helpful and comforting for some, it might be distressing for others, even to such a degree that it might become impossible to proceed with learning. To address this problem, the technique of *patches* is mobilized in spazze (Figures 6.3 & 6.4). The patches are made from different materials such as textile or paint and create a kind of "landing-site" for bodies (Arakawa and Gins). The idea of a patch is not very different from putting something on the floor and see how a cat would go and sit on it. These patches of intensity in the classroom lure a body entering the space, inviting it to land there. The patches, thus conceptualized, are "lures for feeling" (Whitehead 184). The idea is precisely that landing sites can compose an open space of sitting *and* a mode of attention. This landing would often, in co-composition with the rest of the

FIGURE 6.3
Research on *patches* and *landing*
PHOTOGRAPHS BY HALBE KUIPERS, 2020, 2017

FIGURE 6.4   Research on *patches* and *landing*
PHOTOGRAPHS BY HALBE KUIPERS, 2020, 2017

spazze, allow for aspects such as frontality, arrangement, and directness to be curved. Firstly by the lure and its drawing in of attention, secondly by the composing of a landing site by landing. The idea is that bodies in their landing compose the setup of the space, not the other way around. Co-composition is important here because it signals that composing always happens within and through an environment. In other words, there is always more-than what can be seen and composed by those working there. The active making of a patch, for instance, can inadvertently create another patch outside of the marked area. The unforeseen dimension of these techniques requires what Manning calls an "artfulness" in that the techniques deployed keep a certain openness (*Always More* 93).

This coincides with the fact that no technique works for every body. It thus necessitates a continuous honing to new bodies that enter and raise new problems. For instance, while these patches might be deployed as landing sites—implying a certain for-ness in luring bodies to land—for many bodies it will not work this way at all. In fact, it turned out that after making these landing sites and removing all chairs, at some point the chairs were missed by some of the bodies that had entered; some simply need a chair to accommodate their body. The composing of landing sites had gotten so focused on making patches that it was forgotten that chairs might also be certain landing sites themselves. But bringing a chair back into the classroom now makes it a landing site among others and no longer a basic element of the setup. The main point is that the above mentioned "entertainment of modalities of relation" here cannot be reduced to merely one mode, nor can it be reduced to a subject's body. The different modes parse their own manner of attention, so to say, and this also shapes the learning processes.

In this classroom, learning becomes more than knowledge transfer precisely because the environment is always co-composing every mode. It is no longer reducible to a subject, be it a reflective or an intentional one. With every thought it becomes precisely a question *what* thinks along. We can say that "spazze" as a concept here does its work: it folds the classroom and pedagogy together to foreground the modalities of relation by learning, always asking what kind of bodies are created in studying. The environmental takes prominence in all learning; hence we can only speak of the engagement with its abstractions as lived and material engagement. And if they are *lived* abstractions indeed (Massumi, *Semblance*) then we cannot but speak of them as in the world. That might be the closest we can get to a genuine *worlding*, which could even be seen as worlding our brains insofar as brains mark the mental dimension of any process of engagement. Moreover, we can now finally grasp what occurs in spazze when people suggest: "why don't you ask spazze?" The "virtual" is just another term for affirming that there is always more-than what we tend to think is there, and this *more-than* affects every process, including the process of learning.

References

Baggs, Mel. "If We Were Real People." *Ballastexistenz*, 24 Mar. 2010, https://ballastexistenz.wordpress.com/2010/03.

Bergenmar, Jenny. "Autism and the Question of the Human." *Literature and Medicine*, vol. 33, no. 1, 2015, pp. 202–21.

Bergson, Henri. *Time and Free Will: An Essay on the Immediate Data of Consciousness*. Dover Publications, 2001.

Biermeier, Mary Ann. "Inspired by Reggio Emilia: Emergent Curriculum in Relationship-Driven Learning Environments." *Young Children*, vol. 70, no. 5, 2015.

Corwin, Anne. "Interview on Growing Up, Autism, and Other Things—Part I." *Existence Is Wonderful Blog*, 28 July 2008, http://www.existenceiswonderful.com/2008/07/interview-on-growing-up-autism-and_5644.html.

Costendi, Moheb. "Against Neurodiversity." *Aeon*, 12 Sept. 2019, https://aeon.co/essays/why-the-neurodiversity-movement-has-become-harmful.

Dahlberg, Gunilla, and Peter Moss. "Introduction: Invitation to the Dance." *Art and Creativity in Reggio Emilia: Exploring the Role and Potential of Ateliers in Early Childhood Education*, edited by Vea Vecchi, Routledge, 2010, p. xiv-xxiii.

Deleuze, Gilles. *The Fold: Leibniz and the Baroque*. University of Minnesota Press, 1993.

Dinishak, Janette. "The Deficit View and Its Critics." *The Disability Studies Quarterly*, vol. 36, no. 4, 2016.

PEDAGOGY AND NEURODIVERSITY

Freire, Paulo. *Pedagogy of the Oppressed*. 1970. Continuum, 2000.

In My Language. Directed by Mel Baggs, 2007, https://www.youtube.com/watch?v=JnylM1hI2jc.

Johnson, Neal F. "The Role of Chunking and Organization in The Process of Recall." *Psychology of Learning and Motivation*, vol. 4, 1970, pp. 171–247.

Kapp, Steven K., editor. *Autistic Community and the Neurodiversity Movement: Stories from the Frontline*. Springer, 2020.

Lapoujade, David. *Les Existences Moindres*. Les Éditions de Minuit, 2017.

Manning, Erin. *Always More than One: Individuation's Dance*. Duke UP, 2013.

Manning, Erin. *The Minor Gesture*. Duke UP, 2016.

Manning, Erin. "How the Minor Moves Us: Across Thresholds, Socialities, and Techniques. A Conversation with Erin Manning." *Open! Platform for Art, Culture, & the Public Domain*, 20 Feb. 2019, https://onlineopen.org/how-the-minor-moves-us-across-thresholds-socialities-and-techniques.

Manning, Erin. *For a Pragmatics of the Useless*. Duke UP, 2020.

Manning, Erin, and Brian Massumi. *Thought in the Act: Passages in the Ecology of Experience*. University of Minnesota Press, 2014.

Massumi, Brian. *Semblance and Event: Activist Philosophy and the Occurrent Arts: Technologies of Lived Abstraction*. MIT Press, 2011.

Massumi, Brian. *What Animals Teach Us about Politics*. Duke UP, 2014.

Meyerding, Jane. "Thoughts on Finding Myself Differently Brained." 1998. *Autonomy, the Critical Journal of Interdisciplinary Autism Studies*, 25 July 2014, www.larry-arnold.net/Autonomy/index.php/autonomy/article/view/AR9/html.

Pripas-Kapit, Sarah. "Historicizing Jim Sinclair's 'Don't Mourn for Us': A Cultural and Intellectual History of Neurodiversity's First Manifesto." *Autistic Community and the Neurodiversity Movement*, edited by Steven K. Kapp, Springer, 2020, pp. 23–39.

Rancière, Jacques. *The Ignorant Schoolmaster: Five Lessons in Intellectual Emancipation*. Stanford UP, 1991.

Sacks, Oliver. *An Anthropologist on Mars: Seven Paradoxical Tales*. Vintage Canada, 1996.

SenseLab-3e | a Laboratory for Thought in Motion. https://senselab.ca/wp2/.

Singer, Judy. "'Why Can't You Be Normal for Once in Your Life?': From a 'Problem with No Name' to a New Category of Difference." *Disability Discourse*, edited by Mairian Corker and Sally French, Open University Press, 1990, pp. 59–67.

Stenning, Anna. "Understanding Empathy through a Study of Autistic Life Writing: On the Importance of Neurodivergent Morality." *Neurodiversity Studies: A New Critical Paradigm*, edited by Hanna Bertilsdotter Rosqvist et al., Routledge, 2022, pp. 108–24.

Trento, Francisco. "On Unconditional Hos(Pi)Tality: Thinking-Doing Strategies for Dis/Abling Arts Education." *Journal of New Materialism Research*, vol. 2, no. 1, 2021.

Walker, Nick. "What Is Autism?" *Neuroqueer. Dr. Nick Walker's Notes on Neurodiversity, Autism & Self-Liberation Blog*, 2014, https://neuroqueer.com/what-is-autism.

"What Is: Neurodiversity, Neurodivergent, Neurotypical." *Disabled World*, Nov 29, 2022, https://www.disabled-world.com/disability/awareness/neurodiversity/.

Whitehead, Alfred North. *Process and Reality: An Essay in Cosmology*. Edited by David Ray Griffin and Donald W. Sherburne, Free Press, 1985.

PART 2

Narrative Entanglements

∴

CHAPTER 7

Personification as *Élanification*

Agency Combustion and Narrative Layering in Worlding Perceived Relations

Marco Bernini

"Nature is a temple in which living pillars
Sometimes let slip some confused words;
Man there passes through forests of symbols
Which look at him with understanding eyes."

BAUDELAIRE, Correspondences

∙ ∙ ∙

"[Nature]: Did you really think that the world had been tailored to your needs? Now learn that in my structure, order and operations – with few exceptions – I never had any intention to make humans neither rejoice nor suffering."

GIACOMO LEOPARDI, 'Dialogue Between Nature and an Icelandic Traveller' (my translation)

∙ ∙
∙ ∙

1   Introduction

Reviewing recent frameworks in cognitive science (Rowlands), philosophical panpsychism (Goff; Skrbina), new materialist (Bennett), and cognitive literary studies (Hayles) in the still palpable aftermath of social isolation and pandemic constraints can be quite comforting. All stress how, as human cognizers, we are not, and cannot be, alone. Rather we are entangled, coupled, enmeshed, tied, assembled—to use but a few of the new conceptualizations of the subjective mind—with the world, in a net of constitutive relations. When we are born as selves and organisms, as environmental philosopher Arne Johan Vetlesen puts it, "we come into this world expecting it—all of it—to be alive" and that "means to participate in this aliveness that is encountered everywhere and in

© KONINKLIJKE BRILL NV, LEIDEN, 2023 | DOI:10.1163/9789004681293_009

everything" (16). We join a world of relations as *joints*: intersubjective hubs of looping feedback, experiential mediators between inner and outer worlds. These connections between individual human minds and social or material actors are there, we are told, regardless of our awareness. This is why we need to be made aware of them, as ecological thinkers are urging, to be responsible agents in this dense network.

Connections, however, are there because we establish them, and keep renewing them, through our actions and perceptions (or perception as action; Noe). Our feeling of belonging to the world is enhanced by our worlding of outer elements, from human to non-human and inorganic or even imagined matter, into meaningful spheres for actions and interactions. Without the possibility of touching in depth on the ethical, ecological, or epistemic concerns of these recent frameworks, the present chapter wants to contribute to the debate by focusing on one specific worlding mechanism, *personification*, by providing an account of its dynamic interplay in the human "dance" of agency with the external world (Malafouris 208). It will reflect on the working of personification by advancing two proposals: first, that personification might be a cognitive process that uses individual agency as its fuel (what I will call *agency combustion*); second, that this combustion of agency unfolds in time, and that narrative might play a role in progressively layering mentality and intentionality into real or imaginary beings or objects. In addition, I will argue that, conceived this way, personification should be reconsidered (together with, but as I shall claim importantly distinguished from, anthropomorphism) as part of a broader process whereby humans spontaneously or intentionally structure phenomenological relations with their world (a process that I will call, after Bergson's concept of "élan vital," *élanification*). It will also suggest that the give and take between personification and combustion of individual agency occurs in a wide range of experiences, from literary writing or reading and child play to religious and hallucinatory phenomena.

2   Personification as Agency Combustion

The relationship between personification and agency is phenomenologically obscure, energetically dynamic, and conceptually still underinvestigated. This is partly due to the fact that there is a plurality of agencies that should be considered. A common factor across varieties of agencies, however, is that they can either operate undetected below phenomenological awareness or they can be consciously perceived: an optional awareness that makes of agency something that can be felt or sensed (and accordingly also misperceived). To place a selective list of the variety of agencies operating in human experience within

PERSONIFICATION AS ÉLANIFICATION   115

a spectrum, this would go from a maximum of (either perceived or factual) subjective internalism to a (either perceived or factual) worldly externalism:

1. *Individual agency*: (the feeling of) being the initiator, deviser, and master of an action (see, e.g., Davidson)
2. *Shared agency*: (the feeling that) agency is distributed between yourself and other individuals (see, e.g., Hutchins)
3. *Relational agency*: (the feeling of) someone or something having the capacity of acting for, against, upon you (see., e.g., Westlund)
4. *Material agency*: (the feeling that) when you interact with a variety of technologies, from pottery to writing to computers, these material elements have an agency of their own which contributes to the action (see Malafouris; Bernini, "Supersizing")
5. *Independent agency*: (the feeling that) imaginary beings like children's imagined companions or fictional characters have autonomous desires, intentions, and behaviors independent from your imaginative activity (see Taylor et al.; Fernyhough et al.)
6. External agency: (the feeling that) animate or inanimate elements of the real world, from people to objects, have an agency of their own (see, e.g., Gallagher, "Socially"; Krueger).

When phenomenological awareness is present, the first three kinds of agency seem to involve a consistent feeling of selfhood (as yourself, or yourself in a group, or yourself in relation to), whereas the second half of the list progressively gives rise to a harboring feeling of otherness (a cooperating technology, an imaginative being, or actual externalities). Within this spectrum, the more individual agency diminishes, the more traces of otherness appear. Here there seems to be already some potential ground for linking individual agency and personification in an inverse proportion.

Before making this move, though, it is important to consider the two notions (or phenomena or processes) as separated. Loosely speaking, agency is about doing, and personification is about being. However, the distinction is not symmetric, and as far as I can see there can be a recognition of agency without personification, but hardly personification without ascribed agency. I can feel or note that my way of walking is "affected by" these new shoes; that this weather "has a negative power" over me; that the oil and vinegar "do not mix"; that water "extinguishes" fire. Even if all these cases can be easily turned into personifying statements (e.g., these "vindictive" shoes are "killing" me), as they are, they point just at agency without personification.

On the other side, personified elements are, for what I can see, always bearers of agentive features (as beings capable of acting). For instance, I can say or note that a "shy" squirrel is "escaping" from my camera; or that those waves seem "happily playing" with each other. Here I am projecting mental states over, or based on, detectable behaviors: shortly, I am personifying elements to account for, or imaginatively expanding on, agents' features and actions.

Agency as a prerequisite for personification (and not vice versa), however, is quite a coarse conceptualization of their relationship. Can we account for the interplay between agency and personification in more dynamic and interacting terms? This is what my first proposal aims to do. To the best of my knowledge, individual agency and personification have never been put in what I would call a *resource* or *energetic coupling*. Individual agency has been treated as something present, diminished or lost, yet independently co-existing with processes of personification (see, e.g., Gallagher, "Multiple"). I would instead suggest to think of agency as a limited cognitive resource (on a par with attention or working memory; see Oberauer); and of personification as a process combusting internal agency as its fuel. Call it the *personification as agency combustion* (PAC) principle. Applying this principle to the spectrum of agencies that I had singled out, *the more individual agency decreases the more personifying dynamics are fueled.*

The PAC principle seems able to account for—and empirically validated by scientific research on—a variety of experiences across cultural, technological, psychological, and religious domains. Take the case, for instance, of the so-called "illusion of independent agency", whereby literary writers report that fictional characters in the writing process seem to be taking up an agency of their own in terms of volition, beliefs, emotions, and decision-making (Taylor et al.). Here the individual agency of the writer (her intentions, imaginative behavior, and creative control) diminishes in the unfolding of the creative process (see Bernini, "Supersizing"). As a result, characters emerge as autonomous, personified agents (see Foxwell et al.). PAC seems to hold true also for the reverse process of reading. The process of immersion in a fictional world entails the backgrounding and partial fading of the reader's self and agentive control over the unfolding events. This fading of agency is inversely proportional to the vividness and immersivity of readers' simulations, including the simulated relationship with personified fictional characters (Alderson-Day et al.). The emergent autonomy and personification of characters through narratively scaffolded PAC in writing and reading can acquire a quasi-hallucinatory feeling that can be traced back to children's relationship with imaginary companions (Taylor), and which can approximate the borders of proper hallucinatory experiences such as voice-hearing (Woods et al.) and felt presence (e.g., Nielsen). Voices people hear in their head are often accompanied by a feeling of loss of individual agency (it is not me initiating the speech) and by an inversely proportional (and temporally mounting) heightening of personification (the voices often become experienced as an external consciousness, relationally opposed to the voice-hearer; see Wilkinson and Bell).

In writing and reading, however, subjects do not loose entirely ontological weighting of the real world. They rather maintain a "split loyalty" (Ryan) and, I would add, a split agency between fictional and actual worlds. By contrast, in conjuring up imaginary companions and hallucinatory personified presences (on the relationship between the two see Fernyhough et al.), personification is magnified to the point of consuming, sometimes entirely, the phenomenological sense that subjects are agentively responsible for the perceived, personified agents. PAC therefore should be considered as a principle measurable in various degrees of agency combustion, thus able to account for all these variety of personification experiences.

Even some religious experiences, with personified relationship with gods, can be thought of following a similar PAC dynamic. Simone Weil, the French mystic and philosopher, was already reflecting on the inversed proportion between agency and personification, when she wrote that "the soul, like a gas, tends to occupy the whole of the space left open to it." In order to let God's grace enter our life, we need, Weil says, to "create a void" (198). If we substitute here "soul" with a sense of self and individual agency, we can similarly think of a feeling of God (as a personified relation) entering our everyday perception if and only if the level of selfhood and agency within us is diminished (either actively or, as Weil notes, as a passive consequence for instance of traumatic events), letting evaporate an amount of agency that can create an energetic void fueling personified presences such as God's (see also Luhrmann).

We will come back soon more in detail to the scaffolding role of narrative in PAC dynamics. It is worth noting now, however, how all the experiences mentioned have narrative as a possible *catalytic force* in PAC. Writing or reading literary storyworlds, exploring narrative scripts while playing with imaginary companions, relating to intrusive hallucinatory agents or comforting gods that are often shaped by cultural and stereotypical storyworlds and typified characterization (Woods et al.): all these are experiences textured by narrative patterns, plot expectations and story-guided predictions (on the latter see Kukkonen). Somehow countering the idea that narrative is a force that keeps together, albeit illusorily, our self as the agentive center of a story (Dennett), here narrative becomes a (intentional or spontaneous) scaffolding process for lessening agentive control towards the emergence of personified relations. Narrative, due to its well-studied immersive potential (Ryan), lowers our subjective sense of agency, thus liberating an ontological feeling of autonomous worlds and personified presences. We can say that narrative becomes a polyphonic catalyst, whereby, as Mikhail Bakhtin suggested for polyphonic authors such as Dostoevsky, we move from the hierarchically isolated pedestal of the authoring level down to the level of characters in a storyworld, of which we become but one of the perceived, living inhabitants.

I will come back to this hypothesis in the conclusion. For now, it is enough to say that thinking of agency as a limited resource that, once combusted by personifying processes that can be narratively scaffolded, becomes less available to sustain a sense of self, can create a more complex, energetic understanding of personification too. Before going any further, however, I should provide a working definition of what I mean by personification, and this will lead me to place it within a broader human capacity for worlding perceived relations.

3   Élanification and the Worlding of Semiospheres: Biomorphism, Zoomorphism, Anthropomorphism, and Personification

In its widespread usage, the term personification is commonly treated as a synonym of anthropomorphism. Anthropomorphism, as Waytz and colleagues sum up, "goes beyond providing purely behavioral or dispositional descriptions of observable actions (such as noting that a coyote is fast or aggressive); it involves attributing characteristics that people intuitively perceive to be uniquely human to nonhuman agents or events." They also explain how it "includes both *physical features*, such as perceiving a religious agent in a humanlike form, and *mental capacities* that people believe are uniquely human, such as the capacity to have conscious awareness, possess explicit intentions, or experience secondary emotions (e.g., joy, pride, shame, guilt)" (58; emphasis added).

This is a quite generous definition, encompassing each case in which we are to a certain degree imbuing non-human objects and beings with human-like mental states or forms. However, I think personification should be profitably considered as a distinct process that can be *activated* by anthropomorphic projections or pattern recognitions, yet that is not exhausted by, or limited to them. With the term personification I aim at describing the temporal process whereby we *progressively* ascribe specific psychological traits and phenomenological life to an individual being—either real, imaginative, or fictional. In this respect, the target of personification can either be anthropomorphized objects or beings (either real or fictional), as well as real people and fictional human characters (who don't need anthropomorphizing activation).

When we read a novel, in fact, we are not presented with all the characteristics, both physical and mental, of a character. We only slowly gain knowledge, make inferences, and gather information from a variety of sources in order to shape what Alan Palmer has called a "continuing-consciousness frame" (175–82) for a character. This constructive (and constructivist) process occurs in social cognition too, and it is *recursive*: the personified frame we construct for a person, imaginary friend, or fictional being is constantly under expansion and revision, and we can have numerous epistemic fallbacks in our personifying process due to new inconsistencies emerging. Both for fictional and human beings, we (consciously or not) build on our past experiences of human encounters (a repertoire of "models of person," according to Herman, *Storytelling* 193–215) in order to keep layering and constantly adjusting personified traits, which keep modulating worlded relations with the perceiver.

In short, I would suggest that anthropomorphism is a temporally shorter process having as target non-human agents, whereas personification is a longer process having as a target both anthropomorphized non-human agents as well as human beings. Anthropomorphism serves as a shorter process and threshold of activation, projection, or recognition of personhood in non-human entities. Once this process is complete, what were originally non-human entities can *then* become personified through the longer, ongoing, potentially endless process of personification. In human agents (both real and fictional), anthropomorphic activations are not needed, yet richer layers, drafts, and revisions of personifying ascriptions are what keep them relationally lively in diachronic open, intersubjective, and enactive interactions. More importantly, though, my proposal would be to consider both anthropomorphism and personification as dynamics belonging to a broader gamut of processes sharing a common feature: the contingent or diachronic imbuing, perceiving, and worlding of a richer life energy into the world.

Adapting the concept of "élan vital" from Henri Bergson (the "vital force," or "life force," or "vital impulse" which, for him, was the substance of consciousness and nature), I would call this wider umbrella of processes *élanification*. By this term, I want to refer to the capacity and drive of human beings to attribute to inorganic matters, non-human animals, and human beings richer layers of cognition and vitality. Bergson's concept of *élan vital* has already been used by new materialist thinkers like Jane Bennett in her influential book *Vibrant Matter*. My use of the term, however, is partly antithetical, partly complementary to Bennett's agenda. To necessarily oversimplify Bennett's argument, her use of the concept intends to point at a vitality beyond the human (to make humans aware of how everything in the world actually *is* entangled and vibrant). Its application here instead wants to conceptualize élanification as an eminently human faculty, whereby humans *make* the world vibrate (or world vibrations into the world). In other words, my use is noncommittal to how the world really is in terms of a polyphony of agents (an ontological thesis); I only theorize how our interaction with outer elements can be worlded as a polyphony of agencies and perceived relations (a phenomenological and operational framework). Whether élanification as a human process can reveal, detect, or recognize something of the real ontology of our world is beyond the scope of this chapter. I can just briefly signal my sympathy for such view, with some provisos I will flesh out in the conclusion.

As for the complementary component of my proposed view, within my framework new materialist accounts can be considered not as theory of élanification, but as elanifying theories: theoretical and conceptual views that can both promote élanification as well as guide human beings to a better practice of it. If critics of Bennett's work such as Katherine Hayles have rightly focused on the paradox that new materialist theories, while fighting anthropocentric views, are still made by and for human beings (Hayles 66), I see them as implicitly recognizing the potentially revolutionary role of some practice of élanification; a process that, while being eminently human, can world beings and relations towards a richer universe of actions and perceptions.

Now that the scope of my borrowing from Bergson is specified, let's review élanifying possibilities, visualized here in a range that goes from minimal to more substantial forms of biological and cognitive endowments whereby human beings world agents and perceived relations (Figure 7.1).

At its most basic form, elanification starts with *biomorphism*, which consists in the perception, creation, or recognition of forms or images that, while abstract, nevertheless refer to, or evoke, living forms such as plants and the human body. Biomorphic forms have been widely explored by early 20th century artists such as Kandinsky, Miro, Henry Moore, and Barbara Hepworth. The second process in the elanification trajectory is *zoomorphism*, which is the perception, creation, or recognition of animal traits in non-animal objects or beings. And then we have *anthropomorphism* and *personification*. By linking these four processes under the same dynamic, I think we can achieve a better account of the continuity and fluidity between them; as well as a better understanding of their common features.

Describes the perception, creation or recognition of forms or images that while abstract nevertheless refer to, or evoke, living forms such as plants and the human body.	It is the perception, creation or recognition of animal traits in non-animal objects or beings.	It involves attributing characteristics that people intuitively perceive to be uniquely human to nonhuman agents or events	The target of personification can either be anthropomorphized objects or beings, as well as people and fictional human characters.
BIOMORPHISM	**ZOOMORPHISM**	**ANTHROPOMORPHISM**	**PERSONIFICATION**

ÉLANIFICATION

FIGURE 7.1   Diagram of Élanification processes (Marco Bernini)

For instance, all these elanifying processes can be either passive or active. When passive, elanification is largely a matter of *perception*: we spontaneously perceive or recognize a richer degree of vitality, agency or cognition in some external entity. When actively performed, elanification can be a matter of *design, conception, imagination* or *simulation*, whereby we devise or project richer layers of vitality into objects or beings. Activity and passivity can take turns, and an intentionally anthropomorphized object can then become passively perceived as autonomously disclosing new anthropomorphic traits. In other words, once activated by élanification, a target can both move and be moved further in the trajectory (e.g., a biomorphized stone worlded[1] as a vital agent can then start behaving in our imagination as an animal or a human being, which can be then personified with complex psychological traits).

In addition, thinking of élanification as a spectrum can show how many examples can be classed as boundary cases, at the edge between one modality and another. For instance, the Sage auditorium in Newcastle-Upon-Tyne, designed by Norman Foster, lies in-between a biomorphic and zoomorphic architecture (and, according to the latter, was spontaneously renamed by people "the caterpillar"). Novels such as *Animal Farm* by George Orwell (1945) also exploit both zoomorphic and anthropomorphic dynamics.

Regardless of its stage in the élanification trajectory, however, once vitality is activated possible relations between the outer agent and the human perceiver are worlded. This relational field can be characterized as a semiotic field of possible signals and communicative interactions, close to an intersubjective version of what Russian semiologist Juri Lotman called a "semiosphere": or "the semiotic space necessary for the existence of languages [...]. Outside the semiosphere there can be neither communication, nor language. Of course, the single-channel structure is reality" (123–24). If we extend, as semioticians would do, the concept of language beyond its verbal or linguistic component to include any kind of relational signals (e.g., behavioral, intentional, emotional, and so on), the concept of a semiosphere is quite fit to express the explosion of possible communicative relations that élanification can generate in the perceived reality.

---

1 In using "world" as a transitive verb throughout the essay I am endorsing, on the one hand, Heidegger's idea that humans are makers of worlds (in a worlding process defined with the verb "welten" in Heidegger; for reference and application of this usage to literary minds see Bernini, *Beckett*, 122–65); on the other hand, in linking worlding dynamics with human narrative scaffolding I am expanding on Herman's idea (2015) that, both in everyday and textual cognition, we "world stories" by adding ontological weight to narrative universes.

As Lotman phrases it, the internal space of the semiosphere is always a meeting of "boundaries" between the perceiving subject agent and the other communicative agents, thus creating a space that is "unequal yet unified, asymmetrical yet uniform" (131). According to the PAC principle, however, we have seen how in personification in particular (and élanification in general) the balance of symmetries can shift, when the perceiving subject is stripped away of her agency, thus becoming unaware to be the source of personified relations within her semiosphere. We noted how narrative can become a key catalyst for the levelling and bridging of boundaries between a human perceiver and perceived agents in the élanified, worlded semiosphere. It is now time to look briefly more into detail at how narrative élanification works.

4 Prompters and Narrative Percolation in Worlding Perceived Relations

Narrative indeed seems to play a role in élanifying processes, either by prompting, paralleling, or following active or passive élanification. Narrative élanification can be prompted by different triggers, from behavioral to morphological features, and lead to a different granularity in terms of personified psychological traits. For instance, in the landmark experimental study on anthropomorphism and "apparent behavior" conducted by Fritz Heider and Marianne Simmel in 1944, the two scientists showed to the participants a short video with moving geometrical figures (one big triangle, one small triangle, and a circle). In this video, the small triangle and the circle are approaching the rectangle, which has an open door, but they are stopped and obstructed repeatedly by the larger triangle. There is more, but even this brief description, already showing signs of *storied* anthropomorphic ascriptions, is enough to understand how most of the participants reported what happened in a narrative form, resorting to anthropomorphized characters as intentional agents. They interpreted the scene by layering a quite conventional narrative script of a fight between two lovers on one side (the small triangle and the circle) and a strong and violent third man on the other (big triangle). Here the direction of élanification has gone from *behavior recognition* (these forms are intentional moving agents) to a *morphological mapping* (e.g., the big triangle is stronger because bigger; the two triangles are men) to a proper *mentalization* leading to personification of their traits (the bigger triangle is a jealous partner).

This is not the only possible dynamic in élanification. Another possibility is to find morphological prompters. For instance, below is a picture I have taken in the woods behind my house in Durham in the United Kingdom (Figure 7.2).

PERSONIFICATION AS ÉLANIFICATION 123

FIGURE 7.2   Woods in Durham, UK
              PHOTOGRAPH BY MARCO BERNINI

Can you see something more than a tree in it? The morphology of the tree prompted almost instantaneously in me the image of an elephant (from morphology to zoomorphic projections). This morphological recognition then activated in me a wealth of *possible behaviors* in my mind (Can he move? Can he talk? Can he feel or judge or hide? Can he see me?). This array of intentional possible behaviors and relational actions (or what Gallagher calls "operational intentionality," *Enactivist* 80) disclosed by my worlded semiosphere has spontaneously scaffolded richer narrative ascriptions of a mentality with personality traits (he seems calm and wise; rather at home than lost; I wonder where his parents are?). Here my élanifying direction followed from morphology to behavior to mentalization.

Sometimes, pure mentalization seems to occur, with no particular links to morphology or behavior. For example, when the protagonist in Proust's *Recherche* is struggling to fall asleep in an unfamiliar room, he suddenly perceives the "*hostility* of the violet curtains and of the *insolent indifference* of a clock" (12; emphasis added). Here Marcel, due to his fragile mood, is anthropomorphizing and then personifying elements of his room with no particular relation to their forms or behavior.

Finally, other times élanification can also have what I would call, building on Charles Sanders Peirce's theory of sign (1932–37), an *indexical prompter*. In his sign theory (*Writings*, vol. 2), Pierce distinguishes between an icon and an index: if an icon is a sign which has a formal relation to its object (such as a painting to the house it represents), an index bears a physical and causal relation to its object (for example, smoke is an index of fire). I would suggest that in voice-hearing, for instance, we can see an *anthropomorhization by indexicality*. Voice-hearers perceive some, often confused, quasi-auditory stimulus. They then tend to interpret this as an index of a voice, which in turn prompts further ascriptions and personification of this sign (i.e., if there is a voice, there must be a mentality, with some kind of intentions—usually negative and tormenting ones).

This brief and condensed survey of possible prompters for élanification should be sufficient for you to grasp to what extent narrative can be involved in the process. In all these different élanifying experiences, with different perceptual prompters, subjects are scaffolding personifying processes with narrative possibilities. To apply David Herman's cognitive account of the work of narrative to élanification, different prompters are leading subjects at the same time to "story the world" (i.e., narrativizing behavioral patterns, morphology, inorganic hostility, or auditory indexical signals), and "worlding a story" (towards emerging universes filled with relational jealousy, magic, indifference, or persecution). Narrative seems therefore to be one of the main vehicles for ascribing further levels of vitality and mentality or, in Herman's terms, a "heterophenomenological density" (*Narratology* 226–230) to the target objects or beings. Through narrative, we can either actively create or passively perceive denser levels of cognition and vitality in the object or being we relate to. The link between narrative and élanification is possibly even tighter, since they seem to work in very similar ways.

If we turn to Kendall Walton's seminal "pretense theory" of narrative and fictionality (1990), in fact, we seem to find a good candidate to explain processes of élanification as well. For Walton, fictional narratives are props in games of make-believe. Suppose that some children play a game in the woods in which they imagine tree stumps to be bears. In Walton's terminology, in this game the tree stumps are "props" and the convention that the children establish by their agreement that stumps 'count as' bear is a "principle of generation"(38; see also Toon). If we apply this to the experience of the elephant in the wood, the tree functioned spontaneously as a perceptual prop, then becoming a principle of generation of what we can call a wider *narrative percolation* (this elephant can think and talk, this wood might be magic, therefore a lot of other magic beings are probably around and anything can happen). Importantly, and thanks also to the PAC principle lessening subjective agency, once a prop has fired and a principle is established it might be difficult to go back to the previous perception of the world. *Elanification, thanks also to the role of narrative in the PAC*

PERSONIFICATION AS ÉLANIFICATION   125

principle, might be difficult to reverse. Once a richer perception of the world
is unleashed, the Pandora vase might be hard to reseal. In psychotic experiences, this can be a very distressing constraint, leading to a further loss of
agency in their everyday experience. I want therefore to conclude by contrasting the widespread view that sees anthropomorphism only as a biased process empowering human control. Worlding semiospheres of relations rather
unleashes a vitality that lessens human individual agency towards what can
become exposed, frightful interactions with emerging otherness.

5   Between Aliveness and Indifference: towards a Theory of
       Élanification

The two epigraphs to this chapter well summarize the fragile area occupied
by human beings as joints, bridges, hubs for the élanifying and worlding of
perceived relations. On the one hand, we have Baudelaire's poem, which epit-
omizes the fascination for blossoming correspondences in élanified, worlded
semiospheres between man and nature. On the other we have the 18th-century
poet Giacomo Leopardi, who has written extensively on the suffering resulting
from the indifference of nature for human concerns (albeit he does person-
ify and narrativize Nature as an agentive, relational interlocutor in the cited
story). A theory of élanification might help exploring how humans cannot
rest in either options, destined as they are to keep navigating between signals
and silence, aliveness and indifference: if the former takes away agency and
rewards with a (sometimes intruding or terrifying) vitality, the latter leave us
in charge, but of a disenchanted world. Regardless of the ontological truth
captured by new materialist or panpsychist views, the proposed theory can be
seen as aligned with panpsychist calls for "re-enchanting' the universe" (Goff
217). It also aimed at showing, however, how the PAC principle in élanification
in general, and personification in particular, can have distressing outcomes (as
in hallucinatory experiences), with percolating, narrativized presences men-
acing the ontological stability of our individual world. If a theory of élanification is not committal to what world lies beyond the human, it can foster the
understanding of the shared relational drive, exposed fragility, and narrative
inventiveness behind human worlding.
   A theory of élanification can thus provide a common framework for interdisciplinary research on individual ways of worlding relations across the
everyday, creative, literary and clinical domains. The intuition that élanification can be informative of the human mind was already at the core of Hermann Rorschach's test, whereby patients worlded inkblot cards into élanified

presences (notably animals or human-like presences) and narrativized relations (see Searls). This chapter wanted to account not only for the reception of outer inkblot signs, but for the very process whereby humans cannot restrain from worlding semiospheres by spreading (actively or spontaneously) layers of agentive and narrative ink from their individual tanks out on the book of the universe.

References

Alderson-Day, Ben, et al. "Uncharted Features and Dynamics of Reading: Voices, Characters, and Crossing of Experiences." *Consciousness and Cognition*, vol. 49, 2017, pp. 98–109.

Bakhtin, Mikhail. *Problems of Dostoevsky's Poetics*. Translated by Caryl Emerson, U of Minnesota P, 1984.

Bennett, Jane. *Vibrant Matter: A Political Ecology of Things*. Duke UP, 2010.

Bergson, Henri. *Creative Evolution*. 1907. Translated by Pete A. Gunter, UP of America, 1984.

Bernini, Marco. "Supersizing Narrative Theory: On Intention, Material Agency, and Extended Mind-Workers." *Style*, vol. 48, no. 3, 2014, pp. 349–66.

Bernini, Marco. *Beckett and the Cognitive Method: Mind, Models, and Exploratory Narratives*. Oxford UP, 2021.

Davidson, Donald. "Actions, Reasons, and Causes." *The Journal of Philosophy*, vol. 60, no. 2, 1963, pp. 685–700.

Dennett, Daniel C. *Consciousness Explained*. Penguin, 1993.

Fernyhough, Charles, et al. "Imaginary Companions, Inner Speech, and Auditory Verbal Hallucinations: What are the Relations?" *Frontiers in Psychology*, vol. 10, art. 1665, 2019.

Foxwell, John, et al. "'I've Learned I Need to Treat my Characters like People': Varieties of Agency and Interaction in Writers' Experiences of their Characters' Voices." *Consciousness and Cognition*, vol. 79, art. 102901, 2020.

Gallagher, Shaun. "Multiple Aspects in the Sense of Agency." *New Ideas in Psychology*, vol. 30, no. 1, 2012, pp. 15–31.

Gallagher, Shaun. "The Socially Extended Mind." *Cognitive Systems Research*, vol. 25, 2013, pp. 4–12.

Gallagher, Shaun. *Enactivist Interventions: Rethinking the Mind*. Oxford UP, 2017.

Goff, Philip. *Galileo's Error: Foundations for a New Science of Consciousness*. Rider, 2019.

Hayles, N. Katherine. *Unthought: The Power of the Cognitive Unconscious*. Chicago UP, 2017.

Heider, Fritz, and Marianne Simmel. "An Experimental Study of Apparent Behavior." *The American Journal of Psychology*, vol., 57, no. 2, 1944, pp. 243–59.

Herman, David. *Storytelling and the Sciences of Mind*. MIT Press, 2017.

Herman, David. *Narratology Beyond the Human: Storytelling and Animal Life*. Oxford UP, 2018.

Hutchins, Edwin. *Cognition in the Wild*. MIT Press, 1995.

Krueger, Joel. "Schizophrenia and the Scaffolded Self." *Topoi*, vol. 39, no. 3, 2020, pp. 597–609.

Kukkonen, Karin. *Probability Designs: Literature and Predictive Processing*. Oxford UP, 2020.

Lotman, Yuri M. *Universe of the Mind: A Semiotic Theory of Culture*. Translated by Ann Shukman, Indiana UP, 1990.

Luhrmann, Tanya M. *When God Talks Back: Understanding the American Evangelical Relationship with God*. Knopf, 2012.

Malafouris, Lambros. *How Things Shape the Mind: A Theory of Material Engagement*, MIT Press, 2013.

Nielsen, Tore. "Felt Presence: Paranoid Delusion or Hallucinatory Social Imagery?" *Consciousness and Cognition*, vol. 16, no. 4, 2007, pp. 975–83.

Noë, Alva. *Action in Perception*. MIT Press, 2004.

Oberauer, Klaus. "Working Memory and Attention – A Conceptual Analysis and Review." *Journal of Cognition*, vol. 2, no. 1, 2019, pp. 1–23.

Palmer, Alan. *Fictional Minds*. U of Nebraska P, 2004.

Peirce, Charles S. *The Writings of Charles S. Peirce: A Chronological Edition. Volumes 1–6*, edited by Peirce Edition Project, Indiana UP, 1982.

Proust, M. *Swann's Way*. 1913. Translated by C.K. Scott Moncrieff and Terence Kilmartin, Vintage, 2005.

Rowlands, Mark J. *The New Science of the Mind: From Extended Mind to Embodied Phenomenology*. MIT Press, 2010.

Ryan, Marie-Laure. *Narrative as Virtual Reality 2: Revisiting Immersion and Interactivity in Literature and Electronic Media*. Johns Hopkins UP, 2015.

Skrbina, David. *Panspychism in the West*. MIT Press, 2007.

Searls, Damion. *The Inkblots: Hermann Rorschach, his Iconic Test, and the Power of Seeing*.

Taylor, Marjorie. *Imaginary Companions and the Children Who Create Them*. Oxford UP, 1999.

Taylor, Marjorie, et al. "The Illusion of Independent Agency: Do Adult Fiction Writers Experience their Characters as Having Minds of Their Own?" *Imagination, Cognition and Personality*, vol. 22, no. 4, 2003, pp. 361–80.

Toon, Adam. "The Ontology of Theoretical Modelling: Models as Make-Believe." *Synthese* vol. 172, no. 2, 2010, pp. 301–15.

Vetlesen, Arne Johan. *Cosmologies of the Anthropocene: Panpsychism, Animism, and the Limits of Posthumanism*. Routledge, 2019.

Walton, Kendall L. *Mimesis as Make-Believe: On the Foundations of the Representational Arts*. Harvard UP, 1990.

Waytz, Adam, et al. "Social Cognition Unbound: Insights into Anthropomorphism and Dehumanization." *Current Directions in Psychological Science*, vol. 19, no. 1, 2010, pp. 58–62.

Weil, Simone. *The Notebooks of Simone Weil*. 1956. Vol. 1, translated by Arthur Wills, Routledge, 2004.

Westlund, Andrea C. "Rethinking Relational Autonomy." *Hypatia* vol. 24, no. 4, 2009, pp. 26–49.

Wilkinson, Sam, and Vaughan Bell. "The Representation of Agents in Auditory Verbal Hallucinations." *Mind & Language*, vol. 31, no. 1, 2016, pp. 104–26.

Woods, Angela, et al. "Experiences of Hearing Voices: Analysis of a Novel Phenomenological Survey." *The Lancet Psychiatry*, vol. 2, no. 4, 2015, pp. 323–31.

CHAPTER 8

Cognitive Formalism

Or, How Presence Machines are Built

Karin Kukkonen

1 Introduction

The notion of the text as a "presence machine," which I take from the title of a novel by the Norwegian author Gunnhild Øyehaug, might come as a surprise in a volume devoted to "worlding the brain." Doesn't the metaphor of machines and devices belong to a different critical tradition, namely that of formalism? This article argues for the possibility of a cognitive formalism, a dialogue between 4E approaches to cognition and early 20th century Russian formalism about the relationship between literature, language, and world. Literary novels are machines to think with, I am going to argue, because they lead to misreadings, break down expectations, and provoke us to change points of view. Literary language and narrative draw on our most basic embodied and embedded cognitive capacities, while the literary form (which I am going to conceptualize as a "probability design") extends the mind further. The "presence machine" of the literary text achieves its effects through artificial ways for making everyday cognition break down productively.

2 Misreadings

Mistaking one word for another is a familiar glitch in all our reading processes. If we notice, it is easily fixed, as we read the sentence anew. We are fluent readers, for example, when we have learnt not to analyze the combinations of letters that we see now, but when we are able to predict, within a certain margin of error, what the next couple of letters are likely going to be because we know the regularities of written English (Norris). Typos are often overlooked, because our predictions repair them in advance, so to speak. When we misread, we usually go back to double-check and correct. The prediction error leads to a small-scale revision of expectations. In most cases such misreadings are hardly noted, because these processes are highly automated (Snell and Grainger).

© KONINKLIJKE BRILL NV, LEIDEN, 2023 | DOI:10.1163/9789004681293_010

In Gunnhild Øyehaug's novel *Presence Machine* (original title: *Presens Maskin*), however, reading something wrong has enormous consequences; indeed, an unacknowledged misreading becomes the main drive of the narrative. As the protagonist Anna sits in her garden and reads a poem by Tua Forsström in the original Swedish, she mistakes the word "trädgård" (tree garden) for "tärdgård" (38-39). The word "tärdgård" does not exist in Swedish or Nynorsk (the language in which Øyehaug writes her novel); it comes into being only because Anna "reads" it. As the word emerges in Anna's mind, Øyehaug also makes it emerge in the novel's world, because that world is built from words. She splits her narrative into two different strands. "When Anna read the word 'tärdgård' and looked down on the paper and hesitated for a few seconds, there opened that what *might have been found* literally as a new world, a parallel universe, and her daughter, Laura, at two and a half years on her tricycle cycled now in a 'tärdgård' in another world, in the same garden" (39–40).[1] In one world, the word "tärdgård" exists; in the other world, it does not. Anna and Laura's paths are separated in this moment in the novel, and two narratives develop in parallel for the remainder of *Presence Machine*.

The misreading is the first major plot event in Øyehaug's novel. Among theories of cognition, in particular the approach of predictive processing underlines the value of such "prediction errors." We thereby learn about mistakes in the probability projections that we make about the regularities of the world and can eventually amend false expectations. On sentence level, readers might have first passed over "tärdgård," but they can reread the passage when the narrator points it out. On the level of the entire novel, readers will also realize that their expectations about the narrative of the novel as a mostly realist prose story were mistaken, and it shapes their further expectations about what is likely to happen and how important metafictional reflections are going to be as *Presence Machine* develops. Anna, the character, however, is not made aware of her mistake, her "prediction error." As she continues to perceive her world in these mistaken terms, also Øyehaug continues to generate narrative situations and events that follow from it. *Presence Machine* establishes its probability design, that is, the artificial structure through which readers' predictions and prediction errors are guided by the text (see Kukkonen, *Probability Designs*), on the tension between mended and un-mended misreading.

In her depiction of Anna's misreading, which extends over three pages in the printed version of the novel, Øyehaug artificially slows down an instantaneous process. The narrator details how a misreading leads to a new word and, from

---

1   All translations from the Nynorsk are my own. KK

COGNITIVE FORMALISM 131

the new word, to a new fictional reality to which it refers. In a way, all our reading works on this principle. Øyehaug gives readers awareness of this process, when she makes the misreading "literal" ("bokstavelig" in Nynorsk, foregrounding the letters, "bokstaver," on the page), as she puts it herself in the passage quoted above. The prediction error is not silently repaired but spun further and turned into the principle underlying the entire novel. The word "tärdgård" will reappear throughout the novel and signal this principle of the tension between the two worlds to readers. For the rest of *Presence Machine*, Anna will think that she might have had a daughter, and her daughter Laura will feel the lack of her mother who disappeared out of her life's story. Hence, deep and phenomenologically rich engagements emerge from a rather abstract metafictional twist. At the end of the novel, Anna turns back to Forsström's poem. Øyehaug now presents another prediction error that replaces the abstractness of Anna's first prediction error with phenomenological presence. While reading Forsström's *Efter att ha tillbringat en natt bland häster* (*After Having Spent a Night Among Horses*), Anna smells the ammonia mentioned in the poem and starts looking for it in the country house where she is staying. In the process, Anna comes to realize anew the power of words to create worlds. At the end of the chapter, she sees a young woman in the city of Bergen (whom readers know to be Laura). She senses that young woman to be familiar but does not recognize her as her daughter.

It appears that "presence machines" run on misreadings that create both abstract and experiential effects. These misreadings can be explicitly represented in the actions and experiences of characters or they can be inscribed in the form of text as it gives shape to readers' inferences in the probability design. Indeed, the designed prediction errors of plot events, focalization shifts, unusual semantic and stylistic formations, etc. reconfigure the probabilistic predictions through which readers approach the text, even when it is less metafictional than Øyehaug's novel. These misreadings are not random (as prediction errors in an everyday context would be). Rather, they emerge from a sensory stream of words where prediction errors are in-built at multiple levels to scaffold readers' meaning-making processes.

In the case of *Presence Machine*, Øyehaug closes the probability design by taking up the original prediction error and revising it. The presence machine of the novel creates, on the one hand, linguistic structures that can be referred back to, analyzed, and manipulated through striking metafictional inventions, and on the other hand, the book also demonstrates how language provides a strong sense of presence for readers. The sensory stream that enters into a feedback loop with our predictive thought structures is reproduced in literary language and creates a counterfactually rich, embodied environment (Seth;

Kuzmičová). At the same time, however, the sensory stream that readers get from literary narrative is also clearly different from the sensory stream that we get from the world around. Its letter-based, low-bandwidth nature in literary narrative can be designed to reflect back onto itself through the ways in which it names, conceptualizes, and directs attention with language (Lupyan and Clark). Literary language can create both counterfactually rich, bodily engaging worlds *and* draw attention to its own abstractions—within the probability design of the literary text.

3   Algorithmic Narratives

Poetry is a main aesthetic reference point for Øyehaug's prose writing. We have already seen how Forsström's poetry has a profound effect in *Presence Machine*, but poetry provides not only a reference point for phenomenological richness. For conceptual structuring, the Danish poet Inger Christensen becomes relevant and is frequently mentioned by Øyehaug.[2] Christensen's collection *alfabet* (*alphabet*) is built on the principle of the Fibonacci numbers: each poem has a number of lines increasing along the logic of the algorithm. Related to the golden mean, Fibonacci numbers are a way to describe (aesthetic) regularity in nature. Christensen's collection, one might argue, reverse-engineers nature's Fibonacci numbers in the artificial probability design of her poems. Each poem is devoted to a letter of the alphabet, and the number of lines of the poems increases (more or less) on the principle of Fibonacci numbers. As the structures of meaning multiply, connections get more and more complex, but they can always be traced back as emerging from the shorter, simpler poems at the beginning of the collection. The algorithm of the Fibonacci sequence ($Fn = Fn\text{-}1 + Fn\text{-}2$) becomes the building principle of Christensen's collection, executed in the alphabet and in the world-creating power of literary language (see also Christensen). Christensen ends her collection with an outlook of nuclear annihilation in the middle of the poem for the letter N. The formal principle of the connected progressions of the alphabet and the Fibonacci numbers feeds into a profound statement on the relationship between humankind, world, and language, as at the letter "N" (which can of course stand for "nuclear") the stream of meaning comes to a halt.

---

2   As far as I can see, there is no direct reference to Christensen in *Presence Machine*. However, the prominent sentence "Maybe the word already exists" (Kanskje ordet allereie finst, 60) in the reflections on language seems to echo the first sentence of Christensen's *Alphabet*: "Apricot trees exist, apricot trees exist" (11).

COGNITIVE FORMALISM 133

It might appear that prose narratives are not as easily used to deploy algorithms, because they are not as precise in their lines, feet, and syllables as poetry is. Christensen's novel *Evighedsmaskinen (Eternity Machine)*, might serve as an illustration as to how this might be achieved. Christensen retells the story of the Evangelium in the present day through chapters that are numbered exponentially. Chapter 1 is followed by chapter 1 to the power of 1, by chapter 1 to the power of 2, and so on. The chapters expand their thematic reach, and the number of characters involved, as the size of the exponent increases, but the focus on the One (a god-like, messianic figure here called "Ulrik") who keeps returning is maintained.

Øyehaug chooses a different but related device in *Presence Machine*, entangling form and meaning. As the two strands of the narrative develop in parallel, readers learn that both Anna and Laura are preparing to participate in a performance of Erik Satie's *Vexations* (1893–1894). *Vexations* is a very short, complex piano piece, which is performed by repeating the piece 840 times in sequence, often by a series of pianists taking over from one another. On May 30, 2020, a performance by a single pianist, Igor Levit, took twenty hours (and was presented as a response to the experience of the Covid-19 pandemic). In Øyehaug novel, *Vexations* is an event in the Norwegian town Volda, where amateur pianists are invited to play one iteration of the piece each. Anna and Laura, in their different worlds, take part.

Vexations has a double function in *Presence Machine*. On the one hand, it develops the narratives of Anna and Laura in parallel across the two different worlds. They are both preparing to play the same piece and go through the same (or highly similar) actions in preparing. Repetitions of the same phrases in the description of Anna's and Laura's actions give the narrative a kind of rhythm that runs across the novel whenever Satie is mentioned. Moreover, the piano piece also depends on the notion of sequence that cuts across the parallel nature of their worlds. The chapter in which Satie's piece is introduced is called "The Relay Race" (Stafetten). In the closing chapter, Øyehaug presents first Anna and then Laura, in the following paragraph, as preparing for the performance. They both sit "in the same room, at the same moment, in a parallel universe" (152), and take the same turn in the sequence of the performance, carefully coordinated both by organizers of the event and by Øyehaug's probability design, as they take the same piano seat at the same time.

Satie's *Vexations* give rhythm and structure to *Presence Machine*. It is not a regular rhythmic piece that is easy to tap along to, but rather moves against our expectations and literally "vexes" them. Rhythm in music is closely tied to the listener's emotional experience and has been approached through predictive processing (see Huron). The rhythm of Øyehaug's presence machine is established, among other things, through the mentioning of Satie's *Vexations* and through the role the piece and its performance play in the narrative itself. "This little piano piece, which once she thought was the essence of all time, because it is repetitive and immediately transient (because one does not manage to remember it), now sits in her fingers," Anna reflects at the end of the novel (152). At the beginning, Anna, herself an author, had noted the same observation in writing while listening to a recording of *Vexations* (25). Now she is performing the piece herself. The piano piece comes to stand for the multiple dimensions of time in the novel, running in parallel and in sequence, exactly because it is embodied in the fingers and the bodies of the two characters, as they play the piece. This rhythm is not just an abstract principle but embodied in character's actions and, arguably, in the embodied experience of readers' in the reading process. It literally sits in their "fingers."

The underlying structure of Øyehaug's and Christensen's texts is an algorithm. The term algorithm refers to "any set of mathematical instructions for manipulating data or reasoning through a problem" (Finn 17). The Fibonacci principles structure the configuration of Christensen's poem, while the principle of Satie's *Vexations*, a number of chords to be executed in sequence, structures the configuration of Øyehaug's novel. While algorithms tend to depend on numerical data (and tend to be executed by computers), they also come to be mapped onto the natural world, for example in the famous image of the curve of the snail's house that cuts through squares increasing in size according to the logic of the Fibonacci sequence (see Figure 8.1).

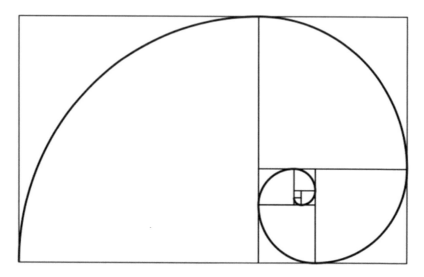

FIGURE 8.1   Curve of a snail's house according to the logic of the Fibonacci sequence

COGNITIVE FORMALISM 135

In their probability designs, literary narratives deploy similar algorithms as the underlying principles of giving structure to prediction errors in the sensory stream of the narrative. The points where predictions change can be identified, as can the principles according to which they change, and these principles can give the probability design an algorithmic structure. Just as prediction errors can unfold on every level of the narrative, as we have seen for the "tärdgård"-misreading in *Presence Machine*, so can these algorithms lead to a configuration across multiple different levels of structuring the temporal sequence of narratives. The length of chapters, the rhythm of plot events, changing focalizations, and the logic according to which characters relate to each other: all these narrative elements can be arranged according to an algorithmic principle that shapes readers' predictions for the coming sentence, pages, and chapters and that lets readers to recognize an entire "probability design" throughout the reading process.

Even though the matter of a literary text is not reducible to numerical values, understanding a narrative can be seen as the act of grasping its generating principle. Ed Finn's *What Algorithms Want* discusses algorithms as part of a "culture machine" that includes computational principles, human attributions of agency, and imagination. "The algorithm is an idea that puts structures of symbolic logic into motion. It is rooted in computer science, but it serves as a prism for a much broader array of cultural, philosophical, mathematical and imaginative grammars" (41). Within this "broader array," it is important to distinguish in how far exactly the notion of algorithm applies to literary narrative in a more than metaphorical sense.

Two aspects differentiate the Fibonacci sequence from the algorithmic narratives in Øyehaug and Christensen. First, the Fibonacci sequence continues forever, given enough computational power. Christensen chooses to break off in the middle of the letter N, interrupting the generative principle, to achieve an aesthetic effect and to comment on the devastating potential of nuclear power that can bring natural sequence and proliferations to an end. Also Øyehaug brings her narrative to an end, when Anna and Laura play *Vexations*, even though the performance itself would continue. The main conclusion, as far as the narrative and its probability design are concerned, has been drawn. The algorithm is integrated into the probability design of the novel or the poem. It contributes to the overall gestalt of the narrative and forms part of its design, but it does not determine that design. The second difference between algorithmic sequences and Fibonacci narratives lies in their mode of abstraction. Algorithms provide a highly abstracted mode for perceiving the world. Literary narratives embed this abstraction into embodied language and phenomenologically dense narration. They let readers perceive, certainly in the case of Øyehaug, both the curve generated from the Fibonacci sequence and the materiality of the nautilus' house, whose structure it describes. Indeed, the abstract principle does not need to be grasped in the abstract by readers, because the probability design will correlate it consistently with the sensory flow of characters' perceptions, choices, and actions. In *Presence Machine*, it is embedded in Anna's and Laura's preparations and performance of *Vexations*. The probability design then scaffolds, in the Vygotskyan sense of support through social and cultural structures, readers' meaning making doubly: It provides an experiential dimension in which characters act and experience, and it provides (more or less explicitly) a plot principle that drives the generation of the action and that keeps it coherent.

4 Cognitive Formalism

Øyehaug's entire oeuvre (as also her essays attest; see Øyehaug, *Miniatyrlesningar*; Øyehaug, *Stol og Ekstase*) engages with the tradition of Russian Formalism, in particular with Viktor Shklovsky's notion of estrangement (1917/2015). Indeed, one might identify the combination of phenomenological detail on Anna's slowly blinking eye, when the misreading occurs, and of the foregrounding of a literary device when the fictional world split as a prime instance of how Shklovsky envisages that art slows down the perception of the world. The notion of estrangement turns into the major plot device in *Presence Machine*, and Øyehaug consequently entitles the chapter in which the misreading occurs "The Fabula" (*Fabelen*), referring back to another term popularized by Shklovsky. Formalist approaches may appear to lie in conflict with the notion of "worlding the brain," because they foreground "literariness" and the difference between everyday and literary perception and thought. It is a misconception, however, to think that Russian Formalism would have nothing to say to an embodied, embedded, extended, and enactive cognitive studies.

The early statements of Russian formalism establish literary studies as autonomous from psychology, history, and related topics. Shklovsky and also Jury Tynianov criticize in particular the tendency in scholarship (of the early twentieth century) to assign importance to an author's or a reader's psychology. Boris Eichenbaum writes, in "How Gogol's 'Overcoat' is Made" (1917/1976), that the "customary procedure of identifying some given statement with the contents of the writer's 'psychology' is false in scholarship" (287). What Shklovsky, Tynianov, and Eichenbaum argue against, however, is not the relationship between literature, cognition, and the life-world *tout court*.

"How Gogol's 'Overcoat' is Made" takes its point of departure from anecdotes about Gogol's life, his desperate requests to Pushkin to "do me a favor

COGNITIVE FORMALISM

and give me a plot" (270), to his recitations and improvisations. Eichenbaum's point is that Gogol might take up everyday speech in his discourse as a narrator, but that this speech has been transformed. It is "articulated sound—a phonic gesture" (279). Eichenbaum carefully traces how Gogol achieves this through sound repetitions, puns, and sentences concluded not on the basis of meaningful logic, but on the basis of sound patterns. Also the famous passage in Gogol's "Overcoat", where the extensive conversations around the naming of Akaky Akakievich are recorded, feeds into Eichenbaum's argument that Gogol "makes" his short story, "The Overcoat", from the material of language, but refashions this material entirely as he turns language into literature. Such refashioning leads to a text in which the parts relate to the whole in the systematic fashion that Tynianov was to foreground, while it also leads to the de-automatization of readers' perception of the world here, in particular modes of oral speech, along the lines of Shklovksy's "defamiliarization."

While this is a rather potted survey of the Russian Formalists,[3] it goes to show, I hope, that their basic ideas are very much in tune with the view of the world established in 4E cognition. In particular one "E," the notion that the mind is *extended* into the environment leads to two conclusions: (1) first, our thinking unfolds in dialogue with the affordances of the world around us; and (2) we create the world around us so that it supports and scaffolds our thinking and our actions. This mutual relationship can be conceived in terms of parity (where elements of the environment take a functionally equivalent position to mental capacities, as with a notebook replacing memory) or in terms of complementarity (where elements of the environment are brought to bear in ways that exceed the functions available to us without it; see Sutton). Complementarity in the extended mind is only beginning to get discussed in greater detail. However, one could do worse than looking at the statements of the Russian formalists for finding suggestions how literature works as a complementary element in extended cognition, taking our thoughts into reaches that have no functional equivalent outside of literature. In that sense, literature needs to be considered independently of psychology, history, sociology, etc., but it does not mean that literary studies would not be informed by these other fields.

Form is the element that shapes language and that makes literary language and literary narrative complementary to everyday language. What is important here is not where exactly the dividing line between literary and everyday language runs (a discussion that has run into several dead ends, as far as I can see). Instead, what formalists like Eichenbaum are interested in is the process, the "formation," when everyday language turns into literary language

---

3 See Sini for an excellent treatment of Eichenbaum's poetics in particular.

(and what effects this has on readers). In "How Gogol's 'Overcoat' is Made," Eichenbaum goes through several examples of Gogol's earlier manuscript drafts and explains formal choices and effects from the changes and revisions that Gogol made on his linguistic material. We could say that Gogol is indeed developing the probability design of "The Overcoat", beginning with the vowel sounds of the names of his protagonists, continuing to the extravagant "phonic gesture" in letting the description of Akaky Akakievich end with "the sort of complexion that is known as hemorrhoidal" (279), and on to other aspects of the grotesque narrative. In the rather general description of the low-ranking government official Akaky Akakievich, the word "hemorrhoidal" stands out as a possible prediction error, making readers wonder whether they have misread Gogol, only to find that it is part of a larger comic-grotesque strategy of the narrator. "Hemorrhoidal" does not split the narrative into two strands, as does "tärdgård" in *Presence Machine*, but it signals early on to readers that the Saint Petersburg we are going to encounter in "The Overcoat" is designed differently from the real-world city on the Neva.

Øyehaug thematizes the writing process itself, as a way to relating oneself to the world and as a means of relating oneself to what Tynianov calls the "system of literature." In *Presence Machine*, her character Anna is an author and wants to write a "novel about language" (44). Øyehaug relates this ironically to the current quest for authenticity in literary writing, certainly Knausgård's epic *My Struggle* series, when Anna's husband comments, "nobody wants to read about *language*! We want to read about what you had for breakfast! Who you had sex with in the nineties! Someone *meets* someone, and something *happens*. That we want to read about" (44). Anna, on the other hand, is rather interested in disappearing herself from the text entirely, imagining herself as a "text machine," because she writes under a pseudonym (45). The idea that language writes itself also comes to the fore in Inger Christensen's essays. "When I write poems, I sometimes pretend it's not me but language itself that's writing" (*The Condition of Secrecy* 61). Anna, Øyehaug, or Gogol never entirely disappear behind the language that they write. However, their language can be understood as an element of the machines they construct, and, within the construction of these machines, their authors shape and reshape language, and they gain presence along the way.

∵

The cognitive formalism that I propose, then, foregrounds how literary language designs and extends embodied experiences. It draws on principles of

COGNITIVE FORMALISM 139

4E cognition, according to which language can evoke embodied resonances in readers and shape their embodied experience (Kukkonen and Caracciolo). It also draws on predictive processing for the dynamics between the sensory flow from the world and its integration in our understanding of the world, through re-adjusting our inferencing processes from misreadings. And, finally, it takes up the methods from the Russian Formalists that depend, on the one hand, on close attention to the ways in which texts are built, formally, and on the other hand, on an understanding of how this form has emerged in the creative process. (Indeed, the next step in an account of literature based on predictive processing will be to develop a better understanding of creativity within this framework).

Both Christensen's *Eternity Machine* and Øyehaug's *Presence Machine* use the formal devices in their novel to underline the ways in which their narratives are entangled in the world. Christensen ends *Eternity Machine* with Ulrik setting out to tell his story: "even if he thought it was wrong to start in the mode in which one tells a story, he didn't find a different way to start, one that was better, and he went around and whispered into one ear after another, and what he whispered spread like wildfire: There once was an eternity machine..." (153).[4] Readers had listened to Ulrik's whispers, in a way, throughout the entire novel, that now takes another iteration, another multiplication of the one. Just as the story of Christ is repeated every year from Christmas to Easter (and beyond), so does the eternity machine of Christensen's book continue running in the ears of readers, even after they stop reading. Meanwhile, the performance in *Presence Machine* takes place in 2019, which lies in the immediate future for readers who took up the novel when it was published in 2018. Thereby, the relay of *Vexations* not only links parallel worlds within the novel, where daughter and mother coexist and take over from one another, but establishes also a similar double similarity and continuity with the readers' world. In the form of Øyehaug's *Presence Machine*, readers might come to reflect that, on the one hand, the probability design enables them to trace how the experience unfolds, in parallel to the characters, while they also continue after the completion of the novel, perhaps, when remembering how they read, or remembering an element from *Presence Machine* when they take up their next book. If the literary text is a "machine to think with,"[5] then it is a machine that has multiple open interfaces with the world.

---

4   The translation from the Danish is mine.
5   The phrase is I.A. Richards'. He uses it to refer to the book rather than the literary text and its designs.

Acknowledgments

Work on this article was supported by LCE – Literature, Cognition and Emotions (FPIII Program at Humanities Faculty, University of Oslo, 2019-2023).

References

Christensen, Inger. *Evighedsmaskinen*. Gyldendal, 1964.

Christensen, Inger. *Alphabet*. Translated by Susanna Nied, Bloodaxe Books, 2000.

Christensen, Inger. *The Condition of Secrecy: Selected Essays*. Translated by Susanna Nied, New Directions, 2018.

Eichenbaum, Boris. "How Gogol's 'Overcoat' Is Made." *Gogol from the Twentieth Century*, edited by Robert A. Maguire, Princeton UP, 1976, pp. 267–291.

Finn, Ed. *What Algorithms Want: Imagination in the Age of Computing*. MIT Press, 2017.

Huron, David. *Sweet Anticipation: Music and the Psychology of Expectation*. MIT Press, 2006.

Kukkonen, Karin. *Probability Designs: Literature and Predictive Processing*. Oxford UP, 2020.

Kukkonen, Karin, and Marco Caracciolo. "What is the Second Generation?" *Style*, vol. 48, no. 3, 2014, pp. 261–74.

Kuzmičová, Anezka. "Presence in the Reading of Literary Narrative: A Case for Motor Enactment." *Semiotica*, vol. 189, 2012, pp. 23–48.

Lupyan, Gary, and Andy Clark. "Words and the World: Predictive Coding and the Language-Perception-Cognition Interface." *Current Directions in Psychological Science*, vol. 24, no. 4, 2015, pp. 279–84.

Menary, Richard. "Writing as Thinking." *Language Sciences*, vol. 29, 2007, pp. 621–32.

Richards, I.A. *Principles of Literary Criticism*. Routledge, 2001.

Norris, Dennis. "The Bayesian Reader: Explaining Word Recognition as an Optimal Bayesian Decision-Making Process." *Psychology Review*, vol. 113, no. 2, 2006, pp. 327–57.

Seth, Anil. "A Predictive Processing Theory of Sensorimotor Contingencies: Explaining the Puzzle of Perceptual Presence and Its Absence in Synesthesia." *Cognitive Neuroscience*, vol. 5, no. 2, 2014, pp. 97–118.

Shklovsky, Viktor. "Art as Device." Translated by Alexandra Berlina, *Poetics Today*, vol. 36, no. 3, 2015, pp. 151–74.

Sini, Stefania. *Contrasti di forme: Boris Ejchenbaum teoretico della letteratura*. Ledizioni, 2018.

Snell, Joshua and Jonathan Grainger. "Readers Are Parallel Processors." *Trends in Cognitive Sciences*, vol. 23, no. 7, 2019, pp. 537–46.

Sutton, John. "Exograms and Interdisciplinarity: History, the Extended Mind and the Civilising Process." *The Extended Mind*, edited by Richard Menary, MIT Press, 2010, pp. 186–225.

Tynianov, Jurij. *Die literarischen Kunstmittel und die Evolution der Literatur*. Suhrkamp, 1967.

Øyehaug, Gunnhild. *Presens Maskin*. Kolon, 2018.

Øyehaug, Gunnhild. *Miniatyrlesningar. Essay*. Kolon, 2017.

Øyehaug, Gunnhild. *Stol og Ekstase: Essay og noveller*. Kolon, 2019.

CHAPTER 9

"Watchman, What of the Night?"

Reading Uncertainty in Djuna Barnes's Nightwood

Shannon McBriar

In the central chapter of Djuna Barnes's novel, *Nightwood* (1936), protagonist Nora Flood makes a late-night visit to Dr. Matthew-Mighty-grain-of-salt-Dante-O'Connor, seeking relief from her anguished uncertainty as to why her lover, Robin Vote left her. Upon asking him, "What am I to do?," the doctor replies enigmatically: "Ah, mighty uncertainty!" (83). In an answer that borders on invocation, O'Connor not only expresses an important, stubbornly persistent, and complex part of meaning-making in the world, but also the axis upon which much of the novel turns. Uncertainty is at the heart of the love triangle between Nora, Robin, and Jenny Petherbridge, also called the "squatter," a character of borrowed solidity, who appropriates the lives, objects, and loves of others. Uncertainty is also at the heart of the existential crisis that underpins the novel, which is both observed and performed by the cross-dressing Tiresian figure of the doctor, a "fisher of men" whose world consists of declarations, digressions, verbal alchemy, and advice that is at once ironic and profound (87). Significantly, the "uncertainties" we encounter here are formidable: they are driving forces, capable of garnering earthly and symbolic power, and seem resistant even to the possibility of resolution. Complicating these uncertainties still further is the "mighty uncertainty" of the modernist text itself. As Jeanette Winterson points out, "this is not the solid nineteenth-century world of narrative; it is the shifting, slipping, relative world of Einstein and the modernists, the twin assault by science and art on what we thought we were sure of" (Winterson x). In its formal qualities, *Nightwood* exemplifies the spirit of experimentation spurred by the sense of alienation, fragmentation, and loss that marks the assault of modernity on life and mind (Lewis; Kannenstine; de Laurentis). For the reader, navigating diverging streams of consciousness that bend and break and stop abruptly, characters who are "tricks of the light" (Winterson x), and a peculiar, persistent physicality in the text that stubbornly pulls back and confounds the "inward turn" to consciousness (Waugh 95), creates a sense of confusion, unpredictability, and instability—a multiplication of uncertainties rather than the gradual resolution of them.

© KONINKLIJKE BRILL NV, LEIDEN, 2023 | DOI:10.1163/9789004681293_011

The lack of predictability in this text raises two sets of entangled questions: The first centers on what it means to "read" uncertainty: Why, given this difficulty, does the reader persist (if she does)? What is the appeal of uncertainty? The second is concerned with exploring these questions in a literary text and what this could reveal in terms of challenges and complications more specifically of interest to cognitive and neuroscientists researching uncertainty within the predictive processing framework: How is uncertainty encountered and expressed? What does it look like? Why does it matter? In opening up these questions, I would like to draw not only on cognitive approaches in literary study, but also think with cognitive and neuroscientists about the rich and complex relationship between prediction and uncertainty.

With regard to literary criticism of this novel, and perhaps modernist criticism generally, uncertainty rarely appears as an object of study in its own right but is often absorbed into the larger dynamics of the "inward turn" in which "Cartesian geographies of the mental as an interior, immaterial domain" have primarily been explored (Herman 249). The emergence of more embodied "geographies" in literary studies that privilege the situatedness of representations of cognitive activity in the world has not only complicated this turn, but also allowed for more fruitful intersections with areas of scientific research, such as distributed cognition and predictive processing (Oulanne; Garratt; Kukkonen; Caracciolo et al.). According to Bayesian accounts of prediction, uncertainty, whether encountered in the environment or generated as a result of our interaction with it, functions as a continuous trigger, a catalyst for the interloping process of perception and action that allows humans to navigate their worlds (Knill and Pouget; Vilares and Kording). According to this view, encounters with uncertainty engage both our bottom-up sensory perception of the world as we move through it, and our top-down ability to generate probabilistic predictions of that input based on our "stored knowledge" about the world (Clark 8, 13). This knowledge consists of both "low-level" and "high-level" priors, which represent a range of increasingly abstract hypotheses, beliefs, and conceptualizations and is itself affected by "unpredicted input," the so-called prediction errors (Clark 30). Depending on the nature and weighting of the error signal, cognitive agents engage in a continuous, complex process of adjustment in making and reshaping predictions (Clark 25, 57–59). This process is expressed in a cognitive agent's multilayered "generative model" of the world, which projects how sensory input is generated by causal and material relations in that agent's environment. This model is constantly revised on the basis of new input and an organism's key means of intelligent "guessing" what might be expected next (Clark 9).

As Andy Clark points out, "there are many possible architectures, and possible ways of combining top-down predictions and bottom-up sensory information" in the brain. The possible architectures he offers are largely schematic models within the broader purview of prediction-related study, ranging from neuro-physiological and neural network models to cognitive psychological accounts of prediction-based learning (Clark 298). In this chapter, I will focus not on the structure of the brain and the neural implementation of these models but rather on what literary texts might be able to tell us about the "possible ways of com-bining" top-down and bottom-up signals within predictive processes. In other words, my focus will be on exploring the affordances emerging from the textual environment of *Nightwood* and what they reveal about the combination and disjuncture of these signals within literary texts. As the performance of uncer-tainty within the text and in our reading of it suggest, uncertainty emerges as something more than a trigger or catalyst for action and the continuous updat-ing of generative models. It is, in addition, a real and persistent presence, one that infiltrates the predictive process, destabilizing the relation of both top-down and bottom-up inputs and disrupting the orchestration between them. It accomplishes this in various ways throughout the novel, rendering the "stored knowledge" and hierarchies of priors unstable. This instability manifests itself in the language of the text in a way that resists reading within the temporal cas-cades of "probability design" (Kukkonen 2–3) and instead invites a more open-ended reading that is distributed within the affordance structure of the text, one that allows a "single conspectus" while refusing to "efface or suppress the seething mass of particular things that inhabit" those affordances (Cave 50). Read in terms of its affordance structure, the text allows multiple possibilities to be ambiguously co-present across the entire range of levels of prediction.

1 Uncertainty, Prediction, and the "Designer Environment" of the Text

Human beings possess, in Andy Clark's words, "uncertainty-sensitive machin-ery" (xiv), that is, they have developed highly evolved ways of structuring their response to a rapidly changing, uncertain, and often disorientating world. Pre-diction is commonly held to be a central feature of that response, in that it is through a continuous process of anticipation and prediction error minimi-zation that we develop new patterns, "learn about the world around us and [...] engage that world in thought and action" (Clark xiv). Clark's primary con-cern is with prediction as the "automatically deployed, deeply probabilistic, non-conscious guessing" (2) that allows cognitive agents to navigate their envi-ronments, solve problems, and complete tasks, but in the final chapter of his monograph *Surfing Uncertainty*, entitled "Being Human," he opens up space to reflect on a more expansive conceptualization of prediction, one not confined to epistemological problems, but one that moves closer to problems of meaning and interpretation. Within the framework of the "prediction-driven" and "action-oriented engagement machine" (Clark xiv, xvi) Clark here considers questions of meaning-making and problem solving in cultural practices and artefacts, or "designer environments" (Clark 274). Central to these questions are the upper layers of generative models that attempt to predict the activity of sensory processing at lower levels, meaning that they are able to generate "virtual versions" of the world (Clark 93). In what he playfully refers to as "The Imaginarium," bottom-up input is not even required to project a world of interacting causes, which is particularly helpful when dealing with "complex structures of hidden causes in domains characterized by noise, ambiguity, and uncertainty" (Clark 94).

It is not a far jump with either of these elements to see how their role in the predictive process outlined above might be applied to the "designer environment" of literary texts. For Michael Burke, patterns of anticipation, whether latent or expressed, underpin the "continuous process" of "the literary reading loop" (Burke 109). Likewise, as Paul Armstrong argues in *How Literature Plays with the Brain*, there are similarities between patterns of anticipation and "the circularity of interpretation" or "hermeneutic circularity" (Armstrong 54, 3). In his reconsideration of reader response theory within a contemporary neuroaesthetic framework, Armstrong argues that the "description of reading as an anticipatory and retrospective process of building consistency and constructing patterns" can take on new significance (54). According to this model, "reading is not a linear process of adding sign to sign, scanning one after the other in a sequential manner. Rather, the reading of a text requires the recognition of patterns, and a pattern is a reciprocal construction of an overall order and its constituent parts, the overarching arrangement making sense of the details by their relation to one another, even as their configuration only emerges as its parts fit together" (Armstrong 54). For Armstrong, a neuroaesthetic approach to the hermeneutic circle reveals an inherent tension between the stability of accumulated knowledge required to generate patterns as we move through a text, and the "changeableness of its inputs" (Armstrong 65)—in predictive processing terms, the error signals that point to the unreliability or insufficiency of previous knowledge.

In her book, *Probability Designs*, Karin Kukkonen takes up this tension in persuasively arguing the case for the relationship between prediction and textual design in literary criticism. In adapting the predictive processing framework for literary study, she proposes an alternative to the "patterns of anticipatory and retrospective practice of reading" that underpin the hermeneutic circle, which, she argues is fundamentally "flat" (Kukkonen 143) and unable to account for the various embodied and interpretative dimensions of literary reading. According to Kukkonen's model, there are three inter-looping "cascades" of first, second, and third order probability designs that we encounter as a reader in working through a literary text. In the first order, prediction error "plays out at the level of plot," thus taking on a structural function within the narrative (4). In the second order, as "embodied readers," we assess the *reliability* of prediction errors we encounter, which can create a "sense of flow" in the engagement with the text (4, 9). In the third order, readers draw on "intertextual connections" and cultural constructions such as genre for gaining an awareness of the relevance of the shifting probability expectations that the text offers (4–5). Imagined as "cascades" that are temporally fluid rather than fixed, Kukkonen's conception of probability design "retain[s] the accumulative aspects of the hermeneutic circle, where ... knowledge increases as the individual moments are related to the whole and vice versa" but also "allows us to include the feeling of reading a familiar novel 'for the first time'" (Kukkonen 144). As readers, this model allows us to continue to be piqued by the uncertainties that emerge in the text despite the accumulative knowledge gains that are made in reading it. Significantly, whether the circle is flat or multidimensional, this literary interpretation of "self-organized instability" (Clark 265) takes place in a looping process in which prediction errors provide information for revising expectations "towards greater accuracy" (Kukkonen 3). As Kukkonen puts it, "predictions from more general, abstract levels can prefigure perceptions, while prediction errors on the lower, faster levels of perception or movements easily feed up to revise higher-level predictions" (3).

This model raises a number of questions worth exploring in a literary context, especially in relation to uncertainty-minded texts such as *Nightwood*. For example, these models suggest the "stored knowledge" that we rely upon to generate top-down predictions is accumulated, retained, adjusted, and updated; but what happens when the text deliberately subverts this process and constantly calls attention to the instability of that knowledge? What if the "knowledge" readers acquire is not structured as "knowledge" at all, conventionally speaking, but appears as a series of exposures, affordances that remain simultaneously open, multiplying, rather than restraining outcomes? How does this impact not only the quality of, but even our ability to generate "top-down" predictions at all? And finally, what happens when error signals remain intentionally unresolved, suppressed, or alternatively, become the default mode of engagement—when the text itself seems to be a "burst of error" (Clark 89)? What, then, do readers hold onto?

2 Conceptual Confusion, Unresolved Errors, and the Affordance Structure of the Text

In exploring these questions and what they might open up in terms of how we experience the affordance structure of the text in relation to uncertainty, it is worth returning to the observation about *Nightwood* made by Jeanette Winterson:

> *Nightwood* is demanding. You can slide into it, because the prose has a narcotic quality, but you can't slide over it ... There is much more to this book than its story, which is light, or even its characters, who are magnificent tricks of the light. This is not the solid nineteenth-century world of narrative; it is the shifting, slipping, relative world of Einstein and the modernist, the twin assault by science and art on what we thought we were sure of. (Winterson x)

As we have seen, on first reading, Winterson firmly situates *Nightwood* in its broader cultural and scientific moment of uncertainty. As a modernist text, it exemplifies the spirit of experimentation spurred by the assault of modernity on life and mind (Lewis 3). It is rife with confusion, unpredictability, and instability and is obsessed with opening up the unknowable so far beyond its boundaries as to preclude the very possibility of knowledge. It requires and invites, as T.S. Eliot observed, more than a single reading (xvii). However, it is Winterson's framing comment, that you can "slide into it ... but you can't slide over it" that is most significant here. While "sliding into" a text suggests a sense of immersion, the idea of "sliding over" is more complex, particularly in the context of uncertainty, in which potential affinities with Andy Clark's central metaphor of "surfing" are present (xiv). For Clark, world-engaging prediction is like surfing the waves of ambiguous and noisy sensory stimulation, always staying just ahead of the place where the wave breaks. On this view, "sliding over" means to reach several points in succession where one can revise previous predictions accurately enough to be carried along for the time being, resulting in the experience of "flow" (Kukkonen 4). But there also is another kind of "sliding over" in *Nightwood*, one that the text itself seems to invite, particularly in moments where it seems impenetrable, where we encounter complex metaphorical constructions, internal contradiction, and digression, and where it seems to willfully disrupt the predictive process. Indeed, sometimes the difficulty of the text almost *makes* the reader slide over it, forced on by sheer momentum, word tumbling over word—a kind of reading that feels very much like being in free fall. In these moments, readers may be unable to stay "in the pocket" of the waves of sensory stimulation (Clark xiv). When they break, it seems readers are left without even the vague promise of something to hold onto. It forces us, in other words, to endure a state of uncertainty long beyond that with which we are comfortable.

In exploring what is at stake in *this* sense of "sliding over," like Kukkonen, I take as a foundational assumption the claim that the "designed sensory flow" coming from literary texts can be thought of in a complementary way to the "sensory flow of the real world" (Kukkonen 5). This flow has a lower "bandwidth" than the sensory flow from the real world, as it largely appeals to the senses via written words, but it can nevertheless elicit embodied resonances in the reader and, unlike the real world, present prediction errors in a "carefully crafted sequence" designed by the author (Kukkonen 10, 5) Employing this complementary (rather than parity-based) model of world and text may also, in turn, allow us to more fully complicate the role of uncertainty in the relational hierarchy between sensory input and conceptual inference at the heart of the predictive process. According to Clark, in predictive processing there is a "deep functional asymmetry between forward and backwards pathways— functionally speaking 'between raw data seeking an explanation (bottom-up) and hypotheses seeking confirmation (top-down)'" (Clark 29). In the textual world of *Nightwood*, I argue, this asymmetrical movement between "forward and backwards pathways" is complicated by constant disjunctures between sensory and conceptual levels of prediction. This confusion destabilizes the hierarchy of "low-level" and "high-level" priors within top-down processing itself, resulting in a sense of being stuck in uncertainties rather than moving to resolve them. Perhaps this is partly what Winterson was referring to when she wrote that one simply *cannot* "slide over" the text.

Such disjunctures frequently emerge in the interplay between embodied imagery, mixed metaphor, and abstraction in the novel, which continue to upend what we think we know. Throughout *Nightwood*, sensory images relating to the anatomy of the human body ("kidneys," "guts," "gall," "bones," "blood," and "bowels") or to beasts (the "night fowl that caws" or hounds that "claw" and "howl") appear with force, often suddenly and unexpectedly. The visceral quality of these images, particularly when beast and human overlap, creates a kind of conceptual confusion, an uncertainty in how we "read" and anticipate the sensory information emerging from these composite figures. In these moments, what might strike the reader as an "error signal" is highly deliberate, allowing sensory images to increasingly bear conceptual weight. This confusion between the sensory and the conceptual spurs a forward movement toward the revision of expectations; yet this movement is also constantly deflected and frustrated.

WATCHMAN, WHAT OF THE NIGHT? 149

These dynamics can be traced in the following passage, in which Nora's former lover Robin is described indirectly as a "beast turning human":

> The woman who presents herself to the spectator as a 'picture' forever arranged, is, for the contemplative mind, the chiefest danger. Sometimes one meets a woman who is beast turning human. Such a person's every movement will reduce to an image of a forgotten experience; a mirage of an eternal wedding cast on the racial memory; as insupportable a joy as would be the vision of an eland coming down an aisle of trees, chapleted with orange blossoms and bridal veil, a hoof raised in the economy of fear, stepping in the trepidation of flesh that will become myth; as the unicorn is neither man nor beast deprived, but human hunger pressing its breast to its prey.
>
> Such a woman is the infected carrier of the past: before her the structure of our head and jaws ache—we feel that we could eat her, she who is eaten death returning, for only then do we put our face close to the blood on the lips of our forefathers. (33–34)

Moving quickly from the promise of something fixed—"a 'picture' forever arranged"—to the more vital, transformative image of a "beast turning human," and then to the sensory uncertainty of a "mirage" and the historical ambiguities implicit in "racial memory," this passage is framed by an almost self-reflexive gesture toward the slippery nature of its design. In the first sentence alone, there is a strange disjuncture between the static nature of the picture, the observational tone of the narrator, and the increasing tension that attends the phrase "chiefest danger." This disjuncture continues to build throughout the passage, at once confirming, upending, and redirecting the patterns of anticipation created by the reader, for whom knowledge becomes increasingly unreliable. Conflicting sensory and conceptual signals emerging from the cross-attribution of beast and human reinforce this sense of disjuncture, as we encounter the visually rich image of an animal bride, an "eland" moving down a forest aisle "chapleted with orange blossoms and bridal veil." The formation of this already conceptually challenging image and its implication in myth-making is immediately arrested and deflected not only by concrete bodily action ("a hoof raised"), but also the functional and almost anti-mythical phrase "*economy of fear*" (my emphasis). Within the framework of predictive processing, such sudden changes of register are seen as "precision shifts" (Kukkonen 84–95), i.e., as moments that give rise to a re-evaluation of the reliability of prediction errors. With each turn in this building image of transformation, the parameters of what counts as relevant and reliable information change.

Such shifts continue to occur between the physically disturbing and the conceptually abstract that follow. We are forced into the sensation of "stepping" into "the trepidation of flesh," which itself is transformed into myth, recalling the mythic creature of the unicorn and hereby activating a new conceptual image to guide us, before we are suddenly subjected to the sensory punch of "beast", followed by the violent, embodied abstraction of "human hunger pressing its breast to it prey." These tensions culminate in the final sentence of the passage, in which the sensory, animalistic, and strangely scientific image of "the structure of our head and jaws" suggests new conceptual relevance. When forced further into this impossible sentence, embodied readers might recoil at the phrase "we could eat her, she who is eaten death returning." The structure of this phrase is peculiar as we rest on the comma separating "her" and "she"— stuck, for a moment, in the transition from object to subject, only to stumble, unexpectedly, at the word "eaten." One might expect the repetition of "eat" and "eaten" to carry that rhythm forward, but instead the peculiarity of the phrase "eaten death" causes confusion and disruption in the reader. We are suspended in the sentence, possibly experiencing another error signal produced by this latest turn of imagery. This is reinforced rather than resolved in the directional confusion of "returning," the final word of the sentence, which is related in temporally complex ways to the prefix "fore" in "forefathers," itself suspended between past and present and nevertheless positioning us in closest physical proximity to these ancestors ("blood on the lips)."

These various disjunctures or precision shifts mostly play out at the level of "second-order probability design" (Kukkonen), i.e., at the level of the interaction of the embodied reader with the affordances of the text. According to Kukkonen, bodily descriptions, motion verbs, indications of direction, and other literary devices are able to activate "embodied resonances" in the reader that support the development of a predictive model of the text (Kukkonen 94). Preparations of a character to leap out of a window, for instance, can resonate with her previous actions of jumping and climbing and with the reader's own sensorimotor experience, thus giving "cues" for the interpretative exploration of the text (Kukkonen 62–72). Importantly, Kukkonen does not regard the storyworld of novels as a stable and coherent construct that directs readers' expectations; for her, it is precisely the constant update of expectations in precision shifts that creates the sense of "flow" in the engagement of the reader with a work of fiction. Yet, her approach also operates on the assumption that in "surfing the complexity of the text" readerly expectations can "yield a sound inference" with a given model of the text (Kukkonen 84, 81).

In the passage above, the very possibility of such soundness seems in question. The multi-sensory imagery of the passage, including the disturbing allusion to hunting human flesh, arguably can spawn strong embodied resonances

WATCHMAN, WHAT OF THE NIGHT? 151

in the reader, but it is much less clear what kind of "cue" they form. They seem to have next to no predictive value for what comes next—except, maybe, for the paradoxical expectation of unpredictability. The passage oscillates between the literal, the figurative, and the conceptual ("stepping in the trepidation of flesh") as well as between different registers (myth, science, wisdom, nightmare), making it hard (or impossible) to revise a generative model "towards greater accuracy" (Kukkonen 3). The assumption that predictions from more abstract levels can "prefigure perceptions" and that prediction errors on the lower level of perception "easily feed up to revise higher-level predictions" (Kukkonen 3) only seems to hold in a very limited sense for this text. I therefore argue that the novel creates a peculiar, open-ended affordance structure in which uncertainty is a constant and real presence and "stored knowledge" for probability assessment is constantly undermined. In other words, the affordance structure of the novel cannot be reduced to its supportive role in the development of a probabilistic model of the text.

This open-endedness is also reflected in the story world itself. In his dress and manners Baron Felix acknowledges uncertainty by preparing himself for contrasting outcomes, in a seeming attempt to avoid prediction errors and their emotional consequences altogether. He is dressed, for example, "as if expecting to participate in some great event, though there was no function in the world for which he could be said to be properly garbed; wishing to be correct at any moment, he was tailored in part for the evening and in part for the day" (8). In dressing "in part" for both the evening and the day, the Baron creates his own certainty as he navigates an uncertain social world to which he has questionable claim. This is further entrenched in his manner of address to those he meets in the street. We find Felix

> still spatted, still wearing his cutaway, bowing, searching, with quick pendulous movements, for the correct thing to which to pay tribute: the right street, the right café, the right building, the right vista. In restaurants he bowed slightly to anyone who looked as if he might be "someone," making the bend so imperceptible that the surprised person might think he was merely adjusting his stomach. (8–9)

In tailoring his dress, his manners, and himself to cover all possibilities, Felix bypasses the very possibility of error. His inability to commit reveals the persistent unreliability of his store of knowledge, as he reads his environment not according to any top-down conception of its overall design, or his place within it, but rather from "sign to sign" (Armstrong). This executive failure also underpins Felix's failed marriage to Robin. Unable to form an overarching "idea" of Robin and reading her, too, sign by sign, he could never really know her, but only ever form an "image" of her. When, in a reflective mood, he declares that "an image is a stop the mind makes between uncertainties" (100), he posits uncertainty as the inextricable backdrop of all experience.

3   Uncertainty as Literary Affordance

As we have seen in these examples, the frequency of prediction errors and precision shifts in *Nightwood* suggest that uncertainty may be complicated in unexpected ways. Rather than conceiving uncertainty as a cause for action and probability assessments, the novel encourages us to think about how it operates as a real presence, and nowhere is this more evident than in the complex image of the night itself. In seeking relief from the uncertainty regarding her failed relationship with Robin, Nora asks Dr. O'Connor to tell her "everything about the night" (71). In doing so, she asks him what is, on the surface, an empirically driven question about the night that Robin met Jenny, the third part of their love triangle. Yet, the question is deliberately open-ended, as Nora inquires not only after that specific "night of nights" (80), but also "the night" as an entity in general. While the doctor turns her question back onto her, his digressive meditation begins to sprawl, gathering in pace and incoherence throughout the chapter. The night is at once expansive, encompassing "other times ... and foreign countries" (73); it partakes of the "torment" of time, the "remembrance of things past" (81); it is visceral, animating the bodies of "beasts," sheltering the "night fowl that caws," and is yet figured in the "heart," "bones," "skin," and "flesh" of the living and the dead (76); it is ephemeral, as the fantastic realms of dream and sleep guarded by the night, proffer "unknown lands," "darkness," and "estrangement" (79); it is, significantly, unpredictable, as the "tree of night ... drips a pitch against the palm that computation has not gambled" (75). In the doctor's digressions, the night does not build so much as unravel—it becomes an unpredictable pulse, displacing "stored knowledge" with a series of flashing exposures, disjointed, incoherent, and at times positively opaque, which we slide over and into as we read the text. Significantly, as the doctor wanders in his thoughts and words, he works at generating uncertainty, rather than resolving it. He proposes that Nora does the same, advising her to "think of the night the day long, and of the day the night through, or at some reprieve of the brain it will come upon you heavily—an engine stalling itself upon your chest, halting its wheels against your heart; unless you have made a roadway for it" (75). The almost crushing conceptual weight borne by the sensory image of the night as an "engine stalling upon your chest" can recall Clark's "action-oriented engagement machine," but here forward movement and reduction of uncertainty are not a matter of course at all (Barnes 32; Clark xvi).

But how, then, does uncertainty function as a textual affordance? How are we to "read" it? As an alternative to reading in terms of probabilistic design models, which assume temporal flow, the relevance of stored knowledge, and the weighting of error signals, I have proposed that we think about uncertainty in terms of the affordance structure within the text itself. This structure allows for the co-presence of multiple latent possibilities, sporadically emerging, receding, and disappearing, firing into view and fading, depending on the situation or indeed their "relevance" (Cave 51). It also allows for a looser, more underspecified arrangement that accounts for persistent, unresolved ambiguities and the instability of stored knowledge. This open-ended affordance structure is reflected in Dr. O'Connor's direct discussion of uncertainty with which this chapter began. When Nora asks the doctor "What am I to do?," he replies:

> "Ah, mighty uncertainty!" [...] "Have you thought of all the doors that have shut at night and opened again? Of women who have looked about with lamps, like you, and who have scurried on fast feet? Like a thousand mice they go this way and that, now fast, now slow, some halting behind doors, some trying to find the stairs, all approaching or leaving their misplaced mouse meat, that lies in some cranny, on some couch, down on some floor, behind some cupboard; and all the windows, great and small, from which love and fear have peered, shining and in tears? Put those windows end to end and it would be a casement that would reach around the world; and put those thousand eyes into one eye and you would have the night combed with the great blind searchlight of the heart."
> Tears began to run down Nora's face. (Barnes 83)

In this passage, uncertainty seems itself to have become an open-ended affordance, something that, like language, can be "offer[ed] for improvised use" (Cave 54). Like the women scurrying on "fast feet," searching for their "misplaced mouse meat," Nora too searches for this crumb of certainty. The accent falling equally on each syllable, this small but oddly visceral phrase holds us back as we slide over domestic imagery, which we think will hold, but does not. As we read, the doors that "have shut at night and opened again," become existential portals through which lights flicker and fade in the dark distance, and windows bear the weight of affect, "love and fear" peering through them, "shining and in tears." Uncertainty itself remains underspecified within this affordance structure, drawing out a thousand doors, a thousand windows, and a thousand eyes, culminating in the profound image of the "great blind searchlight of the heart." As it "combs" an existential landscape, moving from sign to sign, the sheer sensory and conceptual breadth of this image makes it feel as though the imaginarium has lost all predictive layering and structure.

As this passage suggests, the heart that searches for certainty does so in error, but it is an error, as Hibbitt suggests, "in the sense of wandering … definitely not in the sense of mistake" (Hibbitt 28). In making this argument for uncertainty as an affordance, it is this attendant sense of directionlessness, open-endedness, and underspecification (Cave 51) which allow us to open up Bayesian accounts of prediction within a literary context. Through rethinking design-based models that assume intact hierarchies between high and low-level priors, stored knowledge that is updated, revised, and retained, and through drawing out the richness of error signals in their own right, we might be able to reach a more ambiguous picture of the ways in which bottom-up, or sensory perception and top-down conceptual processing combine. In doing so, we may move closer to opening up cognitive paradigms, thinking with those in cognitive and neuroscience who are exploring similar assumptions that underpin a linear, or "monotonal" conception of how we deal with uncertainty (Hasson 6) and with those who are attempting to understand how uncertainty is represented in the neural system itself, especially in assuming inefficiency rather than "optimal" efficiency to be at work in this process (Vilares and Kording 11). Of course, this is not to say that *Nightwood* cannot be richly read within the frameworks of probabilistic design, just that the presence of uncertainty both in the novel and in one's reading of it could benefit from the open-endedness that an affordance structure provides. Uncertainty, it seems, can be disruptive in ways that these models may not fully account for. Perhaps a sense of this pressed on T.S. Eliot, when he wrote in his Preface to *Nightwood*, that "in trying to anticipate a reader's misdirections, one is in danger of provoking him to some other misunderstanding unforeseen" (Eliot xxi).

References

Anderson, Miranda, et al. *Distributed Cognition in Victorian Culture and Modernism*, Edinburgh UP, 2020.

Armstrong, Paul B. *How Literature Plays with the Brain: The Neuroscience of Reading and Art*. Johns Hopkins UP, 2013.

Barnes, Djuna. *Nightwood*. 1936. Faber and Faber, 2007.

Burke, Michael. "The Rhetorical Neuroscience of Style: On the Primacy of Style Elements during Literary Discourse Processing." *Journal of Literary Semantics*, vol. 42, no. 2, 2013, pp. 199–215.

Caracciolo, Marco, et al. "The Promise of an Embodied Narratology: Integrating Cognition, Representation and Interpretation." *Emerging Vectors of Narratology*, edited by Per Krogh Hansen et al., De Gruyter, 2017, pp. 435–59.

Cave, Terence. *Thinking with Literature: Towards a Cognitive Criticism*. Oxford UP, 2017.

Clark, Andy. *Surfing Uncertainty: Prediction, Action, and the Embodied Mind*. Oxford UP, 2016.

Eliot, Thomas Stearns. "Preface." *Nightwood*, by Djuna Barnes, Faber and Faber, 2007, pp. xvii–xxii.

Garratt, Peter. *The Cognitive Humanities: Embodied Mind in Literature and Culture*. Palgrave Macmillan, 2016.

Hasson, Uri. "The Neurobiology of Uncertainty: Implications for Statistical Learning." *Philosophical Transactions Biological Sciences*, vol. 372, art. 20160048, 2016.

Herman, David. "1880–1945: Re-Minding Modernism." *The Emergence of Mind: Representations of Consciousness in Narrative Discourse in English*, edited by David Herman, U of Nebraska P, 2011, pp. 243–72.

Hibbitt, Richard. "Reflections on the Fruitful Error." *Textual Wanderings: The Theory and Practice of Narrative Digression*, edited by Rhian Atkin, Legenda, 2011, pp. 27–36.

Kannenstine, Louis F. *The Art of Djuna Barnes: Duality and Damnation*. New York UP, 1977.

Knill, David C., and Alexandre Pouget. "The Bayesian Brain: The Role of Uncertainty in Neural Coding and Computation." *Trends in Neurosciences*, vol. 27, no. 12, 2004, pp. 712–19.

Kukkonen, Karin. *Probability Designs: Literature and Predictive Processing*. Oxford UP, 2021.

De Lauretis, Teresa. "Nightwood and the 'Terror of Uncertain Signs.'" *Critical Inquiry*, vol. 34, suppl., Winter 2008, pp. 117–29.

Lewis, Pericles. *The Cambridge Introduction to Modernism*. Cambridge UP, 2007.

Oulanne, Laura. "Affective Bodies: Nonhuman and Human Agencies in Djuna Barnes's Fiction." *On_Culture*, vol. 2, 2016.

Vilares, Iris, and Konrad Kording. "Bayesian Models: The Structure of the World, Uncertainty, Behavior, and the Brain: Bayesian Models and the World." *Annals of the New York Academy of Sciences*, vol. 1224, no. 1, 2011, pp. 22–39.

Waugh, Patricia "Thinking in Literature: Modernism and Contemporary Neuroscience." *The Legacies of Modernism: Historicising Postwar and Contemporary Fiction*, edited by David James, Cambridge UP, 2011, pp. 75–95.

Winterson, Jeanette. "Introduction." *Nightwood*, by Djuna Barnes, Faber and Faber, 2007, pp. IX–XV.

CHAPTER 10

The Unfolding Now

Narrative Sense-Making from a Neurocinematic Perspective

Pia Tikka and Mauri Kaipainen

1 Introduction

Written and performative storytelling, more generally narration, is a cornerstone of human society, woven into cultural, legal, and political subsystems of the society, among others. Narration can be defined as the storied expression of the world's complexity, captured in relations between events, entities, and things perceived, sometimes implying causation, sometimes hierarchy. We consider the act of narration a key means of constructing and imposing coherence and consequence on the world, which would otherwise remain an unstructured phenomenal chaos. While the most commonly conceived function of narration may be intersubjective and cultural communication, we suggest that its primary function is *autonarration*, the experiential function of *making sense of the world* and situating oneself in the world so structured. Our first aim is to explore the sense-making function of narration with respect to its embodiment, in particular in the nervous system, and to consider the cinematic medium as a means of simulating the world. The second aim is to suggest how the *subjective* sense made in such a way translates further to *intersubjective* narration.

The foundation of our approach to narrative sense-making lies in the holistic theory of enactive cognition by Francisco Varela, Evan Thompson, and Eleanor Rosch, according to which the human organism *enacts* the world, while itself being inseparable from that world. "Laying down a path in walking" is their metaphor for such enactment.[1] The "human mind"—in this enactive sense—is conceived of as one integrated brain-body-world system. In line with the research mission of neurophenomenology (Varela "Neurophenomenology"; Varela et al.)—which proposes to integrate established methods of cognitive neurosciences with those of phenomenological inquiry—our objective is to identify key perspectives on the dynamical emergence of the narrating

---

1 The metaphoric depiction of the relation between enactive subject and the world seemingly originates from the Spanish poet Antonio Machado. *Caminante, son tus huellas / el camino y nada más; / caminante, no hay camino, / se hace camino al andar* (Machado).

© KONINKLIJKE BRILL NV, LEIDEN, 2023 | DOI:10.1163/9789004681293_012

THE UNFOLDING NOW   157

mind from said system. One of these perspectives opens from *neuroimaging*, a psychophysiological means of observing neural activity associated with narrative sense-making. Another is *phenomenological inquiry,* which enables access to the experiential aspects of the brain-body-world system, which can be described as a "great blooming, buzzing confusion," as William James suggested (488).

2 Autonarration

By *narration* in general we refer to the arrangement of this "confusion" performed by the individual in a manner that allows it to be *experienced* in terms of events or objects and their mutual relations unfolding in time, including causal, hierarchical or other types of relation. In distinction from *intersubjective narration* we let *autonarration* refer to an individual's embodied pre-inguistic sense-making, i.e., the mental moment-to-moment simulation of the world, which also is a precondition for one's own actions. From an enactive point of view, we suggest that autonarration plays a specific role in mediating between the body-brain system's biological dynamism (*homeostasis*) and the dynamical emergence of self (*awareness*). In our *autonarration hypothesis* we state that autonarration provides the connection that Varela describes as the "link between mind and consciousness that seems both obvious and natural: the *structure* of human experience itself" ("Neurophenomenology" 330; added emphasis in italics).

Drawing from Varela's neurophenomenological interpretation of Edmund Husserl's time-consciousness—which distinguishes between primary impression, backward-looking *retention,* and forward-looking *protention* (Husserl; Varela "The Specious Present")—we have previously proposed a neurocinematically informed computational model of *narrative nowness* (Kauttonen et al.; Tikka and Kaipainen "Phenomenological Considerations"). In its terms, autonarration can be regarded as a retentive tail in which earlier experiential events gain significance according to a momentary priority, while past events of less significance keep decaying as a function of passed time, corresponding to fading memory. In this way, retention serves as the context and condition of nowness, i.e., that what is at hand and perceived in the passing moment of time. As the main function of the subjective experience of nowness we regard an organism's orientation to the future or, in Husserlian terms, protention. This model of a continually unfolding nowness describes the experiential structure of autonarration but, as we will argue, it can also serve as a means for formulating hypotheses for neuroimaging experiments.

With regard to language, autonarration in our understanding is akin to Lev Vygotsky's idea of "inner-speech," the kind of internalized communicative speech which enacts the influence of sociality in the development of language. However, if the human mind is conceived of in terms of a broader mind-brain-world dynamics, "internalizing" alone does not explain the opposite influence, namely the ability of the narrating brain to facilitate the intersubjective sharing and "externalization" of language. Without going into theories of how language emerges, we suggest that autonarration may play a role there, without necessarily requiring a linguistic basis. Instead, autonarration can be assigned the function of projecting embodied situatedness into language, as George Lakoff and Mark Johnson have suggested, perhaps in combination with a Vygotskian internalization of sociality through language. In other words, while autonarration is motivated by the urge to make sense of one's situatedness in the world, this situatedness is also dynamically constructed, or enacted, in autonarration. This hypothesis fits the picture of contemporary narrative psychology (see Sarbin; Bruner; Monteagudo; Vassilieva), which assigns (auto)narration the key role in constructing identity. With our hypothesis we emphasize the dynamical function of autonarration and suggest that identity-constructing life-stories ultimately emerge from continuous moment-to-moment autonarration.

This view is in line with the influential bio-philosophical perspective of Humberto Maturana and Francesco Varela's *autopoiesis*, implying that autonarration can be considered as a dynamical function that serves the self-definition of a living organism as a unity in the world. For a biological being, autopoiesis involves the emergence of a boundary like a cell membrane or skin that constitutes a distinction between self and other and thereby identity. It involves systemic metabolic flow of substances and energy across the boundary, but only as long as the process of life goes on, after which the systemically maintained identity will collapse. Correspondingly, autonarration keeps maintaining the identity of the embodied nerve-equipped individual as long as it lives. In this sense, the primary function of autonarration is to maintain the identity of the individual by keeping track of—and making sense of—her situatedness and keeping her adaptively oriented towards the surrounding world. The implication is that, even when reading a book or viewing a movie, narrative sense-making involves physiological engagement. This systemic view aims to close the gap between cognition and experience: inherently entangled and based on the same bodily foundation, both cognition and experience, neurophysiology and autonarration serve the purpose of making sense of the world and the self.

THE UNFOLDING NOW   159

3 Intersubjective Narration

If autonarration is strictly subjective, how then is intersubjective narration possible? How does autonarrative sense-making translate to intersubjective communication? Since others belong to an individual's world, human beings are evolutionarily equipped for interacting with each other by means of various mechanisms. While every individual experience is unique, it also makes internal reference to a range of embodied brain-body-world faculties that are shared across the species, thereby forming a repertoire of affordances for individual experiences.

The mechanisms of intersubjective mapping of individual experiences include, we propose, *mirroring, theory-of-mind* (mentalizing) and *deixis.* Firstly, neural mirroring can be described as an embodied simulation of other people's actions supported by "premotor neurons that fire both when an action is executed and when it is observed being performed by someone else" (Gallese 519). It therefore is likely that watching a handshake on the screen will activate the same neural circuitry that is active when actually shaking hands with someone. It has been suggested that this mechanism is the basis of empathy and social identification (Gallese 519). Secondly, the *theory-of-mind* approach (Frith and Frith; Mar) describes cognitive processes of *mentalizing,* i.e., the ability to imagine other people's intentions, motivations, and future actions. Metalizing is context-dependent, relying on previous experiences and predicting events based on these experiences. It translates to inferences of the type "knowing this person's background, I would not trust the sincerity of this handshake." While mirroring and mentalizing facilitate the prediction and coordination of actions they don't necessarily require direct interaction with others.

With the term *deixis* we refer to the social function that determines a minimal event of direct interaction (Tikka and Kaipainen, "Intersubjectivity").[2] It is the innate, biologically grounded capability that enables *pointing at,* and *confirming,* a common reference via a shared gaze. Humans are equipped to track the focus of another person's eyes via joining the same action—such as petting a cat and sharing its soft and hairy warmth—as well as semantic devices of language (talking about the same cat), which may be termed *deixis.* In the case of film, we extend the idea of deixis to an intersubjectively shared focus on the same narrative event, whether the subjects are watching the film

---

2 Merriam-Webster's definition of "deixis" is: "the pointing or specifying function of some words (such as definite articles and demonstrative pronouns) whose denotation changes from one discourse to another" ("deixis").

together or separately. The experiences, often deliberately designed by the filmmakers to catch everybody's attention, belong to each individual's world while being anchored to the embodied ground of the species. Such deictically shared narrative experiences allow to further observe corresponding activities in individual brains.

In the following, we examine three interrelated and mutually intertwined aspects of narrative sense-making and experience through the lens of neuro-imaging: (1) the neural aspect of enactment in the narrative world, (2) experiential aspects of the enactment and (3) the deictic aspect, describing how this enactment is shared. In order to bring these three aspects of narrative sense-making together, we focus on the narrative medium of cinema. In particular, we discuss findings from neuroimaging experiments with the method of functional magnetic resonance imaging (fMRI) in order to unveil hints of the three aspects, and their contribution to phenomeno-physiological sense making, or the "enworlding" of the brain.

4   Neurocinematic Findings about Narrative Experience

Films make perfect stimuli for neuroscientific experiments because they present compact characterizations of framed world events. Tikka describes films as simulations of the world (*Enactive Cinema*). They therefore have two remarkable advantages for multidisciplinary study of narrative experience. First, experiences and their psychophysical manifestations are time-locked with reference to exact time frames and can therefore be cross-referenced against each other. Second, the restricted duration of a film allows for a temporal window into the aggregated experience (and memory) that may extend to an entire lifetime.

Originally, the term *neurocinematics* referred to the interdisciplinary endeavor of neuroscientists and filmmakers to study in neuroimaging experiments how brain functions of film viewers are affected by specific cinematic events, allowing filmmakers to evaluate artistic decisions and develop new cinematic methods (Hasson et al., "Neurocinematics"). The approach is firmly associated with the paradigm of naturalistic neuroscience, which employs films as sources of time-locked narrative events that offer more ecologically valid stimuli for functional brain imaging than still images or check-board patterns that are traditionally used in such experiments (for review, see Jääskeläinen et al.). Neuroimaging, as well as other physiological measures, allow describing the physiological dynamics of narrative sense-making with

THE UNFOLDING NOW 161

statistical means and correlating these with time-locked annotations of stimulus content. However, the naturalistic paradigm is also limited in its focus on mapping event-based stimulus category labels against brain functions, for instance when mapping the representation of faces in film on activity in the brain's face area (fusiform gyrus). In considering complex worldly events in films, we find the explanatory power of the category labeling approach unsatisfactory, at least in the typical cases in which the labels refer to objects in narrow time windows without relating them to their broader narrative context. For example, it is not enough to label a picture with "gun" without context. It makes a decisive difference in the experience whether the context builds a fear of murder, a plan for murder, or a murder that has taken place. Context fully considered would imply expanding the set of category labels to a hierarchy of infinite depth in two dimensions, one in time (three-part temporality), and one in subjective experience at each specific time-point (nowness model). This is very close to the fourfold structure of nowness proposed by Varela ("The Specious Present" 303).

The autobiographical aspect of autonarration considered, it is likely to hold that the longer the contextualizing autonarration, potentially referring to biographical, cultural experiences and whatever flavors the individual context, the more unique the individual experience. In traditional neuroimaging laboratory settings this would translate to non-viable complexity in terms of the number of variables and subjects. This is among the reasons why subjective experience, intentionality, and consciousness have largely been inaccessible to neuroscientific methods. Associated concerns have been seminally discussed by Varela in "Neurophenomenology: A Methodological Remedy for the Hard Problem." In this paper, he calls for studying the co-determined mutual constraints between neuroscientific data and phenomenological first-person data. With the purpose of advancing the understanding of the interplay of the neural and phenomenal aspects of narrative sense-making, we deliberately deviate our conception of neurocinematics from that of naturalistic neuroscience, and instead consider it as a subproject of neuro-phenomenology. By emphasizing the phenomenological dimension of neurocinematics we aim beyond merely confirming the mapping of specific time-locked events on the screen on activities of specific brain regions or networks, and towards describing the viewer's holistic sense-making in a temporally and contextually extended manner. As a consequence, the primary interest turns to modelling the holistic experiential interplay within the brain-body-world system—i.e., the *enactment* of the world—while only secondarily studying the anatomy and functionality of the brain regions.

Phenomenological inquiry traditionally relies on subjective verbal accounts of the experience under scrutiny. When associated with unfolding cinematic narrative and neuroimaging data by timecoding, the phenomenological descriptions of the structure of experience may open insights into the embodiment of autonarration. Echoing a previous collaboration with Varela, Claire Petitmengin together with her colleagues has elaborated the method of the micro-phenomenological interview to identify general structures of experience triggered by specific events. This method allows assessing first-person experiences in a systematic manner in order to describe (a) the dynamical relations between the temporal unfolding of experience (diachronic elements) and (b) the experiential features characterizing a given moment of time, such as a type of attention, emotional tone, perceptual position, or sensorial modalities (synchronic elements) (Petitmengin et al. 702).

We argue that a holistic and world-embedded view of narrative experience requires engaging test subjects with contexts long enough to cover the meaningful unfolding of narrative, as well as considering subjective autonarratives from short situational contexts to long durations, ultimately at the scale of life-stories. This implies that meaningful narrative contexts of extended timescales are a necessary condition. How micro-phenomenologically informed approaches to intersubjectively shared structures of experience could contribute to neuroscientific studies of the autonarration hypothesis remains for future studies to determine.

For the search of an intersubjectively shared phenomeno-physiology of narrative sense-making, the functional magnetic resonance imaging (fMRI) method has several advantages over other neuroimaging methods,[3] not least the fact that it covers the entire anatomy of the brain and thus allows the observation of broad activation networks that are or can be involved in narrative processing. Notably, we interpret the findings of different studies as spotlights on the broad field of embodied narrative experience. They are addressed as intersubjectively shared manifestations of sense-making beyond mere reactive responses to the physical sensory stimulus. Functional MRI methods have advanced rapidly from the early 2000s, when the free viewing of longer films in

---

3 The paradigm of neurocinematics is by no means constrained to the method of fMRI and its limits. Depending on the research question, any brain imaging technique, such as magneto-encephalography (MEG), electroencephalography (EEG), or positron emission tomography (PET), among many other, can be applied, allowing reliable inferences from smaller groups of subjects, or even individuals, thereby relating more closely to the domain of idiosyncratic experiences. Psycho-physiological observations including heart rate and electrodermal conductance of skin as indicators of emotional state (valence) and excitement (arousal) may add relevant understanding of context-related physiology of narrative sense-making.

the fMRI scanner was still challenged by technical limitations of managing big data sets which restricted scanning time. Therefore neuroscientists typically used short film clips as stimuli. It is an important step towards neurophenomenology to instead present the test subjects full length films and to adopt an exploratory data analysis approach instead of the conventional variable-minimizing methodology.

5 Intersubject Correlation

The benchmark finding of neuroimaging studies using films as stimulus is *intersubject correlation* detected in brain activities of viewers engaged with the same narrative (Hasson et al., "Intersubject Synchronization"; see Jääskeläinen et al. for review). Intersubject correlation means that there are significant similarities between the brain activities of different individuals in response to the same events, apparently allowing for generalizability over individuals. To our knowledge, Iiro Jääskeläinen and colleagues are to be credited for creating the first ever experimental setting of this kind in which volunteers continuously watched the full-length film *Crash* (directed by Paul Haggis 2004), the first 72 minutes outside and the remaining 36 minutes inside the fMRI scanner (Jääskeläinen et al.). The study provided some hints as to where in the brain narrative sense-making activity takes place, given full-length film stimuli. They reported higher intersubject correlations on the right frontal parts than on the left regions of the brain (19), suggesting the dominance of right hemisphere in narrative comprehension, a finding that many other researchers using long-durational stimulus have since confirmed (Mar; Kauttonen et al.).

Several fMRI studies have revealed that narrative sense-making overrides the effect of the storytelling medium. Apparently, the human mind is able to generalize understanding from phenomenal events and event structures regardless of how the narratives are mediated. One of our studies compared reactions to viewing a drama film episode of a young girl witnessing her mother's nervous breakdown (*Heartbeats*, dir. Saara Cantell), *and* reading the same dramatized events in the screenplay text (Tikka et al.). In this comparison we identified what we call a set of narrative comprehension networks that were synchronized across subjects in both textual and audiovisual conditions. The study is in line with others in showing that the broad socio-emotional context of narratives engages "higher-level" brain areas in a holistic manner, i.e., beyond the "lower-level" sensory modalities that activate based on media-specific visual or auditory qualities of the stimulus of the linguistic difference between languages (Deniz et al.; Honey et al.). In a study by Mai Nguyen and colleagues the test subjects had been either viewing an ambiguous animation film (dynamically moving shapes) or listening only to a verbal description of the story, narrating the movements of the shapes as social characters. The participants were then asked how they interpreted the narrative they had been engaged with. The data analysis revealed intersubject correlations between brain activations of those subjects who shared understanding of the story, *independent* of listening, viewing, or retelling the story in their own words (Nguyen et al. 167). These findings suggest that deep cognitive sense-making overrides effects of the medium. Importantly, in our view these results also highlight the interrelation of autonarration (subjective experience) and intersubjective narration.

These findings may not reveal much of the phenomenological experience per se, but they might capture what we refer to as *deictic enaction* at its deepest level, the one of embodied faculties shared by the human species, and situated in a world filled with intersubjectively shared narratives. Christopher Baldassano and his team were able to identify brain areas sensitive to shared temporal structures that relate to information not only from the on-going narrative, but also from high-level situation models, i.e., schematic event scripts, such as restaurant or airport experiences (2018). Reaching beyond any film narrative's time-locked temporality, such experiential contextualization can be seen as long-tailed (even life-long) retention in Husserlian terms. Even though new light has recently been cast on the precuneus—a brain area typically involved in movie viewing—and its role utilizing contextual information for the retrieval of temporal order in films (Foudil et al.), the ways in which memory and lived experiences affect moment-to-moment narrative sense-making still require more study.

Zacks and his coworkers have shown that in complex life-like settings there is an automated recognition of the border of events in the brain that supports cognitive sense-making through the anticipation of the duration of events (Zacks et al.). Any human annotation of contextual events synchronized in time-locked manner with a test subjects' functional brain data (Lahnakoski et al.; Kauttonen et al., "Model of Narrative"; Kauttonen et al., "Optimizing Methods") can be assumed to emerge from such automated event recognition processes. On the dynamic view of the brain-body relation, there are no isolated "events" as such; events only exist in the context of the enactment of a world as a whole, during an emergent momentary expression of a living system. To tackle this complexity, we selected the puzzle film *Memento* (dir. Christopher Nolan, 2000) as stimulus in one of our fMRI studies on the neural basis of narrative sense-making (Kauttonen et al., "Brain Mechanisms"). What makes the film both challenging and captivating for the viewers is that the narrative scenes of *Memento* unfold

THE UNFOLDING NOW   165

in reverse chronological order. Could the context-dependency of specific temporally distant, yet time-locked events be detected in brain behavior? Our study focused on fifteen short sequences, each of which is repeated once at some point of the story, thereby anchoring it to another previously presented scene with the same image. Every repetitive image reveals new information of the previously seen scenes to the spectator in a kind of aha moment. We propose that by perceiving temporally distant but partly overlapping scenes as continuous, the viewer re-constructs the story anew at each of these moments. The scrutiny of these repetitive manifestations of the same phenomenon allowed us to identify a unique functional brain network that arguably represents a neural fingerprint pattern for narrative sense-making, related to integrating previous and freshly gained information (Kauttonen et al., "Brain Mechanisms"). However, the question remains what exactly takes place at the narrative sense-making level during these repetitions that is specific for the unique neural network we identified. What makes our finding intriguing—and raises new questions—is that all 15 event pairs are totally different in terms of their auditory and visual features, and in terms of the narrative content they convey.

Narrative sense-making in different contexts can be studied by priming the viewing in varying ways to activate distinct perspectives on the same narrative scenes—such as different autobiographical contexts—and compare the neural activations and/or verbal descriptions between different groups. In a study by Juha Lahnakoski and colleagues, two groups of viewers were primed to watch the same film scenes either as interior decorators or crime detectives. Eye-tracking showed that the subjects simulating the perspective of interior decorator mainly watched the environment and objects around the characters, while the perspective of crime detective focused mainly on the faces of characters. Both groups were presumably engaged in cognitive mirroring and mentalizing processes, however, the given tasks guided them to either focus on objects or social cues, both processed in two relatively well distinguished functional networks in the brain. This behavior resulted in clear differences in the brain signals (Lahnakoski et al., "Synchronous Brain Activity"), thus highlighting the crucial role of context-awareness beyond the audiovisual cues. Another study by Orit Furman and colleagues sheds light on the context-dependency of retentive event decay on a long temporal scale. They show that the movie plot and social relations are the best remembered features of films after several months, while the memory of decontextualized jokes declines in a few weeks' time (Furman et al.). In sum, contemporary neuroimaging has a valuable repertoire of methods at its disposal to study narrative context dependency. In our view, this justifies expectations for the experimental observation of autonarrative retention as a key to sense-making.

While the context-dependency of retentive aspects is a challenge for neuroscientific studies, the protentive dimension is even harder to investigate. However, it is possible to study this dimension from a neurocinematics perspective as well, as shown by Gal Raz and Talma Hendler. Based on an fMRI study, they suggest that movie-viewing may involve two functionally separate empathy networks that operate depending on the temporal status of the narrative event in question: When the anticipated death of a character will take place in the distant future, the viewer's *cognitive empathy* processes seem to correlate with mentalizing capacities to predict other people's future fate. *Affective empathy*, in turn, emerges in the embodied simulation processes of the viewer when making sense of the character's on-going painful situation (Raz and Hendler). As in life outside cinema, in the lived moment of narrative nowness the shocking news of someone's death calls for different embodied sense-making strategies than death taking place in the past or in the future. These are encouraging research results for the project of binding together the experiential structures of retention, protention, and narrative nowness from a neurophenomenological perspective.

In different ways, the studies we discussed in this section explore phenomeno-physiological aspects of narrative sense-making and allow us to argue for cinematic narrative as a particularly advantageous medium for the study of narrative experience. First, films can be conceived of as a simulation of complex events in the world and are therefore well fit to be applied as stimuli for neuroscientific experiments aiming at understanding the encounter of the brain and the world. Secondly, full-length films can simulate temporally extended narratives and are therefore relevant for the study of autonarrative, contextualized sense-making at scales far beyond short and limited events. Thirdly, due to its temporal nature, the medium allows for the synchronization of shared annotations, self-described experiences, and psychophysiological enactment of the unfolding narration in a time locked manner, facilitating a reciprocal analysis of the data.

6   Conclusion

Departing from the enactive mind approach and neurophenomenology, we have put forward the idea that the root of narration lies in subjective sense-making of the world, or autonarration, and that it manifests itself at both a neural and experiential level. Both autonarration and intersubjective narration rely on a range of embodied faculties—such as mirroring and mentalizing—and on the worldly affordances common to the human species, therefore supporting the prediction and understanding of actions and intentions of others. From these embodied dynamics, we have turned to the intersubjective world by elaborating on the idea of deixis as the shared focus and joined action that bridges individually embodied experiences via synchronized encounters with others.

While the current findings are only precursory, they point towards a future research program in which the understanding of the brain-body-world system can be increased via a triangular epistemology: Although a direct mapping from experience to psychophysiology is not possible, experience can be studied indirectly via observable deictic foci (interpersonally shared pointers to events of the world). New insights about a story's experiential effects can be generated by means of interpreting authored narration as deliberately designed deixis. And while reported first-person experiences do not go hand in hand with context-annotations of film, experiments with variously induced autonarrative contexts may shed light on systemic regularities among subjective experiences and their intersubjective shareability.

In sum, the "worlding the brain" perspective for us implies a two-directional approach. On one hand, the world is continuously simulated by means of individual autonarration, i.e., the brain is being "worlded" inwards. On the other hand, a worlding of the brain also happens when autonarratives of subjective nature are extended to the intersubjective domain via embodied faculties common to the human species; hence, autonarratives are also "worlded" outwards.

Acknowledgments

The work has been funded by the EU Mobilitas Pluss Top Researcher Grant (MOBTT90), Estonian Research Council in association with the Baltic Film, Media, Arts and Communication School, Tallinn University.

References

Baldassano, Christopher, et al. "Representation of Real-World Event Schemas during Narrative Perception." *Journal of Neuroscience,* vol. 38, no. 45, 2018.

Bruner, Jerome. "Life as Narrative." *Social Research*, vol. 54, no. 1, 1987, pp. 11–32.

Crash. Directed by Paul Haggis, Lions Gate Films, USA, 2004.

"Deixis." Merriam-Webster's Learners Dictionary, *Merriam-Webster*. www.merriam -webster.com/dictionary/deixis.

Deniz, Fatma, et al. "The Representation of Semantic Information across Human Cerebral Cortex during Listening cersus Reading Is Invariant to Stimulus Modality." *Journal of Neuroscience*, vol. 39, no. 39, 2019, pp. 7722–36.

Foudil, Samy-Adrien, et al. "Context-Dependent Coding of Temporal Distance between Cinematic Events in the Human Precuneus." *Journal of Neuroscience*, vol. 40, no. 10, 2020, pp. 2129–38.

Frith, Chris, and Uta Frith. "Theory of Mind." *Current Biology*, vol. 15, no. 17, 2005, pp. 644–45.

Furman, Orit, et al. "They Saw a Movie: Long-Term Memory for an Extended Audiovisual Narrative." *Learning & Memory*, vol. 146, 2007, pp. 457–67.

Gallese, Vittorio. "Mirror Neurons, Embodied Simulation, and the Neural Basis of Social Identification." *Psychoanalytic Dialogues*, vol. 195, 2009, pp. 519–36.

Hasson, Uri, et al. "Intersubject Synchronization of Cortical Activity during Natural Vision." *Science*, vol. 303, no. 12, 2004, pp. 1634–40.

Hasson, Uri, et al. "Neurocinematics: The Neuroscience of Film." *Projections*, vol. 2, no. 1, 2008, pp. 1–26.

Heartbeats. Directed by Saara Cantell, Pystymetsä Productions, Finland, 2009.

Honey, Christopher J., et al. "Not Lost in Translation: Neural Responses Shared across Languages." *Journal of Neuroscience*, vol. 32, no. 44, 2012, pp. 15277–83.

Husserl, Edmund. *The Phenomenology of Internal Time Consciousness* [*Zur Phänomenologie des inneren Zeitbewusstseins* 1893–1917]. Translated by J.S. Churchill, Indiana University Press, 1964.

Jääskeläinen, Iiro, et al. "Inter-Subject Synchronization of Prefrontal Cortex Hemodynamic Activity during Natural Viewing." *The Open Neuroimaging Journal*, vol. 2, 2008, pp. 14–19.

Jääskeläinen, Iiro, et al. "Neural Processing of Narratives: From Individual Processing to Viral Propagation." *Frontiers in Human Neuroscience*, vol. 14, art. 253, 2020.

Jääskeläinen, Iiro, et al. "Movies and Narratives as Naturalistic Stimuli in Neuroimaging." *NeuroImage*, vol. 224, art. 117445, 2021.

James, William. *The Principles of Psychology*. Vol. 1, Holt, 1890.

Kauttonen, Janne, et al. "Model of Narrative Nowness for Neurocinematic Experiments." *Proceedings 5th Workshop on Computational Models of Narrative*, Dagstuhl Publishing, 2014, pp. 77–87.

Kauttonen, Janne, et al. "Optimizing Methods for Linking Cinematic Features to fMRI data." *NeuroImage*, vol. 110, 2015, pp. 136–48.

Kauttonen, Janne, et al. "Brain Mechanisms Underlying Cue-Based Memorizing during Free Viewing of Movie Memento." *NeuroImage*, vol. 172, 2018, pp. 313–25.

Lahnakoski, Juha M., et al. "Stimulus-Related Independent Component and Voxel-Wise Analysis of Human Brain Activity during Free Viewing of a Feature Film." *PLOS One*, vol. 7, no. 4, 2012.

THE UNFOLDING NOW 169

Lahnakoski, Juha M., et al. "Synchronous Brain Activity across Individuals Underlies Shared Psychological Perspectives." *NeuroImage*, vol. 100, 2014, pp. 316–24.

Lakoff, George, and Mark Johnson. *Metaphors We Live By*. U of Chicago P, 1980.

Machado, Antonio. "Proverbios y Cantares XXIX." *Selected Poems of Antonio Machado*, translated by Betty Jean Craige, Lousiana State UP, 1978.

Mar, Raymond A. "The Neural Bases of Social Cognition and Story Comprehension." *Annual Review of Psychology*, vol. 62, 2011, pp. 103–134.

Maturana, Humberto, and Francisco Varela. *Autopoiesis and Cognition: The Realization of the Living*, Reidel, 1980.

Memento. Directed by Cristopher Nolan, 2000.

Monteagudo, José González. "Jerome Bruner and the Challenges of the Narrative Turn: Then and now." *Narrative Inquiry*, vol. 21, no. 2, 2011, pp. 295–302.

Nguyen, Mai, et al. "Shared Understanding of Narratives Is Correlated with Shared Neural Responses." *NeuroImage*, vol. 184, 2019, pp. 161–70.

Petitmengin, Claire, et al. "Discovering the Structures of Lived Experience. Towards a Micro–Phenomenological Analysis Method." *Phenomenology and the Cognitive Sciences*, vol. 18, no. 4, 2018, pp. 691–730.

Raz, Gal, and Talma Hendler. "Forking Cinematic Paths to the Self: Neurocinematically Informed Model of Empathy in Motion Pictures." *Projections*, vol. 8, no. 2, 2014, pp. 89–114.

Sarbin, Theodore R. *Narrative Psychology: The Storied Nature of Human Conduct*, Praeger Publishers, 1986.

Tikka, Pia. *Enactive Cinema: Simulatorium Eisensteinense*. Publication Series of the University of Art and Design, Helsinki, 2008.

Tikka, Pia, and Mauri Kaipainen. "Phenomenological Considerations on Time Consciousness under Neurocinematic Search Light." *Cinema&Cie*, vol. 14, no. 2–3, 2014, pp. 91–103.

Tikka, Pia, and Mauri Kaipainen. "Intersubjectivity, Idiosyncrasy and Narrative Deixis – a Neurocinematic Approach." *Narrative Complexity: Cognition, Embodiment, Evolution*, edited by Marina Grishakova and Maria Poulaki, U of Nebraska P, 2019.

Varela, Francisco J. "Laying down a Path in Walking." *Gaia: A Way of Knowing*, edited by William Irwin Thompson, Lindisfarne Press, 1987, pp. 48–64.

Varela, Francisco J. "Neurophenomenology: A Methodological Remedy for the Hard Problem." *Journal of Consciousness Studies*, vol. 3, no. 4, 1996, pp. 330–49.

Varela, Francisco J. "The Specious Present: A Neurophenomenology of Time Consciousness." *Naturalizing Phenomenology: Issues in Contemporary Phenomenology and Cognitive Science*, edited by Jean Petitot et al., Stanford UP, 1999.

Varela, Francisco J., et al. *The Embodied Mind: Cognitive Science and Human experience*, MIT Press, 1991.

Vassilieva, Julia. "The Narrative Turn in Psychology." *Narrative Psychology: Identity, Transformation and Ethics*, edited by Julia Vassilieva, Palgrave Macmillan, 2016, pp. 9–47.

Vygotsky, Lev S. *Mind in Society: The Development of Higher Psychological Processes.* Harvard UP, 1978.

Zacks, Jeffrey M., et al. "The Brain's Cutting-Room Floor: Segmentation of Narrative Cinema." *Frontiers in Human Neuroscience*, vol. 4, art. 168, 2010.

PART 3

Figuring the Brain

CHAPTER 11

Set and Setting of the Brain on Hallucinogen

Psychedelic Revival in the Acid Western

Patricia Pisters

1 Introduction: the Psychedelic Renaissance

Hallucinogenic and other brain stimulants have been part of human culture for ages. Varying from the use of peyote in Native American tribes to psilocybin in Mexican *curandera* practices and ayahuasca in Amazonian rituals, hallucinogens in indigenous cultures are deeply rooted and integrated in practices of wisdom and healing (Davis; Adelaars et al.). European cultures, however, have labeled altered states of consciousness and alternative knowledge systems related to plant medicine and practices that are not aligned with patriarchal laws of State and Church as work of the devil, as phenomena that must be eradicated, as in the case of witch hunts (Papasyrou et al.). The secret and sacred traditions of altering consciousness met again in psychedelic research and culture of the 1960s, when psychedelics were used in clinical experiments as well as in counter-cultural settings. In the United States and other Western cultures, Nixon's War on Drugs declaration in 1971 put an end to many of these practices in the ensuing decades, when scientific use of mind manifesting drugs was banned and went underground in subcultural circles (Greer) and was partially continued in the rave culture of the 1980s and 1990s, although XTC and MDMA are considered empathogens rather than hallucinogens. In Latin America and among indigenous cultures in other parts of the world there was no such radical rupture in the legal and cultural status of hallucinogens.[1]

Recent suggestions of a *psychedelic renaissance* refer to the revival of hallucinogen research in the West that picked up again in the 1990s and which has evolved rapidly during the last two decades. In *Neuropsychedelia* (2013), Nicholas Langlitz maps out how this research has progressed in the decade of the brain, while Michael Pollan's *How to Change Your Mind* (2018) situates the popularization of the psychedelic revival in a broader cultural context.

---

1 In Peru, for instance, ayahuasca officially belongs to the national heritage. One also has to note here that the Spanish conquistadors did eliminate many indigenous cultures and shamanic practices in the colonialization of the Americas.

© KONINKLIJKE BRILL NV, LEIDEN, 2023 | DOI:10.1163/9789004681293_013

Langlitz focuses on the rise of neuropsychopharmacology as a field of research centered on neuroscientific and psychiatric clinical studies on the therapeutic effects of ketamine, MDMA, psilocybin, and LSD to treat depression, post-traumatic stress, and other mental conditions, a development that is slowly but surely changing the field of psychiatry (Tullis). However, contrary to symptom-suppressing medications such as anti-depressants and anti-psychotics, the use of psychedelics raises philosophical and religious questions about the human soul and its relation to nature, the world, and the cosmos. Because of their healing, spiritual, and entheogenic potential that open new "doors of perception" (Huxley), psychedelics demand a more holistic and transdisciplinary approach that goes beyond the scope of the bio-medical sciences.[2]

Moreover, as Eric Davis argues in *High Weirdness*, the extra-ordinary perceptions and experiences that come with psychedelics are "weirdly mediated a lot of the time," often through myths, stories, and images in popular culture and media technology (31). Hence, to gain a better understanding of the novel questions raised by the current psychedelic renaissance, it is vital to interrogate the past and present of the media forms and repertoires in and through which new psychedelic understandings emerge. In the following, I will examine emblematic and historically changing cinematic reflections on psychedelia through the lens of one specific popular film genre, the so-called "acid Western." The choice of this subgenre is pragmatic, in the sense that its relation to psychedelics and its peculiar manifestations is explicit, even if sometimes only generic.[3] Many other relations between film and drugs can be made (James), but these are beyond the scope of this chapter. By considering acid Westerns as a type of fictional trip reports that resonate with broader developments in society, I will ask how this genre helps to trace a "worlding of the brain on hallucinogens" that is indicative of the psychedelic renaissance.[4]

---

2 The other scientific fields that are strongly involved in the psychedelic renaissance are anthropology and ethnobotany (see Adams et al.; Luke and Spowers).

3 The term "acid" refers to LSD, but as a genre reference it is often taken as a more generic term, taking LSD as prototypical psychedelic, even if other psychotropics are often referred to in the films that are designated by this term, especially in its transformations after the 1970s.

4 See Doyle 2013 for an extensive study on the value of trip reports as scientific method. By "worlding of the brain" I refer to the scope of this volume to stage an encounter between bio-medical and cognitive science of the brain and social and cultural disciplines.

SET AND SETTING OF THE BRAIN ON HALLUCINOGEN   175

2   Collective Set and Setting of the Hippie Exploitation Film and the
     Acid Western

After Timothy Leary introduced the concepts of *set* and *setting* in psychedelic
experiments, they have become an integral part of psychedelic practices and
discourse. Set, or mind set, refers to personality, expectation, and intention
of the person taking a psychedelic substance. Setting indicates the social,
physical, and cultural environment in which the experience takes place. In
his book *American Trip*, Ido Hartogsohn has proposed that set and setting are
not only important for individual experiences but also have an important collective dimension. Across several large sets and settings (such as the experimental psychosis movement in psychiatry or experiments by the CIA and
Silicon Valley psychedelic innovation workshops), Hartogsohn demonstrates
that the effects of psychedelics are "predominantly the result of sociocultural
tendencies and interpretations" (12). Hartogsohn argues, for example, that the
notorious *bad trip* became more prominent as an experience "after the media
started to report more on this phenomena and societal and political consensus moved towards the war on drugs" (206). Hence, psychedelic experience
are shaped by multiple feedback loops between psychedelic substances and
(mediated) cultural repertoires in society.

   The creative and artistic field of the 1960s is the pre-eminent example of
the close entanglement of psychedelic manifestations with their societal and
collective set and setting (Hartogsohn; Davis; Das and Metzner). As a cultural
style we are all familiar with the cliché curly letters and patterns on psychedelic posters, the flower power hippie-look, and the typical dreamy or acid
music styles, ranging from the Beatles to Jefferson Airplane and Jimmy Hen-
drix. Moreover, the 1960s saw experiments with artistic creativity by adminis-
trating LSD to painters, writers, musicians, actors, and filmmakers (Hartogsohn
131); many artists self-experimented with psychedelics, as did tech-innovators
in Silicon Valley (Markoff; Turner *Counterculture*). As one organizer of a psychedelic training workshop explained: "We said, for instance, you can try to
identify with the problem from other vantage points than you'd usually use.
You can see the solution. Visualize the part. Go inside the various parts of the
physical apparatus. (...) You can see it in fresh perspectives" (Hartogsohn 157).
LSD, mescaline, or psilocybin were not seen as an easy fix for problems of creativity but certainly as potential mental boosters. As creative catalysts, psychedelics generated varying stylistic repertoires in different cultural contexts.
Hartogsohn mentions the difference, for instance, between the rowdy acid
tests of the West Coast's sunny beaches and the grittier New York variation of
psychedelia, more related to speed and the artistic underground scene (142).

Cinema has played an important role in the popularization of ideas about psychedelia and forms its own collective set and setting. While trippy science fiction films like *2001: A Space Odyssey* (Stanley Kubrick, 1968) and drug-infused road movies such as *Easy Rider* (Dennis Hopper, 1969) were shaping and shaped by a particular *zeitgeist*, many of the controversies around psychedelics also found their way in the B-genre of the so-called hippie exploitation film.[5] After the CIA's loss of interest in LSD as potential mind control weapon, the rising scandals around the figure of Timothy Leary, and the association of drugs with anti-government protests and rebellion during the Vietnam War, the discourse on these mind expanders got marked by larger societal narratives of disapprobation. Michael DeAngelis cites a 1963 article in the *Saturday Evening Post* entitled "The Dangerous Magic of LSD" as exemplary for the way in which a general fear for LSD was provoked and associated with pathology and mind control (130). The portrayal of psychedelics in films such as *Hallucination Generation* (Edward Mann, 1966), *Riot on Sunset Strip* (Arthur Dreyfus, 1967), *The Love-Ins* (Arthur Dreyfus, 1967), and *Psych-out* (Richard Russ, 1968), catered to a young generation, yet eventually subscribed to the cultural consensus of the older generation that tripping is bad and thus by and large followed the general consensus of the dominant set and setting of the War on Drugs. Only a few films, such as *The Trip* (Roger Corman, 1967) and *Skidoo* (Otto Preminger, 1968) give more nuanced perspectives on the potential dangers but also therapeutic benefits and entheogenic or spiritual insights produced by psychedelics. *The Trip* was praised for its authentic depiction of the experiences of its tripping protagonist Paul (Peter Fonda), who at one point exclaims that an orange is like holding the sun in his hands, and that he can see right through his own brain. Paul also confronts his marriage problems, emphasizing the therapeutic value of his psychedelic journey (DeAngelis 139–140). Hence, these 1960s films can be considered time capsules that embody the generation conflict over psychedelics.

The *acid Western* is a subgenre within the domain of countercultural hippie films that appropriates the repertoire of the Western to translate the psychedelic mindset by stretching the rules of the genre. The Western is pre-eminently bound up with the emergence and development of Hollywood film culture itself. André Bazin called the Western "cinema par excellence" (141). Defined by its setting in the frontier towns and vast landscapes of the American West and

---

5   While the "hippie" is considered an American invention, it is a transnational phenomenon. European hippie "trash" or cult films include, for instance, *A Lizard in a Woman's Skin* (Lucio Fulci, 1971) and *Performance* (Nicholas Roeg, 1970). See also the documentary *Soviet Hippies* (Terje Toomistu, 2017).

SET AND SETTING OF THE BRAIN ON HALLUCINOGEN 177

by the iconic figure of the cowboy as the image of heroic masculinity, the genre is (not unproblematically) associated with mythological adventure and conquest. John Ford's *Stage Coach* (1939) is often cited as the prototypical Western and demonstrates, in Bazin's words, a "maturity of a style brought to classic perfection" (149). The genre has been revised both from within Hollywood (the revisionist Westerns of Arthur Penn, for instance, create more space for Native American perspectives, albeit still mediated by a white male protagonist) and from outside Hollywood, as in the famous spaghetti Westerns of Sergio Leone that present a more cynical view on the violence and monetary motives of its heroes.

The aura of absolute freedom associated with the cowboy, and even the cowboy aesthetics, nevertheless also resonated with the countercultural generation. A case in point are Dennis Hopper's hippie cowboy looks and the transformation of the Western image of freedom into the road movie in his film *Easy Rider*. The acid Western resonates with the psychedelic rebellious counter-cultural spirits of the time, when psychedelics were already on the list of forbidden substances, the bad trip had gained prominence and when the ideals of freedom and flower power had moved into more vehement political protests and demonstrations against the Vietnam War and for sexual liberation and racial equality. In a way, the acid Western can thus be understood as a stylistic protest genre against the established rules. It designates a subgenre of the Western that puts genre conventions completely upside down in combining the masculine violence of the classic western with the absurd to "conjure up a crazed version of auto-destructive white America" (Rosenbaum). Alejandro Jodorowsky's *El Topo* (1970) and Dennis Hopper's *The Last Movie* (1971) were released around the same time and point to different aspects of the connections between psychedelics and cinema in the rebellious spirit of the late 1960s and early 1970s.[6]

The term "acid Western" was coined by film critic Pauline Kael after the release of *El Topo* in 1971, describing how the film turned into an instant cult phenomenon that was shown for months in packed midnight theaters in New York (Rosenbaum; Mikulec). Kael's term actually referred to the doped midnight audience that was watching Jodorowsky's film and not to the film itself. Nevertheless, *El Topo* came to designate certain transformations of the Western genre associated with the acid aesthetics of the counterculture. Working

---

6   *El Topo* was the first film marked as acid Western. Later other (also earlier) films have been added, such as *The Shooting* (Monte Helmann, 1966), *Zachariah* (George Englund, 1971), *Greaser's Palace* (Robert Downey Sr., 1972). *Walker* (Alex Cox, 1987) and *Dead Man* (Jim Jarmush, 1995) have also been labelled acid Westerns.

outside Hollywood, and shooting in Mexico on an extremely low budget, Jodorowsky transformed the exploitation genre in his own idiosyncratic way by creating images that "create a mental change" in a film that "is LSD without LSD" (Jodorowsky in Ivan-Zadey).

Jodorowsky himself plays El Topo, the black leathered cowboy who goes on a bizarre symbolic and spiritual quest in the desert which, halfway into the film, leads to his rebirth in a cave where he helps to escape the wretched of the nearby town by digging a tunnel. There is plenty of blood, sex, and violence in the mise-en-scène, but in the end one realizes that this is all part of a process of soul searching that involves both virtues and vices. By putting all genre rules upside down, remixing with incredible affective intensity the collective ideas and images about masculinity and femininity, violence, and sexuality, Jodorowsky proves to be a mind bending artist who bypasses the collective norms of the time by creating his own set and setting that therefore gains perennial qualities. *El Topo* undermines genre conventions by brewing all its elements in a surreal and alchemical transformation, which creates a psychedelic experience without any drug. The images themselves are colorful, extreme and hallucinatory, disturbing and insightful at the same time. And as such, *El Topo* reflects both the insubordinate spirit as the weirdness of the collective psychedelic set and setting of the 1960s and early 1970s.

3   **Blowing up Hollywood: *The Last Movie's* Hallucinatory Sexism and Racism**

While Jodorowsky came to the film industry as an outsider and used the Western genre as an entrance point to create his own peculiar psychedelic universe, Dennis Hopper was an insider of Hollywood who unraveled genre conventions from within the system. *The Last Movie* feels like a feverish bad trip. However, unlike other hippie exploitation films, this is not a film *about* drugs but rather a film made *on* drugs. Much of the chaos and of the sex, drugs, and alcohol that we see consumed in front of the camera reflects the crew's behavior on and off set (Chinchero was famous for its cocaine production at the time). The psychedelic nature of the film is conveyed by the unruly, jagged editing and the wildly looping self-reflexive and hyperbolic style of the mise-en-scène (Kohn; Ayd).

Hopper himself plays the lead in *The Last Movie,* similar to Jodorowsky's appearance in *El Topo.* Hopper is Kansas, a disillusioned and depressed stuntman of a Hollywood Western that was shot in the Peruvian Andes. Kansas stays in the Peruvian village after the production is wrapped and hooks up with a local prostitute Maria (Stella Garcia). The villagers use the décor of the film for reenacting their own version of the script, using film equipment made out of wooden sticks and replacing fake violence for real violence. On this meta-level, *The Last Movie* seamlessly mixes the actual shooting conditions, the genre of the Hollywood Western, and the version of the Western shot by the locals to question the role of cinema. By demonstrating how real violence and actual violence bleed into one another, *The Last Movie* questions the influence of Hollywood tropes and stereotypes. The few scenes in "the film in the film" that is produced by the Hollywood crew consists only of shoot outs and extreme violence: everybody shoots everybody, laying bare the deeply rooted violence of the conquest of the West. This violence in and of (Hollywood) filmmaking is shown to the point of troubling absurdity in the mise-en-scène of guns and falling and bleeding bodies. Moreover, by dismantling the entire grammar of the plot by presenting the events in non-chronological order (even the titles of the film appear at several moments throughout the film), *The Last Movie* explicitly shows the distressing building blocks of sexism and colonialism.

Hence, on this very concrete level of the mise-en-scène and editing of the film, *The Last Movie* both confirms and destroys the myths of the Western and thus reflects the revolutionary protest spirits of the counterculture. As a masculine genre, the Western actually exemplifies the entire Hollywood industry and a society dominated by the white male gaze, much criticized by the emancipation movements of the 1970s. By calling his film *The Last Movie*, Hopper shows the destructive extremes of dominant (Hollywood) culture, while also participating in it. The depiction of women as worthless objects is painful to watch. Even if one scene shows how Kansas himself is hit by a woman, this does not make up for the evident sexism and violence against women in the film. The colonial gesture of the invasion of a Western film crew in the Peruvian village Chinchero cannot be ignored either. The fact that the indigenous natives re-enact the movie-making ritual reinforces the notion that Hollywood also colonizes peoples' mental spaces with these violent ideas. The film can certainly be seen as subscribing to all these problematic dimensions of the Western. And yet, because of all its subversive elements in style and production, the message of *The Last Movie* at the same time also feverishly announces the end of an era by dismantling the Hollywood film industry and its inherent power structures.

Where the violence in *El Topo* is surreal and symbolic and part of a trajectory of spiritual death and rebirth, the violence in *The Last Movie* is allegorical, exposing the Western (and Hollywood more broadly) as part of Western patriarchal colonialism that is based on the desire for conquest. Because of this, both films are at times hard to watch, and yet, they are also quite remarkable acid Westerns that each in their own way refract the conventions of filmmaking and open new perspectives. They remain unique sign posts in cinema, that mark the end of the countercultural era where the collective set and setting of psychedelics was colored by the disillusion of the flower power movement and its insistent association with the bad trip. In the meantime, the war on drugs and the ban on psychedelia had stopped most clinical studies on the use of psychedelia. Culturally, the hippie scenes everywhere in the world were replaced by other subcultures and youth scenes, including the ravers of the 1980s and 1990s, when XTC took over from the classic psychedelics of the 1960s counterculture. More recently, with the emergence of a new psychedelic renaissance since the 2000s, there has been a remarkable return to the tradition of the acid Western. Tracing the similarities and difference between these recent examples and the acid Westerns of the psychedelic revolution in the 1970s helps to understand the shifting but persistent critical potential of genre subversion.

4   *Blueberry*'s Ayahuasca Gold Rush and the "Western" Quest for Shamanic Healing

Since the 2000s, a growing number of clinical and neuroscientific experiments in the therapeutic properties of psychedelia are prudently set up. Such experiments need to be carefully monitored and mediated to gradually counter the longstanding controversial imago of psychedelics (Langlitz; Calvey; Pollan). Recent documentaries such as *Trip of Compassion* (Gil Karni, 2017) and *From Shock to Awe* (Luc Coté, 2018) show the experiences of several patients with severe symptoms of trauma when they receive treatment with MDMA or ayahuasca. They present deeply moving insights in the remarkable effects these drugs have on patients and the different approach they demand from doctors, psychiatrists, or shamans, who guide the patients in their journey toward healing. In these and other popular media productions, such as the Netflix feature *Have a Good Trip* (Donic Cary, 2020), there is a noticeable shift in the way drug culture is portrayed that resonates with larger societal changes towards the brain on hallucinogen. Additionally, in fiction film there is also renewed attention for narratives about substance use and the integration of an immersive psychedelic style. Contemporary versions of the "acid Western" reveal a number of updates to the genre. One striking revision is that, more explicitly than before, the typical American genre of the Western has become a "global genre" (Costanzo 204).[7] Two contemporary acid Westerns provide particularly

---

7   Jodorowsky and the spaghetti Western were mentioned before. The Wuxia, Samurai, and Kung Fu films made in China, Japan, and Hong Kong have influenced and been influenced

SET AND SETTING OF THE BRAIN ON HALLUCINOGEN 181

salient expressions of the new cultural dimensions of the contemporary psychedelic revival: Jan Kounen's ayahuasca Western *Blueberry* (2004) and Kleber Mendonça Filho and Juliano Dornelles's psychotropic Western *Bacurau* (2019).

Kounen's *Blueberry* can be considered a film that previsions the current psychedelic revival, which is commonly marked by a large 2006 symposium on LSD in Basel, organized on the occasion of the 100th birthday of Albert Hofmann, the inventor of LSD. *Blueberry* is loosely inspired by the *Moebius* comics of Jean Giraud (started in the 1960s) and presents the story of Mike Blueberry (Vincent Cassel), nicknamed Broken Nose. The film is shot in the Mexican desert, featuring typical Western elements such as cowboys, saloons, greedy gold rushers, and Native Americans. However, contrary to the previous recalcitrant acid Westerns, in *Blueberry* the Amazonian ayahuasca rituals feature as the film's "mind set," based on Kounen's experiences with these sacred ceremonies during his frequent visits to Peru in the 1990s. In his 2015 book *Visionary Ayahuasca*, Kounen presents the notes of his inner journeys to meet healers and to undergo "a few hundred ceremonies" (1) that he practices with the indigenous Shipibo people. He is therefore dubbed a "cineaste ayahuasquero" (1), a filmmaker who embraces ayahuasca. The journey notes are composed as a "metaphysical drama, constructed in flashback mode" (4), in which Kounen himself is the hero, much like his hero in *Blueberry*.

Looking at *Blueberry* in relation to the 1970s acid Westerns of Jodorowsky and Hopper, it is striking to see that the iconography and the grammar of the Western remains more intact compared to the crazy and intense transformative symbolism of *El Topo* and the wild achronological self-reflexive and self-destructive structure of *The Last Movie*. *Blueberry* stays closer to the traditional storyline of the genre: a stranger arrives in a typical Western town, enters into a conflict and, after several duels and shoot outs, there is a resolution of the conflict. However, in *Blueberry* the sought after gold is not the precious stone of the traditional goldrush but the secret and holy ayahuasca brew that creates deep insights and is the source of healing. Ayahuasca, as spiritual gold, has been integrated into the narrative where Blueberry confronts the villain Blount (Michael Madsen) inside the Sacred Mountain, where they challenge each other in a trip. In this sense, it is possible to read *Blueberry* as a visionary allegory of the current psychedelic revival, which sometimes is indicated as the psychedelic goldrush, referring to the countless capital ventures and startups that have discovered psychedelics as a new "gold mine" (Farah). Obviously, the development of entrepreneurship and patents is not without

---

by the Western. *The Good, the Bad, the Weird* (Kim Jee-Woon, 2008) is a Korean translation of the spaghetti Western.

risks of appropriating and stealing from indigenous communities that are not included in these ventures (Gerber et al.).

At the same time, *Blueberry* also reflects another dimension of the psychedelic revival. Rather than being focused on countercultural rebellion, the European and North American cinematic manifestations of the psychedelic renaissance are directed towards healing. Kounen's Western is a healing journey in which Blueberry confronts his traumatic memories with the help of the spiritual guidance of his Native American friend Runi (Temuera Morrison), whose family took care of Blueberry after he was found wounded. While the theme of a white man growing up with Native Americans is not new—in fact, it is a central fantasy in revisionist Westerns such as Arthur Penn's *Little Big Man* (1970) and Kevin Costner's *Dances with Wolves* (1990)—the emphasis on traumatic memories and healing via plant medicine is clearly a new dimension that is part of the current psychedelic revival, previsioned by *Blueberry*. In the film, the ayahuasca visions are represented in splendidly immersive images, full of graphic details in golden mandalas, bird's eyes perspective in flight, and (scary) confrontations with totemic and archetypical animals that guide the hero to see the painful and repressed truth of his memories.[8] Only when Blueberry confronts his own inner demons, he can fight his opponent. Rather than subversively undermining the genre of the Western, Kounen opens it up to inner visions and spiritual growth. It could thus be argued that *Blueberry* is exemplary for the psychedelic renaissance: instead of resonating with a rebellious counter-culture, the film reflects a spirit of integration into existing practices.

As in other Westerns, the role of women has not changed much (it is the favorite prostitute of both Blueberry and Blount who is the direct cause of their conflict; and because she dies, she is also the source of Blueberry's trauma). In regard to gender, the rules of the genre basically remain the same. In turn, the colonialism that is part of *The Last Movie* has now been replaced by implicit references to Westerners looking for spiritual healing via the plant wisdom of the Amazon. As Kounen indicates in his book, since he started traveling to Peru in the 1990s, spiritual tourism grew exponentially, which prompted him to write a manual included in *Visionary Ayahuasca* (143–250). In the film, as in reality, the Native Americans hold the wisdom to this ancient knowledge, decimated in the conquering of the West. By including these deep insights into knowledge of the soul, *Blueberry* points towards the growing importance of ayahuasca in the psychedelic revival as important healer for PTSD and other

---

8 Recently, Kounen has reinvigorated these immersive qualities in a VR-experience titled *Ayahuasca Kosmik Journey* (2019).

SET AND SETTING OF THE BRAIN ON HALLUCINOGEN 183

traumas (Adelaars et al.). As indicated before, there is a danger that this may lead to neo-colonial practices of a new "gold rush" (Farah) or simply to renegade tourism that does not respect indigenous rules and ritual. Such dangers need to be addressed critically (Williams and Labate). Yet, we can sense here that within the confinements of Western culture, self-criticism, modesty, respect, and a desire for transcultural and transhuman (plant) knowledge is opening up. In this sense, *Blueberry* constitutes a different type of "acid Western" as "aya Western," a novel variation of the genre that resonates with larger developments in the world marked by the psychedelic renaissance.

5   Shooting Back and Collective Action in Psychotropic Western *Bacurau*

While most variations of the acid Western have white, male, and heterosexual characters in the lead (even though their position is also undermined and sometimes literally shot to pieces), the film *Bacurau*, as the latest addition to the acid Western subgenre tree, brings to the fore an important new perspective. Not only is the US setting of the frontier town transposed to Brazil, but importantly, the film is also told from the perspective of minorities that have not been central to the Western: indigenous people, the colonized, refugees, black populations, women, and non-binary gendered characters (see also Zang). They are the central characters in *Bacurau*, which the Western is appropriated to express resistance and self-esteem.

Bacurau is a remote and isolated town in the hinterland, the sertão (the "wild West") of Brazil, where the action takes place. A resident, Teresa (Bárbara Colen), returns to her hometown for the funeral of her mother, when the town is attacked by a group of armed, drone-assisted foreigners looking for entertainment and opening the hunt. But the residents hit back. Writers and directors Mendonça Filho and Dornelles use the conventional semantic elements of heroes and villains (Altman), but they turn all the iconic archetypes of the Western upside down: not one brave man but an entire village becomes the collective hero of the film. The genre rules are stretched further by hallucinatory images. The village seems to have its own psychedelic means of fighting: "we have taken a powerful psychotropic, you are going to die," one of the villagers tells the villains in a final shootout scene. This non-specified psychedelic, and the entire revisionist story of the film, can be read as an allegory that offers an important political commentary.

As a political allegory, the film operates on at least three levels of resistance. First, the corruption of Brazilian politics is addressed. The local politician Tony

Jr. (Thardelli Lima) regularly arrives in town to buy votes by distributing cheap and outdated food and addictive painkillers, while at the same time putting pressure on the village by cutting off water supplies and by allowing American tourists to come in for shooting games (thus silencing, quite literally, the villagers). The hypocrisy and corruptness of the politician is explicitly revenged by the united villagers at the end of the film. Second, another level of resistance marked by references to the Western is directed towards the masculine figure of the cowboy. The gun crazy and ruthless "cowboys" that come in to hunt are tricked to enter the village museum that holds many Western memorabilia, including old shotguns. By taking revenge on these structural elements of the Western shoot out, the villagers change the traditional rules of white masculinity: they call in the non-binary gendered local rebel Lunga (Silvero Pereira) to help out in the counter strike. Moreover, by completely bending the rules of the genre's hero narrative, the film retaliates against the position of the Western (and of Hollywood film more generally) in our collective unconscious. Third, by referring explicitly to the devastating addictive effects of big pharma medication, expressed most explicitly by the town's doctor Domingas (Sonia Braga), and the emphasis on the community's own plant medication, the film references key themes of the psychedelic revival. The status of symptom-suppressing, conventional medicines versus the more profound healing properties of psychedelics are an important part of current debates.

Bacurau also addresses a vital aspect of the psychedelic renaissance that has not yet been mentioned: the necessity to change the balance of power in the world. While *Blueberry* shows the danger of Western "treasure hunters" of all sorts going to the Amazon to get gold, *Bacurau* gives voice to those who have never been heard in the mythology of the Western and for whom the psychedelic renaissance is not a renaissance at all, but an ancient tradition. By way of these genre revisions, transformations and appropriations, *Bacurau* addresses the need for active resistance to old and engrained power structures that tend to return, as well as the importance of agency from the perspective of a range of diverse characters that have always been placed in minority positions. This aspect of the indigenous and ancient traditions and wisdom of the psychedelic revival currently receives increasing attention and *Bacurau*, as a "psychotropic Western", makes a case in point in this respect.

6   The Weird and the Disturbing in the Psychedelic Revival

The genre of the acid Western that emerged within the set and setting of the psychedelic counter-culture of the 1960s and early 1970s offers "weird mediations"

(Davis) and imaginative translations of the brain-on-psychedelics. Its transformations and adaptations in more recent times resonate more clearly with concerns of the current psychedelic revival. Taken together, these films offer, in their historical variation, a cultural prism that reflects larger cultural and political questions entangled with the past and present psychedelic movements. Jodorowsky's surreal *El Topo*, with the midnight crowds it inspired, as well as Hopper's *The Last Movie*, with an explosive and disillusioned force that marked the end of an era, are connected to the rebellious spirit of the counterculture. This type of rebellion has been replaced by the integrative qualities of *Blueberry*, which returns to the classic language of the Western but transforms it into a quest for healing and plant wisdom that is prevalent in the current psychedelic renaissance. And the resistance of *Bacurau*, as a hybrid psychotropic Western, addresses the power and agency of indigenous views and diverse minority perspectives to battle traditional power structures. These new generation of acid Westerns also implicitly warn against neo-colonial practices that threaten to spur a new psychedelic gold rush in cultural and neuropharmacological medical practices today. In any case, these films demonstrate that the confrontation with the weird, the disturbing, "the good, the bad and the ugly" are necessary for both individual and collective healing in the set and setting of the psychedelic renaissance.

References

Adams, Cameron, et al., editors. *Breaking Convention: Essays on Psychedelic Consciousness.* Strange Attractor Press, 2013.

Adelaars, Arno, et al. *Ayahuasca: Rituals, Potions and Visionary Art from the Amazon.* Divine Arts, 2006.

Altman, Rick. "A Semantic/Syntactic Approach to Film Genre." *Cinema Journal*, vol. 23, no. 3, Spring 1984, pp. 6–18.

Ayd, Jade, and Jennifer Ayd. "The Last Movie: Dennis Hopper's Curiously Frustrating Experiment." *Moving Image*. 30 July 2019, https://walkerart.org/magazine/dennis -hopper-the-last-movie.

Bazin, André. *What is Cinema?* Essays selected and translated by Hugh Gray. Vol. 2, U of California P, 1971.

Bittencourt, Ela. "Rise Up! Interview with the Makers of *Bacurau*." *Film Comment*. March-April 2020, https://www.filmcomment.com/article/rise-up-bacuarau-kleber -mendonca-filho-and-juliano-dornelles/.

Calvey, Tanya, editor. *Psychedelic Neuroscience.* Elsevier, 2018. Progress in Brain Research 242.

Costanzo, William. *World Cinema through Global Genres.* Wiley and Blackwell, 2014.

Davis, Erik. *High Weirdness: Drugs, Esoterica, and Visionary Experience in the Seventies.* MIT Press, 2019.

Das, Ram and Ralph Metzner. *Birth of a Psychedelic Culture.* Synergetic Press, 2010.

DeAngelis, Michael. *Rx Hollywood: Cinema and Therapy in the 1960s.* State University of New York, 2018.

Doyle, Richard. *Darwin's Pharmacy: Sex, Plants, and the Evolution of the Noosphere.* U of Washington P, 2013.

Farah, Troy. "Psychedelic Gold Rush? Psilocybin Startup Compass Pathways Goes Public at More than $1B." *Double Blind,* 29 Sept. 2020 (updated 12 Mar. 2021), https://doubleblindmag.com/compass-pathways-goes-public-psychedelic-gold-rush/

Gerber, Konstantin, et al. "Ethical Concerns about Psilocybin Intellectual Property." *ACS Pharmacology & Translational Science,* vol. 4, no. 2, 2021, pp. 573–77.

Greer, Christian. *Angel-Headed Hipsters: Psychedelic Militancy in Nineteen-Eighties North America.* 2020. U of Amsterdam, PhD dissertation.

Hartogsohn, Ido. *American Trip: Set, Setting, and the Psychedelic Experience in the Twentieth Century.* MIT Press, 2020.

Huxley, Aldous. *The Doors of Perception.* Chatto and Windus, 1954.

Ivan-Zadeh, Larushka. "El Topo, the Weirdest Western Ever Made." BBC *Culture,* 23 July 2020, https://www.bbc.com/culture/article/20200723-el-topo-the-weirdest-western-ever-made.

James, David. "The Movies Are the Revolution." *Imagine Nation: The American Counterculture of the 1960s and 1970s,* edited by Peter Braunstein and Michael William Doyle, Routledge, 2002, pp. 275–304.

Kohn, Eric. "The Last Movie: Dennis Hopper's Misunderstood Masterpiece Deserves a Second Chance." *Indiewire,* 2 Aug. 2018, https://www.indiewire.com/2018/08/the-last-movie-dennis-hopper-restoration-1201990114/.

Kounen, Jan. *Visionary Ayahuasca: A Manual for Therapeutic and Spiritual Journeys.* Park Street Press, 2015.

Langlitz, Nicholas. *Neuropsychedelia: The Revival of Hallucinogen Research since the Decade of the Brain.* U of California P, 2013.

Luke, David, and Rory Spowers, editors. DMT *Dialogues: Encounter with the Spirit Molecule.* Park Street Press, 2018.

Markoff, John. *What the Dormouse Said: How the Sixties Counterculture Shaped the Personal Computer Industry.* Penguin, 2006.

Masters, Robert, and Jean Houston, editors. *Psychedelic Art and Society.* Grove Press, 1968.

McLuhan, Marshall, and Quentin Fiore. *The Medium is the Massage.* Penguin, 1967.

Mikulec, Sven. "A 1971 Interview with Jodorowsky on 'El Topo,' the Psychedelic, Genre-Bending Midnight Movie." *Cinephilia & Beyond,* https://cinephiliabeyond

SET AND SETTING OF THE BRAIN ON HALLUCINOGEN

.org/1971-interview-alejandro-jodorowsky-el-topo-psychedelic-genre-bending-midnight-movie/.

Papasyrou, Maria, et al., editors. *Psychedelic Mysteries of the Feminine: Creativity, Ecstasy, Healing.* Park Street Press, 2019.

Pollan, Michael. *How to Change Your Mind: The New Science of Psychedelics.* Allen Lane, 2018.

Rosenbaum, Jonathan. "Acid Western." *Chicago Reader,* 27 June 1996, https://www.chicagoreader.com/chicago/acid-western/Content?oid=890861.

Shulgin, Alexander and Ann Shulgin. *Pikhal: A Chemical Love Story.* Transform Press, 1991.

Taylor, Rumsey. "Acid Westerns." *Not Coming to a Theater Near You,* 1 Apr. 2013, http://notcoming.com/features/acidwesterns/.

Tullis, Paul. "How Ecstasy and Psilocybin are Shaking up Psychiatry." *Nature,* Jan. 27, 2021, https://www.nature.com/articles/d41586-021-00187-9.

Turner, Fred. *From Counterculture to Cyberculture: Stewart Brand, the Whole Earth Network and the Rise of Digital Utopianism.* U of Chicago P, 2006.

Turner, Fred. *The Democratic Surround: Multimedia and American Liberalism Form World War II to the Psychedelic Sixties.* U of Chicago P, 2013.

Williams, Monica and Beatriz Labate. "Diversity, Equity and Access in Psychedelic Medicine." *Journal of Psychedelic Studies,* vol. 4, no. 1, 2020, pp. 1–3.

Zang, Pam. *How Much of These Hills is Gold?* Riverhead Books, 2020.

CHAPTER 12

Modeling the Model

Reflections on a 10-Year Documentary about the Blue Brain Project

Noah Hutton

After I graduated from university and started working in documentary film, I daydreamed about someday making a documentary film about neuroscience. But neuroscience proved to be an elusive subject. For even as individual scientific studies yielded tantalizing results, the eventual cures for diseases or the ultimate answers to age-old existential questions were dangled in the discussion sections of papers and concluding chapters of bestselling books but always eventually punted off over an indefinite horizon. Though I wanted to figure out some way to explore the world of neuroscience in a film, I worried that the narrative structure implied by feature-length filmmaking would suffer from the inevitable lack of a third act, requiring the fracturing of the film into a series of short vignettes. And then I saw a TED talk.

The esteemed neuroscientist Henry Markram's infamous 2009 presentation at TED Global sent a shockwave through the neuroscience community. In the talk, Markram announces that he is setting out to simulate an entire human brain on supercomputers within a decade, has worked out a proof of concept on a small piece of a rat brain, has been granted the machinery for the endeavor by IBM, and will, once successful, send a hologram from the fully-simulated human brain back to TED in ten years to give a talk of its own. Finally, I thought: here is a neuroscientist willing to stake out an actual narrative timeline that I, as a filmmaker, could latch a film production timeline to. At age 22, ten years both felt like long enough for anything to happen but also short enough that I could imagine actually finishing the film someday.

Funding myself through freelance video work in New York City, I started making yearly trips on my own to Lausanne to visit Markram's Blue Brain Project and capture the team's progress. During one of my first visits, I was led to the visitor screening room at the Blue Brain Project and shown a fly-through video of the small piece of rat neocortex that the project had already simulated (Figure 12.1). Set to Strauss' *The Blue Danube*, the video was a neuro-aesthetic marvel. On the level of neuroaesthetics itself—the scientific study of aesthetic response—it's worth considering how the Blue Brain Project's visuals cast a unique sort of spell on me, a dual interpretation of Vessel et al.'s concept of

---

© KONINKLIJKE BRILL NV, LEIDEN, 2023 | DOI:10.1163/9789004681293_014

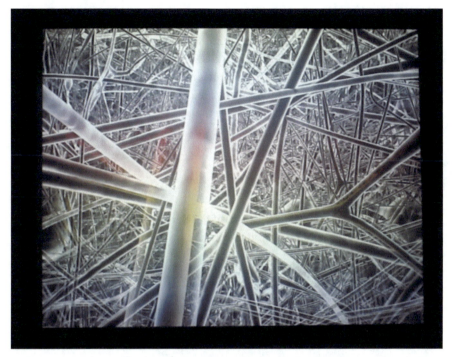

FIGURE 12.1   Fly-through of the rat neocortex as projected in the Blue Brain Project's visitor screening room in 2010
COURTESY OF COUPLE 3 FILMS

aesthetic objects that are "so well-matched to an individual's unique makeup that they obtain access to the neural substrates concerned with the self—access which other external stimuli normally do not get. This mediates a sense of being 'moved,' or 'touched from within'" (1).

It is this sense of being "touched from within" which forks into two meanings, for to be immersed inside the brain is to implode the notion of first-person perspective as established during the revolutions in visual perspective during the Renaissance, where the art object is set out at a quantifiable distance away from the viewer's gaze. Instead, in fly-throughs of the human brain, we are taken inside the very substrate of that gaze, giving the notion of being "touched from within" an added layer of meaning. What I would come to realize over time, however, was that crafting brain-like imagery through sophisticated visualization software based on averaged data from millions of experiments was not yielding the direct, unmediated glimpse of a neural substrate that I had imagined it to be (and to a degree, had been led to believe it was). From color choices to camera angles, the animations produced by the Blue Brain Project were carefully rendered artworks that depicted a level of representation of the brain deemed acceptably salient by its creators, shedding degrees of physical detail in the process that the Project had decided were superfluous to their pursuit of biological reality. These visuals were calibrated for maximal (neuro) aesthetic response in viewers like me, and far from imploding the Renaissance notion of perspective by attaining a pure, objective merging with our interiors, their assumptions and liberties of representation set them at a crucial distance from the inner sanctums of biological life.

1   Multiplying Screens

Over the years, an increasing awareness of the sharp criticisms of the Blue Brain Project—then later its scaled-up flagship spawn, the Human Brain Project— yielded an oscillation within my own perspective. When I talked to the critics, I would leave feeling critical. When over eight-hundred scientists signed onto an open letter calling for Henry Markram to step down from his leadership role of the Human Brain Project, even more so ("Updated"). But when I would then talk to Henry Markram, usually I would have believed in his vision again, trusting that the esteemed scientist who had authored papers assigned in classes I took as a neuroscience student was fundamentally correct that full-scale "in silico" neuroscience was the way of the future and that everyone else was just slow to the game or toiling on incomplete models. The same voice in the back of my head that also tells me there's a kernel of truth in every cliché would alert me to the possibility that Henry was right about himself as a misunderstood maverick who, as he states in my film when confronted with heated criticisms of his work, "needs a bullet-proof vest."

After a reaffirming interview with Markram, I'd then go downstairs to see the latest visuals, and usually would have believed even more. But something else was starting to creep in. A sense of multiplying touch screens, curved screens, high-tech headsets, but a lack of meaning to anything and anyone outside this glass and steel building in Geneva. When I had first shown up in late 2009, the Project had been housed in a modest academic building on the campus of École Polytechnique Fédérale de Lausanne, right next to the architecture department. Three years in, they had moved from the center of the EPFL campus to an "innovation park" on the school's outskirts. By my sixth year making the film, this identity-by-proximity journey had reached its logical conclusion, and I found the Project housed inside Campus BioTech, a looming office building in Geneva shared with banks, pharmaceutical lobbying firms, and private sector health startups, an aesthetic sibling of the EU headquarters in Brussels or any number of other technocratic hubs within twenty-first century

MODELING THE MODEL   191

capitals. If once the cardboard and wooden architecture models lining display cases on the EPFL campus had served as the best faith analogues to the digital brain models the Blue Brain Project was building down in the basement, the business directory at Campus BioTech now felt like an apt representation for what Blue Brain had become: a Silicon Valley-styled startup with a European twist.

If the outside world wasn't convinced by Blue Brain's scientific papers attesting to the reality of their model, the idea seemed to be that the visuals could be made to look real. As I walked around a gallery of poster-sized images meant to show off the Project's latest work on the ground floor of Campus BioTech, one image in particular caught my eye: a representation of a single neuron, stained dark against a parchment-toned background (Figure 12.2). I asked about this image, and Blue Brain Project graphic designer Nicolas Antille explained that "The fleshy tone is fake. We also chose a stain that is not a pure black because pure black is not a stain you often see … that's what tricks people into believing this image." We were looking at a digitally reconstructed neuron: a neuron not plucked from any single brain, but rather one built from an algorithm that had used weighted averages across millions of data points to determine the shape its branching dendritic arbor should take. Then, to assuage any remaining doubts and to reinforce "belief," the neuron was given an aesthetic cloak to help it look like the stained neurons we're used to seeing from real biological

FIGURE 12.2   Graphic designer Nicolas Antille regards "Virtual Golgi Staining," a poster in the lobby of the Blue Brain Project's headquarters in Geneva
COURTESY OF COUPLE 3 FILMS

tissue. What kinds of additional cloaks would be constructed along the way, and what would be lost as a result? Ultimately, this episode presented a question of identity: when we talk about building a digital model of *the* human brain, whose brain are we deciding to build?

2   Neural Normality

The funding rationale for large-scale brain research endeavors like the Blue Brain Project and the Human Brain Project has always been tethered to the great societal cost of brain-related disease and disorder. Indeed, a recent report on the Human Brain Project from the European Commission leans on the same statistic about brain-related economic impact as was used in the initial proposal for the project I read back in 2012, which Henry Markram also reiterated to me in our on-camera interviews: "In 2011, the global cost to European health-care budgets was estimated to be around EUR 800 billion per year and is set to only increase further as Europe's population ages and becomes more susceptible to brain disorders" (European Commission 2). Framed in economic terms, the disordered and diseased brain becomes a site for bureaucratic management, and neuroscience is enthusiastically folded into the toolkit of neoliberal austerity. Insights from neurobiology can make computers better, too, perhaps finally achieving a much sought-after toe up on Silicon Valley: "The [Human Brain Project]'s twofold vision is mutually reinforcing: To utilize advanced ICT in neuroscience to better understand the brain and its diseases, while drawing inspiration from biology to improve ICT" (12).

When scientists studied the human heart to such a degree they could instrumentalize its functions into the machinery of a pacemaker, working equally well in your body or mine, it was quite clear what the criteria for that model should be, and what we wanted it to do. But when governments and private entities earmark vast sums to neuroscience research in order to cut medical costs and gain insights from cognition to drive our technologies, who gets to decide what the ideal brain should be? What is a generic brain—an ideal, healthy, productive, and safe brain?

Half of the initial investment in Obama's US BRAIN Initiative came from DARPA and IARPA, secretive agencies within the Defense Department that are known to fund basic research for military applications. In early meetings of the Ethics & Society subproject of the EU's Human Brain Project, I witnessed conversations where the American dependence on "dual-use" research was explicitly frowned upon—"dual use" research being basic scientific research (good) that could one day be used to hurt or harm people (not good), such as improving the cognitive function of soldiers or helping drone operators forget their remote-controlled deeds. As long as basic research was free of this type of American-style military funding, an assumption of scientific purity shunted the ethical considerations in these meetings to the "what if" terrain of science fiction.

The problem is that all research is ultimately dual-use: it's just a question of speed. As long as modern capital is at stake, scientific insights into the brain revealed by any sector of society will either be absorbed for use by the state directly through American-style funding arrangements or developed in parallel by the state once published in academic journals anywhere in the world. Look no further than the announcement in late 2020 by the French military that they would be pushing forward on developing neural implants for soldiers to aid in resisting pain, an endeavor that will draw upon decades of existing research on sensory systems in primates and humans (Comité D'Éthique de la Défense 2). In her speech announcing the new supersoldier program, French Minister of the Armed Forces Florence Parly explained that "everyone has our scruples, [but] it is a future for which we must prepare" (Parly 4). Even the most well-intentioned ethics committee appears power-less in the face of a future that is already always here, into which we must adapt or be left behind. In this way, ethical relationships with human brains are built on present-tense pronouncements of the inevitable, allowing for conscientious objections so long as they never seriously threaten the tides of history that find us always already in deeper waters, where ethical com-promise is suddenly necessary to compete on the global stage. In France, and surely many other countries soon after, the road to brain-augmented supersoldiers will be paved with the well-intentioned scruples of ethics com-mittees and the non-objections of the scientists who contributed the basic research to get us there.

But it's not just military applications, cost reduction for late-stage disease intervention, and insights for better computer chips that are driving many of our scientific entanglements with brains. As Nikolas Rose and Joelle M. Abi-Rached note, an "emerging style of thought" is advising governments that in order "to reduce the economic burden of mental disorder, one should focus not on cure but on prevention. And prevention means early intervention, for the sake of the brain and of the state" (14). Early intervention means establish-ing the norms that the intervened-upon brain has transgressed. In this sense, models of the brain take on the world-making force described by Paxson and Helmreich, "not just as representatives, standards, or experimental objects, but also as moral exemplars—models that are not simply descriptive, but that might simultaneously be prescriptive" (171).

The process of building prescriptive models seems benign enough in real-time, detail by detail: massive datasets are parsed for features that describe the most "typical" shape, say, for a basket cell in the cortex of a mouse brain. The modeler asks: what rules can we discover in the data that will best capture the wide variability of basket cell shapes? Or on a systems level, the question might be: what activity best represents the interplay of cortex and cerebellum for the behavior at hand? For each parameter, this becomes a game of middle-of-the-curve rule discovery. Writ large and perhaps one day applied to a digital reconstruction of an entire human brain, this process of averaging across variability becomes an industrial-scale act of Foucauldian normalization, as miniscule determinations of typicality come to one day embody what we believe to be *the* human brain, even as we dutifully file our conscientious objections to gender, racial, and other forms of bias inherent in such algorithmic extractions. As Foucault pointed out in a lecture at Collège de France in 1977, long before microchips were to be fitted into the brains of French soldiers, who were at that time busy fighting for France's colonial interests in Western Sahara, "Disciplinary normalization consists first of all in positing a model, an optimal that is constructed in terms of a certain result, and the operation of disciplinary normalization consists in trying to get people, movements, and actions to conform to this model, the normal being precisely that which can conform to this norm, and the abnormal that which is incapable of conforming to the norm" (57). The codification of psychiatric disease and disorder in the DSM was a precursor to what the normalized brain model's prescriptions could mean for medical, educational, or even disciplinary intervention. And in an age of personalized technology, those prescriptions may no longer be bound up in a psychiatrist's dusty tome but rather built into the code of a job listing app or mortgage approval portal intent on gathering a few more metrics to make its decision.

Catherine Malabou asks the key question in the title of her short but eviscerating book *What Should We Do with Our Brain?* "To ask 'What should we do with our brain?'," Malabou explains, "is above all to visualize the possibility of saying no to an afflicting economic, political, and mediatic culture that celebrates only the triumph of flexibility, blessing obedient individuals who have no greater merit than that of knowing how to bow their heads with a smile" (79). "Saying no" to the already-normalized and then outwardly-normalizing model of the brain means we ought not to "replicate the caricature of the world" (78). Malabou points to the plasticity of the nervous system as the site for radical resistance to these encroaching norms around us: "To talk about the plasticity of the brain means to see in it not only the creator and receiver

MODELING THE MODEL

of form but also an agency of disobedience to every constituted form, a refusal to submit to a *model*" (6).

3   Reliably Plastic

In my seventh year filming at the Blue Brain Project, I was intrigued to hear that the Project had received a grant from the Argonne National Laboratory in Chicago to run their brain simulations on "Mira," one of the world's fastest supercomputers, and, for the first time, to model a few seconds of plasticity in their digital slice of cortex. The announcement on the EPFL website piqued my curiosity: at Argonne, the Blue Brain Project would "simulate biophysical synaptic plasticity in reconstructions of the neocortical microcircuit to discover their synergistic functional principles" (Blue Brain Project).

I traveled to Argonne to capture this first foray into full-scale digital plasticity, still hopeful that I might see a revelatory breakthrough occur during the decade I was making my film. But instead, I recorded hours of establishing shots of supercomputers and flashing lights, hallways and banal open work environments. There was no evidence of any discoveries of "synergistic functional principles" of plasticity in my interviews with Argonne researchers or in any publications or news media that followed in years to come. In a 2018 report issued by Blue Brain Project leaders about the work at Argonne, the conclusion was predictably more interested in lessons learned about computers than about human biology: "[These developments] will allow BBP to be fully equipped to move its INCITE workload from Blue Gene/Q to KNL Theta over the years to come" (Delalondre 8). And the report's "use-case" section, meant to detail their specific use of the computing power at Argonne to purportedly investigate neuroplasticity, contained a telling line: "In particular, we never tested the rewiring dynamics and the proposed models are mostly placeholders" (11). The Principal Investigator in charge of the work at Argonne, Eilif Muller, would leave Blue Brain two years later to join an artificial intelligence firm in Montreal.

Malabou's definition of neuroplasticity as a radical space for resisting the conformity of the model had held its ground at Argonne. The digital brain model wasn't capable of true plasticity yet, and its practitioners seemed locked into cycles of PR salesmanship only to bury their admission of a shortcoming in dense reports, punt their "discovery" to the next generation of supercomputers, and gather what was learned in the process for potential applications to artificial intelligence. In documentary film, a narrator is deemed unreliable if gaps in truth emerge between their statements and actions, or just between two of their statements themselves. If we take each new statement at face value, we lose our autonomy as critical viewers—this is the unreliable narrator's path to victory. I had started making the film because the public narrator of the Blue Brain Project, Henry Markram, had attached his bold idea to a timeline. But as that timeline drifted further and further into the future, with the human brain gradually scrubbed from PR materials and replaced by the mouse brain as the end goal, my narrator's reliability was thrown into question. So to ensure the reliability of my film-model in the years after Argonne, I made a conscious effort to try to stop buying the PR pronouncements of its subjects at face value and instead to let the realities in front of me dictate what the film should be interested in next.

Though this search came to form the third act of my film, it was perhaps seeded much earlier by a question Princeton neuroscientist Sebastian Seung had posed to me during an interview in my third year of filming. "I would ask you this," Seung had begun, asking me about my time so far filming at the Blue Brain Project. "They showed you a simulation of some neural activity inside this. Suppose it looked different, how would you know that that was wrong or right?" Sitting behind the camera, I replied, "Well, *I* wouldn't know." Seung reiterated: "Right, how would *anybody* know what was a wrong activity pattern or right activity pattern?"

His question echoed years later as one impugning the reliability of the model itself. The "right" activity pattern was the much sought-after outcome of modeling the brain, and the scientists at the Blue Brain Project were quick to explain to me how they constantly checked the simulation against the results of real experiments on brain tissue performed "in vitro" (in a dish) or "in vivo" (inside the living organism) to ensure their model was mimicking biological realities. If successful, "in silico" neuroscience (experiments performed on a silicon computer) could emerge as an equally valid methodology. And to do that in a way that would be helpful to any number of questions, you'd want to know that your activity patterns inside the simulation were "right."

The problem arrives when one begins to interrogate what "right" would entail, for simulating a profoundly noisy biological system inside the circuits of a perfectly programmed machine seems to eventually reach an a priori, foundational impasse. If biology runs on a motor of unpredictable, noisy "mistakes" known as mutations that, through interactions with the environment, have driven evolutionary change through natural selection, how could the determinate system of software running on digital computers—where structural mistakes, known as "bugs," are quickly fixed to make way for the perfect code (even the perfect code to model the biological "mistakes")—ever capture the truly unpredictable mistakes of biology seen at every level of description in brains? Proponents of

MODELING THE MODEL

deep learning in artificial intelligence research enjoy using the language of bio-logical evolution to describe their software, but beneath superficial similarities there is a fundamental platform issue. It's the server farm that instantly shuts down because of a tiny issue with its power supply—rendering its intractable cloud of data suddenly all too tractable—versus the organism that finds a new way of living because of a tiny "mistake" in replicating its genetic code.

Though the scientists at the Blue Brain Project whom I interviewed over the years shared a range of perspectives on the thorny issues of noise and chaos in the simulation, they all stood firmly behind their methods, which leaned on "state of the art" random number generators to inject artificial noise into the simulation in hopes of approximating the general network effects of the stochasticity seen in biology. Richard Walker, the in-house science writer for the Project, was bluntly dismissive of any such problem with this approach, "Because as long as it's random, I just need a thing which jumps me into the next thing. I don't really think it matters much. And random is all the same. I suspect actually simulating exactly the right sort of chaos doesn't really matter very much." Indeed, in my final year of filming at Blue Brain, Henry Markram announced at a Blue Brain all-hands meeting that "The one thing you can be absolutely sure of is that [the model] can only get better. There is a perfect reconstruction lying at the end of that railroad track."

The idea of a *perfect* reconstruction of biology struck me not only as poor marketing but also as a Sisyphean quest so long as it was performed on digital computers. Since the variability seen in biology is fundamentally unpredict-able—you can measure the probability of a synapse firing, but never be com-pletely sure it will fire in response to the same input *in vivo*—I wanted to get to the root of the Blue Brain Project's confidence in a full-scale, bottom-up digital simulation of variability. Finally, when I asked Lida Kanari, a more junior sci-entist at the Project working on reconstructing the morphologies of cortical neurons, I heard an answer that cut through the positivist PR gloss. Asked how she approached the extraction of morphological constants from the highly variable shapes of neurons found in the cortex, Kanari explained that she uses "the features that are consistent, and exploits them... so [we] generate struc-tures that have the same main topology, but also add some noise. Add the vari-ability that you see in biology." I then asked: "How do you add the right kind of variability?" To which she replied: "That's a good question, because the right kind, we can never know what's the right kind of variability."

In order to answer Sebastian Seung's provocation (*How would anybody know what was a wrong activity pattern or right activity pattern?*) in the affir-mative, one would need to reliably know that the variability being simulated was the *right* kind of variability. In 2019, the Blue Brain Project published a paper entitled "Cortical reliability amid noise and chaos," in which they simulated "prominent sources of noise" found in the brain, and ultimately found that their simulated circuit can "overcome these noisy and chaotic network dynamics ... and produce reliable patterns of activity" (Nolte et al. 2). This paper presents simulated forms of variability in the network being "overcome" by a simulated form of a neuron. If, according to Kanari, we can never know the *right* kind of variability, it seems that what we're really talking about is not necessarily a reconstruction of the biological brain but rather a digital system that ultimately does exactly what its creators want it to do. Malabou observes that there "is today an exact correlation between descriptions of brain functioning and the political understanding of commanding" (32). Like the profusion of brain-inspired artificial intelligence, brain-inspired computational neuroscience is gradually leaving biological brains behind in search of the "perfect reconstruction," a non-biological, algorithmic fiction that purports to replicate the variability of biological beings but in actuality replicates assumptions of normality that can be programmed into a perfect software package, inching ever-closer to translations for political and economic forces eager to add its commanding potential to their toolkit. Max Nolte, lead author on the "Cortical reliability" paper, has since left the Blue Brain Project to work on "neuroscience-inspired machine learning in the AI industry" at INAIT, an "EPFL spinoff" owned by Henry Markram.

4   Horizon Twentysomething

During my final trip to the Blue Brain Project, I was invited into the Project's conference room to film a meeting. Print-outs of many of the same visualizations I had seen over and over again through the years were neatly laid out on the table. Markram and other project leaders entered and began milling around, rearranging the images. Once everyone had arrived, the lights dimmed, and a video began to play on a large flatscreen in the room: a slide presentation showing storyboard images for a new film the Project would soon be making about their work. Over stock imagery of data-infused brains and 3D mannequins emulating talking heads, a series of on-screen text captions appeared one after the next, detailing the visual flow that would accompany their forthcoming film's scripted narrative:

> [Data-driven building from ground up: not Disney/fantasy animations but realistic biology]
> The brain image transitions into a simulation

MODELING THE MODEL   199

    That slowly dissolves
Into mathematical equations
That reveal a supercomputer and the computational aspect
[For all parts, heavily rely on zoom-ins, 3D & fly throughs, keep audience
attention with simple explanations and cool visuals]
Discuss results and achievements so far, emphasize neuroscience
But include some computing implications for the future of neuroscience
research, improving the human condition
END

After ten years, this would be the closest thing to the hologram sent back to TED I would see: a model of a film-to-be, a script for the future of brain simulation. If I thought I was making a documentary about simulating a human brain on supercomputers, I knew now that the endeavor was still at concept stage, with both of our projects sounding like science fiction—that genre so enamored with representations, simulacra, and transmutations of humanity into other forms. It may have been a mistake to take the TED talk seriously and start making the film in the first place, but it was a mistake that, in laying bare the unreliability of the "computational aspect," had revealed to me the only truly reliable force in our world: the unpredictable noise of brains, a sacred terrain of political potential.

References

Blue Brain Project. "Timeline and Achievements." *EPFL*, https://www.epfl.ch/research/domains/bluebrain/blue-brain/about/timeline/.

Comité D'Éthique de la Défense. "Opinion on the Augmented Soldier." *French Ministry of the Armed Forces*, 21 Aug. 2020, https://shorturl.at/mwBUY.

Delalondre, Fabien, et al. "Large-Scale Simulation of Brain Tissue, Blue Brain Project, EPFL: Technical Report for the ALCF Theta Early Science Program." *Argonne National Laboratory*, May 2018, https://publications.anl.gov/anlpubs/2018/11/148038.pdf.

European Commission. "How the Digital Revolution is Transforming EU-funded Brain Research." CORDIS EU *Research Results*, 2019, https://cordis.europa.eu/article/id/401587-cordis-results-pack-on-the-brain.

Foucault, Michel. *Security, Territory, Population: Lectures at the College de France 1977–78.* Picador and Palgrave Macmillan, 2007.

Malabou, Catherine. *What Should We Do with Our Brain?* Fordham UP, 2008.

Nolte, Max, et al. "Cortical Reliability amid Noise and Chaos." *Nature Communications,* vol. 10, art. 3792, 2019.

Parly, Florence. "Ethics and Augmented Soldiers." *Speech delivered during Digital Defense Innovation Forum*, Paris, France, 4 Dec. 2020, https://www.vie-publique.fr/discours/277612-florence-parly-04122020-ethique.

Paxson, Heather, and Stefan Helmreich. "The Perils and Promises of Microbial Abundance: Novel Natures and Model Ecosystems, from Artisanal Cheese to Alien Seas." *Social Studies of Science*, vol. 44, no. 2, 2014, pp. 165–93.

Rose, Nikolas, and Joelle M. Abi-Rached. *Neuro: The New Brain Sciences and the Management of the Mind*. Princeton UP, 2013.

Seung, Sebastian. *Connectome: How the Brain's Wiring Makes Us Who We Are*. Mariner Books, 2013.

"Updated: European Neuroscientists Revolt against the E.U.'s Human Brain Project." *Science*, 10 Dec. 2017, www.sciencemag.org/news/2014/07/updated-european-neuroscientists-revolt-against-eus-human-brain-project.

Vessel, Edward, et al. "Art Reaches within: Aesthetic Experience, the Self and the Default Mode Network." *Frontiers in Neuroscience*, vol. 7, art. 258, 2013.

CHAPTER 13

A Monk in the Office

Mindfulness and the Valuation of Popular Neuroscience

Ties van de Werff

1 Introduction

It is that nagging feeling, lingering in the back of your mind. The cause of those painful knobs in your shoulders, and it is probably the reason why you snarled at your daughter at breakfast this morning. It is what some seem to wear proudly as a "badge of honor," but most of us wish we could do without: stress. Stress is occupational hazard number one, as chronic stress can lead to all kinds of health problems, ranging from anxiety and heart diseases to burnout, depression, and other mental illnesses. Work-related stress seems to be the biggest obstacle to working and living well in our contemporary work culture.

In recent years, one peculiar antidote to stress has become increasingly popular: mindfulness, a form of meditation originating from Buddhist contemplative traditions. More and more corporations and organizations in Western affluent countries have started to encourage their employees to start meditating. While *mindfulness-based stress reduction programs* (mbsr) took flight at Silicon Valley corporations such as Google, Twitter, and Facebook, the trend quickly trickled down to local (and less trendy) institutions such as banks, universities, local municipalities, and the tax office. Mindfulness is fast growing into a common practice at the workplace and a standard element in the toolkit of HR managers.

How did mindfulness emerge as something desirable in the context of work? Taking a look at flyers of training programs, one justification for this unlikely marriage stands out: the plastic brain. Training programs and popular books on mindfulness invoke knowledge of the plastic brain to diagnose problems at the workplace and herald the benefits of meditation. Popular mindfulness coaches invite participants to take control of and change their brain functioning, promising new ways to prevent stress and achieve happiness and well-being. The combination of an age-old form of meditation with cutting-edge science draws considerable media attention, by which the idea of mindfulness as brain training—or what I will refer to as the mindful brain in this chapter—quickly entered Western mainstream culture, including the workplace.

© KONINKLIJKE BRILL NV, LEIDEN, 2023 | DOI:10.1163/9789004681293_015

In this chapter, I explore how a neuroscience understanding of mindfulness is made valuable to address concerns and ideals of working well, focusing on white collar office work in the United States and the Netherlands. How did neuroscientific knowledge enable the rise of mindfulness in the workplace of knowledge workers? What kind of good employee do you become by practicing mindfulness? I explore these questions by looking at the ways a neuroscientific understanding of mindfulness travels from scientific papers and press releases to advice literature, self-help literature, and expository works (Mellor 509), such as mindfulness books, programs, and brochures, as well as public discourse on the mindful brain in the context of work in the Netherlands.[1]

The mindful brain holds the promise that neuroscience knowledge comes with certain moral changes: changes in the ways and ideas we can and should improve ourselves through particular ways of perceiving of and acting upon our brains. Such a promise of neuro-induced moral change underlies the current debate on understanding the implications of the increasing societal import of neuroscience knowledge. While proponents and enthusiasts—e.g., popularizers of neuroscience knowledge and some scholars in the humanities and social sciences—value neuroscientific knowledge as a potential liberating and empowering force, critics warn of a reiteration of an ethic of neoliberal self-care (Pitts-Taylor), "neuro-governance" (Papadopoulos 450), or a new brain-based biomedical citizenship, (Rose and Abi-Rached). All too often in this debate—especially regarding applications based on brain plasticity, such as the mindful brain—both enthusiasts and sceptics seem to imply that neuro-moral changes are imminent, whether they are valuated desirable or not.

In this chapter, I demonstrate that disseminators, appropriators, and translators of neuroscience knowledge are not merely passive recipients of that knowledge. A neuroscience understanding of mindfulness allows management coaches and mindfulness advocates to turn mindfulness into a desirable intervention for dealing with a variety of concerns, challenges, and ideals at the modern workplace. I show how the plastic, mindful brain is made valuable by deliberate efforts of de-ethicization and re-ethicization, efforts I dub *value work*. I argue that the case of the mindful brain indicates that we cannot assume a transformative potential of the neurosciences: in order to explore possible ethical and societal implications of neuroscientific knowledge, we need to empirically study how knowledge of the brain *is made valuable* and normatively mobilized in specific societal contexts in the first place.

---

1   This chapter is based on my dissertation, titled "Practicing the Plastic Brain: Popular Neuroscience and the Good Life" (2018), available at www.tiesvandewerff.nl.

2 A Monk at the Office: Stress and the Mindful Brain at the Work Place

In 1979, molecular biologist Jon Kabat-Zinn (University of Massachusetts Medical Center, US) decided to turn the meditation lessons of his Zen teacher into a practice to help people cope with chronic pain ("An Outpatient Program" 33). This practice became known in the Western world as *mindfulness*. Kabat-Zinn describes mindfulness as "the awareness that emerges through paying attention on purpose, in the present moment, and nonjudgmentally to the unfolding of experience moment by moment" ("Mindfulness-Based Interventions" 145–46). In this popular definition, mindfulness is the training of attention by focusing on the present and becoming aware of how thoughts, emotions, and bodily sensations emerge—without being judgmental. The mindfulness program of Kabat-Zinn, including his definition of mindfulness, became known as "mindfulness-based stress reduction" or mbsr (*Full Catastrophe Living*).[2]

Since the 1990s, a group of enthusiastic psychologists and neuroscientists—with the help of the Dalai Lama's Mind and Life Institute—have made mindfulness and meditation topics worthy of scientific inquiry.[3] The rise of fMRI scanning techniques accelerated neuroscience research on mindfulness and meditation in the 2000s, which was soon dubbed *contemplative neuroscience*. Besides Kabat-Zinn, scholars such as psychologist Richard Davidson (founder of the Center for Healthy Minds at the University of Wisconsin-Madison, US), cognitive scientist Antoine Lutz (Waisman Lab for Brain Imaging & Behavior at the University of Wisconsin-Madison, US), psychologist and science journalist Daniel Goleman, and many others have been influential in establishing a neuroscience-based understanding of mindfulness and making their research valuable to both general and professional audiences.

The "hard" knowledge of the neurosciences has made mindfulness acceptable as a scientific object, for lay audiences and experts alike (Tresch 60). However, as we know from debates around emerging science and technologies, such scientization is not a self-evident process. As a body of work in Science and technology studies (STS) shows, new science and technology often come with value-laden vistas of promises, hopes, concerns, and expectations

---

2 Kabat-Zinn offers these programs in his Stress Reduction Clinic at the University of Massachusetts Medical School (US). I focus in this chapter not on the clinical use of mindfulness but rather on the use of mindfulness in the context of work.

3 There are many different forms and traditions of (Buddhist) meditation practices, of which mindfulness can be seen as a specific one. Often, neuroscience studies focus on a particular form of meditation, which later (when disseminated) becomes described as mindfulness. In this sense, mindfulness has become a popular metaphor for a variety of meditation practices.

about possible usages and desirabilities (Lucivero 129; Van Lente 769). For example, valuations are enacted in what some have called *stake-making* or *concern-making*: addressing certain challenges or issues and translating these to (neuro)scientific knowledge, linking matters of fact to matters of concern (Dussauge et al. 10; Latour 225). Only after addressing the problem, and giving a specific diagnosis of that problem, can a solution be promised—a solution that often takes the form of action programs (what to do) or ideals (what is desirable). Promises and expectations form the bridge between the "inner and outer worlds of techno-scientific knowledge communities and fields" (Borup et al. 286) and link the technical realm of science with societal issues. Public and scholarly deliberation about emerging technosciences such as the neurosciences are therefore often characterized by recurring patterns of moral argumentation (Borup et al. 295; Swierstra and Rip 4).

In the following, I trace the journey of mindfulness from the lab to the context of work, by explicating the (recurring) strategies by which a group of key scholars and translators make a neuroscience understanding of mindfulness valuable to specific audiences and to specific ends.[4] I specifically focus on how the mindful brain is aligned to concerns (and the identification of these concerns), action programs (what to do), and ideals (values or virtues). I describe these strategies that scholars and translators of neuroscience engage in as *value work,* a notion inspired by a body of work in the field of sociology of valuation (Dussauge et al.; Helgesson and Muniesa; Lamont).

3 From Buddhist Practice to Brain Training: De-Ethicizing Mindfulness

A major strategy of value work is coordinating the normative uptake of the research. Studies on meditation and mindfulness—including those by Davidson and his colleagues—are not uncontroversial.[5] For example, in a radio

---

4 The selection of these influential, yet limited group of scholars is obviously neither exhaustive nor representative of the whole emerging field of contemplative neuroscience. These scholars, however, present an interesting case to study value work, as their research is not only often cited in academic debates but also draws considerable media attention; their work is a frequently cited source in mindfulness programs and books.

5 There is, for example, discussion about the methodological quality and a lack of replication of results (Tang et al.). Furthermore, because many influential neuroscience advocates of mindfulness (including Davidson, Lutz and others) are enthusiastic meditators themselves, their affirmation of mindfulness has been questioned (Tang et al.; also see Van Dam et al.).

A MONK IN THE OFFICE

show, Kabat-Zinn reflects on how he made mindfulness accessible to a wider audience:

> Because it's often freighted, even the word "meditation" is freighted with so much cultural baggage and so much, really ideological baggage and sort of belief baggage that the essential beauty of it is often really not apparent to people until long after they have somehow wandered into the domain of it. (...) And so I tried to create a kind of glide path into meditation that would be so common-sensical and accessible and based on what people really need and also fear and are challenged by, that we could at least empirically test whether, if it was framed in that kind of way, regular mainstream Americans would take to meditation. (Kabat-Zinn, qtd. in Tippett)

The "ideological and belief baggage" Kabat-Zinn refers to is the Buddhist context of mindfulness. In Buddhist traditions, especially Theravada Buddhism, mindfulness is generally considered to be a form of insight-meditation or *vipassana*, in contrast to forms of meditation focused on concentration. Mindfulness, often described by Buddhist scholars as the heart of Buddhist meditation, is about cultivation, especially the cultivation of the habit of attention, as a means for gaining deep insights into the laws or nature of the mind, emotion, and suffering (Dalai Lama). In Buddhist ontology, suffering is part of our human condition, as humans typically suffer from three destructive emotions, or "poisonous diseases": greed, hatred, and ignorance (or unawareness). To focus attention inwards through meditation ideally results in a "deeper" understanding of these emotions and thoughts through which a more "fulfilling" or "wholesome" way of being can be found (Dalai Lama). Mindfulness is traditionally part of a wider conceptual, ethical, and metaphysical framework, including the ethical prescript of non-harm, the moral imperative to engage in virtuous action, and the disciplined training of the mind to prevent suffering and to increase compassion and kindness (Kabat-Zinn, "Mindfulness-Based Interventions" 146; Sun 4–5).

Advocates of the mindful brain coordinate the uptake of mindfulness by occasionally dismantling it from this traditional context and *de-ethicizing it*. Scholars such as Kabat-Zinn and Davidson do this by displacing the Buddhist context of mindfulness and by translating Buddhist values onto the brain. For example, Kabat-Zinn argues that "there is nothing particularly Buddhist" about mindfulness and instead describes the practice as an "inherent human capacity," a "deep inquiry" having to do with attention and awareness as universal human qualities (*Mindfulness Meditation for Everyday Life* 15;

"Mindfulness-Based Interventions" 145–46). In these examples, Kabat-Zinn values mindfulness as not specifically Buddhist, religious, or philosophical but rather as having certain *epistemic* values. The goal of this tactic of displacing spiritual and metaphysical connotations ("enlightenment") and the ethical context of virtuous living and non-harm is to show that Buddhism and science are more similar than different. Such an anti-metaphysical and empirical reading of Buddhism, a recurring theme in Western society, has some benefits: It makes the practice compatible with atheism and other religions, and it makes research eligible for public funding (Lopez 2; Tresch 60; Sun 19). Only after doing away with its metaphysical, religious, and spiritual connotations can mindfulness be established as a neutral, non-spiritual form of mental training.

A second tactic of aligning mindfulness with science consists in redefining Buddhist concepts and values in terms of the brain, shifting mindfulness-as-mental-training to mindfulness-as-brain-training. In order to make mindfulness fit the neuro-lab and to study the effects of mindfulness and meditation on the brain, the holistic practice of mindfulness is split into separate, measurable mental states and functions. To give an example, in the studies of Lutz et al. awareness is associated with gamma-band synchrony ("Long-Term Mediators" 16369), and compassion is linked to the insula and cingulate cortices in the limbic region ("Regulation of the Neural Circuitry" 2). While authors present a nuanced and limited definition of these concepts in their research articles, the (moral) connotations of these terms are reintroduced when their results are communicated to a wider audience. In the press release for Lutz et al.'s study ("Regulation of the Neural Circuitry"), in which the researchers found that expert meditators showed increased activity in the insula and an increase in the temporal parietal juncture, the conclusion is translated and linked to both happiness and compassion: "The findings support Davidson and Lutz's working assumption that through training, people can develop skills that promote happiness and compassion" (Land). As Davidson states in a university news item and press release: "People are not just stuck at their respective set points [of happiness and compassion]. We can take advantage of our brain's plasticity and train it to enhance these qualities" (Land). Compassion, empathy, and well-being are no longer described as Buddhist or secular ideals to strive for but become naturalized as attainable qualities of the brain.

Through these tactics of de-ethicizing mindfulness—displacing the Buddhist context and translating values onto the brain—the meaning of mindfulness changes: what was once a Buddhist practice becomes the scientific training of particular brain traits. After redefining Buddhist notions in terms of the brain, some connotations of the Buddhist roots of mindfulness can be re-introduced. By carefully balancing scientific novelty with the idiom of an age-old contemplative tradition, continuity between modern neuroscience and ancient Buddhist traditions is enacted. Once mindfulness is presented as brain training, mindfulness advocates can more easily appeal to concerns of non-Buddhists and propose mindfulness as a promising solution without having to anticipate conflicts about the perceived religiousness or spirituality of mindfulness. Once de-ethicized, dislodged from its Buddhist context and turned into brain-training, the mindful brain appears malleable and versatile enough to be adapted to a variety of societal contexts, including the corporate world of office work.

4 The Mindful Brain at the Office: Re-Ethicizing Mindfulness

Inspired by the work of scholars such as Kabat-Zinn, Davidson, and many others, a variety of mindfulness programs that cater to the needs of employees and managers emerged in the past decade. Popular programs and books include Google's Chade-Meng Tan's *Search Inside Yourself* (2015), David Rock's *Your Brain at Work* (2009), Michael Chaskalson's *The Mindful Workplace* (2011), Daniel Goleman's *Focus: The Hidden Driver of Excellence* (2013), and Houagaard et al.'s *One Second Ahead: Enhance Your Performance at Work with Mindfulness* (2016). Mindfulness has become a business, with consultancies offering expensive, tailored, in-house programs for corporations and organizations, extensive eight-week management courses, self-help manuals, and mindfulness smartphone apps. As I will show, a neuroscience understanding of mindfulness allows consultants, coaches, managers, and other mindfulness advocates to make mindfulness compatible with a range of concerns, needs, goals, and ideals of both employees and managers.

Mindfulness advocates in the context of the workplace employ a different strategy of value work. While researchers on mindfulness focus on de-ethicizing mindfulness and making it compatible with contemporary science, advocates in the context of work *re-ethicize* mindfulness again by aligning the mindful brain to different context-specific values of working well. In the valuation of the mindful brain in this context, advocates articulate specific concerns facing the modern-day employee and manager and promise to demonstrate how specific ideals of working well can be achieved through mindfulness as brain training. Based on the analysis of the valuation of the mindful brain in a variety of Dutch mindfulness programs, books, consultants' websites, and public discourse, two recurring patterns of valuations of the plastic, mindful brain can be distinguished. Each of these repertoires of working well with a mindful brain consists of its own set of concerns, diagnoses, action programs, and ideals.

5   Mindfulness as Cognitive Enhancer

In the first repertoire, the mindful brain is presented as a *cognitive enhancer*. The central concern of employees and managers in this repertoire is the influence of digital technologies on contemporary working practices. The continuous distractions and bombardment of information through smartphones and email, and the accompanied high work pace and working style of multitasking, are major concerns for contemporary employees, freelancers, and managers alike, who fear a loss of productivity and a burnout through stress. Mindfulness is presented in this repertoire as a necessary competency for a digitized workplace.

The main diagnosis in this repertoire is that our brains are not suited for the twenty-first century workplace, with its high technology and fast pace. The distractions of the digital workplace are put forward here as resulting in a "brain overload": a state of stress that is deemed unnatural, since our brain "hasn't had time to properly evolve" in relation to new screen technologies (Alidina and Adams 152). Digital technologies and multitasking make us inefficient and stressed as we suffer from "the frontal assault on our focusing ability from the mounting tide of distractions" (Goleman, *Focus* 23). Brain overload is explained as a result of the fight/flight response: the ruling of the parasympathetic and sympathetic brain systems over the prefrontal cortex. Mindfulness as promissory solution is geared towards increasing cognitive performance through training of the "attentional muscle" to manage "unruly emotions." The problem of the "amygdala hijack," as Goleman famously puts it (Goleman, *Emotional Intelligence* 13–29), is that it happens automatically, and that we are unaware of it, especially when it is experienced over a long period of time. Awareness is an important part of all mindfulness programs; awareness of your bodily sensations, of your fleeting or recurring thoughts, of storming or tucked-away emotions. In contrast to awareness of the three poisonous emotions (i.e., greed, hatred, and ignorance), as the Dalai Lama puts it, awareness in this case is directed towards the workings of our brain: only by paying close attention to the deep influence of our brain can we change its harmful functioning. Action programs in this repertoire are thus focused on training "at the level of physiology" (Tan 28). Chade-Meng Tan, Google's in-house mindfulness advocate and founder of the popular *Search Inside Yourself* mindfulness program, describes this process as follows:

The simplest way to do it is to bring mindfulness to your body all the time. Every time you bring mindful attention to your body, you create conditions for neurological changes that allow you to become even more perceptive of your body, and consequently, of the process of emotion. (Tan 76)

Thus, mindfulness is described in this repertoire as "much more than work techniques and mental strategies" because it's about "moment by moment, rewiring the neurological pathways of your brain" (Hougaard et al. 165) and "rebalancing the nervous system" (Alidina and Adams 266). Generic action programs, such as breathing techniques, small thought experiments, the labelling of emotions, and "body scans"—standard techniques in most mindfulness programs—are presented as solutions, precisely because they allow for neurological changes. In this repertoire, mindfulness is seen as a form of manipulation of old and rigid structures in the brain.

Buddhist idiom is carefully avoided and replaced with economic valuations and metaphors. Mindfulness advocates in this repertoire describe desired neurological changes in terms of values such as *productivity* and *efficiency*, which are not only presented as promised results of mindfulness but also described as inherent and desirable features of the changed, mindful brain itself. Authors of mindfulness books talk about mindfulness as "increasing the throughput of your brain" (Koole 9), "increasing the power output of the regulation systems," and "upgrading the operating efficiency of our brains" (Tan 47, 93). Mindfulness optimizes our "limited energy supply" (Alidina and Adams 92, 276), and strengthens the prefrontal cortex, often described as the "CEO of the brain." The mindful brain in this repertoire is an *efficient* and *productive* brain. Working well here receives the meaning of being able to productively function in a techno-induced workplace—learning to be resilient enough to prevent stress and burnouts and endure changing demands.

6 Mindfulness as Soft Skill

Next to a repertoire of productivity and resilience, the mindful brain is also made valuable through a repertoire of well-being. Here, the mindful brain is presented as a soft skill, resulting in a sociable attitude. Actors use the mindful brain to articulate values such as compassion, kindness, empathy, and well-being and tailor them to the workplace. The major concerns for employees in this repertoire are an uneven work-life balance and a lack of job satisfaction, both resulting in stress. For managers, job absenteeism, talent retention, and employees' motivation in times of economic crisis are issues for which mindfulness is seen as a solution.

The diagnosis of stress in this repertoire is similar to the first repertoire, but it emphasizes a different effect of our evolutionary-grown and rigid brains. Here, stress is a result of the so-called *negativity bias*: our brains are said to be prone towards negative information because avoiding dangers was key to our survival. This negativity bias causes stress and makes us feel we "are losing control and that the things people do or say are threatening and negative" (Chaskalson 65). To regain control over the emotional responses of the limbic system, action programs of mindfulness in this repertoire are focused on practicing emotion regulation and cultivating positive emotions in order to counteract our negativity bias and to create and foster more positive experiences. Positivity is presented as "a natural mechanism that prevents our brains from functioning on too primal a level" (Hamburger and Bergsma 23).

In contrast to the generic mindfulness techniques, mindfulness as brain training in this repertoire consists of action programs such as exercises in emotion labelling, letting go, acceptance, and "learned optimism." Thoughts and emotions that are difficult to let go should be seen as "opportunities to rewire your brain" (Hougaard et al. 163). To create "more positive pathways," meditations and thought experiments in this repertoire are directed towards cultivating values such as kindness, compassion, and empathy. Echoing the research of Davidson and others, these values are described as attainable qualities of the brain: happiness, kindness, compassion, and empathy "come preinstalled in our brains; we are all hardwired to be empathic" (Tan 145). Kindness becomes described as "the direct neurological opposite to unpleasant states of mind" (Hougaard et al. 136), and by practicing kindness it can become "our default neurological reaction" (Hougaard et al. 137). Plasticity here is used to justify the claim that "real" self-transformation is possible and that happiness, compassion, and kindness are within our reach, as trainable brain traits.

Cultivating compassion, kindness, and empathy through mindfulness is seen as beneficial for communal life at the office. Managers and leaders are specifically addressed. Empathy and kindness, for example, improve managerial qualities. Kindness has the possibility to "create trust and understanding," by which managers become more able to "skillfully negotiate and manage their [employees'] concerns" (Tan 128). Similarly, happiness and well-being are associated with job satisfaction and are presented as prerequisites for workplace values such as creativity and innovation. Positive emotions "widen our attention and our receptiveness to the new and unexpected" (Goleman, "The Focused Leader") and allow for creativity and "flow." Well-being also strengthens the company culture as employees become more motivated, engaged, and

A MONK IN THE OFFICE

"are less inclined to search for other jobs [because] they value their co-workers more, and they feel in general more satisfied and happier at work" (Dewulf 133). In contrast to the Dalai Lama's eudemonic view of happiness as a "wholesome, fulfilling life, in harmony with one's self and surroundings" (Dalai Lama), happiness and well-being in this repertoire become defined hedonically as the absence of negative affect and the affirmation of positive affect. Instead of necessary competence to remain productive, as in the first repertoire, mindfulness here becomes a soft skill, a social attitude that improves working life both for the individual and the company culture. Working well in this repertoire means being positive, creative, kind, compassionate, and empathic.

The two repertoires of the mindful brain in the context of work help to show how mindfulness has gained ground in the business realm. Using a neuroscience understanding of mindfulness, advocates of mindfulness in the first repertoire are able to address concerns of productivity in a digitalized workplace, aligning mindfulness to a register of individual, economic values. In the second repertoire, a neuroscience understanding of mindfulness is used to address concerns of well-being and communal life at the workplace, using the mindful brain to propagate social values such as compassion, kindness, and empathy— virtues that are not traditionally seen as part of the office world—into the context of work. The mindful brain gains traction in the context of work precisely because it can be re-ethicized in multiple ways, aligning to economic ideals of increasing cognitive performance and efficiency as well as to ideals of achieving personal well-being and a satisfying and inviting company culture. The popularity of the mindful brain therefore lies not solely in its (performed) scientific credibility and authority but rather in its promise to fulfill the conflicting demands of our highly technologized, neoliberal knowledge economy, both for employees and managers.

7   Conclusion

In this chapter, I have explored how neuroscience helped mindfulness to travel to the workplace. A neuroscience-based understanding of mindfulness indeed has made mindfulness accessible to a wider audience, as its enthusiasts and critics both agree (Cederström and Spicer; Davies; Purser; Tresch).[6] However, this is not an automatic process: it is through efforts of value work,

---

6   The scope of this article does not allow me to evaluate the possible neuro-moral changes of mindfulness in the context of a contemporary work environment, for example relating it to a history of work ethic or historical practices of neuroascesis (Ortega; also see Van de Werff).

of deliberate strategies of de-ethicization and re-ethicization, that mindfulness becomes seen as acceptable and desirable in the workplace. Robbed of his characteristic robes, left with brain training as a bare, yet moldable form of ascesis, the monk in the office reflects the ideal of working well in our contemporary highly technologized work culture.

What does the case of the mindful brain imply for understanding the societal impact of the neurosciences? As we have seen, a neuroscience understanding of mindfulness does not speak for itself: technical brain facts have to be made valuable, for specific audiences and for specific ends. The possible ethical meaning and relevance of neuroscientific knowledge are the outcome of deliberate, practical, and contextual processes of valuation. By appealing to the perceived concerns and challenges of a specific audience, and by linking neuroscientific knowledge to their hopes and ideals, advocates of the mindful brain not only attribute (moral) relevance to scientific claims but also prepare the ground for a normative appropriation of these claims. Ignoring these deliberate efforts of value work can result in overlooking the multiplicity and entanglements of brain claims and values in practice. Understanding and explicating how values and valuations are part of the translation of science to wider audiences might make it easier to direct the focus of our critique: both towards the implicit moral labor of scientists, science journalists and other translators, and towards our own willingness to accept certain moral stories over others.

References

Alidina, Shamash, and Juliet Adams. *Mindfulness at Work for Dummies*. Wiley, 2014.

Borup, Mads, et al. "The Sociology of Expectations in Science and Technology." *Technology Analysis & Strategic Management*, vol. 18, no. 3/4, 2006, pp. 285–98.

Cederström, Carl, and André Spicer. *The Wellness Syndrome*. Polity Press, 2015.

Chaskalson, Michael. *The Mindful Workplace: Developing Resilient Individuals and Resonant Organizations with MBSR*. Wiley-Blackwell, 2011.

Dalai Lama. "Science at the Crossroads." Annual meeting of the Society for Neuroscience, 12 Nov. 2005, dalailama.com/messages/buddhism/science-at-the-crossroads.

Davidson, Richard J., et al. "Alterations in Brain and Immune Function Produced by Mindfulness Meditation." *Psychosomatic Medicine*, vol. 65, no. 4, 2003, pp. 564–70.

Davidson, Richard J., and Antoine Lutz. "Buddha's Brain: Neuroplasticity and Meditation." *IEEE Signal Process Mag.*, vol. 25, no. 1, 2008, pp. 174–76.

Dewulf, David. *Heartful Leven, Mindful Werken*. Lannoo, 2014.

A MONK IN THE OFFICE

Dussauge, Isa, et al. "On the Omnipresence, Diversity, and Elusiveness of Values in the Life Sciences and Medicine." *Value Practices in the Life Sciences and Medicine,* edited by Isabelle Dussauge et al., Oxford UP, 2015, pp. 1–28.

Goleman, Daniel. *Emotional Intelligence: Why it Can Matter More Than IQ.* Bloomsbury, 1996.

Goleman, Daniel. "The Focused Leader." *Harvard Business Review,* 1 Dec. 2013, https://hbr.org/2013/12/the-focused-leader.

Goleman, Daniel. *Focus: The Hidden Driver of Excellence.* HarperCollins, 2013.

Hougaard, Rasmus, et al. *One Second Ahead: Enhance Your Performance at Work with Mindfulness.* Palgrave Macmillan, 2016.

Hamburger, Onno, and Ad Bergsma. *Happiness at Work: Improve Your Self-Leadership Skills to Flourish at Work.* Boom/Nelissen, 2013.

Kabat-Zinn, Jon. "An Outpatient Program in Behavioral Medicine for Chronic Pain Patients Based on the Practice of Mindfulness Meditation: Theoretical Considerations and Preliminary Results." *General Hospital Psychiatry,* vol. 4, no. 1, 1982, pp. 33–47.

Kabat-Zinn, Jon. *Full Catastrophe Living: Using the Wisdom of your Body and Mind to Face Stress, Pain, and Illness.* Dell, 1990.

Kabat-Zinn, Jon. *Mindfulness Meditation for Everyday Life.* Piatkus Books, 2001.

Kabat-Zinn, Jon. "Mindfulness-Based Interventions in Context: Past, Present, and Future." *Clinical Psychology: Science and Practice,* vol. 10, no. 2, 2003, pp. 144–56.

Kabat-Zinn, Jon. *Coming to Our Senses: Healing Ourselves and the World Through Mindfulness.* Piatkus Books, 2005.

Koole, Wibo. *Mindful Werken.* Business Contact, 2013.

Land, Dian. "Study Shows Compassion Meditation Changes the Brain." University of Wisconsin-Madison, 25 Mar. 2008, news.wisc.edu/study-shows-compassion-meditation-changes-the-brain/.

Lamont, Michèle. "Towards a Comparative Sociology of Valuation and Evaluation." *Annual Review of Sociology,* vol. 38, 2012, pp. 201–21.

Latour, Bruno. "Why Has Critique Run Out of Steam? From Matters of Fact to Matters of Concern." *Critical Inquiry,* vol. 30, no. 2, 2004, pp. 225–48.

Lopez jr., Donald S., *Buddhism and Science: A Guide for the Perplexed.* U of Chicago P, 2008.

Lucivero, Federica, et al. "Assessing Expectations: Towards a Toolbox for an Ethics of Emerging Technologies." *NanoEthics,* vol. 5, no. 2, 2011, pp. 129–41.

Lutz, Antoine, et al. "Long-Term Meditators Self-Induce High-Amplitude Gamma Synchrony during Mental Practice." *PNAS,* vol. 101, no. 46, 2004, pp. 16369–73.

Lutz, Antoine, et al. "Regulation of the Neural Circuitry of Emotion by Compassion Meditation: Effects of Meditative Expertise." *PLOS One,* vol. 3, no. 3, 2008.

Mellor, Felicity. "Between Fact and Fiction: Demarcating Science from Non-Science in Popular Physics Books." *Social Studies of Science,* vol. 33, no. 4, 2003, pp. 509–38.

Ortega, Francisco. "Toward a Genealogy of Neuroascesis." *Neurocultures: Glimpses into an Expanding Universe,* edited by Francisco Ortega and Fernando Vidal, Lang, 2011.

Papadopoulos, Dimitris. "The Imaginary of Plasticity: Neural Embodiment, Epigenetics and Ectomorphs." *The Sociological Review*, vol. 59, no. 3, 2011, pp. 432–56.

Pitts-Taylor, Victoria. *The Brain's Body: Neuroscience and Corporeal Politics.* Duke UP, 2016.

Purser, Ron. "Cutting Through the Corporate Mindfulness Hype." *HuffingtonPost*, 22 Mar. 2016, huffingtonpost.com/ron-purser/cutting-through-the-corporate-mindfulness-hype_b_9512998.html.

Rock, David. *Your Brain at Work: Strategies for Overcoming Distraction, Regaining Focus, and Working Smarter All Day Long.* HarperCollins, 2009.

Rose, Nikolas, and Joelle M. Abi-Rached. *Neuro: The New Brain Sciences and the Management of the Mind.* Princeton UP, 2013.

Sun, Jessie. "Mindfulness in Context: A Historical Discourse Analysis." *Contemporary Buddhism*, vol. 15, no. 2, 2014, pp. 394–415.

Swierstra, Tsjalling, and Arie Rip. "Nano-Ethics as NEST-Ethics: Patterns of Moral Argumentation about New and Emerging Science and Technology." *Nanoethics*, vol. 1, no. 1, 2007, pp. 3–20.

Tan, Chade-Meng. *Search Inside Yourself: The Unexpected Path to Achieving Success, Happiness (and World Peace).* HarperCollins, 2012.

Tang, Yi-Yuan, et al. "The Neuroscience of Mindfulness Meditation." *Nature Reviews Neuroscience*, vol. 16, no. 4, 2015, pp. 213–225.

Tippett, Krista. "Jon Kabat-Zinn: Opening to Our Lives." *On Being*, 27 Dec. 2012, https://onbeing.org/programs/jon-kabat-zinn-opening-to-our-lives/.

Tresch, John. "Experimental Ethics and the Science of the Meditating Brain." *Neurocultures: Glimpses in an Expanding Universe*, edited by Francisco Ortega and Fernando Vidal, Lang, 2011, pp. 49–68.

Van Dam, Nicolas T., et al. "Mind the Hype: A Critical Evaluation and Prescriptive Agenda for Research on Mindfulness and Meditation." *Perspectives on Psychological Science*, vol. 31, no. 1, 2018, pp. 36–61.

Van de Werff, Ties. *Practicing the Plastic Brain: Popular Neuroscience and the Good Life.* 2018. Maastricht University, PhD dissertation.

Van Lente, Harro. "Navigating Foresight in a Sea of Expectations: Lessons from the Sociology of Expectations." *Technology Analysis & Strategic Management*, vol. 24, no. 8, 2012, pp. 769–82.

CHAPTER 14

Figuring Thought

Between Experience and Abstraction

Ksenia Fedorova

1 Introduction

The chapter is inspired by an old philosophical problem: what is at stake when the act of thinking a thought is captured or represented? While neuroscientists attempt to identify areas in the brain responsible for a certain bodily and mental activity, the operation of thinking—the act of making sense of the world—eludes mechanical capture and may arguably be more appropriately tackled by philosophy and the arts. Part of the puzzle is that thought is directly tied to an experience: it stems from an amalgam of intuition, memory, knowledge, and bodily conditions, among other elements. The significance of the form in which a thought is expressed and communicated, discursive or non-discursive, should also not be underestimated. In what follows, I will approach the process of thinking through the concept of figuring. There are reasons why comprehension, or thinking something through in order to understand it, is often called "figuring out." I will treat "figure" in this text as situated in between an image (something visible), a diagram (a non-symbolic means for expression of logical relations), and a schema (a cognitive capacity of linking objects of experience to abstract concepts). I will argue that figuring is an active process that does not only represent what is already there (either as an abstract notion or part of an experience) but also is instrumental in generating and making manifest new forms of thought. Particularly, I will consider two experimental ways of figuring thought processes—graphically, through creative diagrammatics in the work of Austrian artist Nikolaus Gansterer, and bodily, through embodied action and interaction in both Gansterer's work and in selected workshops of the "Experimenting, Experiencing, Reflecting" interdisciplinary research project. I will thus discuss what these different approaches to representation and imagination as an active experience can evince about thinking processes.

Gansterer's artistic research in the field of figuring thought presents a thought-provoking case. Having studied large amounts of existing diagrammatic images, he "internalized," as he put it, the key motifs and set off to explore visual ways of constructing knowledge and developing his own grammar of

© KONINKLIJKE BRILL NV, LEIDEN, 2023 | DOI:10.1163/9789004681293_016

graphic notation (Gansterer, "Preface" 21) (Figure 14.1). Reflecting on the making of his diagrammatic images, he asks: how are these figures "to be read, given their ambivalent nature between image, symbol, and drawing. Moreover, how do they in turn configure our thought processes? What narrative forms can be found in these drawn figures of thought? And what happens when figures are removed from their original context? What poetic, performative and speculative action potential is then liberated?" ("Preface" 21). Gansterer's collection of drawings and the resulting publication *Drawing a Hypothesis: Figures of Thought* (2011/2017) intrigues me by its agenda that bridges image-making and thinking as a process. Extending these ideas, Gansterer subsequently collaborated with writer Emma Cocker and dancer Mariella Greil in a project titled *Choreo-graphic Figures: Deviations from the Line* (2014–2017), which brings forward the value of embodied experience in thinking. In this project, thought processes are situated in a special relational environment: the participants were encouraged to contemplate their relations to other objects or people in space while performing certain scores.

I use the term "embodied figuration" to explain how creative practices like Gansterer's helps us to conceptualize thought as a temporal experience that can be activated by physical action. I follow here the idea of embodied diagramming, initially proposed by the artist and his collaborators, putting it in the broader context of figuration as an epistemic practice of figuring out, but with the engagement of the body. To gain a better understanding of the idea of embodied diagramming, I also examine experimental workshops on cognition and perception, including those that are part of the multi-year research project "Experimenting. Experiencing. Reflecting" run by neuroscientist Andreas Roepstorff at the Interactive Minds Center (Aarhus) in collaboration with Studio Olafur Eliasson (Berlin). Putting the human body at the center of an intersubjective experience, such group artistic engagements problematize visual interpretation as the dominant way of figuration. In an innovative way, they point at the multisensorial and relational aspects of cognition and thus stress the ambiguity of representation. Ultimately, the chapter argues for a new way of interpreting the "operative" dimension of imagination and the figurative through exploring the connections between abstract thought and embodied, materially grounded, and collective experience.

2　Figuring Thought in the Act

Relations between cognitive processes and the figural have a long and convoluted history within philosophy. It is impossible to do proper justice to the

FIGURING THOUGHT 217

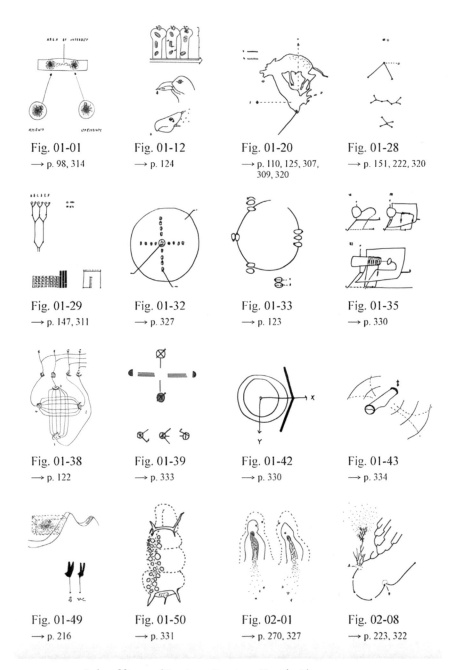

FIGURE 14.1   *Index of figures I* (Gansterer, *Drawing a Hypothesis*)

diversity of approaches to the figural and to the related concepts of mental image or mental representation in this chapter, hence I will only point out at a few aspects that are most relevant to the creative experiments in focus.

We can talk about the figural, first of all, in terms of an image: as belonging to an inner activity of imagination, a mental image, or as an outer expression of that activity that is shareable with others. W. J. T. Mitchell and Gottfried Boehm discuss images through the characteristic of iconicity, a type of correspondence between sign and meaning that goes beyond symbolic language: the meaning is contained within an image. They define this quality as a form of thinking which is both non-symbolic and non-mimetic. Conceived this way, images do not have to correspond to a state of actual affairs (as proposed in the classical picture theory of language by Wittgenstein).[1] In addition to the quality of iconicity, it is important to stress another characteristic: the meaning of an image emerges in the very fact of its presentation, an idea particularly elaborated in the French postmodern tradition. As Jean-François Lyotard put it, the work of the figural is in the act of manifestation and showing.[2] An image can make apparent what is otherwise paradoxical and indescribable, including the non-representable itself (Rodowick 15–16). The figural, thus, has a special place in cognition and transcends discursively and logically constructable thought.[3] The figural as an image also implies an act of perception, it is there to be actively engaged with.

Figuration becomes key to cognition particularly through the work of imagination. In Kant's philosophy, imagination is a capacity that helps to bring together the otherwise disjointed domains of the imperceptible concepts and the perceptible world of experience. Imagination facilitates the work of schemata, which relate abstract concepts to the corresponding empirical phenomena in the real world, yet without tying them to individual images, the appearances of these phenomena. Hence, schema is not the same as image. It should be treated rather as a structural condition for establishing

---

1   The pictures in Wittgenstein's theory are logical forms into which the states of affairs of the real world are projected. The pictorial form (*Form der Abbildung*) of a proposition serves as the main means for the expression of thoughts (Wittgenstein 13).

2   According to Lyotard, the figure gives language its "density" and "thickness" and is responsible for the very ability of expression (40).

3   Elsewhere, I have discussed the importance of the fact that the event of presentation of the image, both mental and given through the senses, should also be cognized (Fedorova). The new software-enabled technologies of visualization bring the role of an image to another level—of providing feedback on bodily and thinking processes that are otherwise invisible and unknowable. The way the feedback is presented plays a crucial role in restructuring and reordering the processes of gaining awareness.

correspondences between abstractions and objects of experience. It helps to reconstitute the experiential data in a way that they could be cognized. It can be argued then that figuration is located somewhere in between the cognitive capacity of schematization and images as sensory phenomena. The figural has the qualities of both: iconicity and making something apparent to the senses (as in images) as well as the capacity to relate to the conceptual and logical dimension (as schema does).

In her discussion of Kant's schematism, philosopher Sybille Krämer stresses another important point for our discussion: "A schema is not simply a visual structure, but rather an action, which [Kant] characterizes as 'figural synthesis'" ("Trace" 21). This means that the schemata are primarily conditioned not by space but by time. For instance, to conceive of a line does not mean the appearance in the mind of an image of a stable demarcation, but rather "the temporal action of its own production (the line is its drawing)" (21). Krämer points to Kant's reasoning in *Kritik der reinen Vernunft* that he cannot imagine any line without drawing it in his mind to make a record of our *Anschauung* (Kant 140, qtd. in Krämer, "Trace" 21): "The schema, which guarantees that abstract concepts take on a meaning within perceptible experience, can itself not be explained through concepts. Thus our graphical, constructive faculty (our capacity for figuration) [is] the originating location for the work of the imagination" (21). Krämer's argumentation helps to recognize why it is important to talk not about the figure or the figural, but figuration and *figuring* as an active process. The relationship between the sensible realm of experience and how we cognize it is actively constructed in the *process* of schematization.

It can be said that thought itself emerges "in the act," i.e., its expression is inseparable from what it is. Aloisia Moser, in her book on the performativity of thought, advocates for the necessity of an account of meaning that is pragmatic (active and situational) in a new sense. She writes: "What makes a proposition meaningful are neither the contents of the atomic bits that we put together nor the pragmatics of putting together bits of language or thought. Instead, the fact that we make sentences or speak or think at all is what gives meaning to thought or language" (Moser 8). Recently, a number of scholars have paid attention to the processuality and performativity of thought, informed not only by process philosophy but other philosophical traditions as well (as exemplified by Moser's analysis of Kant and Wittgenstein) and often in close relation to creative practice (Manning and Massumi). Importantly, such novel process-oriented understandings of thought also pay attention to the fundamental aspect of mediation. How to capture or register these (fleeting) acts of thinking? And how do the modalities and media, in which these acts manifest themselves, affect their meaning? Again, in investigating this question of recording and mediation, research with and through the arts can make an important contribution.

3 Graphical Thinking

Through his creative practice, artist Nikolaus Gansterer develops his own theory of cognition and how it can be understood with the help of visual and performative tools. He writes: "The cognitive act of perceiving, translating and allocating occurs continuously when we compose thoughts and receive or process information. This process of sense-making always happens by establishing relations and through drawing connections" (Gansterer, "Preface" 21). For Gansterer, "drawing mediates between perception and reflection, it plays a constitutive role in the emergence, production and communication of knowledge" (21). Whereas Kant's schemata support the work of imagination but are not easily expressible, "graphical thinking" as proposed by Gansterer can serve as a visual example of the formation of abstract ideas through figuration.

Gansterer's creative interpretation of multiple iconographic patterns demonstrates how mental processes can be represented. Titled "Questions of Order and Relational Characteristics of Figures of Thought" (Figure 14.2), an extensive map of drawings builds up on Gerhard Dirmoser's "Collection of Figures of Thought" that in turn outlines recurrent principles and motifs of "thinking in drawing": knots, cuts, curves, folding, rhizomatic root networks, marking and tracking, silhouettes, cellular setups, and others (Dirmoser). Some of Gansterer's figures are titled: "sequence," for instance, is presented as a row of dashes, with arrows pointing towards them from dotted, cloud-like abstract shapes floating around. Gansterer's collection of drawings, however idiosyncratic and poetic, can be treated as nearly scientific (or definitely inspiring further scientific inquiry). His work goes straight to the heart of the problem (representation of thought processes) and develops its own method that parallels a scientific one.

Gansterer's drawn figures capture dynamics of thinking processes as if approached simultaneously from within and from the outside, as a lived experience (of a certain thought) and as an *object* of a new experience. The intelligible is turned into the perceptible (visual images) only to come back to the intelligible in a different way. His drawings become conditions for the emergence of a new type of *thought about thought*. To use Kant's terms, they serve as a tangible ground for a "synthesis" of an empirical experience of thinking and a potential concept standing for that experience. What gives these fanciful figures epistemological weight is not only the extensiveness of the research

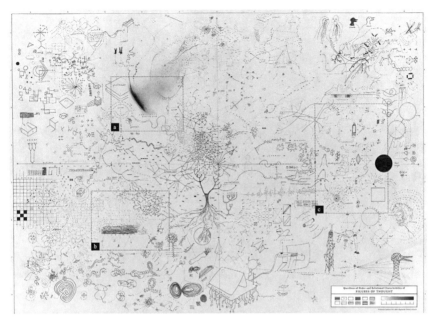

FIGURE 14.2   "Questions of Order and Relational Characteristics of Figures of Thought" (Gansterer, *Drawing a Hypothesis*)

behind them, the ingenuity and imaginativeness, but the very subject matter and form at hand—diagrammatic representation of thought.

A diagram is an instance of the figural and is particularly relevant for our discussion. Positioned in between text and image, the logical and the sensible, a diagram appeals to both rational and aesthetic types of cognition. Diagrams can therefore serve as useful tool for presenting abstract ideas. They provide non-symbolic means for expression of logical relations in the world, making "explicit" the "implicit" abstractions (Stjernfelt). Diagrams are not the same as illustrations, since it is their graphical logic that elucidates the relevant relations and helps in generating the message. They are distributed in space and are perceptible (unlike the schemata, which are still abstract mechanisms) but can stand for whole intuitions and "gestures" of the mind, as suggested by the names of the figures used in another project by Gansterer on *Choreo-graphic Figures*: "Temporary Closing", "Qualitative Moments", "Waves of Intensity", "Hybrid Hiatus" (Figure 14.3). One can think of Rudolf Arnheim's notion that *gestalt*, or spatial form perception and grasping of the "configuration," shapes concept formation.[4] Key to our discussion is that diagrammatic figures do not

---

4   A well-known example is the tree-model as an expression of Charles Darwin's idea of evolution that grants it its full meaning.

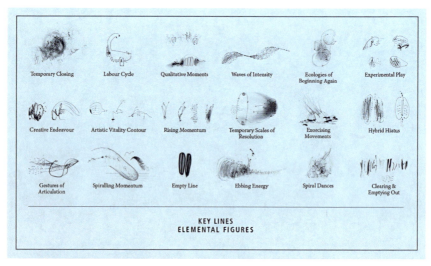

FIGURE 14.3   *Key Lines* (Gansterer et al., *Choreo-Graphic Figures*)

only serve as representation and transmission of knowledge about the objects but help to create such knowledge.

Among the characteristics of diagrams identified by Sybille Krämer (flatness, graphism, homogenization of relation, schematism, referentiality, usefulness) one feature stands out as particularly relevant for our discussion—operativity. As much as they outline the logical connections between elements (however diverse the types of logic), diagrammatic figures can also serve as a set of instructions for action. This way, they do not only re-present but also shape new possibilities for thought and action. Operativity entails a scope of meanings, for instance "to perform a mental operation in such a way that it is liberated from mental activities and can be realized as a mere mechanical process" (Krämer and Ljundberg 6). One of Krämer's examples is the nomogram of a multiplication table, which visually facilitates arithmetic operations. Similarly, the meaning of a music notation is activated when it is performed by a musician and the meaning of a map when it is used in navigating a territory. As Krämer puts it, "operative pictoriality proves to be not only a medium of illustration, but also a tool and an instrument for reflection (*Reflexionsinstrument*)" (*Operative Bildlichkeit* 100).[5] The space that is generated in between the domain of abstractions (represented through visual language) and the

---

5   "Writing, graphs and maps do not only (re)present something, but open up areas where the representable can be handled, observed and explored" (Krämer, *Operative Bildlichkeit* 100, my translation).

FIGURING THOUGHT   223

concrete, to which they can be applied, is where the operation of reflection, the back and forth between the two realms can happen, one informing and proving the other.

Diagrammatic figures like Gansterer's trigger thought, but what about the fact that thought is a durational phenomenon, while a drawing on a piece of paper is a spatial one? There surely are images that present movement and dynamics,[6] but the interesting part about diagrams is that, as scores, they *anticipate* action. They materialize, if only on a flat surface and in points and lines, the imaginary "what if." (What if Leonardo da Vinci's technical drawings were correct and we could build those imaginary machines with contemporary materials? What if the whimsical drawings by Gansterer could be instructions for specific action, e.g., a dance move?). Time is thus fundamentally presupposed in the nature of diagrams: looking at them and reading them happens in time, and the mental representations that they may form also emerge in the course of time. Moreover, as a form of writing, they serve as mnemonic devices: the linear movement of time itself can be "undone" in these still images. In science, but also in creative process, diagrammatic figures and drawings often indicate the initial stage, a model for something to unfold. Such a model, or a draft, attempts to *foresee* (e.g., *Entwurf* in German and *набросок/nabrosok* in Russian literally mean "to throw ahead"). The aim of this space for thinking-in-progress is to register the development of an idea from a proto-form to its full realization in the future.[7] As descriptions of the not-yet-realized, drawings have a hypothetical function: they point towards the possible, which is not yet fully known. As Gansterer's collaborator Emma Cocker elegantly puts it: "Like the hypothesis, drawing is a conjectural operation, the tentative manifestation of an insurgent *if*" (100–102).[8]

Psychologists and cognitive scientists have developed criteria and visions of the "effectiveness" of diagrams and visual forms of information communication in general (Andersen et al.; Isenberg et al.). But what kind of studies should be used that do not address the evaluation of processing information

---

6   The debate about whether an image can adequately represent time goes back to Lessing and his distinction of the arts of time and the arts of space. In his essay "Moment and Movement", Ernst Gombrich importantly argues that perception is always dynamic and durational and that an image should be understood as a process and not as a structure (Gombrich).

7   Diagrams are process-models also because they refer to procedures (Mareis).

8   "The hypothesis signals a transitional state of being between, where things are neither yet proven nor disproved. It is a double-headed arrow. Like Janus, its glance is double-facing, for it always looks towards the conditions of the present-past for stimulus, whilst gesturing forwards to the future, to the (imagined) arrival of clearer understanding, towards the moment of realisation" (Cocker 98).

but the process of *knowledge-in-formation*, i.e., the usage of figures in an active way, as figuring and figuring out? I would like to posit that this is exactly when self-reflexive artistic methodology can be useful. In the hands of an artist, a diagram can leave the flat surface: graphical features can be taken into three dimensions and, moreover, can become alive! Of course, a full living body in the role of a "diagramming agent" has the capacity of being much more than a mere instrument of drawing. The resulting figure of thought also goes far beyond the given spatial boundaries and the temporal dimension. Fully actuated through an embodied physical action, the figure acquires a new level of importance.

4 Embodied Figuration

Embodied action is the next logical step in moving from abstract mental activity (including its interpretation in scientific analysis of recorded brain signals) through the two-dimensional surface of a drawing to the inherently different parameters of the self-reflexive actuations of the living body. Embodied diagrammatics, as conceived by Gansterer and his collaborators, supposes active participation of the body in constructing the image of thought. But what does it mean to imagine with the body? What does the bodily dimension add to the process of "schematization" taking place in imagination? Or does it contribute to a *different* type of figuring, one that moves away from the rationalizable and attempts to capture a different type of logic? The body informs us about what happens when a thought is being thought and can thus be endowed with a key role—a subject of thought. It is not only the brain's intuitions, beliefs, and fantasies that perform a thought, but the full body—through physical gestures and felt sensations.

The collaborative artistic research project *Choreo-graphic Figures* by Nikolaus Gansterer, Emma Cocker, and Mariella Greil intends to explore the "taking place" of "thinking-making." The intuitions behind the flat diagrams of Gansterer's previous work find here a multidimensional, multisensorial, and multi-body expression. The work shows how, within particular material conditions, hypothesizing about the possible leads to that possible becoming real. The operational core of the project is a "Method Lab"—"a hybrid of studio and rehearsal room, research residency and retreat ..., a working context for exploring the nature of 'thinking-in-action' or the 'figures of thought' produced as the practices of drawing, choreography and writing enter into dialogue, overlap and collide" (Gansterer et al., *Choreo-graphic Figures* 25–26). Within each Method Lab the group composed and improvised what they call "scores of

FIGURE 14.4   Method Lab, scores of attention (Gansterer, *Choreo-graphic Figures*)

attention" (Figures 14.4 & 14.5). An action with selected objects (ropes, mirrors, paper, wooden beams, etc.) *becomes* a figure, one that is distributed *through and within* the action, with the bodies of the actors and through their connections with the objects and with each other. Every physical expression becomes meaningful and amounts to the resulting figure: a posture (standing, sitting, leaning, laying), specific bodily gestures and types of movements, including their qualities (tension, balancing, stretching, relaxing), interactions with the objects (holding, throwing, carrying, gathering, watching). Attending to the durations and what the authors call "energies" of the objects and materials is as important for the embodied outlining of the collective figure as observing one's own reactions. The artists explain this process of figuring as "those barely perceptible micro-movements at the cusp of awareness: the dynamic movements of decision-making, the thinking-in-action, the durational 'taking place' of something happening live" (Gansterer et al., *Choreo-graphic Figures* 70).

What is being choreographed and mapped here is purely intuitive and abstract, and yet it scores the space of potentiality, making sensible what is only intuited. The artists are heedful of the temporal nature of their practice. For instance, one of the "elemental figures" represents what they call a

FIGURE 14.5   Method Lab, scores of attention (Gansterer, *Choreo-graphic Figures*)

"spiraling momentum" (Figures 14.6 & 14.7). Both the drawing and the material-relational score of this figure emphasize the need "to set in motion," to rotate, to twist and to embrace the kinetic force of whirling (Gansterer et al., *Choreo-graphic Figures* 268). A moment in time, when related to motion, can also mean "momentum," a contraction of motion that gives it a sense of importance (stillness can be equally potent). The project attempts to cultivate a special type of presence, which they describe in terms of "when-ness" of the "kairotic" time (from the Greek *Kairos*—an opportune moment, which is opposite of *Chronos*—linear time). Kairos does not point at any imminent future, since it exists outside of the parameters of the linear time and is indeterminate (Gansterer et al., *Choreo-graphic Figures* 249–51). This is why, despite of their placement in time, these performative acts are treated as "figures" and scores to be potentially played again.

There is an important conceptual similarity in the agenda of *Choreo-graphic Figures* and the research initiative "Experimenting, Experiencing, Reflecting" (EER) co-run by the Interacting Minds Center (Aarhus) and the Studio Olafur Eliasson (Berlin), 2019–2023.[9] The latter project brings together

---

9   At the moment of the current writing, the research is still ongoing and hence the findings are limited; for more information see www.eer.info.

FIGURE 14.6 "Figure of Spiraling Momentum" (Gansterer et al., *Choreo-graphic Figures*)

behavioral psychologists, neuroscientists, anthropologists, visual artists, and choreographers with the aim to create a dialogical space for the interaction of the first-person approach (usually attributed to the arts) and a third-person scientific perspective. The experiments are designed to examine the key thematic threads both in science and art: perception, decision-making, action, notions of togetherness, collaboration, and the transmission of knowledge. In

FIGURE 14.7   "Figure of Spiraling Momentum" (Gansterer et al., *Choreo-graphic Figures*)

the EER group workshops, which take place in artists' studios and musea, participants shape choreographic scores not unlike the work of Gansterer and his collaborators.

For instance, in the workshop "Uncertainty and Participation," led by cognitive scientist and movement practitioner Asaf Bachrach, the participants were asked to imagine the perspective of an object (a rock, a tree branch, a piece of paper, a chair, etc.) and to locate this object in the room so that it could "observe" the group in a certain way. This task presupposes careful consideration of the physical parameters of the given space and intuiting its atmosphere. The object's "perspective" implies quite literally a line of sight, a "point of view" of the objects directed towards the human bodies. The spatial constellation of the objects and the human participants would reflect emotional attachments, mutual projections, and expectations. Taken together, they compose a figure of the collective state of mind, the state of being present together in a particular moment of time. After having registered this state in a mental but also a physical "figure"—the objects and the human bodies

FIGURING THOUGHT

would form specific constellations in space—the participants were invited to reconstruct this interactive setting in another location, an adjacent room filled with yellow light (one of Eliasson's experiments with atmospheric conditions of perception). Each person would lead a partner, whose eyes would be closed, to the second room through a hall, as if through a tunnel. The figure of collective presence then had to be built anew with the other objects at hand and within other spatial conditions. This challenge to transfer a mental figure reminds us of the communicative dilemma behind both Gansterer's drawings of thought and the neuroscientific agenda to record and analyze brain data during a cognitive performance. How to capture the transient intuition of a thought in a way that it could be re-produced and re-activated? Critical to Bachrach's method are forms of participatory sense-making, the intra-, trans- and pre-subjective ways to create meaning of a shared experience (Bachrach). Spatial organization of the emergent knowledge (through grids or in a spontaneous and unconstrained way, as in this case) may be then a useful alternative to discursive communication.

Another workshop, "Sharing Perspectives," led by anthropologist Joe Dumit and choreographer Dorte Bjerre Jensen, was devoted to a similar challenge— of exchanging memories of the body-mind and relating to space through someone else's perspective. Selected visitors of Olafur Eliasson's exhibition at Tate Modern were invited to consciously place themselves somewhere in space, which itself has already been transformed by Eliasson's installations (differently angled walls, dispersed color, materials of various texture, etc.). They then needed to share their reasons behind choosing this position with two other participants, but they had to do so nonverbally. As the subsequent interviews showed, sharing perspective made people more conscious both of their own experiences and the intersubjective space of possibilities of experience more generally (Dumit and Roepstorff). Reflection on one's experience done through the act of sharing it is thus another way of "figuring out" what that experience was about.

These tasks (the "scores") cannot be described diagrammatically on a flat surface, and yet they similarly involve the mapping of a relational space: lines of sight, positions of physical balance/unbalance, geometrical/topographical and temporal orders[10]—all these elements constitute a figure of thought-in-the-making. As pointed out by cognitive scientist and phenomenologist Claire Petitmengin, the author of another workshop within EER ("Being Aware. Sharpening our Tools"), these kinds of actions are experiments in

---

10   The concept of order can be of interest here as implying both the distribution of elements in space and a command (see Brandstetter).

microphenomenology—attending to the nuances of being present in a relational environment. Petitmengin proposes to design very precise "experiential protocols" that could complement experimental psychological and cognitive (neuroscience) studies. At their core lie "micro-gestures of attention," ways of paying attention, which bring us closer to the present and allow to reflect more accurately on our being in time and associated mental states (Petitmengin).

The value of this project is in its layering and intertwining of the experiential experiments with scientific observation. The scientific lead of the project, neuroscientist Andreas Roepstorff, has previously expressed his concern about the ambitions of cognitive neuroscience to create generalized frameworks. He proposed that human decision-making is based on the ability of "build[ing] shared worlds that are at the same time material and symbolic: worlds that exist outside the individual, and in time-windows, which extend beyond the here-and-now of interaction" (Roepstorff 224). For Roepstorff, sharing is more than the ability of abstract thinking and writing as a means of knowledge transmission. What matters here is the collective nature of subjectivity—thinking beyond one's immediate self-interests. Roepstorff's lab presents an important example of the rigorous analysis of the experiences of awareness in perception and thinking-together that take place in the context of a hybrid artistic-scientific lab. Interviews and surveys about subjects' experiences may give us as much, if not more than the gathered quantitative data, especially when it concerns figuring intersubjective positions not only in mental but in physical space.

My analysis of different ways of figuring thought processes has demonstrated that researching imagination indeed takes imagination, such as in the imaginative artistic research constellations discussed in this chapter. Whether it is "drawing a hypothesis" and outlining "thinking-making" with one's body, or sharing perceptual experiences—the prevalent method is non-discursive. By concentrating on the operation of figuration—in the sense of figuring out, imagining, mapping out and scoring an action—I wanted to stress the epistemic potential of experimenting with a space of possibilities. Thought happens in time, and one of the first stages, supposition and intuiting—and becoming aware of this process taking place—is especially precious. Paradoxically, static images on a flat surface disclose the potential to register the fleeting intuitions, the images of the not-yet-known. Artistically created figures, beyond being enigmatic in terms of their semantics, capture the momentum of the live generative process. They speak of the vitality of inner processes and allow the manifestation of not just being, but of being alive. The relations charted in the experiments by Gansterer and his collaborators, as well as in the "Experimenting, Experiencing, Reflecting" project, represent the abstract logical realm and are at the same time informed by the very material and

FIGURING THOUGHT

physical processes of interaction between the bodies, objects, and space. In fact, the duality between the sensible and empirically given, on the one hand, and the imaginary and the intelligible, on the other, becomes suspended, and the outlined scores of attention can help guiding us through the momentum of this transition, allowing new forms of meaning to emerge. Further experimentation with novel methods of thinking about thinking, particularly those that experiment with understanding (inter)subjective experiences and material conditions, should then unveil new dimensions of the very logic of making sense.

References

Anderson, Erik W., et al. "A User Study of Visualization Effectiveness Using EEG and Cognitive Load." *Proceedings of the 13th Eurographics / IEEE-VGTC conference on Visualization*, edited by Helwig Hauser et al., The Eurographs Association and John Wiley & Sons, 2013, pp. 791–800.

Bachrach, Asaf. Interview with the author. 17 May 2021.

Boehm, Gottfried. *Wie Bilder Sinn erzeugen.* Berlin UP, 2007.

Brandstetter, Gabrielle. "Anordnung (als choreographisches Verfahren)." *Denkfiguren: Für Anselm Haverkamp*, edited by Eva Horn and Michèle Lawrie, August Verlag, 2013, pp. 35–38.

Cocker, Emma. "Distancing the If and Then." *Drawing a Hypothesis: Figures of Thought*, edited by Nikolaus Gansterer, 2nd ed., De Gruyter, 2017, pp. 97–108.

Cocker, Emma, et al. "Choreo-graphic Figures: Scoring Aesthetic Encounters." *Journal for Artistic Research*, vol. 18, 2019, https://www.researchcatalogue.net/view/462390/462398/3265/2867.

Dirmoser, Gerhard. "Collection of Figures of Thought." *Drawing a Hypothesis: Figures of Thought,* edited by Nikolaus Gansterer, 2nd ed., De Gruyter, 2017, pp. 161–76.

Dumit, Joseph, and Andreas Roepstorff. "Sharing Embodied Perspectives, Exploring Interacting Minds in Real Life @ Tate Modern." Presentation at EASST/4S virtual Prague, 19 Aug. 2020, https://youtu.be/hsdNUtvLVRo

Fedorova, Ksenia. "Neurointerfaces, Mental Imagery and Sensory Translation in Art and Science in the Digital Age." *Invisibility in Visual and Material Culture*, edited by Asbjørn Grønstad and Øyvind Vaagnes, Springer, 2019, pp. 91–109.

Fitsch, Hannah. *Dem Gehirn beim Denken zusehen?: Sicht- und Sagbarkeiten in der funktionellen Magnetresonanztomographie.* Transcript Verlag, 2014.

Gansterer, Nikolaus, editor. *Drawing a Hypothesis: Figures of Thought*, 2011. 2nd ed., De Gruyter, 2017. http://www.gansterer.org/img/projekte/drawing-a-hypothesis_web select/Drawing-a-Hypothesis_Figures-of-Thought_Nikolaus-Gansterer_c-2011_sample -pages.pdf

Gansterer, Nikolaus. "Preface: Drawing a Hypothesis." *Drawing a Hypothesis: Figures of Thought*, edited by Nikolaus Gansterer, 2nd ed., De Gruyter, 2017, pp. 21–29.

Gansterer, Nikolaus, et al. *Choreo-graphic Figures: Deviations from the Line*. De Gruyter, 2017.

Gansterer, Nikolaus. *Choreo-graphic Figures: Deviations from the Line*. https://www.choreo-graphic-figures.net/cyclopedia/.

Gombrich, Ernst H. "Moment and Movement in Art." *Journal of the Warburg and Courtauld Institutes*, vol. 27, 1964, pp. 293–306.

Isenberg, Tobias, et al. "A Systematic Review on the Practice of Evaluating Visualization." *IEEE Transactions on Visualization and Computer Graphics*, vol. 19, no. 12, Dec. 2013, pp. 2818–27.

Kant, Immanuel. *Kritik der reinen Vernunft*. 1781/87. Vol. 1, edited by Wilhelm Weischedel, Suhrkamp, 1974.

Krämer, Sybille. "Operative Bildlichkeit. Von der 'Grammatologie' zu einer 'Diagrammatologie'? Reflexionen über erkennendes Sehen." *Logik des Bildlichen. Zur Kritik der ikonischen Vernunft*, edited by Martina Hessler and Dieter Mersch, Transcript 2009, pp. 94–123.

Krämer, Sybille. "Trace, Writing, Diagram: Reflections on Spatiality, Intuition, Graphical Practices and Thinking." *The Power of the Image: Emotion, Expression, Explanation*, edited by András Benedek and Kristóf Nyiri, Lang, 2014, pp. 3–22.

Krämer, Sybille, and Christina Ljundberg. "Thinking and Diagrams: An Introduction." *Thinking with Diagrams: The Semiotic Basis of Human Cognition*, edited by Sybille Krämer and Christina Ljundberg, De Gruyter, 2016.

Le Poidevin, Robin. *The Images of Time: An Essay on Temporal Representation*. Oxford UP, 2007.

Lyotard, Jean-François. *Discourse, Figure*. Translated by Antony Hudek and Mary Lydon, U of Minnesota P, 2011.

Manning, Erin, and Brian Massumi. *Thought in the Act: Passages in the Ecology of Experience*. U of Minnesota P, 2014.

Mareis, Claudia. "Zeitlichkeit des Entwerfens: Visuelle Prozessmodelle und ihre temporale Bedeutung." *Visuelle Zeitgestaltung,* edited by Claudia Blümle et al., De Gruyter, 2020, pp. 114–23. Bildwelten des Wissens 15.

Mitchell, William J. T. *Picture Theory: Essays on Verbal and Visual Representation*. U of Chicago P, 1994.

Moser, Aloisia. *Kant, Wittgenstein, and the Performativity of Thought*. Palgrave MacMillan, 2021.

Petitmengin, Claire. Interview at the workshop "Experimenting, Experiencing, Reflecting. Art and Science at Work in the Public Realm," June 2018, https://vimeo.com/315433122.

Rodowick, David. *Reading the Figural: Or Philosophy after the New Media*. Duke UP, 2001.

Roepstorff, Andreas. "Interactively Human: Sharing Time, Constructing Materiality." *Behavioral and Brain Sciences*, vol. 36, no. 3, 2013, pp. 224–25.

Stjernfelt, Frederik. *Diagrammatology: An Investigation on the Borderlines of Phenomenology, Ontology, and Semiotics*. Springer, 2007.

Wittgenstein, Ludwig. *Tractatus Logico-Philosophicus & Philosophische Untersuchungen*. 1921/1953. Reclam, 1990.

PART 4

Shared Patterns and Discordant Worlds

CHAPTER 15

Circulating Neuro-Imagery:
A Trilogue

Antye Guenther, Flora Lysen, and Alexander Sack

CIRCULATING NEURO-IMAGERY — AN INTERDISCIPLINARY EXERCISE

contributors: ALEXANDER SACK (AS), FLORA LYSEN (FL), ANTYE GUENTHER (AG)

In this chapter, artist-researcher Antye Guenther, cultural historian Flora Lysen and neuroscientist Alexander Sack present a visual and textual exchange on the topic of neuroscientific visualization practices and images of the brain. Our back-and-forth builds on a previous "art-science" project that took place in the Maastricht Brain Stimulation and Cognition research group headed by Sack. Over a period of fifteen months, Guenther conducted interviews, gathered field notes, and was a test subject for various experiments, culminating in a performance in the main auditorium of the brain research department. Throughout this process, Lysen has been a close observer, interrogating the fuzzy dynamics of art-science-in-the-making. All three participants in this unfolding art-science exchange recognize the (implicit) expectations attached to the phenomenon of "art-science." Did this project count as a "collaboration," a "cooperation" or something else entirely? Was this an "interdisciplinary" project, and if so, what kind? Did it generate new practices and new insights, and if so, how? The following pages do not aim to answer such questions directly, but instead demonstrate a process of bouncy inquiry between three researchers. Guenther's observations on brain stimulation and visualization research are the starting point for an exchange that strings together a number of seductively alluring images of the brain, ranging from early modern cracked skulls and 1901 "thought forms" to Dali's automated animation and contemporary fictional user interfaces for brain research. In the process of discussing and commenting, this exchange turns into an "exercise," in which the three participants start to see again more clearly the effects of their own disciplinary backgrounds. Ultimately, it is this "form" — this way of working together — that constitutes the project's core contribution. We end with offering an outline of this exercise for trans- and interdisciplinary exchanges/collaborations.

text reply in regular 10pt
commented part in the text highlighted in white
comments in *italic 9pt*
image adjustments highlighted in black
image credits in regular 8pt

FIRST IMAGE, proposed by: AG
date: 19th of September 2020

AG: I felt caught here. Did I also just want to present attractive images to mesmerize?

AG: exactly. This is what Flora seems to go for.

Dear Antye,
Thank you for sending this smashing visualization collage. To me, this/outer space image conjures immediate associations with the now-fashionable "dark mode" for websites and apps. According to designers, dark mode saves energy and allows images to pop-out in our visual field and stick in our mind. Indeed, looking at these planetary bodies I am immediately drawn to the colourful tractography visualization on the left, which seems to strangely hover over the misty grey brain to which it belongs. Accordingly, the composite nature of the image is even more readily visible. Over the past years, I have encountered similarly brightly coloured images of bundles of nerve fibres printed with popular science articles and books (most recently on the cover over Gina Rippon's The Gendered Brain, where a jungle of pink and blue fibres are partly knotted together). Tractography images (tractograms) are a preeminent example of "seductively alluring" images in neuroscience. Various scholars have argued that such visualizations may overpromise what we currently know about the brain. In an article for the journal Neuroimage, neuro-connectivity

image credits (given separately on extra sheet):https://www.jch.com/volumes/dtifmri.htm / cortex based alignment of MRI brain data, processed in Brainvoyager)

*AG: no one mentioned or won-
dered about the added arrow.
AS: The arrow was a detail I
saw but decided that it is
likely a specific finding from
the study depicted here*

*AG: Flora seemed to go straight
to the parts of the collage
that received a lot of criticisms within academia, leaving
all other parts aside ...*

*AS: Simple: Just thought
I saw the hand area within
the motor cortex*

Dear Antye,
I looked at the image(s). Here is what came to my mind:

- misalignment
- mind without matter
- bad anatomy

- motor omega

- kissing and crossing
- planet on ecstasy
- Andy Warhol

(...)   Is this what you had in mind?
Alex

AG email reply:

-> *I wonder how that might look like*
-> *good and bad anatomy - how not to
think of this in moral terms?*
-> *I tried to imagine what that
could be, but my mind stayed blank*

-> *Why Andy Warhol? And not Phillip
Guston?*

*AG: It actually does not
matter what I had in mind*

researcher Daniel Margulies discusses
the art of creating tractography images (Margulies 2013). Image makers,
he writes, face a number of dilemma's:
should they favour anatomical clarity
over connectomic complexity? Aesthetic
appeal over information content? Thor-
oughness over readability? For Margulies, the best tractogram would be
one that signals its artifactuality. It
would be an "honest depiction of uncertainty" that turns a vast amount of
data in an "intuitive form." But is it
possible to integrate uncertainty and
probability in an instinctively comprehensible image? For Margulies, image
makers should be granted some creative
license to "distort brain space." In
captions, neuroscientists could explicitly state that a figure should not be
taken literally. Yet, for Margulies,
the question remains "to what degree
should a visualization be allowed to
stand alone?" For me it seems, images
never stand alone. The issue raised by
your image is: if we can make visible
the processes of visualization – super-
imposing, collaging, cut-and-paste –
how does this visibility of the process
of making impact the scientific reasoning, practices and institutions of
which it is part?

Regards, Flora

Margulies, Daniel S., Joachim Böttger, Aimi
Watanabe, and Krzysztof J. Gorgolewski.
"Visualizing the Human Connectome." NeuroImage, Mapping the Connectome, 80 (October 15,
2013): 445–61.

AG: This dentation was left outside the image frame giving the impression of a perfect sphere

AG: Residua from the black background are visible when shown with a background other than black

AG: Of course Flora knows the reference and that is immediately her point of reference.

image adjustments before sending:
in Photoshop: left image (downloaded jpg): The object was masked using the magic wand tool, the black background removed, and the image size adjusted to 300 dpi without resampling. right image (screenshot): The object was masked using the magic wand tool, and the interface frame and the white background removed. The saturation of the image was elevated by +10 as well as the brightness by slightly convexing the histogram curve. An opacity of 90% was applied to the image to make it transparent, and the image size adjusted to 300 dpi without resampling.
in Indesign: The two images were arranged within the image frame of 320 by 220 mm, based purely on aesthetic preferences. A dashed, slightly curved arrow was added, which points from one object to an asterisk that was placed on the other assuming a connection between the two objects.

I had to smile a bit when I read her text ....

In lieu of a more elaborate answer (time constraints).

SECOND IMAGE, proposed by: AG
date: 4th of October 2020

This is a tough one.

I first thought about space (like in our galaxy) and clouds or fog surrounding planets. Something far away and beyond our concept of matter. Then I read the legend and wondered whether mental activity can have a form, quite literally, a gestalt, where function or activity becomes a structure , a very transient ephemeral structure. In essence we are searching for a materialization of mental activity, of a thought, of our mind. We think about coding principles but always fail to provide a real being of the mind, a real meaning of this code. Here, we give it a form, a gestalt of electrical activity, this feels intuitive but does it really relate to the function it represents? Can electrical activity create an object or become an object? The second image is even more abstract and makes me wonder whether again and

—Makram's 2009 video "A brain in a supercomputer," is a treasure trove of tropes in popular communication of neuroscience. Galaxies, blue clouds, lighting bolts, the whole shebang. As part of the Blue Brain project, he created visualizations of electrical patterns, calling them "ghostly-like structures" that are like "electrical objects" appearing in the neocortical column. In turn, such "electrical objects," according to Makram, could become "brain coordinates" that could then be extrapolated to know what types of thoughts or actions they were referring to. There is more than a decade worth of criticism of Makram's computational neuroscience and promises of simulating the human brain. In this Worlding the Brain volume, Noah Hutton recounts his ten-year

electrical objects appearing → within the neocortical column.

image credits (given separately on extra sheet): https://www.ted.com/talks/henry_markram_a_brain_in_a_supercomputer#t-795945 / Annie Besant, C.W. Leadbeater. Thought Forms: A Record of Clairvoyant Investigation. London, 1901.

AG: I definitely felt caught out! It felt as if by choosing this particular image I am rather behind, all known and none of these images cutting edge (anymore). Ouch!

documentary project that
followed the Blue Brain researchers. I am excited about
these long-term ethnographic
views of computational neuroscience endeavours (see
for example, Bruder 2020).
Such research can expose the
infrastructural efforts in
strengthening a particular
computational view of the
brain.
– The two images you juxta-
pose, Makram's "ghostly-like
structures" and the "thought
forms" of Besant and Leadbeater (1901, is that correct?) similarly point to
the ongoing promise of materialization of thoughts/
behaviour in some-thing that
can be made visible. Con-
sidering the shape of this
debate on "materialization,"
those early decades of the
twentieth century are an
interesting moment, because
new media of recording and
broadcasting (x-rays, for
example) met with older imaginaries (ether, mesmerism,
magnetism, telepathy, clair-
voyance). Does every new
recording technology fortify
the dream of capturing the
mental?

again we are looking
at the brain and our
mind from the outside,
looking at the surface
without getting any
closer to its actual
core, it's true na-
ture and meaning. It
is all about visualiz-
ing, describing space
and time and rep-
resentation of mental
function, which like-
ly brings us no clos-
er to unraveling it's
mystery. It is like
looking at a light
bulb, taking pictures
with different cameras
and colors and de-
scribing its sub parts
and measuring its
temperature increase
in an attempt to un-
derstand how electric-
ity works, why there
is light. We focus on
what we see and not
how it works.

Best
Alex

→ *AG: I specifically liked how this number seemed disentangled, but in its font referered to somehow ancient times*

→ *AG: Nicely strange comparison, specifically as well due to the connection between brain activity and the light bulb that is going on*

AG: I first thought she meant it had to be much later
FL: I love these images! I have a scanned version of
the book on my computer (from a different date).

Bruder, Johannes. Cognitive
Code: Post-Anthropocentric Intelligence and the Infrastructural Brain. McGill-Queen's
Press - MQUP, 2020.

'Interestingly, the actual 2005
paper that proposes the idea of
"electrical objects" is rather obscure and seems no longer
available online. "Dendritic
object theory: a theory of the
neual code where 3D electrical
objects are formed across den-
drites by neural microcircuits,"
Swiss Soc. Neurosci. Abstr. 196
(2005), mentioned in Markram,
Henry. "The Blue Brain Project."
Nature Reviews Neuroscience 7,
no. 2 (February 2006): 153–60.
https://doi.org/10.1038/nrn1848.

image adjustments before sending:

In Photoshop (screenshots and downloaded jpg): All objects were cut
from their backgrounds using the magic wand and rectangular marquee
tool. The left object in the first image was originally cut at the top.
This top got freely reconstructed using the clone stamp and patch
tool. The saturation of the objects was slightly heightened, and the
image size adjusted to 300 dpi without re-sampling.
In Indesign: The two screenshots were placed on the first page with
cut, copied and rearranged subtitles. The downloaded jpg, which became a .psd file to keep the transparent background, was placed in the
middle of the second page with the original page number on the bottom.
Geometrical forms, straight and circled arrows with dashed and solid
lines were added to both images, on top and behind the frayed objects.

AG: Why again did no one comment the additional structures? Almost
as if they are not existing. Modernis-
tic, old fashioned diagrammatic add-
ons ....

AS: I think this is the too selective attention. I
noticed throughout this excersize that my coments
are characterized by top-down control, filtering,
selecting, prioritizing based on existing knowledge (or the illusion thereof), which limits me in
seeing what else is really there. Antye looks at it
very differently, in a non judgmental way, seeing
also details, giving them equal priority and importance. I wonder whihc one is better, which one represents the expert view of the world?

FL: my attention was also extremely conditioned
by my disciplinary training. I see historical
references, I rush to contextualise. Have I
become blind for things that do not fit my narrative?

FL: Could I add a lightbulb-head image here?
The oldest one I am able to find?

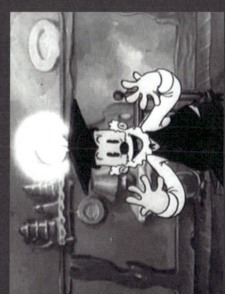

Fleischer, M. (1935). Betty Boop and
Grampy [Cartoon]. Fleischer Studios.
Retrieved from: https://archive.org/
details/bb_and_grampy

THIRD IMAGE, proposed by: AG
date: 18th of October 2020

I asked to comment the first image before looking at the second one in order to not jump to easy conclusions such as two versehrten heads, but then different, one analog, one digital, and then even the one of the (female) artist.

AG: in regards to Flora's comment on fashionable black background I placed these two images (and actually all that follow) on white backgrounds

image adjustments before sending:
In Photoshop: first image: The white point and black point were set for EV compensation with a heightened brightness and contrast of the image. The yellow hues were set with a reduced saturation and an elevated lightness. The overall sharpness of the image was adjusted by applying a high pass filter of 1,5 pixels.
in Indesign: second image: The image was duplicated and the head structure masked, rotated by 89°, enlarged by 105% and placed on top of the interface screenshot, covering the original head structure. Both images were placed on a white background.

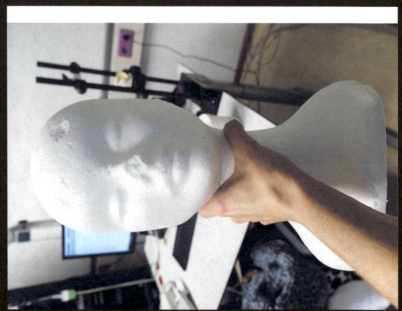

image credits (not given):
digital photograph taken by AG in AS's lab / screenshot of Brainvoyager interface with MRI brain data being reconstructed as a head mesh

AG: simple real picture – I see. ;)

AG: Yes, indeed!

Dear both,
I just looked at figure 1. Here my spontaneous
thoughts :

Ah, nothing reconstructed or modeled or indirectly assumed, but a simple real picture from
my lab. A real hand (probably Antye's left hand)
holding a head made of styrofoam. The styrofoam
head is not intact but shows 3 clear "lesions",
on the left and right forehead as well as on the
tip of the nose. In fact, the tip of the nose is
completely missing. I could think of many funny metaphors describing the limited integrity of
this styrofoam head, yet I can't help but logically conclude that this head was probably used
to demonstrate TMS neuronavigation using ultrasound senders for motion tracking. During the
required co registration between the "real" and
reconstructed head, three miniature ultrasound
senders need to be attached to the real head. For
this we usually choose the left and right forehead and the tip of the nose of our subjects. I
am sure someone tried to demonstrate this procedure using this styrofoam head as the "real" head
and therefore placed 3 sticky ultrasound senders
on its surface. When removing those, the styrofoam came off at these locations leaving the poor
styrofoam model in this disgraceful condition.
Time to buy a new one or change the material.

I will now look at figure 2.
Alex

Hi Antye,
please see my two responses below.

Image 1. Aww. Thankfully that hand is not grip-
ping her neck any tighter. Poor mannequin doll.
Probably manufactured to model wigs or hats and
now demonstrating what happens to experimental
subjects during TMS. The Nefertiti of Neuronavigation. The stimulated styrofoam Sphinx. I could
say that it is not a coincidence that this "model subject" is a female subject. The mannequin
signals a long history of women as ideal neurological subjects to be rendered transparent by a
technological-scientific gaze (Cartwright, 1995).
But perhaps even more interesting for the current
situation in the Maastricht Brain Stimulation and
Cognition group, I wonder if in fact most subjects in this lab are actually women (female psychology students). How does that matter?

Lisa Cartwright, Screening the Body: Tracing Medicine's Visual Culture (Minneapolis: University of Minnesota Press, 1995

*AG: I have to admit and I really wonder what
Alexander had in mind here ...*

*AS: nothing really. just pictured my staff
playing with this studd and breaking off
the nose..*

AG: But what about the metaphors?

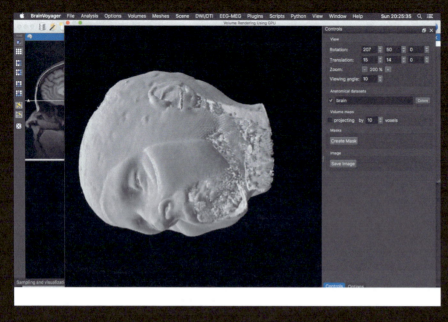

Dear both,
Figure 2:

AG: I take this as a compliment! ;)

AS: You should

I see a head mesh of Antye, quite nice looking head surface. Such reconstructions of the skull itself are nice but mostly without purpose. However, one important function of such head meshs is to localize anatomical landmarks on the reconstructed head. These landmarks can be identified on both, the reconstructed head from a subject (the head mesh) as the real head. This will help the software to bring both heads into the same reference system, as a starting point for any neuronavigation. It is a pity that the ears are a bit squished, probably from the ear protection or cushions used during the mri scan. How can the software now know how much the reconstructed ear is squished as compared to her real ear. This will cause some imperfections in the co registration process between real as reconstructed images. Oh well. Thinking about it. Since this is just about the outer superficial shape of her head, it may be better to just use a high-resolution laser to scan her head and only fmri to really image brain matter and brain activity. Then again, everything is distorted anyways in the scanner.

Best wishes, Alex

Image 2. A digital archaeologist has uncovered a grainy layer of voxels underneath the smooth skin of the head volume. The image makes me think of nineteenth century photographs of "ectoplasm," a type of a spiritual slime that foamed out of mostly female mouths. Ectoplasm was "a viscous substance" emanating "from the body of a spiritualistic medium" ((Oxford English Dictionary)) that could develop into a human form or face. Please "create mask" for this ghostly medium.

AG: I have to admit I do not really understand what "create mask" really means here.

regards! see you soon, Flora

FL: I meant the "create mask" function in the software, which fits beautifully with this foaming mouth.

image credits (both recipients knew the source): Volkskrant ...

Dear Flora,

Great picture! Here my thoughts:

- Innocence - curiosity - wisdom
- Fear - Preservation - Hope

Best
Alex

> *AG: Innocence? Who or what is*
> *innocent here? The patient or*
> *test person? The technique or*
> *the technology? Surely not the*
> *practicioner, right?*
>
> *AS: Yes. The practicioner!*

I have to admit I am looking at the image now not
for the first time. When Flora proposed it I had a
closer look already, and I also briefly discussed
it with her. Why mention this? Is our conversation
protocol corrupted? Should I not have been exposed to the image beforehand? But why would these
standards matter here anyway?
Anyway,what do I see? I see a white space with
plastic covering of electric etc. wiring along the
wall at midriff height. Ugly and very typical for
functional spaces, such as labs and hospital spaces. The lighting is also specific: somehow clinical white light, but then not evenly distributed,
rather leaving a stage like circle of light on the
wall. What kind of lamps are used in this space?
Does the light come from above or is the scene il-
luminated with an extra lamp? A middle aged man is
standing in the centre, which I know is Alexander
Sack, wearing quite casually a white polo shirt,
of what kind of brand is not decipherable. He is
looking, seemingly very concentrated, onto something outside the image with one hand on a black
device that looks like Mickey mouse ears made of
plastic and with the other hand at a knob of a
technical apparatus. The black device, which I believe to be a TMS coil, is supported by a mounting

(made of what looks like a polished stainless steel) suggesting that precision is of crucial importance, meaning holding the device purely by hand would not be sufficient. The black device is placed on the left-upper part of a woman's head, while the head seems to be comfortably placed on a blue-whitish cushion with an unidentifiable structure in the left lower corner. The middle aged woman (why does middle aged sounds in both cases almost insulting?) looks into the same direction as Alexander Sack with a rather tensed or even frightened expression on her face. She is wearing a white cap on her head, a cap that reminds me of a swimming cap, but that I assume to be an EEG cap. But why is there no wiring attached? The woman wears an orange top/dress with a necklace that looks to be made of leather and shells. The colour of the top/dress and the necklace seem to be of a person with an 'alternative lifestyle', of someone closer to nature, healthy eating and gardening etc. than to high-tech and orthodox medicine. Oh, these prejudices! But it made me wonder who this person is/was. A patient? But what about anonymity/privacy then? A test person? But why agreeing to be photographed while people might think one is a patient needing brain procedure? Was this image from the archives provided to the journalist or made for the occasion of the article? In the latter, is the whole scene then staged and therefore also fake (which would explain the missing EEG cables)? The most interesting thing about this image seems to be outside of it. Both persons almost stare towards what: a screen? An output to the procedure? Why do we not see what both are watching? Is this what might be called suspense and what makes this image then also intriguing? Perhaps Alexander Sack will uncover the mysteries around this image in his reflection. Best, Antye

Dear Antye,
great text, eye for detail, like a novel...
here my answers:

- yes, there is an extra light that was used by the camera team who came with the journalist...
- i think it is Banana Republic or Hilfiger, whatever was on sale at the time
- the EEG cap has no wires because it is just used for coil positioning, placing the TMS coil on F3 electrode position. Believe it or not you can now buy EEG caps without EEG wires just for this purpose (totally overpriced of course). So, it is not fake or a mistake in the picture.
- the woman is Christl from the CN secretariat. So, yes, the whole scene is staged. Our real patients did not want to be in a national newspaper as being treated for depression (apparently this is still stigmatised). So we mimicked the procedure with our secretary playing a patient.
- I think I am (we are) looking at, talking to, the journalist who asked questions. But I am not sure anymore. But the journalist talked to me and the real patient and this picture was taken specifically for this article by the newspaper people.

Best wishes, Alex

FL: I confess. I already knew this image was staged. But I wanted to have a little behind-the-scenes peek into the way images of science are constructed (in the multiple senses of the word).

FL: :) perceptive. Makes me wonder about how people with different lifestyles may be open to (or opposed to) using TMS. There is also a DIY TMS community, which might have more connections to spirituality than one would presume (but I am not an expert on this).

FIFTH IMAGE, proposed by: AG
date: 14th of November 2020

AG: Indeed. And I have the feeling I was telling too much during our unrelated meeting!

PHILIPPE HALSMAN
Dalí mit verspiegelter Brille im / Dalí with mirrored glasses at Hotel Saint Regis, New York 1942

Well, I think I see Dalí lying in a bed, wearing mirroring sunglasses.
Very quickly I can't help but lose myself in the meta level of wondering why Antye chose this picture? What does it mean? What is she trying to say? I sense a feeling of being tricked into something... i feel like a fool...

But this is all about me and not the picture ... so focus ... back to the picture. I see Dalí, I think it is him, he looks much younger and nicer as compared to the usual pictures I know of him.

He is lying in bed, it reminds me of a hospital, but the legend reveals a hotel in NYC. Still, I constantly feel like it is a hospital. This is maybe because he is wearing this cap or bandage on his head, with a cable sticking out and disappearing somewhere behind a sort of flip chart. It seems as if he is wired up to something. Of course I immediately think of brain stimulation... The flip chart shows some sketches of random thoughts like a brainstorm.. I see a visual illusion , graphs, formulas, quick and dirty.. he is holding a book or something in his hands but he is more interested in directly looking into the camera, it all seems staged and arranged, not real. On the wall behind him are pictures, the room is decorated, quite nice for a hospital room (you see, it happened again). Why is he wearing mirroring sun-

glasses inside? They don't show anything but
light, illumination, reflection of nothing.
I never was keen on Dali.
Alex

The image amuses me, I am not a fan
of Dali's work, but I like thinking
about his life and art as a kind of
Rorschach image that sparks questions of taste and popular opinion
(my own remark "I am not a fan of
his work" is of course a telling re-
assurance of my own proper cultivation)
Dali mastered self-fashioning as a
form of art.. By the time Philippe
Halsman took this image, I presume
Dali had already become a "brand": a
symbol of the surrealist legacy and
a vain jester artist (who would have
himself photographed laying in bed
in a hotel room). Had Dali started
to work with Walt Disney at this
point? I love the strange hybrid
projects he started taking on after the 1930s, such as advertising
copy and animation (in Hitchcock's
Spellbound 1945).
In this image, the photographer and
the artist have staged a strange
"brain-mirror." Dali's thoughts seem
to be wired onto a drawing board by
means of a cord extending from his
cranium to the paper. This brain
mirror is doubled by the pen in Dali's hand and the pieces of paper on
his lap. The photograph shows us two ways in
which the mind (Dali's unconscious) is trans-

AG: Of course! And I can only vehemently agree
on account of my own proper cultivation.
*

image credits (file name next to the images): both photographs
were taken by AG at the Arp Museum/ Remagen, 2020

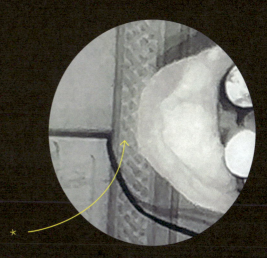

*

a light beam caught in Dali's mirror glasses, another element of reflection that gestures to an onlooker looking inward – literally seeing yourself in the eyes of the other. Likewise, the glass covering this Halsman photograph also shows the faint reflection of the photographer-art-viewer-subject-Antye. My short google search turned up a second image by Philip Halsman that was probably taken in the same sitting session. A small projector sits on Dali's head and seems to take the place of rays of light (and again, a pen in his hand for additional automatic writing). On the right side of the image, we see the leftovers from his (room-service) breakfast. It seems he must have received quite some pennies for his thoughts.

× F

image adjustments/ manipulation before sending:
In Photoshop: The adjustment of both photographs started with removing the perspective distortions to straighten frame and images. Afterwards the black wire was retouched and directly attached to Dali's white cap. After unsuccessful attempts to do so via a copied masked layer, the clone stamp tool proved most suitable. EV compensations and colour corrections were applied to remove the yellow tinges and lighten the images, as well as another high pass filter for sharpening.
In Indesign: Both images were placed on white backgrounds with the file names placed in NotCurierSans 10pt.

The image adjustment (or manipulation as one might say) reflects the way I saw the image for the first time. I thought this cable was atached to his head and I immediatly started to imagine the procedure that was taken place and had been recorded somehow on the board next to Dali. What does it mean when one's perception adds a piece of cable for the pleasure of imagination around brain procedures and thought or brain activity recording?

© Philippe Halsman/Magnum Photos

SIXTH IMAGE, proposed by: AG
date: 29th of November 2020

Hmm, tricky one again.
I see a man looking at a screen. The screen looks like a head up display you have in modern cars. He is looking at various sources of information and data. I see brain scans. I see some sort of code, maybe a genetic code of some sort. I also see a map, looks like the map of the US. Another man on the opposite side of the display watches the scene. It is unclear what is happening. I imagine some sort of diagnostic purpose, a multi dimensional and multi modal assessment leading to a robust and reliable diagnosis I imagine AI and maschine learning algorithms predicting best possible treatment, treatment response, and prognosis. Maybe a new bio-marker is tested for its predictive value. Is this all done with good or bad intention? Has an informed consent been collected? Who is in charge here?

I was wondering what this structure was. Alex might be right, though, as the game is situated on former US territory.

Alex

AG: I am surprised again of what Flora and Alex did either not see or not comment on: e.g. 1lh game Movie, cut scenes therefore are not the scence that where left out. Also, fluid samples together with a brain scan equals lumbal puncture on the go?

image credits: screenshots of DEATH STRANDING All Cutscenes (Game Movie) at 37:36min and at 6:54:47h

My reaction to your image is just one word, and this document: BRAIN FUI!
XF

AG: FUI for federal unemployment insurance? ;)

FL: FUI as in: Fantasy User Interfaces, Fictional User Interfaces, Fake User Interfaces, Futuristic User Interfaces, Film User Interfaces, Future User Interfaces. I think almost all of the interfaces I sent you were made by the same company: KIT FUI. I wonder if this might also explain why some FUI's look so 2000s to me sometimes :)
Could there be a wholly different aesthetic for this? What would it look like?

AG: yes, yes. Of course. The insurance reference was just the first one that came up in my Google search! ;)

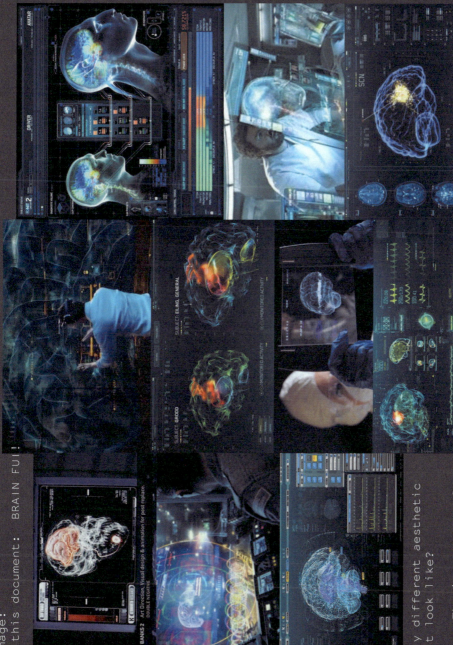

image adjustments before sending:
The brightness and contrast were elevated in both screenshots as well as the 'i' symbols in the right upper corners retouched for pure aesthetic reasons. Afterwords both image sizes were adjusted to 300 dpi without resampling.

AG: *Flora finds these colour schemes very 2000. Does this also apply to the death stranding screenshots? Would it have been important in this regards to have send the 2nd image as well with its pink- turquoise colour scheme? If its still very 2000, what does it say about the developer and programmer of this video game? Who is influencing whom? Could these brain visualisations in the game still be called FUI? The category 'fake' or 'fantasy' seems to make little sense in a completely fictional video game ...*

DEATH STRANDING All Cutscenes (Game Movie) 1080p HD

Until Resuscitation Remaining Time
00:03

6:54:47 / 11:17:07   Für Details scrollen

LAST IMAGE, proposed by: AG
date: 9th of December 2020

image credits (not given): Humani Capitis by Johannes Dryander/Eichmann, 1537 / https::/download.brainvoyager.com/bv/doc/UsersGuide/Segmentation/HeadSkinSegmentationAndReconstruction.html

Dear Antye,

I feel as if I was looking at a rel-ict displayed in a museum. I am just not sure whether it is a museum of modern art or a history museum.

I see a sphere, a mesh where the shrinking algorithm has aborted the calculations for some reason. I see a mouth and the bottom part of a nose, but then just the unfinished sphere like a ball, a balloon. On the surface of this balloon is a painting of a brain like a curtain covering a face, also painted there in an imperfect prolongation of the reconstructed unfinished "real" face. I see script, hair, some tools in the foreground. A painting I would hang in my living room and discuss its elements with random guests over a glass of port.

Best
Alex

scientific visualis-ations as conversa-tion piec-es made by artists. How illus-trative ;)

HVMANI CAPITIS, FIGVRA QVARTA

Hi Antye,

This blow-up brain looks like a balloon that is about to explode (did somebody misplace a comma in a 3-D visualization program?). If a scalpel would only casually touch the dotted line, we would immediately have ac-cess to the alien inside of this head. KA-POW! This really is nothing like the hard work of hammering open a skull that was nec-essary to produce the engraving underneath this image: the Humani Capitis by Johannes Dryander/Eichmann, 1537. Dryander's Capitis image is often described as an early example of a shift, in the mid-sixteenth century, from the medieval diagrammatic representa-tions of the brain (illustrating the ven-tricular system or "cell doctrine") towards

life-like anatomical drawings that aimed at objective naturalism. More recently, a number of scholars have pointed out that this was not a straightforward and linear shift (strange mixes of different approaches persisted for centuries). Moreover, historians of epistemology have emphasised that the ideal of "truth to nature" was practiced in different ways depending on varying historical contexts. Hence, a true-to-life engraving is very much a "cultural hologram" of its time (Martensen 2004, cited in De Rijcke 2010, 41).
Regards! Flora

FL: I like how the concept of the cultural hologram itself is so obviously period-specific.

image adjustments before sending:
In Photoshop: The first image was cropped and parallel aligned, the brightness and contrast heightened, the saturation, specifically of the yellow hues, decreased and the whole image sharpened using a high pass filter on a second layer with applied soft light. The second image was cropped, and the object masked to separate it from its background. As a progress window overlapped the skin reconstruction object, the outer rim on the left upper corner of that object needed to be reconstructed using mostly the clone stamp tool.
In Indesign: The second image was rotated by 13° clockwise and placed on top of the first one with an applied transparency effect of opacity reduction to 88%. A white dashed line of 1pt was added with the vage intention to resemble a cut line, and everything placed on a grey background of K8%.

AG: No comments etc in regards to the image adjustments either, said the artist naggingly ...

The meaning of the "inter" in "interdisciplinarity" projects is often left under-defined, and this art-science project was no exception. Performing this visual and textual exchange underlined the possibility of playfulness between disciplines, yet one that was always scaffolded by a simultaneous disciplinary mode, i.e. a learned way of emphasizing, associating and leaving things unmentioned. Ultimately our exchange showed the outlines of an exercise in interdisciplinarity, or, more precisely, an exercise in response. As a final "contribution," this chapter offers a short manual for this exercise to inspire interdisciplinary exchanges in other research constellation to the pre-presented visual material and the comments it provoked.
 Try to find and imagine items of both obvious vs. ambivalent choices, as you might be surprised by the comments to both categories. Short video clips or short sound pieces could work well as thought-provoking items.
 Both in the short and longer versions of the exercise, the group will need to decide on who initiates the exchange. Will all participants start one of the rounds of commenting or will there be a main or single initiator? Will the process itself reveal the order of initiations and initiators, taking images and comments into consideration, or be pre-determined?

MANUAL OF AN EXERCISE IN RESPONSE:

Decide on a group with participants from different backgrounds and fields of expertise. To ensure intimacy and intensity of exchange, keep group size to three to four people.

Two potential time frames could be fruitful:

A speed version to be performed in one to two hours at a stretch, or a longer, accompanying version, that will unfold over a few months.

In the speed version the participants will each prepare a few images, visualisations, photographs etc. relevant to the topic/ the context of the interdisciplinary project. The long(er) version allows for more refined image-answers in regards

Limit the time period for commenting. As so many of us are on the verge of burnout, keep things light and fun. Encourage your colleagues/ collaborators to contribute what immediately comes to their minds.

Give time to comment on the comments before proposing the next (visual) item. The total number of items should not exceed seven to eleven rounds (keeping the group energy level in mind).

Plan a final online/offline meeting to discuss the process, the findings and to simply enjoy each other's presence.

CHAPTER 16

What Have the Arts and Humanities Ever Done for Us?

Disruptive Contributions and a 4E Cognitive Arts and Humanities

Michael Wheeler

1 Will the Cognitive Arts and Humanities Please Stand Up?

The term "cognitive arts and humanities" refers to an active field of interdisciplinary research that brings the cognitive sciences and the arts and humanities into a mutually productive relationship. Having written this opening sentence, I have to confess that it suffers from two shortcomings. The first is that there isn't really a recognized field of scholarship that is widely referred to in academic circles specifically as the cognitive arts and humanities. So much is true. The term doesn't currently return many complete matches from a Google search, for example, although the term "cognitive humanities" (without the explicit extension to art) does better. However, the failure here is innocuous. The cognitive arts and humanities is (in my humble opinion) a perfectly appropriate moniker for a rich, vibrant, and growing body of interdisciplinary research that unquestionably does exist, the unifying aim of which is precisely to bring the cognitive sciences and the arts and humanities into a mutually productive relationship. There is no space here for any sort of conceptual or historical introduction to this body of work.[1] *Arguably*, it all began with pioneering work by thinkers such as Spolsky (1993) and Turner (1991), among many others, has its strongest roots in the area known as cognitive literary studies (where the relevant links are specifically between cognitive science and literary interpretation—see e.g., Zunshine 2015), and is admirably represented by the ongoing series of international conferences that goes under the name of "Cognitive Futures in the Arts and Humanities."[2] If, for whatever reason, you want to call

---

1 See Anderson et al. for one such introduction that deploys the more restricted term "cognitive humanities" and is oriented towards the particular kind of cognitive science in which we'll be mostly interested in this chapter.

2 There have been nine such conferences so far. The most recent was in Warsaw in 2023 ("Cognitive Futures"). The series-name used to be just "Cognitive Futures in the Humanities," but that under-represented the contributions being made by disciplines such as art, dance, and

---

© KONINKLIJKE BRILL NV, LEIDEN, 2023 | DOI:10.1163/9789004681293_018

WHAT HAVE THE ARTS AND HUMANITIES EVER DONE FOR US? 259

the domain in question something other than the cognitive arts and humanities, that's fine with me, although you'll have to put up with my favored terminology for the rest of this chapter.

The second shortcoming exhibited by my opening sentence is definitely not
innocuous. Indeed, it's potentially toxic to the very notion of a cognitive arts
and humanities, as I have characterized it. I have defined the field in terms
of a *mutually productive* relationship between the cognitive sciences and the
arts and humanities, and that means that we should expect to find in operation a two-way channel of intellectual exchange, a channel, that is, in which
intellectual illumination flows both from the cognitive sciences to the arts and
humanities *and in the opposite direction*. It is perhaps easy enough to see what
cognitive science might do for art, literature, literary studies, performance
studies, history, and so on, by explaining the minds and thus the actions of
the beings who write, choreograph, perform, consume and even figure imaginatively in various artworks, and who take part in the unfolding of history.
However, it is often hard to see what arts and humanities disciplines can do for
cognitive science, beyond perhaps revealing better data to be explained by the
empirical science.

One might wonder what is meant here by the phrase "better data." Consider
the psychology of reading—the scientific study of how human beings extract
information from and make sense of written text. Risking a sweeping generalization, one might think that much of this sub-field of psychology revolves
around the use of relatively simple texts that are specially constructed by the
experimenters concerned. These specially constructed texts are read under
laboratory test conditions by subjects who have no advanced training in literary comprehension or interpretation and whose psychological engagement
with the texts in question is investigated using button-pressing or eye-tracking experimental paradigms. The upshot is (one might argue) a distorted and
superficial manifestation of what reading often is. Of course, no one will sen-
sibly deny that this approach can produce useful knowledge—for one thing,
superficial reading is undoubtedly a genuine phenomenon—but any literary
theorist worth their salt will want to complain that whatever explanations of
reading the psychologists gather in this way will be of limited application to
the so-called deep reading that characterizes our engagement with great novels, great poetry and so on. Such deep reading involves cognitively sophisticated inferential, analogical, and critical reasoning alongside experience and
insight. The key observations for our purposes are, firstly, that these cognitive

performance and theater studies, so it was changed. I have followed suit here with the term
"Cognitive Arts and Humanities."

processes are arguably missing altogether from, or at least invisible within, the experimental context described above, and, secondly, that literary theorists will have the capacity to bring both the complex phenomenon of deep reading and the properties of the texts that reward it into proper view. Although there will undoubtedly be knock-on effects from this in terms of new challenges for experimental design—challenges that may not be easy to address—the eventual upshot, one might reasonably think, will be that arts and humanities researchers will be able to assist in delivering better data for psychologists of reading to explain.[3]

To be clear, revealing better data for cognitive scientists to explain is already a significant contribution to the project of the cognitive arts and humanities. However, if we simply stop there, then our second direction of illumination—the one that flows from the arts and humanities to cognitive science—remains, in my view, under-explored and under-exploited. Unpacking what this last remark means is the task of the rest of this chapter. In what follows, I shall focus our attention on a particular sub-species of cognitive science, so called 4E (*embodied-embedded-extended-enactive*) *cognitive science* (more on this in the next section). I shall argue that once we adopt the 4E framework, the arts and humanities are revealed as potentially doing more in relation to the cognitive sciences than "merely" articulating a better target for scientific explanation.[4] As this argument unfolds, the phrase "doing more" will come to point to a kind of contribution that I shall call *disruptive*. What does this mean?

In general terms, a contribution to science is disruptive when its effect is to shake up the knowledge-shaping assumptions, frameworks, arguments, and/ or procedures of existing thought and practice in the field. Putting this in a recognizably Kuhnian language (Kuhn), without thereby necessarily endorsing every aspect of Kuhn's philosophy of science, one might say that, in such cases, the inertia of normal science is disturbed and a positive momentum is either established or amplified in the direction of some sort of significant theory-change or, more dramatically, a paradigm shift. Of course, as Kuhn famously tells us, this sort of momentum may well be established *within* the science, by a combination of the repeated failure of the existing science to

---

3   There is, of course, much useful work in the psychology of reading that operates between the no doubt idealized extremes of superficial and deep reading. To give just one example, Mak and Willems use an eye-tracking paradigm to investigate the contribution of mental simulation during the reading, by participants who were not screened for advanced training in literary comprehension or interpretation, of existing short stories by acclaimed writers.

4   I am not claiming that more substantive contributions are not available to a cognitive arts and humanities built on a non-4E cognitive science, but rather that the alliance with 4E cognitive science warmly invites such contributions, in a particular form.

WHAT HAVE THE ARTS AND HUMANITIES EVER DONE FOR US? 261

solve some recognized problem and the presence of an alternative, competing theoretical framework to which scientists can turn. However, if I am right, the same sort of momentum within cognitive science may be established or amplified by the intervention of arts and humanities research, when the right platform (theoretical and practical) is found for bringing such research into constructive dialogue with the science.

In bringing the phenomenon of disruption into view, it is important to emphasize two things. Firstly, in the present context, disruption is a *contribution to* the science in question, taken as a whole. In other words, its end-point is not a critique of science, but rather the opening of new doors within science. Secondly (and adapting the Kuhnian requirement that there be a competing scientific framework on offer), for a contribution to count as disruptive, it may draw on alternative currents of thought or unconventional ways of conceptualizing phenomena that are already available within the science, in order to amplify an existing momentum in the direction of change. In so doing it may participate in the development and articulation of those currents and conceptualizations. That is the dynamic that will be to the fore in the treatment that follows, a treatment in which I'll reflect on certain kinds of disruptive contribution that can be made to cognitive science, by arts and humanities research, once we look at cognition from a 4E perspective.

2 Towards a 4E Cognitive Arts and Humanities

4E cognition is the name for a family of inter-related conceptions of psychological states and processes that has made headway in cognitive science over the last 30 years or so. In very general terms, the four Es may be characterized as follows: cognition[5] is *embodied* when psychological states and processes are routinely shaped, in fundamental ways, by non-neural bodily factors; it is *embedded* when the distinctive adaptive richness and/or flexibility of intelligent thought and action is regularly, and perhaps sometimes necessarily, causally dependent on the bodily exploitation of certain environmental props or scaffolds; it is *extended* when it is literally true that the physical machinery of mind (the part of the physical world where a mind is located) extends beyond the skull and skin; it is *enactive* when it unfolds (is enacted) in

---

5 Some philosophers draw a distinction between "cognition" and "mind." I don't. Alongside most empirical cognitive scientists (as far as I can tell), I treat the two terms as equivalent and as synonyms for "psychological states and processes."

looping sensorimotor interactions between an active embodied organism and its environment.[6]

Because the 4E cognition movement is a family, there are often squabbles between its members. Some of these squabbles get resolved, while others reinforce deep and perhaps unassailable divisions. For present purposes, however, this ongoing domestic strife will not matter, because the line of argument that I shall develop appeals only to (a) an issue—namely whether there is *group-level cognition*—that cross-cuts the various Es, and (b) a shared 4E commitment to what, following an increasingly common usage, I shall call *entanglement*. For the moment, let's focus on the latter. For 4E theorists across the board, psychological phenomena such as thought, reasoning, emotion, and experience routinely depend, in various ways, on intimately entangled systems of neural, bodily, technological, and/or socio-cultural elements. Taking the target of cognitive science to be an intimate and intricate entanglement between brain, body, technology, and culture (there's an example coming up soon) contrasts sharply with the neuro-centric orthodoxy in the field. According to the latter, any non-neural factors are customarily depicted as peripheral elements in the great cognitive drama, in that they are no more than (i) sources of essentially passive informational inputs to the inner neural cognitive system or (ii) the implementing means by which, or the stage on which, neurally-specified actions occur. In their shared rejection of this orthodoxy, everyone in the 4E stable embraces entanglement as an explanatory template, even if the details of that entanglement look different to different thinkers.

As an illustrative example of 4E cognition (and thus of entanglement)—one that is firmly in arts and humanities territory—consider what is now a canonical study. Early modern theater companies performed an astonishing number of plays (as many as six different plays each week), with relatively infrequent repetition, very little group rehearsal, each actor playing multiple roles, and in the face of mounting a new play roughly every fortnight. If we imagine a scenario in which each actor was required to store each of these plays internally (that is, neurally), it seems that we would be forced to conclude that early modern actors possessed super-human organic memory capacities. Since this is patently a lousy hypothesis, how on earth did they do it? In ground-breaking work, Tribble argues that the seemingly prohibitive information processing load just highlighted was rendered manageable because a number of tricks and ploys deployed by the companies concerned resulted in that load being distributed over the individual actor and the physical and social environments

---

6   For a proper introduction to 4E cognition, accompanied by references to the formative research in philosophy and cognitive science, see Anderson et al.

WHAT HAVE THE ARTS AND HUMANITIES EVER DONE FOR US? 263

of the early modern theater. For example, and very briefly, stripped-down manuscript parts that excised all unnecessary information (including the other parts, save for sparse line cues) were used in conjunction with what were called "plots"—sheets of paper containing scene-by-scene accounts of entrances and exits, casting, and sound and music cues. This external scaffolding worked by assuming both the particular three-dimensional organization of the physical theatrical space (e.g., the door arrangements on the early modern stage) and certain conventions of movement that were operative in theater at the time (meaning that the door through which an actor is to enter or exit is hardly ever specified in the aforementioned plots). Finally, various guild-like social structures and protocols supported the development of apprentice actors, enabling them to perform progressively more complex roles.

This is not only 4E cognition but the 4E cognitive arts and humanities coming into view: remembering in the early modern theater (a phenomenon of importance for theater historians, amongst others) has been explained as the product of an entangled system of elements spanning the neural (the actors' brains are certainly crucial factors), the bodily (the physical movement conventions for entrances and exits), the technological (the system of plots and stripped down parts), and the socio-cultural (the guild-like social protocols). One should be impressed. So far, however, one might also be tempted to conclude that, when push comes to shove, this remains a case in which the arts and humanities, as represented by historical theater studies, has succeeded "only" in generating better data for cognitive science—albeit a cognitive science of an enlightened 4E kind—to explain. If this is correct, then, as exciting and as compelling as the research remains, the fact is that, in terms of intellectual illumination, the direction of travel is not quite the one for which we are currently searching.

A moment's reflection, however, should indicate that the conclusion just drawn cannot be correct. If Tribble is right, the material vehicles of the processes of remembering in the early modern theater are a diverse assemblage of different elements, and some of those elements are technological and socio-cultural creations whose forms are surely the home-ground of the arts and humanities. For example, literary scholars will have much to say about the stripped down parts and plots, and social historians will have much to say about the guild-like structures of the companies. Of course, even before the 4E turn in cognitive science, arts and humanities researchers were poised to illuminate such things. But with the 4E turn in place, and with entanglement center stage, the highlighted technological and socio-cultural elements are no longer peripheral features about which cognitive science itself can remain largely silent. Rather, they are active causal-explanatory factors that contribute, in subtle and fundamental ways, and as equal (or nearly equal) partners with neural factors, in the process of remembering. So when arts and humanities scholars reveal the properties of those elements, they are mapping out the mechanisms of remembering, and thus are making a direct contribution to cognitive science that goes beyond the enrichment of some still-to-be-explained data.

With this observation, we have arguably moved beyond what Fitzgerald and Callard, in their analysis of the relationship between social science and neuroscience, disapprovingly call "the regime of the inter-" (15–16). In the present context, the regime of the inter- would be a framework in which cognitive science and the arts and humanities are conceived of as separate domains of knowledge which address themselves to different kinds of phenomena. This framework continues to be the conceptual backdrop even for many constructive projects that count as part of the cognitive arts and humanities, broadly conceived (see e.g., Kelleter). However, by reflecting on the messy reality of how experimental neuroscience actually operates in practice, Fitzgerald and Callard argue for a rejection of the very notion of two neatly separated domains of knowledge with proprietary objects or aspects of study, and in favor of what they dub *experimental entanglements* in which objects are, as they put it, "quite indifferent to a bureaucratic division between disciplines" (23). The present treatment recommends a similar indifference in relation to the arts and humanities and cognitive science.[7]

In effect, we have now arrived at a position that has already been productively inhabited by John Sutton in his work on the extended mind. Highlighting the "daunting array of the social and technological systems with which embodied brains can couple" (213–4), Sutton asks "[w]hat would cognitive science be like, how could it continue, if its objects include notebooks, sketchpads, and tattoos as well as embodied brains?" (214). Sampling the 4E literature, he expands his own illustrative list of the objects of cognitive science to cover "other people, scrabble tiles, theater architecture, cocktail glasses, slide rules, incised sticks, shells, languages, moral norms, knots, codes, maps, diagrams, fingers, monuments, software devices, rituals, rhythms and rhymes and roads"

---

7   There are further productive connections here with the recommendations from Roepstorff and Frith that we can deliver progress by "making people from different disciplines do very concrete research projects together, as a way to get out of stereotyped views" (104) and that we should "start out with joint research projects, do things together, and then be sensitive both to the type of facts and the types of contexts produced by going experimental" (108). Later in the present treatment, I shall take a different but, I think, complementary step, by arguing that we should conceive of certain artworks as psychological experiments that explore the causal workings of entangled systems.

(214). To this expanded list (and specifically to Sutton's Tribble-inspired mention of theater architecture) we might now add the plots, stripped down parts, and guild-like social protocols of the early modern theater. Having done this, we can enthusiastically endorse Sutton's own answer to his question, which is that we need to "tap and in turn influence the enormous and diverse scholarship on memory, perception, emotion, and so on in humanities disciplines, to see what might happen if we try to study cognition scientifically and culturally at once" (Sutton 215). I am confident that Sutton wouldn't mind at all if we converted "humanities" into "arts and humanities," just so that we are all explicitly on exactly the same page.

How far have we come? We have learned that the arts and humanities are not "merely" repositories of better data for cognitive science, but may themselves help to map out the causal-explanatory states and processes that enable thought and experience What happens next? We keep going.

3   Group Cognition in Classical Athens: Taking the Edge off Rupert's Razor

If someone uses the term "group cognition," one might initially take the target to be a familiar scenario in which certain psychological capacities that are realized wholly by the neural states and processes of individual people are manifested only in particular social circumstances. The good ideas that one might have during a successful brainstorming session or the emotions that one might experience while part of a crowd at a political rally provide intuitively compelling examples. Understood this way, group cognition is a version of what Wilson calls the social manifestation hypothesis, according to which cognition remains a "property of individuals, but only insofar as those individuals are situated or embedded in certain physical environments and social milieus" (229). While this is undoubtedly a genuine and interesting phenomenon, and one that slots neatly into the 4E world, a different notion of group cognition comes into view once one considers the possibility that groups or collectives may have minds or undergo cognitive states and processes in much the same way that individuals do. On this more radical view, the owner of the relevant states and processes is the group, not the individual, and we should take at face value commonplace statements such as "the team desires a victory" and "the crowd thinks the game is over." In other words, groups, and not merely their individual members, may non-metaphorically be attributed with beliefs, desires, chains of reasoning and so on. From now on I shall use the term "group cognition" to refer exclusively to this more radical view.

Unsurprisingly, perhaps, the claim that group cognition exists also finds a natural place within 4E thought (see, for example, Huebner; Tollefsen). But why is it relevant to our present concerns? In historical research conducted explicitly in light of 4E ideas, Budelmann builds on the observation that, in ancient Athens, group experiences were central aspects of cultural and political life. For example: many Athenian citizens served on galleys propelled by collectively operated oars; communal festivals and processions were routine occurrences; and unanimity played a key role in the ideology of the democratic system. Within this context, two prominent Athenian groups were the *chorus* (in ancient Greek theater, the homogenous group of performers that comments with a single voice on the dramatic action) and the *dēmos* (the governing assembly of citizens in the Athenian state). By analyzing what Athenian authors said about the psychological activity of these groups, Budelmann argues that although "[t]here are significant exceptions [...] the normal unit of thought [in ancient Athens] is the collective, not the individuals of whom the collective is comprised" (192). In other words, the Athenians were entirely comfortable with the idea of group cognition. Here I shall concentrate on Budelmann's analysis of the *dēmos*.

The central institution of Athenian democracy was the Assembly of Citizens, with participation open to men aged eighteen and over who were not slaves and whose parents were Athenian. This membership was referred to as the *dēmos* (roughly, the people understood collectively). Budelmann draws on texts from the time (e.g., the *Old Oligarch*, the *Histories* of Herodotus, Xenophon's *Anabasis*) to provide compelling evidence that the *dēmos* is, by default, treated as a unitary entity. For instance, when voting took place in the Assembly, by the members of the *dēmos* who were present on the day, the standard recording of events does not give details of the voting pattern. Rather, the language is of the whole *dēmos*, as a unitary entity, performing functions such as enacting a decree. Moreover, Athenian politics is, by default, described in terms of disputes and agreements between a unitary *dēmos* and other elements, not as a matter of dealings or associations between sub-groupings or individuals within the *dēmos*. And finally, and strikingly, when instances of a divided *dēmos* do appear in the ancient texts, as in Xenophon's account (in the first book of the *Hellenica*) of the debate in the assembly following the loss of Athenian lives in the naval battle of Arginusae in 406 BC, these are departures from the norm that signal disarray and dysfunction in the democratic system (198–200). Of course, these examples do not yet deliver group cognition: establishing that the *dēmos* is, by default, treated as a unitary entity does not thereby establish that that unitary entity is also attributed with cognitive states and processes. However, such attributions are, in fact, commonplace. Thus, in a

WHAT HAVE THE ARTS AND HUMANITIES EVER DONE FOR US? 267

series of passages quoted by Budelmann (204–6), the *dēmos* is described as having gone mad, as forgetful, as wishing, as displeased, and as being afraid.[8] In other words, the *dēmos* is treated not only as a unitary entity, but as a unitary entity with a mind.

There is an obvious objection here and Budelmann is alive to it. That objection is that Athenian talk of group minds is no more than some sort of metaphorical flourish. Budelmann's response is that although such a deflationary analysis cannot be ruled out altogether, the very fact that groups played such an important role in Athenian society (see above) provides a cultural context in which it becomes plausible that the Athenian point of departure was that the group, rather than the individual, is the default level at which cognitive states and processes are realized.[9] If so, the cited texts may well mean precisely what they say. Putting all this together, Budelmann arrives at the following principle:"[w]hether one accepts that there is such a thing as group minds depends on one's cultural starting point" (208). Let's unpack this idea in more detail.

Largely in passing, Budelmann refers to an argument against group cognition due to Rupert. Launched from the philosophical end of contemporary cognitive science, Rupert's argument wields something like Ockham's razor in the following line of reasoning: if it is always possible to explain group behavior in terms of the cognitive states and processes of the individuals concerned, plus the interactions both between those individuals and between the individuals and the non-cognitive, physical structures that they manipulate, then, assuming that there is no further, independent reason to attribute cognitive states to the group, positing group cognition would be an ontologically profligate move. He then provides evidence that the two antecedent-style conditions in the argument—that it is always possible to explain group behavior in terms of the cognitive states and processes of the individuals concerned and the relevant interactions, and that there is no independent reason to think in terms of group cognition—are satisfied. On these grounds, according to Rupert, we should tentatively conclude that group cognition doesn't exist.

---

8   There is insufficient space here to include all the quotations themselves, but here is one representative example from Thucydides: "The dēmos was at first displeased when it heard the proposal concerning an oligarchy; but when it had been plainly shown by Peisander that there was no other salvation, through fear and at the same time because it expected to make a change later, it yielded" (Thucydides, translation adapted by Budelmann, 205).

9   Although Budelmann does not make this point explicitly, it is this same appeal to the prominent place of groups in Athenian society that plausibly supports the extension of a literal construal of group cognition beyond the political-legal context of the demos to psychological phenomena in general.

For present purposes, the key feature of Rupert's argument is that, driven as it is by considerations of parsimony, it depends on the adoption of a baseline condition against which the dangers of profligacy may be assessed. For Rupert, that baseline condition is that cognition is a property of individuals. The argument then asks whether appealing to group cognition, in addition to individual cognition, is explanatorily necessary. If it is, then we should tentatively conclude that group cognition exists. If it isn't, then thinking in terms of group cognition would be an unjustified ontological extravagance and, as such, to be avoided. Of course, from the perspective of modern orthodox cognitive science, which is steeped in psychological individualism, Rupert's baseline condition is unremarkable. But, if Budelmann is right, that same condition would have seemed bizarre, or at least overly austere, to the residents of ancient Athens, to whom the idea of group cognition was commonplace. Put another way, the idea that psychological individualism is the baseline condition against which the group cognition hypothesis is to be judged is a hidden assumption of Rupert's argument, or at least an assumption that he treats as entirely uncontroversial. Nevertheless, the good Athenians would have been moved to reject that very assumption. Indeed, starting from the baseline of group cognition, they may well have considered an explanation of group behavior in terms of the cognitive states and processes of the individuals concerned, plus certain direct or technologically mediated inter-individual interactions, as unnecessarily complex. And that, I suggest, blunts Rupert's razor (or at least matches it with one that is equally sharp).

To avoid any misunderstanding, it is worth emphasizing that this rebalancing of the scales in the group cognition debate does not deliver us into the arms of any sort of crude cultural relativism. The claim here is not that there is ultimately no truth of the matter as to whether group cognition exists. Neither is it that group cognition existed in ancient Athens simply because people spoke as if it did. The claim is rather that science, including cognitive science, makes various assumptions, many of which are inherited from, or are conditioned by, the historical-cultural context in which the science is performed. This is presumably nigh-on inevitable, because science is a historically and culturally located human activity. Thus, switching to biology for a moment, consider the long-standing sexist distinction between the sperm cell as an active heroic force that burrows through the egg coat to penetrate the egg and activate the developmental program, and the egg cell as passive matter transported along the fallopian tube until it is assaulted and fertilized by the sperm. This distinction was elaborated over many years by experimental work in biology before the egg was finally granted its own active contribution (Martin). In light of examples such as this, one can surely promote the benefits of exposing

WHAT HAVE THE ARTS AND HUMANITIES EVER DONE FOR US? 269

and criticizing the science-shaping assumptions in question as prompts for—
indeed as contributions towards—doing better science, without any of that
posing a threat to the objectivity of scientific knowledge.[10]

This all points us back in the direction of a lesson that we drew earlier, but
which now warrants further emphasis. Budelmann's historical analysis demonstrates that arts and humanities research may expose and interrogate certain
otherwise unquestioned culturally conditioned assumptions that shape cog-
nitive-scientific research. But, as conceived here, the goal of that intervention
is not to mount some external critique of cognitive science that is designed to
tame, restrict, or emasculate that science in relation to its project of understanding human thought and experience (for example, by identifying repre-
hensible social, political, or economic agendas in play). Rather, in revealing
such assumptions, and in subjecting them to critical scrutiny, the goal is to
make a disruptive contribution to the science by helping to clear the way to
new productive explanations within the science.[11]

4   Artworks as Psychological Experiments

I shall end this discussion by more briefly canvassing a different kind of disruptive contribution. Here is a proposal: certain artworks may fruitfully be
conceived as psychological experiments that explore the causal workings of
entangled systems. What does this mean? In this context, the term "experiment" does not indicate "experimental" in the sense of "previously untried."
Rather, it refers to something analogous to scientific experimentation, to something, that is, which is recognizable as part of the routine business of science.
Put very crudely, an experiment is an event in which specified causal factors
are manipulated to see what happens to a target entity, system, or process, in
a procedure which is not blind, but rather guided by structured expectations
shaped by prior experimental results and theory. This definition would not

---

10   For more on the intertwining of history, culture and science, as I understand it, see e.g.,
      Wheeler ("Science"; "Talking") and Vazquez.

11   In the end, what this amounts to is a refusal to give ultimate priority to the aesthetic and
      the sociocultural in their dealings with science. And it illustrates why the project that I am
      endeavoring to articulate is not in total agreement with the critical neuroscience move-
      ment (e.g., Choudhury et al.), the goal of which is to urge neuroscience to become reflec-
      tively aware of the political, cultural, and economic factors that operate as biases and
      constraints on its knowledge production and, in light of that awareness, to understand
      itself as a cultural activity. Here, once again, there are important similarities between the
      position that I am advocating and the view of Fitzgerald and Callard.

survive very long if it were placed under the noses of practice-led philosophers of science, but it will do for now. If one squints just a little, some artworks exhibit something strikingly like this pattern. They are events in which the artist manipulates the entanglement of the viewer (participant, audience) to see what happens to the latter's experience, in a manner which is not blind but rather shaped by structured expectations conditioned not only by prior artistic work and reflection, but also by a host of socio-cultural, political, and/or scientific factors. Of course, artists being artists, the goal of their experiments is often the production of experiential singularities in their "subjects," rather than the uncovering of law-like patterns of shared response. This means that those experiments are disruptive in relation to much orthodox scientific practice in psychology, but then one of the key shifts engendered by a focus on entangled psychological systems in 4E cognitive science is an increasing interest in adaptive intelligence as a real-time dynamic process of brain-body-world coupling in which contingency and chance routinely play their part in creative, improvised, idiosyncratic solutions, that is, in singularities. So, potentially, what we have unearthed here is just another point of symbiosis (this time between art and cognitive science) in the 4E cognitive arts and humanities landscape.[12]

At the moment, my proposal that certain artworks are distinctive psychological experiments is no more than a tempting speculation, and much more work would need to be done to make it secure. In lieu of such work, however, I shall make do with a suggestive example. *Walk, Hands, Eyes* (*Edinburgh*) is a performance artwork developed by Myriam Lefkowitz.[13] In each manifestation of the work, a performer, trained by Lefkowitz, guides a participant on a walk around the city of Edinburgh. The work begins with a preparatory phase that strengthens the participant's trust in the performer. Then, for the vast majority of the walk, and especially while moving, the participant's eyes are kept closed, and navigation is achieved through the almost omni-present touch of the performer (e.g., hand-holding) alongside certain occasional verbal instructions that the performer gives. Walking is interrupted by moments in which the performer stops the participant and asks them to quickly open and close their eyes, providing the participant with visual snapshots of particular city-scenes. Post-walk feedback from participants makes evident the power of the work to

---

12   For a more general discussion of 4E cognition and artistic creativity, see Wheeler ("Talking").

13   See "Myriam Lefkowitz". The piece was presented alongside other artworks in a 4E related exhibition, *The Extended Mind*, held at the Talbot Rice Gallery in Edinburgh, 02/11/2019–01/02/20. See "The Extended Mind." For a longer description of the piece than space here permits, see Clegg et al. The same format has been used by Lefkowitz to create similar location-specific works, such as *Walk, Hands, Eyes* (*Aubervilliers*).

produce new, collaboratively created, deeply affecting, and often transformational awareness of the city space.

From a 4E perspective, *Walk, Hands, Eyes (Edinburgh)* is, among many other things, an experiment in how, and on what basis, resources are dynamically reallocated within an entangled system. What Lefkowitz's piece both reveals and explores is the pivotal role played by trust in this process.[14] It is the relationship of trust between the participant and the performer, as built in the all-important preparatory phase of the work that enables the close embodied coupling between the two individuals to reallocate the available systemic resources so that the performer takes over certain aspects of the participant's navigation and attention-direction. But what is the character of the entangled system so organized? Should we think of the performer as being incorporated into the participant's sensory and navigational systems? Or, in a group-cognition register, even if we think of the experiences as individually owned, should we think of the collective system of two individuals as itself a bearer of some of the cognitive states and processes that figure in, say, the navigational behavior? And how do the answers to these questions bear on the experiential outcomes for different participants? There are surely subtle issues of explanation here, and what emerges as the best explanation may well vary across different manifestations of the work, possibly correlated with the level or kind of trust achieved. Like all the best experiments, then, Lefkowitz's artwork not only enables us to better understand a phenomenon, it raises new and interesting problems to be solved.

5   Concluding Remarks

If the cognitive arts and humanities are to deliver on their promise of bringing the cognitive sciences and the arts and humanities into a mutually productive relationship, we need to understand the kinds of contribution that arts and humanities disciplines can make to fulfilling the explanatory ambitions of cognitive science. In this chapter, and on the basis of adopting a 4E cognition framework in which the intertwining of brain, body, and culture is appropriately emphasized, I have delineated some of the contributions that begin to map out this territory.

---

14   The role of trust is a long-established theme in the extended mind regions of 4E cognition, reaching as far back as the pivotal Clark and Chalmers paper (Clark and Chalmers), but Lefkowitz's artwork investigates the issue in a new and powerful way.

Acknowledgments

Many thanks to Stephan Besser and an anonymous reviewer for their helpful comments on an earlier version of this chapter. Many thanks also to audiences in Amsterdam, Edinburgh, and Stirling for useful feedback and discussion

References

Anderson, Miranda, et al. "Distributed Cognition and the Humanities." *Distributed Cognition in Classical Antiquity*, edited by Miranda Anderson et al., Edinburgh UP, 2019, pp. 1–17.

Budelmann, Felix. "Group Minds in Classical Athens? Chorus and Demos as Case Studies of Collective Cognition." *Distributed Cognition in Classical Antiquity*, edited by Miranda Anderson et al., Edinburgh UP, 2019, pp. 190–208.

Choudhury, Suparna, et al. "Critical Neuroscience: Linking Neuroscience and Society through Critical Practice." *BioSocieties*, vol. 4, no. 1, 2009, pp. 61–77.

Clark, Andy, and David Chalmers. "The Extended Mind." *Analysis*, vol. 58, no. 1, 1998, pp. 7–19.

Clegg, James, et al. "Myriam Lefkowitz. Walk, Hands, Eyes (Edinburgh)." *The Extended Mind. Exhibition Catalogue.* Talbot Rice Gallery, University of Edinburgh, 2019, pp. 41–44.

Cognitive Futures of the Arts and the Humanities – A Reassessment of Results and Articulating New Possibilities. 12–16.07.2023, 2023, https://centrumq.uw.edu.pl/en/cognitive-futures-2023/.

Fitzgerald, Des, and Felicity Callard. "Social Science and Neuroscience beyond Interdisciplinarity: Experimental Entanglements." *Theory, Culture & Society*, vol. 32, no. 1, 2015, pp. 3–32.

Huebner, Bryce. *Macrocognition: A Theory of Distributed Minds and Collective Intentionality.* Oxford UP, 2014.

Kelleter, Frank. "A Tale of Two Natures." *Journal of Literary Theory*, vol. 1, no. 1, 2007, pp. 153–89.

Kuhn, Thomas S. *The Structure of Scientific Revolutions.* 2nd ed., Chicago UP, 1962.

Lefkowitz, Myriam: *Walk, Hands, Eyes* (Edinburgh) 02 Nov 2019–01 Feb 2020, 2019, https://www.trg.ed.ac.uk/exhibition/myriam-lefkowitz-walk-hands-eyes-edinburgh.

Mak, Marloes, and Roel M. Willems. "Mental Simulation during Literary Reading: Individual Differences Revealed with Eye-Tracking." *Language, Cognition and Neuroscience*, vol. 34, no. 4, 2018, pp. 511–35.

Martin, Emily. "The Egg and the Sperm: How Science Has Constructed a Romance Based on Stereotypical Male-Female Roles." *Signs*, vol. 9, no. 2, 1991, pp. 485–501.

WHAT HAVE THE ARTS AND HUMANITIES EVER DONE FOR US? 273

Roepstorff, Andreas, and Chris Frith. "Neuroanthropology or Simply Anthropology? Going Experimental as Method, as Object of Study, and as Research Aesthetic." *Anthropological Theory*, vol. 12, no. 1, 2012, pp. 101–11.

Rupert, Robert. "Against Group Cognitive States." *From Individual to Collective Intentionality: New Essays*, edited by Sarah Rachel Chant et al., Oxford UP, 2014, pp. 97–111.

Spolsky, Ellen. *Gaps in Nature: Literary Interpretation and the Modular Mind*. State University of New York Press, 1993.

Sutton, John. "Exograms and Interdisciplinarity: History, the Extended Mind, and the Civilizing Process." *The Extended Mind*, edited by Richard Menary, MIT Press, 2010, pp. 189–225.

The Extended Mind. Exhibition 02 Nov 2019 – 01 Feb 2020, 2019, https://www.trg.ed.ac.uk /exhibition/extended-mind.

Thucydides. *History of the Peloponnesian War*. Translated by Charles Forster Smith, vol. 4, Harvard UP, 1923.

Tollefsen, Deborah. "From Extended Mind to Collective Mind." *Cognitive Systems Research*, vol. 7, no. 2, 2006, pp. 140–50.

Tribble, Evelyn B. *Cognition in the Globe: Attention and Memory in Shakespeare's Theatre*. Palgrave Macmillan, 2011.

Turner, Mark. *Reading Minds: The Study of English in the Age of Cognitive Science*. Princeton UP, 1991.

Vazquez, Clavel, et al. "Minding Nature: Gallagher and the Relevance of Phenomenology to Cognitive Science." *Australasian Philosophical Review*, vol. 2, no. 2, 2019, pp. 145–58.

Wheeler, Michael. "Science Friction: Phenomenology, Naturalism and Cognitive Science." *Royal Institute of Philosophy Supplement*, vol. 72, 2013, pp. 135–67.

Wheeler, Michael. "Talking about More than Heads: The Embodied, Embedded and Extended Creative Mind." *Creativity and Philosophy*, edited by Berys Gaut and Matthew Kieran, Routledge, 2018, pp. 230–50.

Wilson, Robert A. "Collective Memory, Group Minds, and the Extended Mind Thesis." *Cognitive Processing*, vol. 6, no. 4, 2005, pp. 227–36.

Zunshine, Lisa, editor. *The Oxford Handbook of Cognitive Literary Studies*. Oxford UP, 2015.

CHAPTER 17

Measuring Acoustic Social Worlds

Reflections on a Study of Multi-Agent Human Interaction

Shannon Proksch, Majerle Reeves, Michael Spivey, and Ramesh Balasubramaniam

1 Introduction

Humans are highly capable of tracking complex behavioral dynamics of crowds in our everyday interactions with the world. Imagine the sounds of a crowded coffee shop. Consider how individuals in that coffee shop might be interacting with each other. There may be some small groups or pairs, and many individuals engaging in small, temporary interactions—but these individuals are not *coordinating* with every other individual in a cohesive "coffee shop group." They are just a jumble of individuals cohabiting a shared space.

Now, imagine the audience on the floor of a rock concert, cheering or singing along with the artists on stage. Alternatively, imagine the fan section at your favorite sporting event emerging into synchronous chant, or a chorus of resounding "boos." Imagine how individuals in those large crowds might be interacting with each other. As they cheer, or sing, or chant, or boo, they are sharing similar behavioral states—engaging in similar actions. They are likely sharing similar physiological and neural states as well. These crowds are changing together in time. They are behaving—coordinating—like one large interdependent group. They have formed a synergy.

The differences between this coffee shop crowd and the rock concert audience or the sporting event crowd are trivially easy for you or I to identify. An uncoordinated group of independent individuals, happening to coexist in a shared space versus a coordinated interdependent group of members of a crowd. We can simply *hear* that these two groups of people sound different. Similarly, we can simply *hear* when we are engaged and participating in a collective synergy while we are interacting in a large group of people. Or perhaps, in a very large musical ensemble.

As scientists in the lab, we are able to measure one or many signals from *every individual* in an interacting or non-interacting group. We can measure those signals and, usually, identify which members of the group are sharing the same *behavioral* state by identifying when their movements synchronize with,

MEASURING ACOUSTIC SOCIAL WORLDS

or complement, other members of the group. We can measure the pattern of each individual's heartbeats or electrodermal activity (subtle electrical signals conducted by the skin) to identify when individuals are sharing the same *physiological* state. We can even measure precise patterns of brain activity (EEG, or fMRI) to identify when individuals are sharing the same *neural* state (Balconi and Fronda; Misaki et al.; Schirmer et al.). When individuals are sharing similar behavioral, physiological, or neural states—that is, when individuals' actions, body states, or brain activity are changing together in time—then a collective interpersonal synergy forms (Riley et al.). Each individual starts to behave together as a member of one large group. Measurement of an interpersonal synergy can be indicative of shared social cognition: of joint participation in co-regulating multiple patterns of activity between two or more agents engaged in a social interaction (De Jaegher et al.).

However, as humans going about our everyday lives, we don't carefully measure the individual components of our successful social interactions or the emergence of interpersonal synergies in our joint actions to determine whether we are engaged in a participatory instance of social cognition. We don't carefully monitor our own movement and brain patterns or carefully compare each of these many individual signals that we generate to the many individual signals that our friends, coworkers, or other individuals generate as we are interacting in real time. In fact, we don't even have access to individualized movement, body, and brain data of ourselves and the people with whom we interact on a daily basis.

Scale this up to an interaction between four or five people, or even further to a very large audience attending a concert—and this feat is unmanageable for any single human's sensory system. Often, you might lack even visual access to every member of the group you are interacting in. What you do have access to is a shared and co-created acoustic world (albeit from your own unique point of reference). With this in mind, we turn first to the science of interpersonal coordination, and then to an empirical study evaluating the formation of interpersonal synergy within a set of musicians, who join together in co-creating an acoustic musical world.

2   Interpersonal Coordination

The science of interpersonal coordination has made advances in describing how individuals interact as part of a dyad or a large group by evaluating a multitude of movement, body, and brain signals from each individual in comparison with each other individual.

But what if scientists don't have access to the vast array of recording devices they rely upon in their lab? What if a scientist wants to study how real groups interact in the wild? Can science identify these same differences in an unco-ordinated group of independent individuals versus a coordinated, interacting, and interdependent crowd? This is the question we asked in a recent study of multi-agent interaction within a musical ensemble. These musicians performed a piece that was specifically composed so that the musicians first cre-ate uncoordinated noise for a period of time on each of their instruments, before joining together into a coordinated joint musical performance. Proksch et al. wanted to understand how the musicians were changing their acoustic behavior in time, either independently or *inter*dependently, in the two dif-ferent musical interactions dictated by their musical score. With the under-standing that individuals often do not have unobstructed visual access to every member of an interacting group (let alone physiological or neural data), we restricted our dynamical systems analysis to a single measurement of the shared and co-created behavior generated by the musicians—a raw audio file of the ensemble's acoustic behavior.

The dynamical systems framework in cognitive science allows for the study of the formation of interpersonal synergies. An interpersonal synergy occurs when the movement dynamics of one individual become causally coupled to the movement dynamics of another individual (Riley et al.). This means that the actions of cognitive agents constrain each other, interacting as a single coupled unit. Interpersonal synergies can arise from simple interactions, such as walking through the park engaged in a conversation and finding one has begun walking in step with your conversation partner (Atherton et al.). Subtler interpersonal synergies can arise in conversation when standing still. Even if one cannot see their conversation partner, the mere act of interacting through conversation serves to constrain subtle sway patterns of body movement, such that body movement is distinctly coupled to the movement of the unseen part-ner (Shockley et al.).

Perhaps more immediately observable, however, are the interpersonal syn-ergies which we see and hear in musical interactions. Where conversation partners might incidentally fall into step or sway together in time, a pair or a group of musicians co-creating a musical performance are intentionally coor-dinating their acoustic behavior. It's important to note here that coordinat-ing acoustic behavior in order to engage in a successful musical interaction often involves musicians moving their bodies differently from their musical partners. A trombone player will make different movements than the string bass player, and a trumpet player or pianist will make different movements and perhaps even play more notes in the same amount of time compared to the

MEASURING ACOUSTIC SOCIAL WORLDS

trombonist and bassist. But together, these differing movement dynamics from each musician join to co-create the same shared acoustic social world. The acoustic output of each musician constrains the acoustic output, and motor behavior, of each other musician in the ensemble. In fact, if the low voices (the trombone and the bassist) were to play a continuous drone, one single chord for a prolonged time, then the duet that the trumpet player and pianist improvise together may result in a different "performance narrative" than if the low voices provided a rhythmic bass line. In a study involving duets performed by pairs of skilled pianists, improvising over the unstructured "drone" backing track resulted in increased movement coordination between the two pianists compared to improvisation over the rhythmic bass line (Walton et al.). Specifically, pianists repeated their improvisation partner's note combinations and head movements in longer sequences when improvising over the drone backing track. Further, listeners rated this performance as more "harmonious" than the improvisation over the structured, rhythmic bass line, with listeners giving higher "harmonious" ratings when the musicians repeated each other's note combinations for longer sequences of time (Walton et al.).

Experimental setups are typically designed to identify interpersonal synergies by correlating one or more of the movement/body/neural signals from each member of the interacting or non-interacting group. But in principle—once an interpersonal synergy is formed—it should be possible to analyze group behavioral dynamics from *one* single signal measured from that system. This is due to two factors—dimensional compression and reciprocal compensation (Riley et al.). Dimensional compression within a synergy occurs when the movement of many potentially independent elements (such as the movement of two independent pairs of legs on two independent walking individuals) become coupled so that they move in time together (the two pairs of legs begin to walk in step, as one interdependent walking dyad). Reciprocal compensation, also termed mutual adaptation, describes the ability of movement in one element of a synergy to react to, or adapt to, the movement of another element of the synergy (one member of the walking dyad can adjust their walking speed to ensure they are in step with their walking partner, see Riley et al.). The behavior of the musicians in the improvising piano duets we visited earlier exhibited these features of dimensional compression and reciprocal compensation. The movement of two independent pairs of hands, and two independent heads, on two individual musicians became coupled so that they created music in time together, and the musical behavior of each musician reacted to, or adapted to, the musical behavior of the other musician. The listeners, who rated this musical performance, were able to extract an acoustic signal from that system and attune to differences in how the two duetting pianists coordinated their sound and movement (Walton et al.). If these listeners were able to attune to these differences in coordination in two forms of coordinated music making (improvised duets over two different backing tracks) based on a single acoustic signal—the raw audio of the music performance itself—then perhaps this same feat can be scaled up to a multi-agent interaction of a much larger musical ensemble. And if the motor and acoustic behavior of individuals within a much larger musical ensemble are functioning together in time, so as to have the features of dimensional compression and reciprocal compensations necessary to form an interpersonal synergy, then it should be possible to detect that synergy from something as sparse as a raw audio file.

3   An Empirical Study of Multi-Agent Musical Interaction

We investigated the coordination dynamics of a performance of "Welcome to the Imagination World," composed by Daisuke Shimizu and performed by the Inagakuen Wind Orchestra (Proksch et al.; Inagakuen Wind Orchestra). Specifically, we evaluated the acoustic behavior of this musical ensemble using methods from dynamical systems theory of phase space reconstruction and recurrence quantification analysis. These time series analysis methods allow researchers to detect two features of interpersonal synergies discussed above—dimensional compression and reciprocal compensation—and to measure patterns of this synergistic behavior over time. In this case, we were somewhat playing the role of the listeners of the improvising pianists. The difference was, instead of asking whether one could *hear* differences in coordination, the question was whether one might *empirically measure* differences in coordination using those dynamical systems tools. And importantly, can these differences in coordination be measured using only the raw audio signal of the musical performance, without access to individual recordings of each musicians' acoustic output?

The musical performance was divided into two main coordination categories: uncoordinated and coordinated. This uncoordination was in fact a specific feature of the musical composition itself. Shimizu composed this piece to reflect the "arrival and development of a simple fanfare motif into an accomplished work", beginning with "random ad lib music (…) free of tempo and as expressive as possible" until the musicians invite the conductor on stage as "the horn, tenor, and brass instruments unify into a majestic introduction' (Shimizu). These descriptions are from program notes describing "Welcome to the Imagination World." Listening to a performance of this work, one can easily hear the difference between the uncoordinated improvisations of individual musicians on stage and the coordinated, collective interaction of the musicians as they co-create "an accomplished work." Importantly, however, we were also able to measure those differences in coordination dynamics from the raw audio signal. The results from the time series analysis make clear that there is a detectable difference between the uncoordinated and coordinated portions of the performance. They tell us that when the musicians began to coordinate their actions, such that the actions of each musician became interdependent on the action of each of the other musicians in the ensemble, they formed a single complex system—a collective interpersonal synergy.

4   Discussion

What are the implications of measuring these differences in coordination dynamics between the acoustic behavior of non-interacting uncoordinated musicians gathered on a stage versus the acoustic behavior of the same musicians when interacting and coordinated as a cohesive musical ensemble?

The current pragmatic turn in cognitive science toward action-oriented views of cognition (Engel et al.) provides a useful explanatory viewpoint for discussing coordination as it relates to multi-agent musical interaction. Specifically, we can interpret the collective coordination which emerged in this musical ensemble in terms of sensorimotor contingency theory under the cognitive framework of enactivism. We argue that the skilled coordination of these musicians engaging in joint musical action is grounded in (implicit or explicit) knowledge of sensorimotor contingencies supporting music perception and production. These shared sensorimotor contingencies enable an interacting multi-agent group of musicians to co-create a shared, acoustic social world— forming a single complex system—as the interdependent actions of individual musicians give rise to emergent dynamics of an interacting musical ensemble.

Enactive sensorimotor contingency theory is a theory of perception, which describes perception as a process which is guided by action, emphasizing a "pre-conceptual, pre-linguistic form of understanding related to bodily and motor expertise" (Matyja and Schiavio). Developed originally as an explanation for visual perception (O'Regan and Noë; Noë), the classic example of sensorimotor contingency theory is "seeing the whole tomato." When we see a tomato, we don't just see a two-dimensional gradient of colors and edges, but in some sense, we see the "whole" tomato. Our awareness of the back of the tomato arises from our bodily knowledge of a repertoire of motor actions, the sensorimotor contingencies (SMCs), necessary in perceiving tomatoes: we know that if we were to perform a certain action (turn the tomato around), that we would see the back of a tomato. Enactivist accounts of music cognition place the perception of music in (implicit or explicit) bodily knowledge of a repertoire of motor actions and their effect on associated sensory stimulation or knowledge of sensorimotor contingencies (Matyja and Schiavio). Rather than passive listeners, simply receiving a barrage of acoustic stimuli and later appraising it as musical (as in a traditional, cognitivist account of music perception), we perceive music through skilled action (Maes et al.; Maes). The music listener learns to "manipulate" the barrage of acoustic stimuli she hears through active (attentive) listening and skillful engagement with the musical environment (Krueger, "Enacting"; Krueger, "Empathy"). Musical training or experience enhances her knowledge of the sensorimotor contingencies involved in producing music, which enables her to selectively attend to increasingly more salient musical features when perceiving music. Knowledge of SMCs involves not only knowledge of what sound can be heard given a certain action, but also what action most likely caused or will cause a certain sound. This bidirectional association between action and perception enables individuals to plan and respond to their own action, and also to predict and coordinate with others through joint musical action—as listeners and players at the same time.

A series of studies by Drost et al. ("Hearing"; "Instrument") demonstrate that individuals with musical training were more susceptible to making mistakes in a forced production task due to incongruencies between visually and auditorily presented chords, and that the effect was stronger when the auditory stimulus presented was in the timbre of their own instrument. These studies indicate that musical training leads to more precise sensorimotor representations of the action necessary to produce a sensory stimulus (the heard chord). A number of piano timing experiments demonstrated that pianists (ignorant of the task condition and told that they were performing with a live partner) were better able to play in time with recordings of themselves than of other musicians (Keller et al.) or with others who were matched in terms of preferred performance tempo (Loehr et al.). Each of these studies indicate that higher knowledge of SMCs enhances the participant's ability to be in time in a music production task by enhancing the participant's ability to plan and coordinate with a partner in joint musical activity.[1]

---

1   The original authors' interpretation of these experiments and results was taken as support for the role of cognitive representations of the actions of self and other in musical activity. Thus, by their account, musicians are cognitively simulating the movement and production of the other musician. Under moderate accounts of SMC, these representations may be thought to include knowledge of SMCs, however under more radical accounts of SMC

MEASURING ACOUSTIC SOCIAL WORLDS

Rhythmic interaction in naturalistic music making, such as musical ensemble performance, relies on extending these simple sensorimotor contingencies—knowledge of the sound your instrument will make when you perform an action; knowledge of the sounds you'll hear based on the preferred tempo at which you play music—to more complex SMCs which take into account the dynamics of two or more interacting agents, such as knowing what musical phrase you'll hear from your band mates in a jam session after you've each taken a certain set of musical actions. Humans excel at the precise timing and coordination of motor and acoustic output from multiple musicians in part because they excel at a skill called entrainment, which is where we are headed next.

Successful coordination within and between human individuals in music making may reflect a greater (implicit or explicit) knowledge of the sensorimotor contingencies involved in perceiving and producing musical events. Take our pianists for example, they are better able to synchronize with recordings of themselves (Keller et al.) or with others who are matched in preferred performance tempo (Loehr et al.). This is because the pianist (unknowingly) playing with a recording of herself has a very strong implicit knowledge of what actions it would take for her to produce the sound she hears from the recording. This strong knowledge of SMCs makes it easier for her to predict when and what she will hear, and enhances the strength of entrainment between musician and recording. It is thus easier for the pianist to form an interpersonal synergy alongside their own pre-recorded musical activity. The pianist who is playing with another who prefers similar tempi has a similarly strong knowledge of SMCs involved in producing the sounds they hear at their preferred tempo, enhancing the strength of entrainment at that tempo, and enabling the emergence of a tight interpersonal synergy.

Entrainment, or a specific form of coordination referring roughly to the ability to synchronize or to be together in time with one or more individuals, has been taken to "relate phenomenologically to a sense of social belonging" and has been conceived as one explanation for group cohesion and bonding that emerges from joint activities such as music making (Clayton et al. 14). Our human ability to entrain with others ranges from the subconscious synchrony of repetitive motions (i.e., happening to walk in step with another) to the synchronization of intentional temporal events such as synchronizing melody and harmony in joint musical interaction. In temporal rhythmic processing, it is the *interaction* of the body, brain, and environment which results in the emergent

---

(with no role for representations) these studies may be taken to support the role of bodily knowledge/memory of the SMCs involved in music production and response.

phenomenon of sensorimotor and neural entrainment (Ross and Balasubramaniam). Interpersonal synchronous movement between two or more individuals may be further linked through synchrony of neural oscillations across individuals (Novembre et al.) and has been found to occur in naturalistic social interactions among affiliative partners (Kinreich et al.). Even when referring in part to neural phenomena, such multi-scale and multi-level coordination patterns likely relate to our phenomenological experience of being part of an extended social and cultural environment. Kirchhoff and Kiverstein describe this feeling as "phenomenal attunement—the feeling of being at home in a familiar culturally constructed environment" (Kirchhoff and Kiverstein 2). The interactions of a musical ensemble, specifically when the ensemble is made up of a group of musicians who have engaged in repeated rehearsals and joint musical interactions together, provides an ideally structured social and musical environment for that ensemble to exhibit an extended cognition, if not an extended conscious mind (Spivey; Kirchhoff and Kiverstein).

In perhaps a less enactivist light, shared predictive *models* of sensorimotor contingencies developed during and as a result of group music making may give rise to group identity in a similar fashion to the "predictive perception of sensorimotor contingencies" which are proposed to underlie a sense of self (Seth 104). While radical enactivism maintains a strictly antirepresentational character of the nature of cognitive processes (Hutto and Myin), we do not take a stance in this debate in this chapter. Rather, we argue that enactive SMC theory grounds and enhances aspects of coordination in joint musical action in terms of bodily and environmental states, regardless as to whether these states are represented in the brain as models or wholly constituted by the bodily/environmental states themselves.

Individuals engaged in joint music making often join together in larger groups than these piano duets, ranging from a four-person quartet to a large chorus, orchestra, or even a stadium full of concert goers singing along with their favorite band on stage. Nevertheless, the shared sensorimotor contingencies among multi-agent groups of interacting musicians enable them to co-create a shared, acoustic social world. In doing so, they form collective interpersonal synergies, allowing the interdependent actions of individual musicians to give rise to the emergent dynamics of an interacting musical ensemble. By examining these synergies in the context of 4E cognition (Newen, et al.), we can see them as emerging from groups of agents who are *embodied* and *enactive*, as well as *embedded* in an environment, thus making their cognition *extended* across many interacting elements. That is, when the people and their instruments are well coordinated by virtue of their shared and co-created acoustic social world, they form one complex system that, by itself, bears a substantial statistical similarity to a mind.

References

Atherton, Gray, et al. "Imagine All The Synchrony: The Effects of Actual and Imagined Synchronous Walking on Attitudes towards Marginalised Groups." *PLOS One*, vol. 14, no. 5, art. 0216585, 2019.

Balconi, Michela, and Giulia Fronda. "The Dialogue between Two or More Brains: The 'Hyperscanning' for Organization." *Frontiers in Psychology*, vol. 11, art. 593832, 2020.

Clayton, Martin, et al. "In Time with the Music: The Concept of Entrainment and Its Significance for Ethnomusicology." *European Meetings in Ethnomusicology*, vol. 11, 2005, pp. 3–73.

De Jaegher, Hanne, et al. "Can Social Interaction Constitute Social Cognition?" *Trends in Cognitive Sciences*, vol. 14, no. 10, 2010, pp. 441–47.

Drost, Ulrich C., et al. "When Hearing Turns into Playing: Movement Induction by Auditory Stimuli in Pianists." *The Quarterly Journal of Experimental Psychology Section A*, vol. 58, no. 8, 2005, pp. 1376–89.

Drost, Ulrich C., et al. "Instrument Specificity in Experienced Musicians." *Quarterly Journal of Experimental Psychology*, vol. 60, no. 4, 2007, pp. 527–33.

Engel, Andreas K., et al., editors. *The Pragmatic Turn: Toward Action-Oriented Views in Cognitive Science*. MIT Press, 2016.

Hutto, Daniel D., and Erik Myin. *Radicalizing Enactivism: Basic Minds without Content*. MIT Press, 2012.

Inagakuen Wind Orchestra. "Welcome to the Imagination World." *Youtube*, 2009, https://www.youtube.com/watch?v=-wJ9ZsgO3QI.

Keller, Peter E., et al. "Pianists Duet Better When They Play with Themselves: On the Possible Role of Action Simulation in Synchronization." *Consciousness and Cognition*, vol. 16, no. 1, 2007, pp. 102–11.

Kinreich, Sivan, et al., "Brain-to-Brain Synchrony during Naturalistic Social Interactions." *Scientific Reports*, vol. 7, no. 1, 2017, pp. 1–12.

Kirchhoff, Michael D., and Julian Kiverstein. "Attuning to the World: The Diachronic Constitution of the Extended Conscious Mind." *Frontiers in Psychology*, vol. 11, art. 1966, 2020.

Krueger, Joel. "Enacting Musical Experience." *Journal of Consciousness Studies*, vol. 16, no. 2–3, 2009, pp. 98–123.

Krueger, Joel. "Empathy, Enaction, and Shared Musical Experience: Evidence from Infant Cognition." *The Emotional Power of Music: Multidisciplinary Perspectives on*

Musical Arousal, Expression, and Social Control, edited by Tom Cochrane, Oxford UP, 2013, pp. 177–96.

Loehr, Janeen D., et al. "Temporal Coordination and Adaptation to Rate Change in Music Performance." *Journal of Experimental Psychology: Human Perception and Performance*, vol. 37, no. 4, 2011, pp. 1292–309.

Maes, Pieter-Jan. "Sensorimotor Grounding of Musical Embodiment and the Role of Prediction: A Review." *Frontiers in Psychology*, vol. 7, art. 308, 2016.

Maes, Pieter-Jan, et al. "Action-Based Effects on Music Perception." *Frontiers in Psychology*, vol. 4, art. 1008, 2014.

Matyja, Jakub, and Andrea Schiavio. "Enactive Music Cognition: Background and Research Themes." *Constructivist Foundations*, vol. 8, no. 3, 2013, pp. 351–57.

Misaki, Masaya, et al., "Beyond Synchrony: The Capacity of FMRI Hyperscanning for the Study of Human Social Interaction." *Social Cognitive and Affective Neuroscience*, vol. 16, no. 1–2, 2021, pp. 84–92.

Newen, Albert, et al., editors. *The Oxford Handbook of 4E Cognition*. Oxford UP, 2018.

Noë, Alva. *Action in Perception*. MIT Press, 2004.

Novembre, Giacomo, et al., "Interpersonal Synchrony Enhanced through 20 Hz Phase-Coupled Dual Brain Stimulation." *Social Cognitive and Affective Neuroscience*, vol. 12, no. 4, 2017, pp. 662–70.

O'Regan, J. Kevin, and Alva Noë. "A Sensorimotor Account of Vision and Visual Consciousness." *Behavioral and Brain Sciences*, vol. 24, no. 5, 2001, pp. 939–1031.

Proksch, Shannon, et al., "Coordination Dynamics of Multi-Agent Human Interaction in a musical ensemble." *Scientific Reports*, vol. 12, no. 421, 2022.

Riley, Michael A. et al., "Interpersonal Synergies." *Frontiers in Psychology*, vol. 2, art. 38, 2011.

Ross, Jessica M., and Ramesh Balasubramaniam. "Physical and Neural Entrainment to Rhythm: Human Sensorimotor Coordination across Tasks and Effector Systems." *Frontiers in Human Neuroscience*, vol. 8, art. 576, 2014.

Schirmer, Annett, et al. "Being 'in Sync'—Is Interactional Synchrony the Key to Understanding the Social Brain?" *Social Cognitive and Affective Neuroscience*, vol. 16, no. 1–2, 2021, pp. 1–4.

Seth, Anil K. "A Predictive Processing Theory of Sensorimotor Contingencies: Explaining the Puzzle of Perceptual Presence and Its Absence in Synesthesia." *Cognitive Neuroscience*, vol. 5, no. 2, 2014, pp. 97–118.

Shimizu, Daisuke. "Welcome to the Imagination World." *Wind Repertory Project*, 2016, https://www.windrep.org/Welcome_to_the_Imagination_World.

Shockley, Kevin, et al. "Mutual Interpersonal Postural Constraints Are Involved in Cooperative Conversation." *Journal of Experimental Psychology: Human Perception and Performance*, vol. 29, no. 2, 2003, pp. 326–32.

Spivey, Michael. *Who You Are: The Science of Connectedness*. MIT Press, 2020.

Walton, Ashley E., et al. "Creating Time: Social Collaboration in Music Improvisation." *Topics in Cognitive Science*, vol. 10, no. 1, 2018, pp. 95–119.

CHAPTER 18

Harmonic Dissonance: Synchron(icit)y

A Case Study of Experimentation at the Intersection of the Arts and Sciences

Suzanne Dikker and Suzan Tunca

1   Introduction

We reflect on the conditions, implications, and outcomes of integrating the worlds of art and science in *Harmonic Dissonance: Synchron(icit)y* (2018-present), a collaborative work of DIKKER + OOSTRIK and ICK Dans Amsterdam that explores the measurability of human connectedness, i.e., the elusive sense of "oneness" that lies above and beyond the mere physical presence of another human body (Dikker et al.). As described in more detail below, dancers wear electroencephalogram (EEG) devices that measure their brain-waves while they interact with audio-visual reflections of their movements and brainwave synchrony on stage. This synchrony neurofeedback environment provides a playground not only for performers but, crucially, also for dance researchers and neuroscientists as they question and negotiate the concept of human connectedness.

From an artistic performative perspective, the staging of the scientific decomposition of complexly layered performative states in dance raises questions about the possibility of enhancing the perception, communication, understanding, and the potential significance of these states in the dancers and in the observers/the audience. As such, *Harmonic Dissonance: Synchron(icit)y* makes it possible to bring intuitive body knowledge and organic forms of measurement in dance in dialogue with scientific perspectives on the phenomena of "synchrony" and "synchronicity."

Working with dancers on stage allows investigators to ask how synchronous movements and the coupling of brain activity between people or inter-brain synchrony (Konvalinka and Roepstorff; Czeszumski et al.) map onto experiences of "togetherness," or social "connectedness": between the dancers, between dancers and the audience, and between audience members. We aim to show that such a "real-world neuroscience approach," involving the collection of brain data from (groups of) people in naturalistic contexts, provides a unique opportunity to investigate the neurobiological basis of dynamic, naturalistic social behavior in ways that are impossible in the laboratory (Dikker et al., "Brain-to-Brain Synchrony"; Dikker et al., "Crowdsourcing").

Below, we first introduce the project *Harmonic Dissonance: Synchron(icit)y*, comprising three workshops that led to a performative experiment. We then briefly discuss two fundamental concepts underpinning the project: the notion of "synchrony" in neuroscience and the idea of "synchronicity" in the choreographic language of Emio Greco and Pieter C. Scholten, founders of the dance company ICK. We outline the creative steps and research questions that influenced the performative and experimental design that operates at the intersection of artistic and scientific practice. We close with discussing the creative potentials that emerge in the experimental space between the meaningful interpretation of scientific data, their artistic rendering, and intuitive bodily perception and knowing.

2 Harmonic Dissonance: Synchron(icit)y

Harmonic Dissonance: Synchron(icit)y was developed over the course of three workshops that examined different aspects and dimensions of connectedness in dance. In this section, we explain the methodology of these workshops in some detail to illustrate how joint research questions and approaches emerge at the interface of scientific and artistic inquiry.

During Workshop I (2018), the dancers wore EEG devices that measured their brainwaves and interacted with audio-visual landscapes that were generated by both their brainwave and motion data. Two ICK dancers performed seven choreographed and improvised variations linked to instantiations of synchrony/synchronicity, based on the repertoire of Greco and Scholten. This allowed both dancers and spectators to explore how motion synchrony can be unpacked into different types of joint action ("coordination", "mirroring", "unison", "anticipation", "resonance", "play"); how these relate to the pursued quality of synchronicity in the dance of Greco and Scholten; and how the sense of togetherness that emerges out of this performative quality might relate to the visualization and sonification of synchronization of brainwaves. Through joint movement and brainstorming, the workshop participants co-created a conceptual taxonomy of synchron(icit)y that incorporates both neuroscientific and performance-based concepts and can serve as a point of departure for (neuro)scientific hypotheses as well as for choreographic dramaturgies (Figure 18.1.a; Dikker et al., "Crowdsourcing").

Building on the taxonomy of synchrony and synchronicity developed in the first workshop, Workshop II (2019) focused on developing the parameters of

HARMONIC DISSONANCE: SYNCHRON(ICIT)Y 287

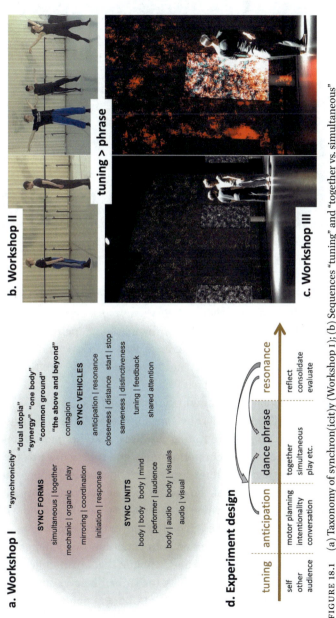

FIGURE 18.1 (a) Taxonomy of synchron(icit)y (Workshop I); (b) Sequences "tuning" and "together vs. simultaneous" (Workshop II); (c) Stills from ID-Lab performance (Workshop III); (d) Experiment design

FIGURE 18.2   Performance of *Harmonic Dissonance: Synchron(icit)y* at the Ballet National de Marseille

an experiment and on translating this setup into performative sequencing, centered on the dichotomy of *simultaneity* versus *togetherness*. This is an intuitive distinction that is not straightforwardly measured, neither scientifically nor performatively. To explore this difference, we tested repeated sequences of "tuning", "anticipation", "movement", and "resonance" with variations on choreographic material (Figure 18.1.b).

For "tuning," we applied for example the dance method Double Skin/Double Mind (ICK, "DS/DM The Method") developed by Greco and Scholten as well as the distinction between positive tuning (towards the other performers), negative tuning (away from the other performers), and tuning towards the self in a standing position (leaning either forward, backward, or finding one's balance in the exact middle line of the central axis of the spine). "Anticipation" was performed and observed by reserving a stable time frame for the mental/physical preparation towards the upcoming movement sequence in stillness. For the "movement" phase, we worked with variations on vignettes based on fragments from the oeuvre of Greco and Scholten that are intended to be performed with the quality of synchronicity (described below). We also worked with improvised explorations around "Pre-Choreographic Elements." Pre-Choreographic elements are a designation for choreographic dance material that has been codified through research in dance notation and made suitable for dance creation; the term refers to the preliminary phase in the choreographic process of Emio Greco and Pieter C. Scholten (ICK, "Home-Pre-Choreographic elements"). With the Pre-Choreographic elements, ICK notates the origins of choreographic statements, which are ideas, metaphors, and images that drive the intentions behind the movement. In addition to working with the synchrony forms, tools, and units from the conceptual cloud (Figure 18.1.a), we also worked with different spatial configurations (e.g., close together facing towards and away from each other, far apart facing towards and away from each other). For the "resonance" phase, the performers simply stood still for a fixed amount of time, allowing both themselves and the observers to gain a palpable sense of the resonance of the preceding movements in their mental and physical interior spaces as well as in the shared space of the performance.

After each iteration of the sequences of "tuning", "anticipation", "movement", and "resonance", observations from the perspective of the dancers and the spectators were shared and documented. The subtle, yet profound distinction between performing with the intentional dispositions of simultaneity versus togetherness crystallized throughout this series of experimentations as the most challenging but also the most potent dichotomy to explore further both scientifically as well as artistically.

During Workshop III (2020, Figure 18.1.c/d), we designed a basic structure of a performative experiment building on the takeaways from Workshop II. For the dramaturgical unfolding of the structure we aimed at finding a dynamic balance between analytically dissecting the layered performative states in linear time (needed for scientific measurement) and giving space to perform the dance in a way that the different layers of awareness ("tuning" towards self, the other, the audience, the dance, the space, the sounds, etc.) can be synthesized in the moment through movement.

The performance/experiment consisted of seven performative vignettes that each constitute an experimentation block (Figure 18.1.d), consisting of the four phases described above: First, dancers "tune" their intentional disposition towards themselves, the other dancer(s), or the audience (Figure 18.1.b/c, left). Second, during "anticipation," dancers internally trace/visualize the movement intentions and spatial development of the subsequent movement phase. Third, during the dance phrase (Figure 18.1.b/c, right), the dancers play with different movement intentions derived from the conceptual cloud representing the scientific/artistic decomposition of synchron(icit)y (i.e., leading vs. following, one body/synchronicity vs. friction, and dissonance; Figure 18.1.a). Finally, during the "resonance" phase, the dancers stand still, either listening to the echo of the "movement" phase inside of their body or evaluating/reflecting on the (mis)match between their predicted movement (as created during the anticipation phase) and the movement itself (see retrospective arrows in Figure 18.1.d). These performative vignettes negotiate the terms synchrony and synchronicity through decoupling and recoupling of movement intentions with choreographic movements and improvised sequences. This sequential approach allows spectators to develop a more nuanced perception of the qualitative differences between different ways of moving together and allows researchers to ask whether different intentions before and after a movement sequence are differentially correlated with inter-brain coupling and movement synchrony. This scientific decomposition—i.e., comparing different performative states on stage—became the basic skeleton for a theatrical dramaturgy. The approach allows the dancers to take an analytical perspective and enables the audience to scrutinize performative states that are usually compounded in the act of dancing, where tuning towards the self, the other, and the audience is happening at the same time.

In sum, through *Harmonic Dissonance: Synchron(icit)y*, we (1) developed a "conceptual cloud" of synchrony/synchronicity that incorporates concepts and vocabulary from both artistic and scientific inquiry; (2) explored how *togetherness* and *simultaneity* can be embodied/measured; and (3) created the dramaturgy for a performative experiment to further investigate human connectedness.

3 Leveraging Conceptual Fuzziness to Generate Working Hypotheses at the Art-Science Interface

Recent years have seen a rise in interest in art-science initiatives. Institutes, workshops, and artist-in-residences are popping up everywhere. These collaborations come in different shapes and forms and are often asymmetric, with a focus on artists becoming part of a (natural) scientific experimentation or investigation. Some scientists have argued, for instance, that working with artists can help in science communication (Zaelzer) or, alternatively, in meeting therapeutic goals (King). With *Harmonic Dissonance: Synchron(icit)y*, we take a different approach. First and foremost, we position artists and scientists on an equal footing and challenge the duality between subjectivity and objectivity that is often associated with art and science respectively. Artists can strive towards replicable observations and experiences as well. In the case of the work of Greco and Scholten this happens through dance notation research that is based on capturing movement intentions (see De Lahunta), while cognitive and social neuroscientists often grapple with connecting supposed subjective phenomena to objective constructs (e.g., the relationship of the mind and the brain). When posing the question how "objective" records of (bio-)physical phenomena (brainwaves, heart rate, movements) can tell us something about the "subjective" experience of feeling connected to others, we find that the ambiguous terms "synchrony" and "synchronicity" can serve as "boundary objects" for interdisciplinary discussion (Halpern). While psychologists and other social and natural scientists have often rejected the term "synchronicity," because of its parascientific connotations, we instead creatively negotiate its diverging definitions in an open dialogue between artistic and scientific perspectives, epistemologies, and modi operandi. As such, the project *Harmonic Dissonance: Synchron(icit)y* leverages terminological frictions as a fruitful ground for discussion and as a fertile space for creative imagination and artistic and scientific invention.

4 Synchrony and the Quest to Measure Togetherness

The term synchrony is derived from the Greek σύγχρονος, an aggregate of the words *syn-* (together) and *chronos* (time). *Merriam-Webster* dictionary defines synchronous as "happening, existing, or arising at precisely the same time," but also includes a definition that associates synchrony with the transfer of information: "of, used in, or being digital communication (as between computers) in which a common timing signal is established that dictates when individual bits can be transmitted and which allows for very high rates of data transfer" (Merriam-Webster). Synchrony in neural oscillations, brain rhythms, or so-called brainwaves, are believed to play a pivotal role in how we understand and interact with the (social) world (Buzsaki). Our biobehavioral rhythms lock to the rhythms of the world around us, mediated by psychological processes such as attention and expectations (Zion Golumbic et al.; Bar), and successful social interactions require tight spatio-temporal coordination between their participants at motor, perceptual and cognitive levels. The latter is shown in recent work on *inter*-brain synchrony in social interactions using so-called "hyperscanning" techniques (for a recent review see Czeszumski et al.). Findings from joint action, music ensembles, teamwork, classroom interactions, and other social tasks have shown that the interpersonal coupling of brain rhythms is linked to social intentions, empathy, performing actions simultaneously, among other factors (Dumas and Fairhurst; Dikker et al., "Brain-to-Brain Synchrony"; Babiloni et al.; Reinero et al.; Dikker et al., "Crowdsourcing").

The "conceptual cloud" or taxonomy of synchron(icit)y (Figure 18.1.a), created during Workshop I, includes a non-exhaustive list of notions, intentions, movements, and potential tools connected to or fostering synchrony. Examples of categories outlined through this conceptual cloud are "objects of synchrony," i.e., ways in which bodies can be synchronized by sound (von

Zimmermann et al.), "forms of synchrony," such as leader-follower relationships (Konvanlinka and Roepstorff), or physical "tools to achieve synchrony," such as alternating between closeness and distance (Dikker et al., "Crowdsourcing"). These categories do not constitute new discoveries—many scholars in both the sciences and the arts have pointed to these terms and issues—yet defining them helps crystallize the research goals. For example, our mind mapping pointed to the importance of notions of anticipation in relation to resonance. Does inter-brain-movement synchrony during the silence leading up to a movement sequence (anticipation) predict the extent to which the movement sequence is completed? And what about the "resonance" stage *after* the movement sequence is completed? Can we distinguish the neural processes underlying movement sequences that are performed simultaneously versus those that are performed *together*, with the intention to *share* an experience? These questions do not apply solely to performance research but extend to the study of joint action more broadly. Working with a performance ensemble such as ICK Dans Amsterdam, who think about joint action, synchronicity, and (in) visible movement at a professional level, provides alternative, more refined angles to address questions that are not directly related to dance but to our scientific understanding of cognition, movement, and behavior more generally. Specifically, how may each of these notions map onto different neuroscientific measures of "synchrony" (Ayrolles et al.; Dumas and Fairhurst)?

5 Synchronicity and Dual Utopia

The artwork *Harmonic Dissonance* builds upon the artistic vision of dance developed by choreographers Greco and Scholten, who understand the term "synchronicity" as related to moving in "synchrony" but also see it as qualitatively above and beyond merely moving at the same time while performing the identical movements. In their approach to choreography and dance, synchronicity denotes a "dual utopia" (a "not yet") as well as a palpable state and multi-layered quality of shared intentionality that is actualized via moving together in dance.

The term "synchronicity" is defined as the "quality of being synchronous," but also, according to the *Merriam-Webster* dictionary, as "the coincidental occurrence of events and especially psychic events (such as similar thoughts in widely separated persons or a mental image of an unexpected event before it happens) that seem related but are not explained by conventional mechanisms of causality—used especially in the psychology of C. G. Jung" (*Merriam-Webster*).

A key principle for the dancers to approximate the quality of "synchronicity" is the notion of moving as "one body." To achieve this quality in a duet (ICK Amsterdam, "TWO, ICK"), the dancers need to cultivate a kind of doubled awareness through which they are both conscious of their own movements as well as the movements of the other dancer, while meeting each other in the same intention behind the movement. This state of moving together is also called "unisono synchronicity," whereby the dancers expand their own individuality, while at the same time making room for the other. Even when "unisono synchronicity" appears to occur, the ideal of a complete unity is never arrived at and the individuality of the dancers becomes even more emphasized (Wijers et al.). It is through the shared intent of reaching towards a utopian quality of becoming "one body" with one or more other bodies during the dance that the pursued quality of experiencing "synchronicity" in dance is generated.

The choreographic language of Greco and Scholten explicitly works with striving towards ideals (for example of body length, spaciousness within the body, speed, togetherness, etc.). It is in the act of striving together towards something that is beyond the (reasonably) achievable that the imagination becomes activated to an extreme extent, thus allowing the body to transcend its limitations. In this vein, dancers aim at becoming "one body" with other bodies in dance, which asks for an extreme expansion and definition of the self, and the expansion of exigent, empathic, and utopian capacities, while simultaneously maintaining a coherent and assembled inner center. In this choreographic language, as Scholten puts it, "the mental state is a physical state and the physical state is a mental state" and the intuitive body in dance is able to "generate a unity between mind and body, a consciousness that evokes the next movement" within split seconds (qtd. in Magnini 115).

Although there is no explicit reference to the famous interpretation of "synchronicity" by C. G. Jung in the work of Greco and Scholten, it is possible to infer some resonances between Jung's ideas of a collective unconscious and archetypes and their work on shared images and metaphors as the basis of achieving "synchronicity" in dance. Whereas a scientific approach towards "synchronicity" would attempt to find evidence of proof of his speculative proposition, the artistic approach focuses on the imaginative, utopian, creative, and connecting potential that is inherent in the ideal of "synchronicity."

In C. G. Jung's definition of "synchronicity," meaning (instead of causation) is a central interpretative tool that suggests an "acausal connecting principle correlating mental and physical events" (Fuchs and Atmanspacher 5). In Greco and Scholten's artistic appropriation of Jung's term "synchronicity" on the other hand, meaning is approached from a different perspective: creativity is understood as incarnated in the body, which implies that the human body is intrinsically able to create time and space and to create different dimensions of meaning independently from externally imposed narratives or conceptual structures. We found the friction caused by the juxtaposition of notions such as "synchronicity" and "meaning"—terms that are frequently used but differently interpreted—very stimulating. We consider these clashes as highly valuable for generating discourse and research questions that can contribute to bridging gaps of understanding between different ways and cultures of knowing.

6 The Brain and the Intuitive Body

In our everyday language, "the brain" is often associated with rationality (evidenced by terms like "cerebral", "brainiac", etc.). However, our brains also allow us to intuitively and performatively tune ourselves to others. Scholars do not yet fully understand how the body moves intuitively and how our brains control the way we relate to the world. *Harmonic Dissonance: Synchron(icit)y* emphasizes that in order to advance our knowledge of how humans achieve a state of "togetherness," it is crucial to acknowledge the intuitive (dancing) body as a highly sophisticated instrument for heightened perception. A focus on the intuitively perceiving body of both dancers and observers may provide significant new insights into the relationship between the brain, movement, and mental (and physical) state that cannot be achieved by technological measurement procedures alone. The intuitive body may perceive, for example, if one is dancing together or simultaneously in ways that are not captured by established scientific registers.

Harmonic Dissonance is thus inspired by the choreographic vision of Greco and Scholten, who work with an intuitive body language that communicates via what they call a "dramaturgy of the flesh" (Wijers et al.). They conceptualize the intuitive body in dance as being sparked by a polarization between instinctive movement and brain-controlled movement (ICK Amsterdam, "Intuitive Body"). In *Harmonic Dissonance*, this intuitive perception and the organic "measurement" of the quality of synchronicity between the dancers (and between the dancers and the audience) is augmented with a visual landscape that transposes the data derived from technological measurement tools. Intuitive performance and perception, scientific measurement, and artistically rendered biofeedback come together to create an experiential landscape that blends wonder and imaginative perception with scientific and performative precision. Through this performative experiment, the artists and scientists involved question how the staging of the scientific decomposition of complexly layered performative states in dance can enhance the perception, communication, understanding, and potential meanings of these states in the dancers and in audience members.

From a neuroscientific perspective, the design laid out in our experimental performance (Figure 18.1.d) allows for the targeted investigation of several research questions pertaining to synchrony. For example, does inter-brain synchrony between dancers during anticipation and/or resonance predict movement synchrony during the dance phrase? Previous research has demonstrated that during action preparation, we develop a neural template, or motor plan, of the anticipated action, such as a movement, a speech act, etc. (Wolpert and Flanagan). During and after a movement, the brain forms a prediction error that describes the (mis)match between the motor plan and the executed action. This information is used to adapt and refine future motor plans with the goal to optimize the match between predicted and actualized actions. One might thus expect that "communicative success" (here: synchrony) in social communication is predicted by the interpersonal similarity in mental representations prior to the communicative act. Previous studies have already reported a relationship between inter-brain synchrony and coupled movement during more constrained joint action tasks (Dumas et al.). *Harmonic Dissonance* thus presents a proof of concept as to how such questions can be asked during naturalistic, real-world joint action.

Crucially, dancers are not used as just a model organism for these scientific questions. Participating in *Harmonic Dissonance: Synchron(icit)y* strengthens the dancers' conscious awareness of specific performative states by engaging in new modes of relating with the audience, with themselves, and with each other. For example, viewers are able to infer the dancers' intentions of togetherness vs. simultaneity, despite the absence of clear visible cues by watching video registrations of three dancers performing the same sequence with different intentions of "tuning" towards each other (positive: towards the other dancers, negative: away from the others or towards the self).

7 Bringing in the Audience

Is it possible to leverage our research questions, technology, and performative decisions to create immersive, interactive aesthetic experiences that allow visitors to gauge and explore their own interactions in a visceral, intuitive way? Incorporating (audio-visual translations of) biophysiological synchrony into the scenography and dramaturgy renders tangible what usually remains invisible and highly subjective in performative and theatrical settings. The intuitive perception of the quality of synchronicity in dance between the dancers and between the dancers and the audience is augmented with a suggestively ambiguous visual landscape based on scientific measurement tools that invites a shared speculation about when, why, and how optimal connectedness occurs or not, and about how connection constitutive or connection disruptive qualities become perceivable and speak differently in a theatrical setting than in a laboratory or in an everyday social situation. *Harmonic Dissonance* brings to the surface the fact that the quality of togetherness can be palpable and intersubjectively verifiable, while remaining extremely difficult to capture scientifically.

In *Harmonic Dissonance*, scientific measurement tools and the interpretation and artistic rendering of data acquired through these measurement tools co-exist with the intuitive and tacit knowledge of the dancers and of the observers in the experimental design; they meet each other in their shared focus on what is actually—visibly and invisibly—happening between the dancers and between the dancers and the observers in the theatrically staged experiment. The neurofeedback environment provides a tangible layer that brings invisible relations between the bodies in the performative space to the foreground.

8   Conclusion

Harmonic Dissonance: Synchron(icit)y aims to exemplify how creative frictions, when met with radical open-mindedness towards different perspectives, can generate new knowledge and experiences. Through three workshops, we (1) developed a "conceptual cloud" of synchrony/synchronicity that incorporates concepts and vocabulary from both artistic and scientific inquiry; (2) explored how *togetherness* and *simultaneity* can be embodied/measured; and (3) created the dramaturgy for a performative experiment to further investigate human connectedness. With this project, we are observing, together with our audiences, what happens when intuitive organic "measurement" (by breath, heartbeat, relation to the space and to each other in the context of choreographed or improvised movement), scientific measurement tools, scientific interpretation of data and their artistic rendering are brought together in the theatrical space of a performative experiment. We see the scientific and artistic perspectives and working modes as complementary to each other. They meet each other in performative and rigorous scientific precision, in ambiguous suggestiveness and playful exploration, in grounded matters of facts and flights of imagination towards the unachievable, together imbued with an endless curiosity towards what we do not know yet. Instead of excluding each other's perspectives, because our working procedures and paradigms may appear to be incompatible, this work recognizes and embraces the challenges and potentials of art-science collaborations in a performative and experimental space. This space then becomes rich in texture and provides multi-faceted and unexpected readings of the work, which can also throw a new light on artistic and scientific research problems.

Acknowledgments

We wish to extend special thanks to Nim Goede, who has been a fantastic colleague, collaborator, and critic of our works, and who has provided us with the opportunity to write this chapter. Interactive media artist Matthias Oostrik is co-creator of the work. *Harmonic Dissonance: Synchron(icit)y* is supported by Stichting Niemeijer Fonds, Creative Industries Fund NL, ICK Dans Amsterdam, Theater de Meervaart, AHK ID-Lab, Doornburgh Buitenplaats voor Kunst en Wetenschap, Ballet National de Marseille, RASL Rotterdam Arts and Sciences Lab, Erasmus University College, ASCA Amsterdam School for Cultural Analysis (University of Amsterdam), Vrije Universiteit Amsterdam, Netherlands Organisation for Scientific Research Award #406.18.GO.024. Choreographic materials: Emio Greco | Pieter C. Scholten. ICK Dancers: Arad Inbar, Sedrig Verwoert, Maxine van Lishout, Hannah Kriesmair, Hiroki Nunogaki, Isaiah Wilson. ICK costumes: Clifford Portier, ICK documentation: Kayla McClellan.

References

Academie voor Theater en Dans. "ICK with Harmonic Dissonance." Academie voor Theater En Dans, 11 May 2020, https://www.atd.ahk.nl/idlab/whats-on/kijk-terug/17-21-february-ick-with-harmonic-dissonance/.

Ayrolles, Anaël, et al. "HyPyP: A Hyperscanning Python Pipeline for Inter-Brain Connectivity Analysis." *Social Cognitive and Affective Neuroscience*, vol. 16, no. 1–2, Jan. 2021, pp. 72–83.

Babiloni, Claudio, et al. "Brains 'in Concert': Frontal Oscillatory Alpha Rhythms and Empathy in Professional Musicians." *NeuroImage*, vol. 60, no. 1, Mar. 2012, pp. 105–16.

Bachrach, Asaf, et al. "Audience Entrainment during Live Contemporary Dance Performance: Physiological and Cognitive Measures." *Frontiers in Human Neuroscience*, vol. 9, art. 179, 2015.

Bar, Moshe. "The Proactive Brain: Using Analogies and Associations to Generate Predictions." *Trends in Cognitive Sciences*, vol. 11, no. 7, 2007, pp. 280–89.

Buzsaki, Gyorgy. *Rhythms of the Brain.* Oxford UP, 2006.

Czeszumski, Artur, et al. "Hyperscanning: A Valid Method to Study Neural Inter-Brain Underpinnings of Social Interaction." *Frontiers in Human Neuroscience*, vol. 14, art. 39, Feb. 2020.

De Lahunta, Scott. (*Capturing Intention*). *Documentation, Analysis and Notation Research Based on the Work of Emio Greco*. Emio Greco PC and AHK/Lectoraat, |PC. Amsterdam: Emio Greco|PC and Amsterdam Hogeschool voor de Kunsten, 2007.

Dikker, Suzanne, et al. "Brain-to-Brain Synchrony Tracks Real-World Dynamic Group Interactions in the Classroom." *Current Biology: CB*, vol. 27, no. 9, May 2017, pp. 1375–80.

Dikker, Suzanne, et al. "Using Synchrony-Based Neurofeedback in Search of Human Connectedness." *Brain Art: Brain-Computer Interfaces for Artistic Expression*, edited by Anton Nijholt, Springer, 2019, pp. 161–206.

Dikker, Suzanne, et al. "Crowdsourcing Neuroscience: Inter-Brain Coupling during Face-to-Face Interactions Outside the Laboratory." *NeuroImage*, vol. 227, art. 117436, Feb. 2021.

Doornburgh Buitenplaats voor Kunst en Wetenschap. "Suzanne Dikker – Op Dezelfde Golflengte." Buitenplaats Doornburgh, 15 June 2020, https://www.buitenplaats-doornburgh.nl/agenda/suzanne-dikker-op-dezelfde-golflengte/.

Dumas, Guillaume, and Merle T. Fairhurst. "Reciprocity and Alignment: Quantifying Coupling in Dynamic Interactions." *Royal Society Open Science*, vol. 8, no. 5, 2021.

Dumas, Guillaume, et al. "Inter-Brain Synchronization during Social Interaction." *PLOS One*, vol. 5, no. 8, Aug. 2010.

Dutch Performing Arts. "BNM FEST 2018." Dutch Performing Arts, www.dutchperformingarts.nl/events/on-the-international-stage/bnmfest-2018/. Accessed 2022.

Fuchs, Christopher A., and Harald Atmanspacher. *The Pauli-Jung Conjecture and Its Impact Today*. Andrews UK Limited, 2014.

Halpern, Megan K. "Across the Great Divide: Boundaries and Boundary Objects in Art and Science." *Public Understanding of Science*, vol. 21, no. 8, Nov. 2012, pp. 922–37.

"Harmonic Dissonance: Synchron(icit)y @ Ballet National de Marseille." Vimeo, https://vimeo.com/312105834.

ICK Amsterdam. "DS/DM The Method · ICK." ICK Amsterdam, https://www.ickamsterdam.com/nl/academy/dansprofessionals/ds-dm-the-method-20. Accessed 1 July 2023.

ICK Amsterdam. "HARMONIC DISSONANCE · ICK." ICK Amsterdam, https://www.ickamsterdam.com/nl/academy/producties/harmonic-dissonance-100. Accessed 1 July 2023.

ICK Amsterdam. "Home – Pre-Choreographic Elements." Pre-choreographic elements, https://pre-choreographicelements.net/. Accessed 1 July 2023.

ICK Amsterdam. "INTUITIVE BODY · ICK." ICK Amsterdam, https://www.ickamsterdam.com/nl/academy/peers-onderzoekers/intuitive-body-11 . Accessed 1 July 2023.

ICK AMSTERDAM. "TWO · ICK." ICK Amsterdam, www.ickamsterdam.com/nl/company /producties/two-51. Accessed 1 July 2023.

King, Juliet L. *Art Therapy, Trauma, and Neuroscience: Theoretical and Practical Perspectives*. Routledge, 2016.

Konvalinka, Ivana, and Andreas Roepstorff. "The Two-Brain Approach: How Can Mutually Interacting Brains Teach Us Something about Social Interaction?" *Frontiers in Human Neuroscience*, vol. 6, art. 215, July 2012.

Magnini, Francesca, and ICK Amsterdam. *Inspiration: Emio Greco, Pieter C. Scholten: The Multiplicity of Dance: Dissemination of Knowledge: Contamination of Cultures: Food for Thought*. Artegrafica, 2015.

Merriam-Webster Online Dictionary. "Synchronicity." Merriam-Webster, www.merriam -webster.com/dictionary/synchronicity.

Merriam-Webster Online Dictionary. "Synchronous." Merriam-Webster, Merriam-Webster, www.merriam-webster.com/dictionary/synchronous.

Phillips-Silver, Jessica, et al. "The Ecology of Entrainment: Foundations of Coordinated Rhythmic Movement." *Music Perception*, vol. 28, no. 1, Sept. 2010, pp. 3–14.

RASL. "International Arts and Science Conference." RASL, https://rasl.nu/rasl-event/. Accessed 1 July 2023.

Reinero, Diego A., et al. "Inter-Brain Synchrony in Teams Predicts Collective Performance." *Social Cognitive and Affective Neuroscience*, vol. 16, no. 1–2, Jan. 2021, pp. 43–57.

Vvon Zimmermann, Jorina, et al. "The Choreography of Group Affiliation." *Topics in Cognitive Science*, vol. 10, no. 1, Wiley Online Library, Jan. 2018, pp. 80–94.

Wijers, Gaby, et al. *Inside Movement Knowledge Documentation Model*. ARTI, Artistic Research, Theory and Innovation & ICK Amsterdam-Emio Greco PC, 2010.

Wolpert, Daniel. M., and John R. Flanagan. "Motor Prediction." *Current Biology: CB*, vol. 11, no. 18, Sept. 2001, pp. R729–32.

Zaelzer, Cristian. "The Value in Science-Art Partnerships for Science Education and Science Communication." *eNeuro*, vol. 7, no. 4, July 2020.

Zion Golumbic, Elana M., et al. "Mechanisms Underlying Selective Neuronal Tracking of Attended Speech at a 'Cocktail Party.'" *Neuron*, vol. 77, no. 5, Mar. 2013, pp. 980–91.

CHAPTER 19

Thanks for Sharing

Local Worlds, Xeno-Patterning, and Predictive Processing

Stephan Besser

1 Introduction

The concept of patterned practices has been introduced into the field of cognitive and cultural neuroscience as an alternative to the generalizing notion of "culture." In their 2010 article "Enculturing Brains through Patterned Practices," Andreas Roepstorff, Jörg Niewöhner, and Stefan Beck note that in anthropology and associated disciplines the use of "culture" as an analytical concept has been rightly criticized for its homogenizing and essentializing effects. Therefore, they observe with some concern that in the emerging field of "cultural neuroscience" the concept is often employed in ways that neglect "intra-cultural variation" and assumes cultures to consist of "homogeneous populations," for instance in research designs that compare "collectivistic" with "individualistic" societies (Roepstorff et al. 1051).[1] Taking conceptual cues from social scientists Pierre Bourdieu and Arjun Appadurai, the authors propose the "middle-range concept" of patterned practices as an alternative (1051; cf. Bourdieu 1977). Patterned practices are activities that are performed by groups of people in concrete, material-discursive environments with a certain regularity; think of practices such as praying, dancing, or making music. Such practices arguably shape neural patterns in the brains of the practitioners and can—through loops of action and perception—create "common worlds" of material, semantic, and symbolic nature between the participants. For the authors, this approach opens new perspectives for the study of the interactive "patterning" of human minds, brains, and bodies that avoid short-circuiting the micro level of brain activity with a macro concept of culture (Roepstorff et al. 1057).

The Patterned practices-paper has been widely cited and particularly influential in research on predictive processing (PP), to which it is explicitly addressed.[2] However, it seems to me that in the PP context the concept

---

1 The authors quote a study by Tang et al. as example.
2 See for instance Clark, "Whatever Next"; Clark, *Surfing Uncertainty*; Taves and Aprem; Kiverstein and Kirchhoff.

© KONINKLIJKE BRILL NV, LEIDEN, 2023 | DOI:10.1163/9789004681293_021

THANKS FOR SHARING 301

of patterned practices is currently also taken into directions that—implicitly or explicitly—reaffirm a more homogeneous notion of culture, albeit at the smaller scale of "local worlds" and socio-cognitive "niches" (cf. Schjoedt; Andersen; Ramstead et al.). Such approaches run the risk of rendering culture as "largely homeostatic," as philosopher of science Andrew Buskell has remarked in his response to a high-profile target paper in the field, Samuel Veissière et al.'s 2020 article "Thinking through Other Minds: A Variational Approach to Cognition and Culture." In Buskell's view, homeostatic processes of keeping some variables in a living system within a specific range are not sufficient as an overall account of culture: radical social change and conflictive forms of social life cannot be plausibly explained if enculturation essentially means "expecting others to stay within the bounds of established behavior" (Buskell 29).[3]

I wonder if the initial pluralization of "culture" through patterned practices is not partly taken back in current extensions of the PP framework to social interaction, resulting in a relative disregard for the "disjunctures" that make up societies in an age of globalization, digitization, and superdiversity (Appadurai). In this essay, I therefore want to think about the relation of patterns to *difference*, both within and across patterned practices. I offer my reflections as the thoughts of a literary scholar who is trained to attend to the dynamics of diversity, intersectionality, and cultural difference but also keenly interested in—and susceptible to—the current fascination with patterns in many fields across the human and social sciences (cf. Bod; Dixon). An important inspiration for me in this regard is the work of literature and science scholar N. Katherine Hayles, who has described the "dialectic of pattern and randomness" as the distinctive epistemic and ontological signature of contemporary techno-culture (Hayles 25). Going back to cybernetics and Gregory Bateson's ideas about pattern and randomness, Hayles claims that the older, metaphysical opposition of "absence"/"presence" is becoming outdated in a world in which things can be absent and present at the same time (as informational patterns) and no stable meanings and identities are guaranteed by a coherent origin (Hayles 283–291). More recently, literary scholar Caroline Levine has made the experience and formation of sociocultural patterns the focus of her work on socio-aesthetics *forms*.[4] Levine is critical of the long-standing

---

3 For this definition of homeostasis see Colombo and Palacios (1). Antonio Damasio has recently proposed an extended conception of homeostasis as the functional principle underlying feelings and culture (Damasio).

4 For Levine, "forms" and "patterns" are essentially synonymous. She defines form as "all shapes and configurations, all ordering principles, all patterns of repetition and difference." In her view, this broad definition has the advantage of addressing the political, aesthetic, and social

tradition in literary and cultural studies to privilege the "formless," i.e., the undoing of structures of oppression through processes of migration, hybridity, liminality, passing, etc. (Levine, *Forms* 9). For Levine, understanding social, political, and cognitive patterns—"what is most likely to be repeated" in a certain context or situation—is essential for improving collective life and attending to the "common good" (Levine, "Model Thinking" 634). But she also stresses that social forms and patterns constantly collide and *clash* (one of her literary examples is the collision of different networks of kinship, social connection, communication, and disease transmission in Charles Dickens's novel *Bleak House,* 1852–53). For Levine, there is no coherent master pattern in contemporary societies; rather, "multiple forms of the world come into conflict and disorganize experience in ways that call for unconventional political strategies" (Levine, *Forms* 17).

Levine and Hayles stand for two different but related lines of thought that I explore in this essay: the notion that patterned practices continuously clash and disrupt each other (Levine) and the idea that patterning *itself* contains an element of randomness that is "the creative ground from which pattern can emerge" (Hayles 286). I address these two ideas—the difference *between* and *within* patterns—in this order and bring them in conversation with the concept of patterned cultural practices in the work of an interdisciplinary research team around Maxwell Ramstead, Samuel Veissière, and Laurence Kirmayer on enculturation from a PP perspective and a work of fiction, Octavia Butler's "Patternist" novel *Mind of My Mind* (1977). In this way, I hope to add a new perspective to current invocations of the "shared world" in PP research and the discourse of embodied cognition more generally (Durt et al.).

2   Bounded Contiguity

The diagram below (Figure 19.1) is the last of six illustrations in the paper "Cultural Affordances: Scaffolding Local Worlds through Shared Intentionality and Regimes of Attentions" by Maxwell Ramstead, Samuel Veissière, and Laurence Kirmayer. It was reprinted in almost identical form in the aforementioned article "Thinking through Other Minds" by the same team of researchers, complemented by philosopher Axel Constant and neuroscientist Karl Friston (Ramstead et al. 12; Veissière et al. 12). Both papers work towards a theory of

---

"affordances" of forms—political organization, narrative order etc.—without privileging any of them (Levine, *Forms* 3, 6–9).

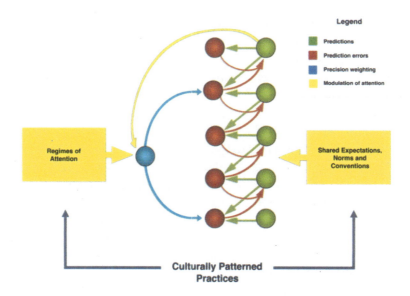

FIGURE 19.1   "Cultural Affordances: Scaffolding Local Worlds through Shared Intentionality and Regimes of Attentions" (Ramstead et al., "Cultural Affordances")

enculturation from the perspective of the PP framework, which conceives of the brain as a "prediction machine" that constantly seeks to predict its sensory input and own states on the basis of probabilistic estimations (Clark, "Whatever Next"). The 2016 article focuses on the ways in which "patterned regimes of attention" (3) mediate the engagement of human agents with *cultural affordances,* i.e., the possibilities for action that are available to humans by virtue of their ability to shape their environments at material and semiotic levels (language, material infrastructure etc.). The diagram offers a summary of key parts of the argument in the form of vector graphics:

Placed at the center of the diagram is the schematic representation of a multi-layered, bi-directional cortical processing hierarchy, in PP parlance also known as a processing "cascade" (Clark, "Whatever Next"). It consists of *prediction units* (green balls), that issue lateral and top-down signals to lower levels, and *error units* (auburn balls), that communicate prediction errors, i.e., mismatches between predictions and input, to higher and lateral levels. The key objective of this mechanism is to minimize long-term prediction error ("surprisal" or "free energy"), which can essentially be achieved in two ways: by altering predictions (*perceptual inference*) or by actions that bring about changes in the world/sensory input (*active inference*). Probabilities are estimated by a multilevel generative model that is realized in the brain; it is called "generative" because it models how sensory input is generated by causal and material relations in the world.[5]

In the diagram, the processing cascade is shown to be affected by two sorts of external influence, namely "Shared Expectations, Norms and Conventions" and "Regimes of Attention." "Shared Expectations" refers to the impact of cultural norms and conventions that are sent "downwards" in the processing hierarchy. Think, for example, of internalized rules regarding how to behave (sit, move, speak, take turns) in shared public spaces such as metros, hallways, university classrooms, bars, etc.: what one has learned to expect others to do in a certain context probabilistically shapes one's prediction of what will happen next in a specific situation (Ramstead et al. 18).

"Regimes of Attention" on the left-hand side of the cascade point to the important impact of "precision weighting" on predictive processing. "Attention" here means factoring in the estimated *reliability* of prediction errors (their "precision") in the processing routine. Visual input in a fog is likely to be assigned less precision than input at clear sight (Clark, *Surfing* 57–58). Similarly, as the authors note, it can be a valid attentional strategy to *not* read behavior and facial expressions of people in anonymized public spaces as reliable indicator of their emotion or character traits (Ramstead et al. 16). "Regimes of shared attention" thus mark specific affordances out as relevant and make predictions errors *count* in a shared cultural context. Finally, both expectations and attention are depicted to be shaped by "Culturally Patterned Practices," rendered visually in a clamp-like position at the bottom of the diagram. As proposed by Roepstorff et al., the authors understand such practices to include rituals, customs, and collective activities but also the shared enactment of narratives, embodied metaphors, and so on. In this way, attentional processes form "a central mechanism through which the individual is *molded to conform* to specific group expectations and participate in forms of cooperative action" (Ramstead et al. 16; my emphasis).

Like every scientific model the diagram involves a reduction and idealization of its target object (Potochnik). It is nevertheless instructive to consider the specific direction into which the idealization is taken and the meaning effects that come with it. In the case of Figure 19.1 it is, first, interesting to note what is *absent* in the visual representation, namely the active engagement of the agent itself with its social and worldly environments. The arrows in the outer layer of the diagram all point in one direction, namely from culturally patterned practices via regimes of attention and expectation *to* the human

---

5   Summary based on Wiese and Metzinger.

THANKS FOR SHARING   305

cognitive agent (rendered metonymically and schematically as a processing cascade).[6] Given the emphasis that most formulations of the PP framework put on active, embodied inference and the ability of human agents to change sensory input to match precisions—which can take the form of changing the world—this *unidirectionality* of the diagram is worth noticing.

A second significant abstraction in the diagram concerns the *uniformity* of these cultural influences themselves. In her landmark study on data visualization, Johanna Drucker has pointed to techniques of spatialization and the visual creation of "discrete bounded entities" as a powerful procedure in knowledge representation (Drucker 132). In the diagram, "Shared Expectations" and "Regimes of Attention" are both named in the plural but represented in bounded yellow boxes. *Conflicting* expectations and cues for precision weighting that a cognitive agent might be confronted with are not represented in the diagram. Therefore, the "culturally patterned practices" at the bottom also can appear as a consistent, unambiguous ensemble, although they are not visually bounded in a box. What emerges is the image of an all-round enclosure and embeddedness of cognitive agents in sociocultural surroundings that "mold" their interaction with affordances in a seemingly homogeneous and comprehensive way.

This focus on the coherence of socio-cultural ensembles is pervasively present in the text of the article as well. The authors use terms such as "local worlds," "local ontologies," "local landscape," and "local niche" to name and delimit distinctive sets or clusters of affordances (Ramstead et al. 1, 3, 12, 14); correspondingly, the term "shared" appears 87 times on the 18 pages of the article. A characteristic remark of this kind reads:

> Social niches and cultural practices generally involve not isolated, individual affordances or expectations, but local landscapes, that give rise to and depend upon shared expectations. We submit that these shared expectations—implemented in the predictive hierarchies, embodied in material culture, and enacted in patterned practices—contribute to the constitution of a given landscape of affordances that characterizes a given community or culture. (14)

This remark treats cultures as discrete entities—"a given community or culture"—with a certain "local" extensiveness; patterned practices are *of* such

---

6   In the 2020 version of the diagram the processing cascade is iconographically represented as residing in the head/brain of the cognitive agent, thereby making the rest of the body disappear (Veissière et al. 16).

a culture rather than a different kind of entity. While Roepstorff et al. voice their doubts about conceptions of culture as a "system of belief and values that are all shared by a particular group" and point to various differentiating factors such as age, sex, and social status (Roepstorff et al. 1055), Ramstead et al. use patterns as a figure of unity, contained within and forming the framework of "a culture." Hence, they speak about the "patterning *of* culture" as if no potential tension between the two terms exists (Viessière et al. 62).

It is important here to be precise about the meaning of the term "local," which does not necessarily imply spatial proximity. The authors work with the notion of a "*landscape*" of affordances," coined by Rietveld and Kiverstein (2014), which emphasizes concrete material settings (architecture, design, urban environments) but also includes a broad variety of affordances that reach beyond specific locations (language, digital environments etc.). Similarly, the trope of the ecological or cognitive "niche" does not necessarily denote a physical space but rather the particular place of a species in a larger ecosystem (Ramstead et al. 5). In a world characterized by real time transcontinental communication, collaboration, and exchange it would indeed seem dubious to define "local worlds" in a spatial sense. Nevertheless, the pervasive use of spatial metaphors—"landscape," "niche," "local"—still supports the notion of a cultural *contiguity* of affordances as forming an integrated whole.[7] For the authors, affordances are not "isolated" or open sets of possibilities for action but cohere in a "scape"; attentional modulation "carves out" a "local field" of affordances in a larger landscape (Ramstead et al. 16). The local and "shared worlds" that the authors describe thus appear in the form of a bounded contiguity, which arguably reflects the bounded contiguity of a processing hierarchy at a "cultural" scale. We are invited to think a multiplicity of niches and cultures but not the multiplicity of the niche itself.

3   Diversity and Homophily

From the perspective of a literary scholar who is used to attend to the polyphony of cultural articulations and identities I find this focus on contiguity most striking in the way in which Ramstead at al. address the topic of cultural diversity. Intriguingly, the authors start their paper by addressing the issue of ethnic and racial bias and posit that their framework might help to understand why children from minority groups already at a young age "show preferences for

---

7 For an approach to "landscapes" of affordances that explicitly includes socio-cultural difference see Rietveld et al.

dominant groups, rather than for persons of their own ethnicity" (Ramstead et al. 1). The authors partly base this claim on research done by psychologists and human rights activists Mamie P. and Kenneth B. Clark in segregated schools in the United States in the 1940s–60s. However, while the Clarks spoke about the "profound conflict" in the personality development of black children and its long-lasting socio-economic consequences (Clark and Clark 350), Ramstead et al. seem to sidestep the issue of permanent intra-cultural tension within groups and individuals by only briefly addressing one example in which a minority is claimed to "acquire" the norms and believes of a "dominant culture" (Ramstead et al. 1). When discussing the issue of enculturation and cultural diversity, it certainly is important to take into consideration the normative, coercive, and even violent dimension of "regimes" of attention and prediction, as the authors do. I wonder, however, if the PP concepts of the hierarchical processing cascade and a unified generative model not also have a dubious streamlining effect in casting "cultures" as equally integrated entities, thereby potentially obscuring the *constant* presence of conflicting priors, different knowledges, and intersectional identities.

In their 2020 target paper on their approach to "Thinking through Other Minds" (TTOM), the authors address the topic of cultural diversity more explicitly, in particular in their response to a number of critical reactions. They outline their "conservative" view of human culture—meaning that culture is seen as ensuring that agents remain within certain "well-bounded" sensory states to minimize long-term *surprisal*—and explain that this implies an understanding of culture(s) as a "a stable, relatively homogeneous social niche" (Veissière et al. 63). But they also acknowledge that "intra-cultural and inter-individual diversity" raise "thorny questions" for their model, which ultimately has to take into account "cultural mobility, hybridity, and the cognitive effects of the constantly changing social niches" (63, 21). The authors also make room for the idea that "bicultural" agents can switch between different generative models—as proposed in a comment by George Christopoulos and Ying-yi Hong (30)—and give some brief examples for the micro-adjustments of cognitive agents to conflicting regimes of attention (Viessière et al. 19).

It is nevertheless fair to say that the paper itself does not answer these "thorny questions" yet. Among the factors that complicate such a response is the way in which the authors employ the theory of mind (TOM), defined as the human ability to ascribe intentions, feelings, and mental states to other agents. For Viessière et al. the "selective patterning" of salience and attention is the result of the estimation of the epistemic authority and social affiliation of others:

> A successful inference about the "sort of person you are" enables a host of conditional inferences, many of which have a direct bearing on "how I should behave." This is particularly true if I infer that "you are like me." (4)

Hence, behavior and predictive processing in human minds are directly and primarily linked to the assessment of the social and epistemic status of others via TOM. Importantly, the authors use the phrase "creatures like me"—also "agents like me," "others like me" etc.—not only in reference to the general human ability of having expectations about other peoples' expectations ("the prior belief that 'I am like you and you are like me—and you believe that I am like you and you are like me" and so on"; Veissière et al. 16). The phrase also signifies, more specifically, the mindreading of people of the same *sort* or *kind*. For the authors, only this more specific type of interaction facilitates cultural patterning and niche construction in a "natural" way:

> We hope to show that these epistemic resources [i.e., the selective patterning of salience and attention, SB] arise naturally from cultural niche construction when, and only when, I share an environment with other "creatures like me." (5)

In her research on network science and present-day algorithmic culture, communication scholar Wendy Chun argues that the concept of "homophily"—which describes the tendency of individuals to bond with those they consider similar—naturalizes the assumption that societies consist of "cultural niches" and "local clusters" of people who are alike (Chun 80, 76). According to Chun, the axiom that "similarity breeds connection" performatively translates from the study of network patterns into social practice through predictive algorithms, computational modeling and datafication: "Networks preempt and predict by reading all singular actions as indications of larger collective habitual patterns, based not on our individual actions but rather the actions of others" (Chun 76, 75). Chun finds manifestations of this development in discriminatory police algorithms as well as in the assumption that socio-economic processes such as gentrification and the movement of minorities to more affordable neighborhoods are *voluntary* actions, caused by a desire to live with similar people (83). For Chun, the relevant insights and recommendations of network science are inherently linked to a neoliberal system that focuses on low transaction costs in human interaction and a predictive analytics of personal fitness, financial reliability, work performance, and so on. She calls for a "queering" of homophily by employing AI technology to create new approaches to intersubjective connection and move beyond the "love of the same" (88–90).

I don't believe that the current rise of the PP framework in cognitive (neuro)science and beyond is inherently related to neo-liberalism.[8] I also don't currently see a close entanglement of PP research with practices of predictive governance—although Veissière et al. declare to be interested in "testable models intent on predicting a person's behavior" (63)—and I acknowledge that the authors, like many researchers in the field, consider cultural diversity an irreducible characteristic of contemporary societies. At the same time, I wonder if the PP notion of "shared worlds"—and the TOM-approach in particular—may not have effects similar to those described by Chun for the field of network science in that it naturalizes cultural homogeneity. The explanation cited above describes the emergence of epistemic resources for prediction error minimization as conditioned by the assumption of *similarity* ("when, and only when, I share an environment with other 'creatures like me'"). This phrasing and other statements in the article mark similarity as essential for the *regular* course of things ("arise naturally"), i.e., the successful, prediction error-minimizing engagement with cultural affordances. The quote does not say what exactly happens when these epistemic resources do not "arise naturally" from the niche construction of like-minded agents, i.e., when we find ourselves in interaction with people that we consider to be *not* like us. But I find it hard not to read this line of argument as an implicit naturalization of cultural homogeneity through the theory of mind.

The PP framework arguably has great value for modeling and explaining phenomena such as implicit stereotypes, cognitive dissonance, and the emergence of ideological "echo chambers" in contemporary societies (Hinton; Kaaronen; Wheeler et al. 195). It seems important, however, not to implicitly and unintentionally turn the study of "social error minimization" (Wheeler et al. 193) into an affirmation of socio-cultural ensembles in which "we all have a common agenda and each play our role, fulfilling each other's expectations," as Maxwell Ramstead has put it elsewhere (*Have We Lost*, 138–39). With the concept of intersectionality in mind, Michael P. Kelly et al. have therefore proposed a social-neuroscience model of predictive processing that departs form a plurality of lifeworlds rather than from the notion of a shared, local world:

> Social environments are heterogeneous and social actors engage not only in differing practices, but the practices taking place in different lifeworlds are constrained by class, age, gender, ethnicity, sexual orientation and geography. These axes of social difference intersect with each other to create the rich and nuanced web of social life in any given society or

---

8 For a brief discussion of the political affinities of Andy Clark's approach to PP see Kukkonen.

culture. [...] Given the variegated nature of the social world, it seems highly probable that the types of ways in which these social networks constrain predictive processing will also be variable in ways that will reinforce current and habituated patterns of advantage and disadvantage. (Kelly et al. 8)

This model does not assume that the alignment of generative models and the minimization of free energy is the primary or main process to look at when exploring PP at a social level. It considers socio-economic inequality, power relations, and intersectionality as equally important factors and shows that, from a PP perspective, patterns can be thought of differently than only as a figure of coherence and unity.[9]

4   Xeno-Patterning

In the conclusion of their article Veissière et al. explicitly "caution against describing cultural ensembles as autonomous systems that maintain their organization and structural integrity through allostasis and homeostasis" (21). I am not sure if this also means that the authors reject a view of "communities" and "cultures" as entities of probabilistic self-realization and free-energy minimization (comparable, in this regard, to individual brains). It rather seems that the emphasis in this sentence is on the term "autonomous," meaning that social systems should precisely *not* be seen as independent from the biological and probabilistic principles of free-energy minimization but as their *expression*.[10] Such a view might explain the authors' strong focus on cultures as bounded entities but arguably also limits the space for interdisciplinary discussions in

---

9   For an intersectional perspective on gender within an enactive and predictivist framework see Albarracin and Poirier.

10   Cf. the phrase "cultural ensembles minimise free energy by enculturing their members so that they are common sets of precision-weighting prior" (Ramstead et al. 13) and Veissière's claim that societies are not autonomous, self-organizing systems (in a social science sense) but should instead be theorized "as natural consequences of free-energy minimization" (Veissière 48). Similarly, Friston et al. suggest that the principles of biological pattern formation and free-energy minimization found in embryogenesis "generalize to larger-scale phenomena such as [...] societies" (Friston et al. 8–9). The free-energy principle is a theoretical framework in biology and neuroscience that regards the minimization of surprisal/long-term prediction error as imperative for all living systems under conditions of increasing entropy.

THANKS FOR SHARING 311

which not all participants may be convinced of the universal applicability of the free-energy principle to biosocial phenomena.[11]

However, my intention here is not to discuss the socio-cultural extension of the free-energy principle. Instead, I now want think a bit more about the different and alien element in biosocial patterning *itself*. I use Octavia Butler's science fiction novel *Mind of My Mind* as a vantage point for my reflections because this work not only intriguingly anticipates some of the key ideas of the TTOM framework but also points to alienness as an important dimension of patterning. The novel tells the story of the formation of the "Pattern," a biosocial community of a special "race" of humans who are able to literally read each other's minds. It is mainly set in Forsyth, a city near Los Angeles, in the 1970s and focuses on the fight between Mary, a young woman of mixed racial background, and her father Doro, a four-thousand-year-old immortal from the Nubia region, who plans to breed a superhuman race of telepaths. When Mary first discovers her extraordinary mental and psionic powers she involuntarily creates the "Pattern," a constant mental connection of herself with seven other telepaths across the United States. Within two years, the Pattern grows into a network of about 1,500 telepaths, organized by rank and social institutions (including "houses," schools, a justice system etc.). When challenged by the cruel and reckless Doro, Mary beats him in a death-or-life battle for mental power and consolidates the "patternist" community, described by Butler in a series of six novels (*The Patternist* series).

In many regards, the Pattern presents an extreme version of the TTOM-model of enculturation and illustrates the "conservative nature of human culture" (Viessière et al.). As a mediating, hierarchical structure, the Pattern defines and polices acceptable behavior and literally prevents the telepaths from self-destruction, social isolation, and killing each other. The price for survival and flourishing is a rigid biosocial organization with Mary at the top. Across various layers of hierarchy—such as the "First Family" and the "Houses"—Mary can give orders to the lower ranks and read everybody's mind (hence the title "Mind of My Mind"). She receives bottom-up objections, and sometimes considers them, but is always able to overrule opposition. (I cannot even begin to do justice here to the highly ambivalent nexus of race, discrimination, and the history of slavery that Butler articulates in the novel). Hence, the Pattern resemblances a predictive processing hierarchy according to the TTOM view, albeit without the probabilistic element: as pervasive mental connection it defines a distinct biosocial group—the patternists—and streamlines behavior

---

11   The problem of the explanatory monism of the PP framework and the free-energy
      principle is addressed, among others, by Menary, and Colombo and Wright.

in a constant loop of top-down and bottom-up processing. As such, it demonstrates the amount of coercion and "social conformity" that can go into the creation of a world shared by people with alike minds (Constant et al.).

At the same time, the novel *also* shows that difference can be "central to the formation of patterns," as philosopher and media scholar Luciana Parisi states in her interpretation of Butler's work (83). Parisi reads the novel as an allegory of the ways in which "incomputables"—i.e., unknown information or randomness—can push systems out of "the autopoetic circuit of self-determination" through a process that she terms "xeno-patterning". New patterns form through "alien" patterns that are not conceptualizable and predictable as such. Parisi currently sees this happing in AI technology, where the deductive logic of "good old-fashioned AI" is replaced by predictive intuition and automated imagination (she cites the famous Move 37 by the AlphaGo computer program in the 2016 match against master player Lee Sedol as an example of the latter). In *Mind of My Mind*, Doro's reign of terror and control represents the old, deductive "master algorithm" while Mary gives birth to a collective intelligence "that can host all kinds of minds" and "invites in the alien imagination for what patterning can become as it mingles with randomness" (Parisi 91, 93).

The PP framework arguably has a profound epistemic affinity with Parisi's argument regarding its insistence on randomness, a shift from deduction to abduction, and the inference of patterns through the projection of causal structures onto data or input stream (Parisi 90). But precisely because of this kinship it might be worthwhile to consider the "incomputable" or alien elements that affect predictive processing and might question its computational premises. Is there a PP equivalent of xeno-patterning? Butler's novel shows that one of the places to look for it might be in the realm of *performance*, in a broad sense of the term. After the formation of the Pattern, various new cultural affordances are created in patternist society, including the "art" of psychometry (the reading of other's minds and feelings from inanimate objects). This practice in itself is not new in the storyworld, but experienced telepath Jan Sholto discovers by chance that she has the ability to isolate and "freeze" particular imprints in objects so that others can lucidly experience particular impressions as well: "A jar [...] held the story of the woman whose hands shaped it 6,500 years ago. A woman of a Neolithic village that had existed somewhere in what is now Iran". This is "better than the movies," Mary rejoices, "because you really live it" (Butler 186–7). The new practice not only enriches the cultural diversity of the Pattern by including alien minds from all historical periods and continents. It also reveals alienness to be an element of patterning itself: the novel affordance and patterned practice arises from a chance performance of something not conceptualized before.

Jan Sholto did not do anything right or wrong, she did something *differently*. I take this as a hint that randomness is not simply a quantifiable entity that

THANKS FOR SHARING 313

can be "reduced" and "minimized" to keep a PP system within "well-defined bounds" but an irreducible presence in biosocial patterning in general. Maybe such patterning inherently exceeds a binary logic of prediction and "error," however refined by notions of precision, attention, and salience? Design theorists Paul Andersen and David Salomon essentially make this point in their discussion of conservative (homeostatic) and dynamic conceptions of patterning across cybernetics, science, and design. They recall Gregory Bateson's notion of the "pattern which connects" mind and nature and his metaphor of pattern as a constant "dance of interacting parts":

> Every instantiation of a choreographed dance is part of an iterative and stochastic system; one that is at once predictable (the noted steps) and random (the interpretation by the dancers). For Bateson, randomness and noise are not nuisances to be eliminated but a necessity to be cultivated. He notes that, "all that is not information, not redundancy, not form, and not restraints—is noise, the only possible source of new patternings." (129; cf. Bateson)

Anderson and Salomon here give an example of "xeno-patterning" as cultural practice: the choreographed dance combines predictable regularity with "noisy" performance. What I suggest to consider here is not the common PP argument that sees cultural innovation and novelty seeking as strategy of a *temporary* increase of prediction error for the purpose of a more "efficient" resolution of uncertainty on the long run (Viessière et al. 12). It is also not the claim that there exists a specific sociocultural *space*—generally speaking, the arts and humanities—where "doubt, uncertainty, novelty, and unknowability" are admitted and humans can explore ambiguity, while anywhere else the unrelenting principle of free-energy minimization rules (Veissière 48–49). Instead, I suggest that patterned cultural practices always contain a performative element that cannot be reduced to a logic of matches and mismatches, prediction and error. Speech acts, writing, symbolic communication, social interaction, and artistic performance all involve, to different degrees, a play of shifting accents, versions, articulations, styles, and enactments that are not fully captured by their error-generating function.[12] Of course, there can be expectations based on social norms, genre conventions, or regimes of attention; I may expect a football teammate to anticipate my passing or a theater performance to look a particular way. But does the process of enculturation not also include the awareness that performance always means doing things somewhat differently, without doing them measurably right or wrong? Conceived of this way,

---

12   My argument here is indebted to Derrida 1988.

performance is an example of an enactive engagement with the world that goes beyond the processing of information and underscores the importance of historicity, contingency, and transition *between* "steady states" that the free-energy principle has trouble accounting for (Di Paolo et al.). With its dynamics of repetition and change it does precisely what Di Paolo et al. call "triggering a swerve in dynamical paths and reshaping dynamical landscapes" of enaction: "Cultural and interpersonal variability in human beings are not statistical noise, but rather necessary consequences of what it means to undergo human becoming" (Di Paolo et al. 23, my emphasis). Considering the profound relevance of performance and performativity in and for social interaction, culture in itself is arguably more "alien" than a hierarchical probabilistic model can capture. Or, as Andersen and Salomon put it: "Ever stochastic, patterns enable the new to emerge out of the same, repeating the difference in them, not only the same we want to see" (Andersen and Salomon 131).

5   Conclusion

Evidently, I don't propose xeno-patterning as a well-defined, elaborate concept. I merely want to offer a terminological incentive to think more acutely about the relevance of *difference* between and within patterned practices and allegedly "shared" worlds. The term *xenos* (other, different, alien) here serves a double purpose: first, to point to the possible collision and interaction of different patterns of practice and expectation, even in the smallest of "local" worlds; and second, to stress the alien component in patterning itself, i.e., the random element of performance that arguably exceeds a comprehensive regime of prediction error minimization. In this twofold and speculative understanding, Parisi's "xeno-patterning" acquires a new meaning that amplifies a key idea of the initial paper by Roepstorff et al., namely to move from a homogeneous view of culture to a performative and partial understanding of common worlds.

Within literary and cultural studies, the notion of xeno-patterning resonates strongly with both Levine's interest in the disjunctures between sociopolitical patterns and Hayles' ideas about the de-essentializing potential of patterns. I think that it is worthwhile and productive to bring these ideas into a dialogue with the exciting developments in PP research. As I have pointed out throughout this essay, there is no single doctrine of PP but a multiplicity of voices that hugely diverge in the ways in which they connect the key idea of the predictive mind to socio-cultural processes. Xeno-patterning might be helpful to make this connection in a way that acknowledges the partiality, ambiguity, and internal multiplicity of all shared predictions.

References

Albarracin, Mahault, and Pierre Poirier. "Enacting Gender: An Enactive-Ecological Account of Gender and Its Fluidity." *Frontiers in Psychology*, vol. 13, art. 772287, May 2022.

Andersen, Marc, et al. "Predictive Minds in Ouija Board Sessions." *Phenomenology and the Cognitive Sciences*, vol. 18, no. 6, 2018, pp. 577–88.

Andersen, Paul, and David Salomon. "The Pattern That Connects." *Acadia10: LIFE in: Formation*, edited by Aaron Sprecher et al., 2010, pp. 125–32.

Appadurai, Arjun. *Modernity at Large: Cultural Dimensions of Globalization*. U of Minnesota P, 1996.

Bateson, Gregory. *Nature and Mind: A Necessary Unity*. E.P. Dutton, 1979.

Bod, Rens. "How to Open Pandora's Box: A Tractable Notion of the History of Knowledge." *Journal for the History of Knowledge*, vol. 1, no. 1, 2020.

Bourdieu, Pierre. *Outline of a Theory of Practice*. Cambridge UP, 1977.

Buskell, Andrew. "Normativity, Social Change, and the Epistemological Framing of Culture." *Behavioral and Brain Sciences*, vol. 43, art. 96, 2020, pp. 28–29.

Butler, Octavia. *Mind of My* Mind. 1977. Grand Central Publishing, 2020.

Christopoulos, George, and Ying-yi Hong. "The Multicultural Mind as an Epistemological Test and Extension of the Thinking through Other Minds Approach." *Behavioral and Brain Sciences*, vol. 43, art. 97, 2020, pp. 29–31.

Chun, Wendy. "Queering Homophily." *Pattern Discrimination*, edited by Clemens Apprich et al., U of Minnesota P, 2018, pp. 59–97.

Clark, Andy. "Whatever Next? Predictive Brains, Situated Agents, and the Future of Cognitive Science." *Behavioral and Brain Sciences*, vol. 36, no. 3, 2013, pp. 181–204.

Clark, Andy. *Surfing Uncertainty: Prediction, Action, and the Embodied Mind*. Oxford UP, 2016.

Clark, Kenneth B., and Mamie P. Clark. "Emotional Factors in Racial Identification and Preference in Negro Children." *The Journal of Negro Education*, vol. 19, no. 3, 1950, pp. 341–50.

Colombo, Matteo, and Cory Wright. "Explanatory Pluralism: An Unrewarding Prediction Error for Free Energy." *Brain and Cognition*, vol. 112, 2017, pp. 3–12.

Colombo, Matteo, and Patricia Palacios. "Non-Equilibrium Thermodynamics and the Free Energy Principle in Biology." *Biology & Philosophy*, vol. 36, art. 41, Aug. 2021.

Constant, Axel, et al. "Regimes of Expectations: An Active Inference Model of Social Conformity and Human Decision Making." *Frontiers in Psychology*, vol. 10, art. 679, 2019.

Damasio, Antonio. *The Strange Order of Things: Life, Feeling, and the Making of Cultures*. Pantheon Books, 2018.

Derrida, Jacques. "Signature Event Context." *Limited, Inc*. Northwestern UP, 1988, pp. 1–21.

Dixon, Dan. "Analysis Tool or Research Methodology: Is There an Epistemology for Patterns?" *Understanding Digital Humanities*, edited by David Berry, Palgrave Macmillan, 2012, pp. 191–209.

Drucker, Johanna. *Graphesis: Visual Forms of Knowledge Production*. Harvard UP, 2014.

Friston, Karl, et al. "Knowing One's Place: A Free-Energy Approach to Pattern Regulation." *Journal of the Royal Society Interface*, vol. 12, no. 105, art. 20141383, Apr. 2015.

Hayles, N. Katherine. *How We Became Posthuman: Virtual Bodies in Literature, Cybernetics, and Informatics*. University of Chicago Press, 1999.

Hinton, Perry. "Implicit Stereotypes and the Predictive Brain: Cognition and Culture in 'Biased' Person Perception." *Palgrave Communications*, vol. 3, art. 17086, 2017.

Kaaronen, Roope Oskari. "A Theory of Predictive Dissonance: Predictive Processing Presents a New Take on Cognitive Dissonance." *Frontiers in Psychology*, vol. 9, art. 2218, 2018.

Kelly, Michael, et al. "The Brain, Self and Society: A Social-Neuroscience Model of Predictive Processing." *Social Neuroscience*, vol. 14, no. 3, 2018, pp. 266–76.

Kirchhoff, Michael D., and Julian Kiverstein. *Extended Consciousness and Predictive Processing: A Third Wave View*. Routledge, 2019.

Kukkonen, Karin. "The Fully Extended Mind." *The Edinburgh Companion to Contemporary Narrative Theories*, edited by Zara Dinnen and Robyn Warhol, Edinburgh UP, 2018, pp. 64–77.

Levine, Caroline. "Model Thinking: Generalization, Political Form, and the Common Good." *New Literary History*, vol. 48, no. 4, 2007, pp. 633–53.

Levine, Caroline. *Forms: Whole, Rhythm, Hierarchy, Network*. Princeton UP, 2015.

Menary, Robert. "What? Now. Predictive Coding and Enculturation." *Open MIND*, edited by Thomas Metzinger and Jennifer Windt, 2015, https://philarchive.org/rec/MENWNP.

Paolo, Ezequiel Di, et al. "Laying down a Forking Path: Incompatibilities between Enaction and the Free Energy Principle." *PsyArXiv*, 19 Apr. 2021.

Parisi, Luciana. "Xeno-Patterning: Predictive Intuition and Automated Imagination." *Angelaki*, vol. 24, no. 1, 2019, pp. 81–97.

Potochnik, Angela. *Idealization and the Aims of Science*. Chicago UP, 2017.

Ramstead, Maxwell. *Have We Lost Our Minds? An Approach to Multiscale Dynamics in the Cognitive Sciences*. McGill University Library, 2019.

Ramstead, Maxwell, et al. "Cultural Affordances: Scaffolding Local Worlds through Shared Intentionality and Regimes of Attention." *Frontiers in Psychology*, vol. 7, art. 1090, 2016.

Ramstead, Maxwell, et al. "Answering Schrödinger's Question: A Free-energy Formulation." *Physics of Life Reviews*, vol. 24, 2018, pp. 1–16.

Rietveld, Erik, et al. "Trusted Strangers: Social Affordances for Social Cohesion." *Phenomenology and the Cognitive Sciences*, vol. 18, 2019, pp. 299–316.

Roepstorff, Andreas, et al. "Enculturing Brains through Patterned Practices." *Neural Networks*, vol. 23, no. 8–9, 2010, pp. 1051–59.

Schjoedt, Uffe. "Cognitive Resource Depletion in Religious Interactions." *Religion, Brain & Behavior*, vol. 3, no. 1, 2013, pp. 39–55.

Tang, Yuchun, et al. "The Construction of a Chinese MRI Brain Atlas: A Morphometric Comparison between Chinese and Caucasian Cohorts." *NeuroImage*, vol. 51, 2010, pp. 33–41.

Taves, Ann, and Egil Aprem. "Experience as Event: Event Cognition and the Study of (Religious) Experiences." *Religion, Brain & Behavior*, vol. 7, no. 1, 2017, pp. 44–63.

Tewes, Christian, et al. "Introduction: The Interplay of Embodiment, Enaction, and Culture." *Embodiment, Enaction, and Culture: Investigating the Constitution of the Shared World*, edited by Christoph Durt, MIT Press, 2017, pp. 1–22.

Veissière, Samuel. "Cultural Markov Blankets? Mind the Other Minds Gap! Comment on 'Answering Schrödinger's question: A free-energy formulation.'" *Physics of Life Reviews*, vol. 24, 2018, pp. 47–49.

Veissière, Samuel, et al. "Thinking through Other Minds: A Variational Approach to Cognition and Culture." *Behavioral and Brain Sciences*, vol. 43, art. 90, 2020, pp. 1–22.

Wheeler, Nathan E. "Ideology and Predictive Processing: Coordination, Bias, and Polarization in Socially Constrained Error Minimization." *Current Opinion in Behavorial Sciences*, vol. 34, 2020, pp. 192–98.

Wiese, Wanja, and Thomas Metzinger. "Vanilla PP for Philosophers: A Primer on Predictive Processing." *Philosophy and Predictive Processing*, edited by Thomas Metzinger and Wanja Wiese, MIND Group, 2017.

Index

Abi-Rached, Joelle M.   3, 193
Addis, Donna Rose   27
Andersen, Paul   313, 314
Appadurai, Arjun   300, 301
Arnheim, Rudolf   58, 221

Bachrach, Asaf   228, 229
Baddeley, Alan D.   27
Baggs, Mel   100
Bakhtin, Mikhail   117
Barnes, Djuna   10, 142
Bartlett, Frederick   27
Bateson, Gregory   301, 313
Baudelaire, Charles   113, 125
Bazin, André   176, 177
Beck, Stefan   300
Bennett, Jane   119, 120
Bergson, Henri   114, 119, 120
Berlyne, Daniel E.   53
Bjerre Jensen, Dorte   229
Boehm, Gottfried   218
Bourdieu, Pierre   300
Budelmann, Felix   266–269
Burke, Michael   145
Buskell, Andrew   301
Butler, Octavia   302, 311, 312

Callard, Felicity   6, 7, 264, 269
Cave, Terence   144, 153, 154
Choudhury, Suparna   4
Christensen, Inger   132, 133, 135, 138, 139
Christopoulos, George   307
Chun, Wendy Hui Kyong   308, 309
Cicero   22
Clark, Andy   2, 5, 8, 9, 50, 144, 147, 148, 152
Clark, Kenneth B.   307
Clark, Mamie P.   307
Cocker, Emma   223, 224
Corwin, Anne   102–104
Costner, Kevin   182

Dalai Lama   203, 205, 208, 211
Damasio, Antonio   301
Danieli, Yael   64, 66, 67, 69
Davidson, Richard   203–207, 210

Davis, Eric   173, 174
DeAngelis, Michael   176
DeGruy, Joy   65, 69, 70, 71
Deleuze, Gilles   4
Derrida, Jacques   313
Descola, Philippe   5, 6
Dickens, Charles   302
Dornelles, Juliano   181, 183
Dostoevsky, Fyodor   117
Drost, Ulrich C.   280
Drucker, Johanna   305
Dumit, Joseph   229

Eichenbaum, Boris   136, 137
Eliasson, Olafur   216, 226, 229
Eliot, T.S.   147, 154

Fechner, Gustav   53
Finn, Ed   135
Fitzgerald, Des   6, 7, 264, 269
Flavell, John   28
Ford, John   177
Forsström, Tua   130, 131
Foster, Norman   121
Foucault, Michel   194
Freedberg, David   35
Freire, Paulo   97
Friston, Karl   50, 302, 310
Frost, Samantha   6

Gallese, Vittorio   31, 35–37, 39–43, 45
Gansterer, Nikolaus   11, 215, 216, 220, 221, 223, 224, 226, 228–230
Giraud, Jean   181
Gogol, Nikolai   136–138
Goleman, Daniel   203, 207, 208
Greco, Emio   286, 288, 290, 292–294
Greil, Mariella   224
Guattari, Félix   4
Guerra, Michele   31, 35, 37, 39–43, 45
Gutman, Herbert George   69

Haraway, Donna   4
Hartogsohn, Ido   175
Hayles, N. Katherine   120, 301, 302, 314

INDEX

Heidegger, Martin 2, 4, 5, 84, 121
Heider, Fritz 122
Heimann, Katrin 35, 37, 40, 41, 43, 44
Hepworth, Barbara 120
Herman, David 10, 124
Herodotus 266
Hibbitt, Richard 154
Hitchcock, Alfred 9, 31, 37, 39–41, 44, 58
Hofmann, Albert 181
Hohwy, Jakob 50
Hong, Ying-yi 307
Hopper, Dennis 176–179, 181, 185
Husserl, Edmund 83, 85–87, 93, 157

James, William 157
Jodorowsky, Alejandro 177, 178, 180, 181, 185
Johnson, Jennell 7
Johnson, Mark 158
Jung, Carl Gustav 292, 293

Kabat-Zinn, Jon 203, 205–207
Kael, Pauline 177
Kandinsky, Wassili 120
Kant, Immanuel 218–220
Kardiner, Abram 69
Kellermann, Nathan 64, 68, 70
Kelly, Michael P. 309
Kirchhoff, Michael D. 282
Kirmayer, Laurence 302
Kiverstein, Julian 282, 300, 306
Kounen, Jan 181, 182
Krämer, Sybille 219, 222
Kraus, Cynthia 7
Kuhn, Thomas S. 260
Kukkonen, Karin 145, 148, 150
Kulechov, Lev 58

Lakoff, George 158
Langlitz, Nicholas 173, 174, 180
Leary, Timothy 175, 176
LeDoux, Joseph 84, 89
Lefkowitz, Myriam 270, 271
Leone, Sergio 177
Leopardi, Giacomo 113, 125
Levine, Caroline 301, 302, 314
Leys, Ruth 63
Littlefield, Melissa 7
Lotman, Juri 121, 122
Lutz, Antoine 203, 204, 206
Lyotard, Jean-François 218

Machado, Antonio 156
Malabou, Catherine 5, 194, 195, 198
Manning, Erin 95–100, 102–105, 107
Markram, Henry 188, 190, 192, 196–198
Massumi, Brian 95, 97–100, 103–105, 108
Maturana, Humberto 158
Mendonça Filho, Kleber 181, 183
Merleau-Ponty, Maurice 2, 84
Meyerding, Jane 99
Miller, George A. 24
Miro, Joan 120
Mitchell, William J. T. 218
Moore, Henry 120
Moser, Aloisia 219
Munsterberg, Hugo 58

Nancy, Jean-Luc 87, 88
Niewöhner, Jörg 300
Nolte, Max 198

Ortega, Francisco 3, 101
Orwell, George 121
Øyehaug, Gunnhild 129–136, 138, 139

Palmer, Alan 118
Parisi, Luciana 312, 314
Paul Armstrong 145
Pearlman, Karen 44
Peirce, Charles Sanders 123
Penn, Arthur 177, 182
Petitmengin, Claire 229, 230
Pitts-Taylor, Victoria 5
Pollan, Michael 173, 180
Proksch, Shannon 276
Proust, Marcel 123

Ramstead, Maxwell 301, 302, 304–307, 309, 310
Rancière, Jacques 98
Rietveld, Erik 306
Roepstorff, Andreas 5, 216, 230, 300, 304, 306, 314
Rorschach, Hermann 125
Rosch, Eleanor 156
Rose, Nikolas 3, 7, 193
Rothe, Anne 63
Rupert, Robert 265, 267, 268

Sacks, Oliver 100
Salomon, David 313, 314

INDEX

Satie, Erik 133
Schacter, Daniel L. 8, 27, 28
Scholten, Pieter C. 286, 288, 290, 292–294
Seung, Sebastian 196, 197
Shimizu, Daisuke 278
Shklovsky, Viktor 136
Simmel, Marianne 122
Singer, Judy 99
Slaby, Jan 4
Sobchack, Vivian 83, 85, 93
Soderbergh, Steven 49
Souriau, Étienne 95, 105
Spivak, Gayatri Chakravorty 4, 5, 8
Spolsky, Ellen 258
Stenning, Anna 100
Sutton, John 264, 265
Swaab, Dick 84, 89

Tan, Chade-Meng 207, 208
Thompson, Evan 156
Thucydides 267
Trento, Francisco 99, 105
Tribble, Evelyn B. 262, 263, 265
Turner, Mark 258

Turvey, Malcolm 31, 35, 36, 42–46
Tynianov, Yury 136, 138

Varela, Francisco J. 156–158
Veissière, Samuel 301, 302, 305, 307–310, 313
Vetlesen, Arne Johan 113
Vidal, Fernando 3, 101
Viessière, Samuel 307
Vroman, Leo 1, 2
Vygotsky, Lev 158

Walton, Kendall 124
Weil, Simone 117
Wekker, Gloria 74
Wheeler, Michael 2, 3, 12
Whitehead, Alfred North 103, 106
Wilson, Robert A. 265
Winterson, Jeanette 142, 147
Wittgenstein, Ludwig 218, 219
Wollheim, Richard 43

Xenophon 266

Zandwijken, Mercedes 63, 67

Printed in the United States
by Baker & Taylor Publisher Services